PLANNING CANADIAN
COMMUNITIES

An Introduction
to the Principles,
Practice, and
Participants

Third Edition

D1457948

Gerald Hodge

 I(T)P Nelson

an International Thomson Publishing company

Toronto • Albany • Bonn • Boston • Cincinnati • Detroit • London • Madrid • Melbourne
Mexico City • New York • Pacific Grove • Paris • San Francisco • Singapore • Tokyo • Washington

I⊤P® International Thomson Publishing

The ITP logo is a trademark under licence
http://www.thomson.com

Published in 1998 by

I⊤P® Nelson

A division of Thomson Canada Limited
1120 Birchmount Road
Scarborough, Ontario M1K 5G4

Visit our Web site at **http://www.nelson.com**

Canadian Cataloguing in Publication Data
Hodge, Gerald
    Planning Canadian communities

3rd ed.
Includes bibliographical references and index.
ISBN 0-17-607379-5

1. City planning—Canada.   I. Title.

HT169.C2H62 1997   307.1'2'0971   C97-931687-1

Publisher   Jacqueline Wood
Acquisitions Editor   Sarah Clarke
Project Editor   Avivah Wargon
Production Coordinator   Renate McCloy
Art Direction   Sylvia Vander Schee
Interior Design   Sylvia Vander Schee
Cover Design   Todd Ryoji
Cover Photographs   (top) Eric Meola/The Image Bank;
                            (bottom) Andy Sacks/Tony Stone Images
Composition   Anita Macklin

Printed and bound in Canada
1 2 3 4 WC 01 00 99 98

The pages in this book open easily and lie flat, a result of the Otabind bookbinding process. Otabind combines advanced adhesive technology and a free-floating cover to achieve books that last longer and are bound to stay open.

*To those who have taught me the importance
of community in community planning:*

*My professors, Fred Adams, Hans Blumenfeld,
John Friedmann, Jack Kent, and Ira Robinson;*

*The citizens who defended and explained their
neighbourhoods to planners; and*

*The three generations who now define my community
—my mother, Marion and Jarrah.*

CONTENTS

PART ONE: THE ROOTS OF CANADIAN PLANNING

Chapter 1: The Need for Community Planning   2

Chapter 2: The Beginnings of Today's Cities   18

Chapter 3: Physical Foundations of Canadian Communities   40

Chapter 4: Establishing the Social Agenda for Community Planning   80

LIST OF FIGURES

ACKNOWLEDGMENTS

The journey of book-writing brings one into contact with many travelling companions. Some share the path; some provide directions; some help with the load. Only in retrospect does it become clear how many people had a hand in seeing one through such a trip. This is even more evident to me the third time over the route.

Of course, the first journey never completely ended. Its residue of memories, mistakes, and remarks of editors, readers, and reviewers quickly reassert themselves. I am more aware now of the gratitude that I owe those who travelled with me through these three excursions, as well as those I've yet to meet. My utmost thanks for their support, kindness, direct help, and thoughtful comments, and that includes those whose names will not come to mind. My apologies, too, for not being able to mention more than a few of their names.

To get to this version was, of course, only possible because of three supportive and patient editors: Peter Milroy, my first editor; Dave Ward on the second edition; and Avivah Wargon, whose enthusiasm and forbearance on this edition demands my special gratitude. The original graphics of Andrew Milos have proved to be durable and much of the present text is little changed from that which emanated from the "typewriters" of Jackie Bell and the late Florence Gore at Queen's University and my daughters Brooke and Clare Hodge. I also remember particularly the literature search done by Lauri McKay and the thoughtful reviews of Kent Gerecke, Bill Perks, and Beth Moore Milroy. They reviewed the book I wrote—not the one they wished I'd written—and their comments continued to guide my hand, as did those of David Amborski (Ryerson), Wayne J. Caldwell (University of Guelph), Pierre Deslauriers (Concordia), and Jeanne M. Wolfe (McGill) this time around.

One other "traveller" deserves special mention. Marion Hodge once again was my companion, proofreading manuscripts, refereeing ideas, and providing the support and ambience for such a project. As any author knows, there are not sufficient words or ways to acknowledge a partner's role.

None of the above bears any responsibility for the content or for any errors. This is my view of community planning, its application, and its potential in the Canadian setting. Sometimes we have realized that potential but, distressingly, too often we have not. The reasons are manifest in the activity itself. Community planning is about agreeing on the best way to build communities, physically and socially. It is nothing if not political in nature. Power and participation are essential ingredients; these are not the makings of a simple recipe. Further, I believe that one of the most important things we can do for our communities is to have ideals—visions—of what they could become, and to work toward achieving them. If a few more Canadians come to appreciate the process better, my hopes will have been realized and probably also the hopes of those who supported me in these three journeys.

G.H.

Denman Island, B.C.

October 1997

PART 1   The Roots of Canadian Planning

Source: Canapress Photo Services

INTRODUCTION

Our communities and the methods we use for improving them are a legacy of the past. Community planning did not grow independently of real urban problems or their solutions as perceived by people, professionals, and governments. Rather it evolved alongside changing urban problems and perceptions of them. But in this evolution various principles learned from past experience were embodied. Long-standing ideals, ideas, and premises regarding the physical form of communities, the social needs of residents, and the institutional means of planning are entwined with our contemporary (post-1950) views of community planning.

Chapter 1 The Need for Community Planning

Think of the things you see in your own city which everyone wishes were otherwise. They might have been otherwise, if there had been careful planning in the past.

Stanley Pickett, 1955

Among Canadian communities, size is no barrier to planning. Baker Lake, Northwest Territories, has its own plan and so does St. Stephen, New Brunswick, right alongside Victoria, Winnipeg, and Montreal. Today few would take issue with the view that planning meets some important needs of communities. Even the periodic confrontations over the building of new shopping centres, high-rise apartments, and highways, or the demolition of historic buildings, or the failure to conserve open space are a measure of the regard in which planning is held. In these contentious situations, the debate is not about the need for planning, but rather the need for better planning—not *whether* but *how* it should be done.

General acceptance of community planning indicates—to use a sociological term—its "institutionalization" in Canadian community life. The act of community planning has come to be strongly valued over and above its immediate achievements. There exists in every province and in both northern territories some form of legislation that both sanctifies the notion of planning and specifies its format in their communities. From coast to coast it is considered a normal and necessary function of public activity.

The fact that we have a plethora of governmental frameworks and legislative means in Canada to facilitate community planning does not tell *why* a community needs planning. The sometimes overwhelming sets of procedures and legalistic steps are not in themselves community planning. They are means, not ends. The need for community planning does not arise because of the formal structures we erect. It arises because people wish to improve their environment. This need has not always been so widely accepted, nor have the concerns over the environment always been the same. In order to appreciate the *raison d'être* for the planning that abounds in most communities, let us begin by focusing on the sorts of actions communities have taken in their pursuit of planning.[1] This will provide a basis for deriving some guiding principles about the need for community planning.

Halifax, Vancouver, and *Montreal* have each developed planning regulations to control the location of tall downtown buildings so as not to spoil public views of important parts of the city environment. In Halifax, planners sought to protect the traditional view of the harbour from Citadel Hill; Vancouver, planners valued views of the mountains; while in Montreal, there was concern over losing views of Mount Royal.

In *Toronto,* residents of the Dundas-Sherbourne area successfully petitioned City Hall to support a proposed infill scheme that would achieve the same number of tenants and the same site coverage as a project that would have torn down their homes and built two high-rise apartment blocks. They thereby managed to keep their community physically and socially intact.

Meadowbrook, on Vancouver's fringe, uses new approaches to zoning to create people-oriented neighbourhoods with an open feeling that also cost less to develop. Houses can be placed anywhere on their own lots, and some have zero-lot-lines, which allows them to be staggered or clustered attractively.

The municipal land bank in *Saskatoon* is justly famous in planning circles. Beginning shortly after World War II, the city began purchasing land on its outer limits that it could then sell in sections to developers in the location and sequence that the community had decided in its city plan.

One of the first municipalities in the country to designate environmentally sensitive areas in its official plan was the Regional Municipality of *Kitchener-Waterloo.* Some of the criteria used there included the presence of rare and endangered species and unusual or high-quality plant life and landforms. One now finds places as far apart as North Vancouver District and Ottawa-Carleton (in its new Greenbelt Plan) using similar critieria.

Edmonton has long had a plan to revitalize the back lanes that cut through many of the city's blocks so that they can be used as walkways and bicycle paths. *London* planners want to use abandoned railway beds to create a bikeway network linking all the parks in the city.

Fermont, a resource town of 5,000 in Quebec's sub-arctic region, has a unique weatherproof downtown core. Like its counterparts in other parts of the country, such as *Tumbler Ridge* in B.C., *Leaf Rapids* in Manitoba, and *Fort McMurray* in Alberta, the planners paid attention to the climate and the need to keep things compact for easy access in all seasons.

As these few samples of planning activity reveal, one of the main concerns of community planning is with the physical environment. From housing arrangements in Toronto and Meadowbrook, B.C., to the banking of land in Saskatoon and the design of transportation networks in Edmonton and the town centre in Fermont, the planning activity deals with elements of a community's physical environment. The planning concerns in these cases, moreover, are not limited to the design and regulation of what is often referred to as the **built environment**. They may also cover the **spatial impact** of various human actions (as in Kitchener-Waterloo's environmental protection proposals) and the **spatial coordination** of different public policies (as in London's plan to integrate its parks and bikeways programs).

Planning actions are taken deliberately to achieve one or more community objectives. For example, Halifax wants to preserve the public's view of the harbour, and London wants to link parks with a bikeway network. Both these planning initiatives embody another important, but often overlooked, characteristic: community planning is about the achievement of a community's preferred future physical environment. This is the backdrop against which the need for community planning arises.

Why should a community be concerned about its future physical environment? The examples of Halifax and London, again, provide helpful insights into this issue. Halifax appears to be responding to an impending problem—new development that might affect historic views—while London appears to be pursuing longer-term aspirations. Either problems or aspirations regarding a community's physical environment (and not infrequently a combination of the two) underlie the need for community planning in Halifax, London, and all other Canadian communities. There are two principal reasons that the need for community planning may arise:

1. A community may wish *to achieve some ideal form of development;* or
2. A community may wish *to solve some problems associated with its development.*

The need may arise for either one or a combination of these reasons. Most commonly, a community faced with the need to solve a particular development problem decides to reassess its preferences for its overall future development.

Planning Issue 1.1

WORLD WATCHES AS BANFF DEBATES ITS FUTURE

BANFF—You'd think being mayor of a picturesque town of 6,000 in the Canadian Rockies would be an exercise in leisure, maybe even a sinecure.

But for Ted Hart, an award-winning Canadian author and historian who is the mayor of Banff, the work is anything but cushy. In fact, these days, being the mayor of the most scrutinized town in Canada requires all the adroitness of an 18th-century French courtier.

Earlier this week, as he presided over a public hearing on the town's future development, the delicacy of Mr. Hart's job was evident. Passions about Banff were in full, if reserved, flight. And so was the sharp disparity in views over what ought to happen.

At issue was a 109-page document several years in the making. It looks innocuous, as so many government-spawned, committee-produced documents do. Even its title, Banff Community Plan, looks dull.

The ideas in the document, however, and their financial and environmental implications, are anything but. The document presents proposals for how much more commercial development ought to take place in Banff, recommending the construction of 650,000 square feet.

For any other city or town, such a plan might spawn a few comments or even a little debate. But in Banff, where the residents have seen a flurry of international and national attention focused on the state of the national park and World Heritage Site in which the town sits, the plan is loaded with meaning. ...

"We're coming to a sort of watershed," Mr. Hart said. "It's unsettling. It's difficult. There are few models to turn to look to."

And as Mr. Hart knows, the stakes are high. "The world is watching," he said. And for what? "To see if people given the precious right to control the town's future are up to it. We can't afford to make mistakes."

The background is complex. Back in 1994, the federal

government decided there were enough concerns about the ecological state of Banff that a task force ought to be set up to examine the park.

Ottawa set up the Banff-Bow Valley Task Force, under the chairmanship of scientist Robert Page of the University of Calgary, and put a moratorium on development until the study was completed.

In the meantime, media from across Canada and from several other countries also began to look at some of the scientific studies that showed the delicate environment of Banff National Park was in jeopardy. There was anger that the park had been brought so low.

The problem, the scientists were saying, was that while the town of Banff is still small—the 1996 census showed it has just over 6,000 residents—it sits in one of the most ecologically crucial parts of the park: the montane.

Just as humans like the flattish, grassy montane, so do animals. For them, the montane is the balmy part of the mountain habitat where they can forage for food in the winter. It also forms the nexus of animals' crossing points, allowing them to travel easily from one part of the

mountains to another.

And small as it is, the town of Banff and some of the other developments alongside it had begun to block these crucial wildlife corridors and damage the biological cradle of the park.

In fact, by the time the Banff-Bow Valley study was released last year, it had found that the park had become ecologically fragile as a result of human activities. It was actually in danger of failing to qualify as a national park.

By the time Heritage Minister Sheila Copps tabled the study's recommendations in the House of Commons just before the federal election was called in late April, she had ordered several impediments to wildlife movement torn down, including a bison paddock, an airstrip and a cadet camp.

She also halted the release of any more land for commercial development, said Banff's population could never exceed 10,000, and said the town could never qualify for city status. As well, she said, the town would have to come up with a new community plan.

At the public hearing on Monday, most of the residents said they were pleased with the general direction of the new plan, which would reduce current development, but they diverged sharply over whether Banff should allow any commercial growth or none at all.

Some businesses that made presentations were angry that their right to engage in commerce would be affected.

One businessman, Oswald Treutler, wrote in a letter read by his son that the plan was immoral and unreasonable.

Another, Ted Kissane of the Banff Springs Hotel, spoke about his concerns over a plan imposing absolutes. Business, he explained, cannot always abide by absolutes. For its very survival, he said, it may need to shift with consumer taste.

Other businesses pointed out that their operations would fall in value. Indeed, one of the themes of the session was how businesses would be financially compensated if their properties lost value as a result of the plan.

Residents and those representing environmental groups had a different take. Jane Newman, who represented Citizens for an End to Commercial Growth, presented the town councillors with a petition her group had begun circulating only 10 days before. More than 1,000 residents had signed it, saying they wanted a complete stop to commercial growth.

Another resident said the time had come for Banff to simply stop and catch its breath. There would be time to build later if need be, he said.

Source: Excerpted from Alanna Mitchell, *The Globe and Mail,* May 30, 1997, A2. Reprinted with permission from *The Globe and Mail.*

THE NEED TO SOLVE DEVELOPMENT PROBLEMS

Of the two basic reasons noted above, a community's need to solve present or future problems in its physical environment is probably the one most people think of first. The problematic situations that spark planning action reflect the concerns and conditions of the time. In the 1980s, for example, the concerns ranged from environmental issues like waste disposal to growth management and affordable housing, while in the 1970s the concerns were very often the effects that new, large-scale projects might have on existing community areas: e.g., apartment-building complexes, expressways, second airports, shopping centres. The 1960s began with major concerns over physical deterioration in communities; urban renewal became the hoped-for solution, until the "bulldozer approach" used to achieve it was called into question. Canadian urban communities in the two decades after World War II were concerned with how to accommodate vast new populations—to provide them with housing, public utilities, schools, and parks, as well as how to cope with their infatuation with the automobile. The problem of housing for the urban poor concerned communities in the 1950s as it had 50 years before and still does today.

In the first decade of the century, cities were suffering from a large influx of newcomers, many of them poor people from abroad. Housing, sanitation, and transportation in most cities at the time were inadequate to handle rapid urban growth. The concerns then, by today's criteria, entailed very elementary city-building standards. Yet the turn-of-the-century concerns, which stimulated the beginning of community planning as a public activity in Canada, also questioned the ability of already established communities to achieve salutary development.

Growth and Development Problems

One common feature that communities have continually expressed is the need for planning to deal with problems associated with growth and development of the community. *Growth* refers generally to a change in the size of population, the number of structures, the space required for the community, or all three. *Development* refers generally to such qualitative changes in the community as the opening up of new areas, the replacement of one land use with another, or the emergence of new modes of building and doing business. But growth and development are always occurring in any community, and always have been. Is planning needed just because there is growth and development in a community?

The answer to this question is that the need for planning depends upon whether the growth and development give rise to problems *for* the community. A typical development situation these days, such as the proposal for a shopping centre on the outskirts of a town or city, often has major implications for a community's established downtown area as well as for its road network. Cities and towns early in this century, however, were often subject to epidemics of disease and prone to extensive fires. Their new populations were not being provided with adequate housing and water, and sewage systems were overloaded, where they existed at all. Both examples indicate that growth and development may generate problems that affect the whole community. Like the proposed shopping centre in today's community, the inadequate housing and servicing of newcomers in communities of 90 years ago posed not only threats to parts of the established community but also uncertainty about the future form and condition of the overall community.

The Public Interest

Earlier, it was suggested that community planning is concerned with the attainment of preferred future conditions in the physical environment, and that the community's preferences are the prime consideration. Community preferences are sometimes referred to as the "public good" or the "public interest." A cornerstone of community planning is that it aims to promote the public interest when coping with the various problems affecting the physical environment. As reasonable as this principle sounds, obtaining community agreement about what constitutes the public interest may not be a simple matter. In 19th-century Canada, decades passed before the public health and safety problems that plagued its cities were recognized and acted upon. If this seems incredible to us today, we need only consider that Rachel Carson, in her book *Silent Spring*, alerted us to the dangers of pollution for our communities more than three decades ago. The reconciliation of interests in the environmental area often still eludes us.

Our communities are composites of privately owned properties, structures, and services, not to mention vehicles, and publicly provided facilities, programs, and means of communication. It is, therefore, not surprising that all the diverse interests involved in maintaining and developing communities do not always coincide in their preferences. Much of community planning concerns reconciling private and public preferences into acceptable community preferences to solve problems caused by growth and development. This is not always accomplished smoothly or quickly, and there is probably no reason to expect either agreement or equanimity all the time in planning issues.

On the private side of the community, those whose interests lie in maintaining a stable, tranquil setting may clash with those who wish to pursue long-held development objectives and rights to change their properties and structures. Or there may be clashes between private interests and the public good, such as proposed development in what the community considers to be an inappropriate location. Halifax's concern that new development might block historic views is a typical case, and so is the concern in many communities over allowing housing developments in flood-prone areas. Sometimes clashes arise over proposals by public bodies to accommodate growth or new technologies, as in the expressway and second airport controversies of the 1970s. Sometimes there are clashes between different public bodies and their interests and aspirations; most recently, governments have clashed regarding where to locate dump sites for toxic wastes.

External Effects

The differences between a community's interests and the interests of others, of the sort described above, usually arise from the expected **external effects** that a proposed development will have on the community. These external effects, which are often called "overspill effects" or "externalities," may be localized, or they may affect the entire community and even beyond. Concerns arise, say, from the expectation that a new professional office building near a low-density residential area may generate traffic and parking needs that can be met only on adjacent streets. A school board's decision to close a neighbourhood school may cause parents to worry that their children will have to walk farther to school and perhaps cross dangerous streets as well. Or there may be concern that the design of a new subdivision's storm-drainage system could cause pollution in a nearby stream that feeds into the community's water supply.

The conception of externalities accompanying development proposals and projects has come to be a central concern in community planning, especially in the past few decades. Earlier community planning tended to focus more directly on overcoming problems of, for example, the lack of housing for the poor or lack of adequate transportation from the suburbs to the centre of the city. Partly owing to greater understanding about how the various parts of a community function and relate to one another, community planning now takes into consideration the potential effects of a low-income housing project on a neighbourhood and on the residents of the project itself. It examines the proposed highway linking the city centre and the suburbs for its effects on the property values, traffic patterns, and air quality of the areas through which it passes. A good deal of community planning is as much about trying to grasp *potential* external effects of development as it is about responding to its direct and immediate effects.

The need to grasp potential problems arising from development proposals has brought with it two other characteristics. The first is the recognition that external effects may not be known from our previous experience—they may have to be guessed at. Moreover, we are beginning to realize that many effects of development may not even be known until well into the future. Community planning today deals to a considerable extent with *predicting* the problems associated with development proposals and other changes in the community as well as with *prescribing* solutions to problems. A second characteristic is the dependence on scientific and technical knowledge to understand the complexity of a community. Arising from this dependence is the need for technical assistance—e.g., the planning professional—to address complex community situations.

To recapitulate, community planning is called upon to determine whether actual or expected problems of development are important for the community as a whole as well as to determine how the community's interest may best be served in solving the problems. When growth and development impinge on community interest, the concern is essentially with the future form and condition that the community aspires to, or at least anticipates. Community planning, therefore, deals not just with solving problems but also with solving them so that the community turns out to be as good as, or better than, it was expected to be. Even in the solving of problems, a community tries through its planning to achieve some of its ideals. In this concern for ideals, we see a connection with the other major reason for community planning—the desire to achieve some ideal form.

THE NEED TO ACHIEVE AN IMPROVED ENVIRONMENT

Community planning is concerned with more than solving the problems posed by current development. Goals are important as well. There is a tradition of idealism that influences much of what is done in the name of community planning. Probably the most quoted aphorism on the subject of idealism is that of Daniel Burnham—"make no little plans"—in the introduction to his 1909 plan for Chicago:

> Make no little plans; they have no magic to stir men's blood and probably themselves will not be realized. Make big plans: aim high in hope and work, remembering that a noble, logical diagram, once recorded, will never die, but long after we are gone will be a living thing, asserting itself with ever growing insistency.

An intrinsic part of most community planning efforts involves the consideration of ideal situations and the aspirations of people for their community. It is a tradition that has its roots deep in the history of city-building. The plans for cities in ancient Greece, Rome, and China, in the Middle East, and in the Americas reveal a concern for the proper location of various functions of the city. The sites of religious buildings and public areas and even the geographical orientation of the streets often were considered symbolic and thus important. Cities themselves were seen as symbols of a society's aspiration to achieve progress and human betterment. As Aristotle noted, "A Citie is a perfect and absolute assembly or communion of many townes or streets in one."[2] Through succeeding eras, the city as a reflection of human aspirations continued to be a major theme in philosophy and culture, although the images changed from the religious to the secular as societies changed.

This tradition is still a powerful one in community planning. The sentiments expressed by Burnham do not encourage just boldness; they encourage the community to express its hopes and ideals in its plans, rather than only deal with solutions to temporary problems or "choose among lesser evils," as David Riesman has stated.[3] Indeed, Gordon Stephenson, a British planner who worked and taught in Canada in the 1950s, unequivocally observes: "I do not believe we can make worthy plans without having ideal conceptions. ..."[4] And, in Canada, there are many examples where the ideals of the plan-makers for human betterment are central to the community plan.

Nowhere is this more striking than on our resource frontier. Kapuskasing, Ontario, planned by Thomas Adams, one of the great planners associated with Canada, and built in the 1920s, is one such place; Kitimat, British Columbia (Figure 1.1), largely designed by the famed American planner Clarence Stein in the 1950s, is another instance of planning to achieve ideal living conditions for an entire community. Both these planners, it also turns out, were well acquainted with the efforts of Ebenezer Howard in England to promote, and eventually build, self-contained Garden Cities. The latter concept of an ideal community is also an extremely powerful model for those concerned with planning and building suburban communities in Canada, from Strathcona Park near Edmonton to Ajax near Toronto.

Other Canadian community plans, while equally idealistic in concept, have striven to improve the environment on a less sweeping scale. One of the most notable is the 1915 plan for Ottawa which aimed to achieve a monumental quality for the nation's capital; of the same genre is the Wascana Centre area around the legislative buildings in Regina. More recently, the planning of Harbourfront in Toronto and False Creek South in Vancouver reflects the aspirations of these communities to create a new but lasting image in their environments. In these examples, something new is designed and built. Rooted in this same theme are the historical conservation programs undertaken by some communities, such as Niagara-on-the-Lake, Ontario, and St. Andrews, New Brunswick, where the desire is to preserve surroundings of special value for future generations.

Whether the planning involves the design for some special new environment or the refurbishing of highly valued older environments, the thrust is essentially the same: creating an image or vision of a possible community environment. At its most dramatic, this facet of planning in modern

FIGURE 1.1   **First Phase of a New Canadian Community: Kitimat, B.C., 1957**
American planner Clarence Stein was commissioned to design a city in northern British
Columbia, ultimately for 50,000, based on the "neighbourhood unit" principle. The eco-
nomic base of the community is a huge aluminum smelter. *Source:* Alcan Smelters and
Chemicals Ltd.

times has produced the impressive capital cities of Brasilia in Brazil (Figure
1.2) and Chandigarh in India. But even less spectacular planning situations
reflect a human need to strive for improved community environments.
There is a utopian element in most community planning, as there has been
since the first communities were planned. But these visions are realizable.
According to an old adage, "A planner is someone with his head in the
clouds and his feet planted firmly on the ground."

   As we have seen, there are two basic reasons for community planning:
one pragmatic (the need to deal with problems in the environment) and
one ideal (the need to strive for a better environment). These approaches
are not mutually exclusive. Those who participate in community planning—professionals or citizens, politicians or developers—seek to reconcile the pragmatic need to solve a problem and the human need to seek a

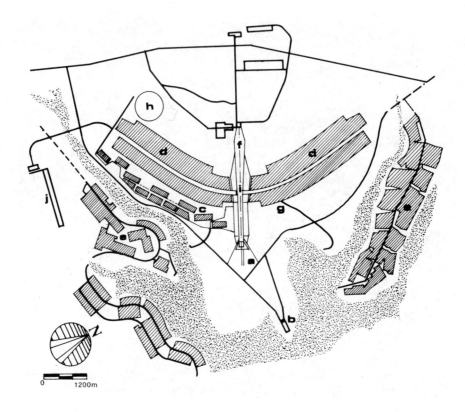

FIGURE 1.2   **Plan for a New Capital City: Brasilia, 1957**
The idea for an inland capital for Brazil dates from its independence in 1822. A competition for a plan was held in 1956, and the curved cruciform plan of Lucio Costa was chosen. Fine buildings were designed by architect Oscar Niemeyer, and the first phase of the highly symbolic city was completed in 1960. *Key:* (a) Main Square, (b) President's residence, (c) foreign embassies, (d, e) residential areas, (f) recreation area, (g) university, (h) cemetery, (i) main traffic interchange, (j) airport.

more fitting environment. The various participants may emphasize one facet over the other, and even change their views over time, but once involved in the planning process, they cannot long avoid the need to recognize the importance of both.

AS THE BOOK PROGRESSES

Planning activity is probably as widespread among Canadian communities as in any other western country. Notably, this planning activity has peculiarly Canadian characteristics, even though it owes much to British and U.S. approaches. The roots, the social purposes, the organizational traits, the professional practice and methods, and who participates in community planning are all entwined in the approach taken in planning in any country. It is the aim of this book to examine the Canadian response to the task of planning for the building and rebuilding of communities large and small in Canada.

The task of planning, which is now so widely accepted as a public function by our metropolitan, city, and town councils, is nonetheless often a bewildering array of actions all taken in the name of community planning. Accommodating new private and public projects, handling applications for rezoning, processing subdivision proposals, designating buildings for historic preservation, and judging the merits of rural land severances or of filling in a flood-prone area are but some of the major planning tasks in Canadian communities. People in all walks and stages of life are affected by the decisions made in the process of pursuing official plans, zoning by-laws, and other land development controls. Both the appearance and functioning of a community are affected; and new concerns—currently, the environment and community quality—are always impinging on community planning.

Despite the venerable history of Canadian community planning, there exists no comprehensive rendering of the origins of the approaches we use in planning today, or of our present-day styles and practices of planning. A basic premise of this book is that community planning in Canada, or elsewhere, may be better understood if one distinguishes (1) the principles and purposes for which planning is pursued; (2) the way in which planning is practised; and (3) the persons and groups who participate in planning activities. These three distinct parts of community planning—the *principles, practice,* and *participants*—provide the focus for the three main parts of this book.

Planning Roots and Principles

Part One examines the roots of Canadian planning. Although the planning of Canadian communities as a conscious public activity is a fairly recent phenomenon, interest in community planning as a way of achieving better communities dates back to the latter part of the 19th century. Community planning is part of our public *culture* in Canada. To have become an integral part of our community life means that it must have roots in long-standing ideals, ideas, and principles about how a community should develop and how it should protect the public interest in the process of development. Important public activities seldom are adopted overnight; they grow out of experience, tradition, and ideals. Four chapters in this section examine three main roots of community planning in Canada: the legacies of the **physical forms** of cities of the past, in other countries (Chapter 2) as well as in Canada (Chapter 3); the array of **social purposes** for which planning is often undertaken and the changing composition of social problems in Canadian communities (Chapter 4); and the evolving **governmental structures** within which public planning decisions are made in this country (Chapter 5). These chapters cover the development of planning through to about 1950 when the activity became more ubiquitous.

Planning Practice

Part Two describes the practice of community planning in Canada at the present time. When community planning goes beyond ideal concepts and social concerns, a mode of practice develops to deal with elements of the environment being planned and to provide the organizational arrangements to conduct public planning. Planning tasks bring forth the need for certain skills, attitudes, expertise, institutions, and tools. Contemporary community planning in Canada has well-developed modes of practice such that planning activity differs little from one part of the country to the other. The form and content of planning practice is described in this part's seven chapters. The **physical environment** and the way planners view it initiate the discussion (Chapter 6), followed by a description of the steps necessary in **making a community plan**, including the typical planning studies that support the plan's proposals (Chapter 7). The **scope and role of the community plan** are then described (Chapter 8), followed by an examination of the **means for implementing** it, e.g., zoning and other land-use controls (Chapter 9) as well as **public policy initiatives** to guide land development (Chapter 10). An examination of how planning works in large communities, metropoli, and regions (Chapter 11) and in quite small ones, such as towns and villages (Chapter 12), rounds out this section.

Planning's Participants

Part Three examines the players involved in making decisions about a community plan. Community planning obliges us to use collective decision-making processes, usually within government, because of the wide array of individuals and groups that may become involved. The procedures that are used, which may be both formal and informal, condition the process of planning in two ways: on the one hand, they define who may participate, and on the other, they define how and when decisions need to be made. The concluding chapters describe two facets of decision making. First, there is an overview of the sequence of **decisions in making a plan** and of the response to development initiatives, including that of the main actors in these initiatives (Chapter 13). Second, an in-depth view of **the main participant**s— from planners to politicians to developers and citizens—is presented (Chapter 14). Planning deals with change and how it affects a community's environment. Some of the issues it deals with today will be supplanted by new ones in the future, just as past issues in planning no longer prevail. Chapter 15 provides a perspective on **past and future planning,** with particular emphasis on the challenges ahead.

Community planning should be seen as a part of the human dynamic. It does not take place in books, but in council chambers, neighbourhood halls, and sometimes in the streets. I have endeavoured to capture some of the drama associated with community planning by introducing a series of case studies called Planning Issues that depict facets of some of the many planning stories that make up the fabric of planning across this country. Regardless of their date or present state of resolution, they are indicative of planning issues communities encounter.

ENDNOTES

1. An older, but still useful source of Canadian community planning initiatives (and one which suggested this list) is Canadian National Committee for Habitat, *The Canadian Settlements Sampler* (Ottawa: Community Planning Press, 1976), especially 14–43.
2. From Aristotle's *Politics* in a 1598 translation, as cited in Helen Rosenau, *The Ideal City* (London:Studio Vista, 1974), 12.
3. David Riesman, "Some Observations on Community Plans and Utopia," *Yale Law Journal* 57 (December 1947).
4. Gordon Stephenson, "Some Thoughts on the Planning of Metropolitan Regions," *Papers of the Regional Science Association* 4 (1958), 27–38.

Chapter 2   The Beginnings of Today's Cities

Such is the tenacity of these simple geometric forms, the circle, the straight line, and the right angle. They survive because of their adaptability.

Hans Blumenfeld, 1943

PERENNIAL ISSUES

When making a plan for a community today, it is safe to predict that the outcome will reflect physical forms from the past. On the one hand, a plan for an existing community will be influenced by the arrangement of streets or the adaptation to the site made by earlier community-building decisions. On the other hand, many modern planning concepts about the physical form and arrangement of a community can be traced to earlier times. These ideas continue to influence plans for today's communities.

Over the approximately 5,000 years since humankind began designing communities, six important issues have recurred for planners. Further, they need to be addressed when it is a matter both of building a wholly new community and of expanding an existing one.[1] They are fundamental to much of what this book is about and need to be arrayed now. The queries that accompany each are key ones for planners to consider, but there will always be others depending upon the community and the era:

1. **The selection of the site.**   Will it be a hilltop or valley, an island or cape, a harbour or some other transportation advantage?
2. **The function (or purpose) of the community.**   What needs is the settlement intended to satisfy? Is it to provide protection, facilitate commerce, act as a political or religious focal point?

3. **The allocation of land uses.**   Where will the people live, do business, govern, worship, congregate for public activities?
4. **Accommodating growth and change.**   Should the community be more intensively developed within its present confines or be extended on the periphery if it needs to grow?
5. **The need for connection.**   How will people and goods circulate and be exchanged among various land uses?
6. **The form of the community.**   What are the aspirations of the populace, the aesthetic considerations of the culture, the functional needs to be served?

These six issues are perennial ones for the planning of all communities, as we said, whether building anew or rebuilding. Although planners must acknowledge all of them, the importance they accord to each will vary depending upon a number of things: the community's values, the human needs, the technology available (especially for building and circulation), and the economic and other functions. Once decisions are made and carried out in any of these issue areas, the physical shape and arrangement of the community will be influenced through all succeeding periods. Consider these points in regard to the various historical cases of city-building and planning described throughout the remainder of this chapter and in those that follow.

Physical forms in a community have a remarkable persistence even though the original function of the place may change. The planner in any period, therefore, works with a *legacy* of past decisions about a community's physical form. Even though Canadian communities are, at most, a few hundred years old, the planner of today's community may work with ideas that come from distant history. Thus, we shall first review briefly important examples of city-building that preceded the actual establishment of communities in 17th-century Canada.

ORIGINS OF CITY-BUILDING AND PLANNING

Cities of the Ancient World

The best knowledge we have about the beginnings of cities indicates that substantial settlements were being built about 3000 B.C. There were village settlements long before 3000 B.C., and villages still abound. But these simple groupings of more or less equal social units are not cities, even though they may possess some regular pattern and have a fairly large population.

As eminent Canadian planner Hans Blumenfeld has noted, "Only where the plurality of social units of a village is combined with the social and functional differentiation found in the castle can we talk of a city."[2] Thus, cities emerge when a society begins to distinguish such social needs as defence, promotion of worship, or symbolizing political control in a region, and then combines these functions with the need to house a large population nearby. The effort to achieve a satisfactory combination of these basic functions at a particular location constitutes the earliest community planning.

Cities of Mesopotamia

The cities of the Tigris and Euphrates Valleys, especially Babylon, provide good examples of planning in ancient times. Babylon (Figure 2.1) was

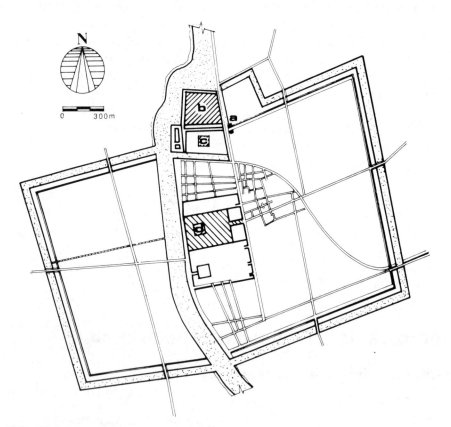

FIGURE 2.1   **Babylon, 6th Century B.C.**
In the time of Nebuchadnezzar, Babylon spanned the Euphrates River, and its walls and moat encompassed an area of about 3 km². Its population was around 10,000. *Key:* (a) main gate, (b) fort, (c) Hanging Gardens, (d) temple.

located in the Euphrates Valley (about 80 km south of present-day Baghdad, Iraq). Its site was a "cape" in the river, which probably provided a good site for defence, transportation, and water supply. The river bisected the city, and a wall encircled both sides, enclosing an area of about 2 km². Powerful emperors lived in Babylon, and during their tenure the city was embellished in many ways. The most famous emperor, Nebuchadnezzar (625–551 B.C.), as well as building the renowned Hanging Gardens, is said by the Greek writer Herodotus to have paved the great processional avenue with "limestone flags."[3]

Of the dwellings of common folk (and the population of Babylon is reputed to have reached close to 10,000 at this time), little can be said. They would have occupied the bulk of the land in the city, but the residential areas seem not to have had any regular layout. Dwellings were arranged within blocks of land perhaps a hectare in size. The housing blocks were not regular in size or shape, and thus the spaces between them, which served as streets, were irregular, although they tended to be rectilinear.

Two factors seem to account for the amorphous form of the interior of these cities. The first is that people moved around mostly on foot (wagons or carts were an exception), a mode of transportation suitable to the lanes that served as streets. The second factor is that the commerce and manufacturing, and even a good deal of the agriculture, were conducted within the dwellings or land in the housing block. Streets were not required to provide easy connections throughout the city for the exchange of goods or for people to get to jobs. This general pattern of cities, comprising dominant public areas, a few major roads leading to monuments and gates, and rather undifferentiated residential areas all within a city wall, was to persist until the Middle Ages in Europe.

Other Ancient City Planning

Ancient Chinese community planning dates at least as far back as the Mesopotamian period. Danish planner Steen Eiler Rasmussen tells us that when Emperor Kublai Khan built his capital in 1268, he chose a location where "five different towns had existed, one after the other, over a period of thousands of years; each one perfectly rectangular and each one oriented exactly north-south and east-west."[4] This precise orientation follows the ancient philosophical principle of *feng shui,* "wind and water," which promotes harmony among various pairs of physical factors within a geographic framework related to the sun. Early Chinese cities had fortified walls with a main gate on the south side. There was usually a great processional road leading from the gate directly north to the entrance of the ruler's palace or to a temple. There were often gates and main streets leading in the other three directions as well. The interior of the city was subdivided into square blocks of land with great families often segregated into special city districts with their own walls.[5] Lanes between housing blocks were narrow and not arranged in a uniform pattern, although the square housing blocks lent a rectilinear form. (See Figure 2.2.)

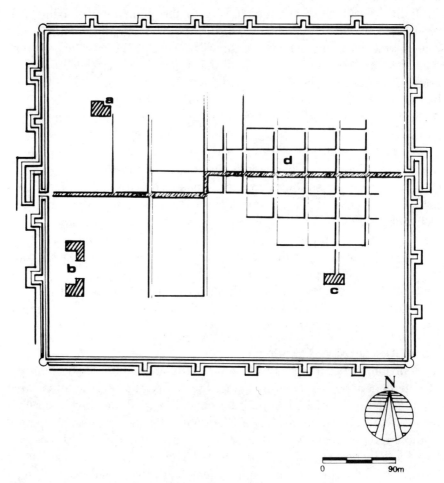

FIGURE 2.2   Khara-Khoto, Early Chinese Colony
This "planted town" in Central Asia employs the planning geometry used in ancient cities in China, with walls and roads oriented precisely north-south and east-west. Roads from the gates are offset to prevent evil spirits from passing through. The town walls enclosed about 0.2 km^2 and held a population of 4,000–5,000. *Key:* (a) tomb, (b) temple, (c) palace, (d) residential compounds.

On the other side of the world from both China and Mesopotamia, and nearly as early, the Aztecs and the Incas were building elaborate cities in Central and South America, in places like the Yucatan, Andean Bolivia, and Peru. The approach of the Incas in planning their communities is best seen in Cuzco, Peru. As American planner Francis Violich describes it, the Incan plan for Cuzco was divided into four sections, with a main plaza at the junction of the four main roads, each of which led to the four great regions of the Empire. Minor plazas were located elsewhere within the city walls and "each city block was an allotment for one city family; its distance from the centre of the city depended upon the degree of relationship to the Inca ruler."[6] The Aztec plan of Tenochtitlan in Mexico bears a strong resemblance to that of Cuzco, even though it is 4,800 km north and in an independent empire and culture. It also has a central plaza and four roads leading to the four points of the compass.

Cities of the Greeks and Romans

The Greek Tradition in Cities

The experience of the ancient Greeks is important in the history of city development and planning because it shows us clearly that early societies did plan and build entire communities along preconceived lines. Greek architects and builders, especially Hippodamus, are usually credited with originating the **gridiron** street pattern, although this is not entirely accurate as we shall see. However, insofar as they attempted to encompass the needs of the entire community, Greek architects and builders probably should be credited with the first comprehensive community plans.

In the Greek community plan, the allocation of land to the individual dwelling was the common denominator. Rectangular blocks of land were arranged to allow the dwellings within them to be oriented to the southern sun, a necessity for houses lacking central heating in the more northerly areas occupied by the Greeks. The location of public buildings and spaces determined the location of major streets. The *agora*, or marketplace, was usually built on one side of a main street, although not necessarily in the geographical centre of the city. Main streets also served the temple, the *pnyx*, an open-air podium where citizens met to consider affairs of state, the theatre, and the stadium. It should be noted that main streets were often only 7–9 m wide and local "streets" were the 3–5 m spaces left between the blocks of housing. Thus, the impression of gridiron street plans for Greek cities is only partly true; the rectangular blocks of land given over to housing, rather than the streets, determined the geometric pattern. Since security was a major need of Greek city populations, most towns were surrounded by protective walls.

The "classic city" of the Greeks, as these plans are often called, was built by the score around the shores of the eastern Mediterranean, into Asia Minor, and on the north coast of Africa. When the Greek colonizers sought sites for their new cities, defence and access to the sea were important; thus they chose such sites as craggy headlands on the ocean. This meant superimposing the geometrical Hippodamian street pattern on rugged sites, with the result that numerous streets were so steep as to be built only as steps. The pattern of streets may resemble today's gridiron, but it is worth remembering that most were not thoroughfares for vehicles. The plan for the town of Priene (Figure 2.3) is a good example of classic Greek city-building.

Towns and Cities of the Romans

From the second century B.C., Rome succeeded Greece as the dominant European power. Over the next 500 years, the Romans extended their control from Britain to Algiers, from Constantinople to the Danube Valley. In this period, they made two contributions to the development of community planning. The first was with the plans for colonial towns. The second was in the planning for the large cities that developed on the Italian peninsula.

In order to sustain power in distant lands, garrison towns were established and connected with roads to facilitate movement of the Roman legions. Thus, the old saying "All roads lead to Rome" aptly captures the extent of Roman domination. Hundreds of today's towns and cities of western Europe owe their location to the sites the Romans chose for their garrisons. The Roman term *castrum,* meaning a military encampment, is found as "chester" in English town names; all such places originated from a Roman camp.

The Roman garrison towns (or *coloniae* as they were called, because they were frequently used to deploy discharged soldiers from the huge armies of the time) all followed a similar pattern. Often rectangular in shape, they were surrounded by walls and dissected by two main streets that met at or near the centre. At this location was the forum. House blocks, or *insulae,* of 0.5–1.5 ha either square or oblong were fairly uniform throughout the area enclosed by the walls. The two main streets were usually oriented so that one ran north-south and the other east-west; it has been conjectured that the latter street pointed toward the spot on the horizon where the sun rose on an important ceremonial day for the town. The plan for Silchester (Figure 2.4) in western England, recreated by historians, is rather typical of Roman colonial towns in layout. Although size varied among such towns, they were usually less than 2.6 km^2 in size and often less than 20 ha. The population of the larger Roman towns seldom exceeded 10,000.

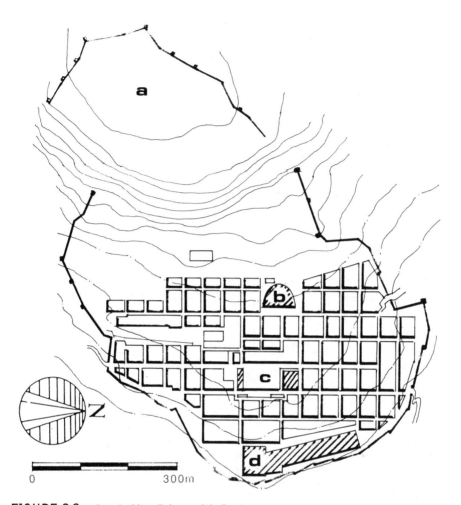

FIGURE 2.3   Greek City: Priene, 4th Century B.C.
The gridiron pattern of Hippodamus is followed in this city of nearly 10,000. It provides for all dwelling blocks to be oriented to the southerly sun and main functional buildings and spaces to be within easy access. *Key:* (a) Acropolis, (b) theatre, (c) Agora or marketplace, (d) stadium.

Such home cities of the Romans as Naples, Pompeii, and Rome itself grew from early villages and without benefit of the deliberate, overall plan used in building their colonial towns. These domestic Roman cities also represent the earliest known examples of planning and managing the development of cities of considerable size. Pompeii, a small city, reached 20,000 population by A.D. 79; Ostia, the port city of Rome, is estimated at

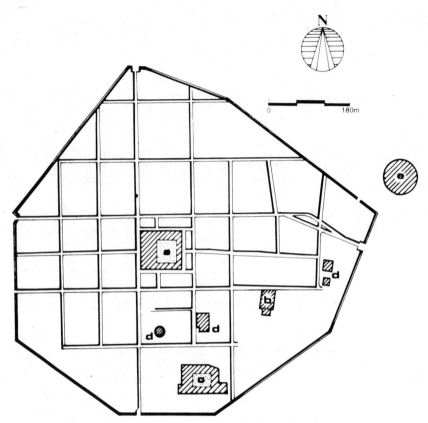

FIGURE 2.4 **Ancient Roman Garrison: Silchester, England**
Roman garrison towns were usually dissected by two main streets, one running north-south and the other east-west; the forum with its shops, temples, and public buildings was near their intersection. The population probably did not exceed 5,000. *Key:* (a) forum, (b) baths, (c) inn, (d) temple, (e) amphitheatre.

50,000 by the 3rd century, and Rome itself reached upward of 1.5 million about the same time. To be able to house populations of this size requires methods of distributing large amounts of water, providing for drainage and sewage, moving people and goods, as well as taking into account shopping and cultural needs.

The Romans solved the technical problems created by their growing cities in unprecedented, and often dramatic, ways. Large aqueducts were built to supply water; Rome needed 14 aqueducts. Underground sewers were constructed that are still considered feats of engineering, and the 29 main highways leading to other parts of the Empire were, in most cases, paved.[7] Canadian planner Robert McCabe has studied how the Romans provided for the shopping needs of citizens. It turns out that they built what correspond to our present-day shopping centres. In conjunction with a city's forum a *macellum* was constructed, a structure for many shops, often on two or more levels. In Rome, the shopping centre portion of the main forum of the city had about 170 shops and covered almost 18,600 m^2.[8] Such a centre compares to the larger shopping centres built in most Canadian communities up to recent years. Smaller planned shopping centres were also built in the various regions (districts) of Rome to provide for "neighbourhood" shopping needs.

The large Roman cities were, undoubtedly, complex communities, in many ways rivalling modern cities. This can be grasped by comparing the population densities. Pompeii occupied about 85 ha and had 20,000 residents; Rome occupied about 26 km^2 and had, possibly, 1.5 million residents. These represent densities around 50,000 persons per square kilometre. Toronto, in its central area, has densities under 8,000 persons per square kilometre and densities of less than half of that in its suburbs.

Summary

Cities in the ancient empires were established much like the "new towns" of modern times; they were often built where no previous settlement had been, or perhaps only a very small one. To quote Rasmussen again:

> [When] faced with the necessity of creating a new town in a strange place they must build it according to a preconceived plan or it will end in chaos. And that plan must, of necessity, be a very simple one, easily laid out, so that everyone with the least possible trouble can quickly discover what he has to do.[9]

Babylon, Peking, Cuzco, and the other ancient cities were planned simply. Their forms reflect the main physical and cultural needs of the society as well as the prevailing technology of the time.

The resulting physical form of ancient cities, indeed of cities until the 14th century, has two fundamental characteristics. First, the arrangement of land uses is, to employ Blumenfeld's term, a "block plan"; **blocks** of land devoted to public and residential uses, rather than **streets**, dictated the form.[10] Second, the surrounding wall limited the community's growth and also tended to give a radial pattern to main streets as they developed to provide access to gates, temples, and markets. This is the first evidence of the **radial-concentric** physical form. It is probably more accurate to describe ancient cities by these two characteristics than to compare them with later cities, where streets and traffic are crucial elements.

ORIGINS OF THE MODERN CITY

It is important that you not see these examples of city-building in the past as static concepts, simply as maps. They were functioning communities that existed over long periods of time, and significantly, they changed during their history: shifting the allocations of land, adding new buildings, making new road connections, even expanding in many cases. They were "continuing" cities, to use the key word from the title of Vance's book.[11] The evolution that occurs in city form and composition would be evident if you were to probe the situation of the ancient cities described above. It should become even more evident as we proceed to describe more modern instances in this section. It is a necessary perspective when one considers not only where a city has come from but also what it might become. You can be sure it will continue to change in the future.

From Dark Ages to Middle Ages

The several hundred years after the fall of Rome in the 5th century, the period called the Dark Ages, are characterized by a general social formlessness and a lack of large settlements in Europe. The political stability and protection provided by the empires of the Greeks and Romans ceased, and large cities could not be maintained; neither their supply of food nor their trade and other basic needs could be assured. The settlement pattern of Europe reverted to one of villages. Only in the stabler empires of Persia, China, and the Americas were cities of considerable size maintained in this period.

As strong kings, princes, and bishops emerged to provide security over larger regions, from the 9th century onward European town life greatly expanded. Many towns and cities began from modest roots in the feudal countryside where, often, some dwellings and a market had been established at the gate of a castle or monastery leading to the extension of the castle walls. Many new towns were also established in this period. All but a few of today's main cities in Europe—Copenhagen, Paris, Vienna, Southampton, Florence, and so on—owe their location and much of their form to the medieval town builders.

The urban historian A.E.J. Morris classifies the towns resulting from the urban expansion of the Middle Ages as being either **organic growth towns** or **new towns**.[12] The former were those places that grew on the sites of old Roman towns, on the sites of fortified feudal villages, or on the sites of agricultural villages. London, Cologne, and Paris grew from such roots and greatly expanded in this period. The physical form of organic growth towns is partly conveyed by the name; that is, they generally lack any overall pattern. Except for a few main roads, the streets meandered, and blocks of land were irregular in shape, as the plan of Carcassonne shows (Figure 2.5). One still finds a residue of this amorphous medieval development at the centre of many large European cities; there are even a few in North America, such as the "Lower Town" in Quebec City.

Morris subdivides the new towns of the Middle Ages into two types: *bastides* and *planted towns.* Both were used to consolidate territorial control by a king or ruling house. Bastides, as the name suggests, were bastions, fortified towns built to a predetermined plan. They employed a clear pattern for streets and blocks of land within rectangular or circular walls. Bastides were built mostly in the 13th century in France, Wales, and England by Edward I, and by other rulers in Germany and Bohemia. Planted towns were new towns developed to promote trade as well as protect territory; New Brandenburg (Figure 2.6) is an example of one such town. Many developed on the sites of existing towns, either with or without a prior plan. Cities like Londonderry in Ireland and Berne and Zurich in Switzerland owe their existence to this form of new town development in the Middle Ages.

More than this, bastides and planted towns would prove to be models that would be used to build cities in the New World, a century or so later. When bastides were first built, there was a need to attract settlers to these regions, and this was done in part by providing the newcomers with plots of land inside and outside the walls. Land-use allocation was much more egalitarian in the bastides than in the past. Their general gridiron pattern facilitated this, and the English, in particular, would come to use this model in their North American colonies.[13]

Whether new towns or those developed from earlier settlements, medieval towns were alike in many respects. The component parts were the wall and its gates, the marketplace, often with a market hall and commercial buildings, the church, and, sometimes, the castle. Main streets connected the main buildings and the market with the gates and joined main areas together. The rest of the land within the wall was allocated in blocks for residences and gardens. When land was needed for, say, a market or church square, either a block of land was left vacant or a street was widened at that point. Most streets were narrow, for movement was largely on foot.

Political necessity and protection were paramount in the town-building of the Middle Ages, but material well-being also improved, and this spurred trade and industry. Tradesmen, artisans, and merchants in many towns became prosperous and powerful enough to challenge the local

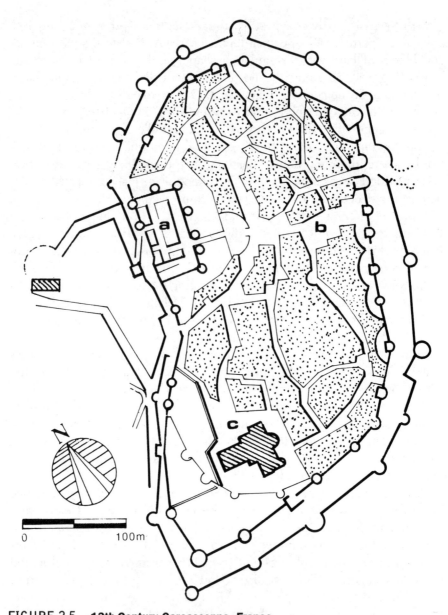

FIGURE 2.5   **13th-Century Carcassonne, France**
Typical of an "organic growth" town of the Middle Ages: the few main streets connect the gates, castle (a), church (c), and market (b) as needed, and the overall pattern is irregular.

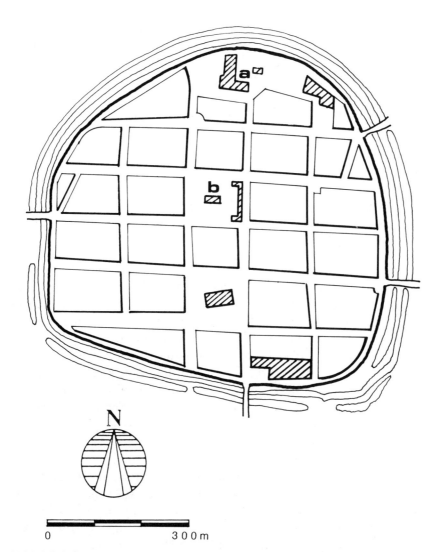

FIGURE 2.6   **Fortified German Town: New Brandenburg, 1248**
Towns such as this one were "planted" for territorial control in the late Middle Ages. They
employed a fairly regular gridiron street pattern. *Key:* (a) church, (b) market square.

rulers and gain citizenship. Especially in northern Europe, they often built guildhalls and a town hall adjacent to the market area of the town to signify the importance of the "burghers," or citizens of the "burg." In the long run of history, these steps to allocate the space of the city among king, church, and citizens were decisive to the development of a modern, segmented, urban way of life. But it should be noted that only a small part of Europe's population lived in towns in the Middle Ages; most people lived in the countryside and engaged in barely more than subsistence agriculture. This would remain the norm until well into the 19th century.

Renaissance and Baroque Cities: The Importance of Design

The period from 1400 to 1800, which encompasses the Renaissance and Baroque eras, is a decisive one in regard to the form of cities today, for this is the period when the compact settlements of medieval Europe were dramatically extended, refined, and restructured. The city became an object of design, a means to express the aesthetic and functional aims of the period. These aims, in short, were a desire for order and discipline and a desire to impress. They can be seen in the designs of the painting and architecture of the time. In turn, they led to the designs for such special features as the Gardens of Versailles, the grand boulevards of Paris, the piazzas of Rome, and the Georgian squares of London. Scores of European cities show the imprint of Renaissance/Baroque city design, as do colonial cities that Europeans took to the Americas and Asia.

The major achievements in city-building in this period came after 1600. They were stimulated by the confluence of five factors: (1) the aesthetic theory and concepts coming from a revival of interest in the classical art forms of Rome and Greece; (2) the invention of printing and improvements in the production of paper; (3) the growth of wheeled traffic as a result of replacing the solid wheel with a lighter one of separate rim, spokes, and hub; (4) the invention of gunpowder, which rendered medieval fortifications obsolete; and (5) the accumulation of immense, autocratic powers by the heads of nation states and city states.

The cumulative effect of these five factors was to turn city planning and development away from the Middle Ages concept of cities being concentric, concentrated, and self-contained. Cities were literally opened up by new avenues, public squares, and new residential districts. Moreover, the planning was a self-conscious undertaking with certain design principles at the forefront: symmetry, coherence, perspective, and monumentality. The informal and somewhat ad hoc arrangements of the medieval town gave way to a "preoccupation," as Morris calls it, "to make a balanced composition" when making a city plan.[14]

Most of the planning activity was devoted to restructuring existing cities, since few new places were created in this period. The planners, who were mainly architects and engineers, employed three main design components:[15] the main straight avenue, the gridiron pattern for local streets in new districts, and enclosed spaces. As Lewis Mumford says:

> The avenue is the most important symbol and the main fact about the baroque city. Not always was it possible to design a whole new city in the baroque mode; but in the layout of half a dozen new avenues, or in a new quarter, its character could be re-defined.[16]

The main avenue, often radiating from a monument or public square, was a functional necessity as much as a Renaissance/Baroque design concept (see Figure 2.7), for in this period wheeled traffic increased tremendously. There was resistance to this new mode of travel, as there would be later to railroads in cities and urban expressways, but the advantages were obvious for the flow of goods, people, and military equipment. Combined with the strong powers possessed by the rulers of the city states, these dramatic changes to street patterns could be achieved with relative ease. The advent of the straight street for moving traffic, both the main avenues and in new districts, marks the beginning of what Blumenfeld describes as the "street plan" for cities.

The public square was just as important in Renaissance/Baroque city design as the straight street. Squares were also conceived on an axial basis, sometimes provided by a main avenue leading to the square. In addition, squares were enclosed spaces; that is, they were designed as three-dimensional spaces to be surrounded by buildings or other landscape features providing an architectural harmony. Even main streets with their uniform facades took on this same sense of enclosure. This quality of architectural coherence, so often lauded by visitors to Europe's cities, probably best epitomizes the notion of urbanity in a city, a quality still sought after in the building of present-day civic centres.

The cities of the 1400–1800 period still needed to be bastions of defence, but owing to the perfection of gunpowder and the cannon new means of fortification had to be found. Because the vertical medieval walls would be breached, the alternative was to increase the horizontal distance between the perimeter of the city and the fortifications. There were countless attempts to create an ideally defensible and livable city through the design of intricate systems of bastions and citadels. Plans for fortified towns, often based on the concepts of French military engineer Sebastian Vauban, were

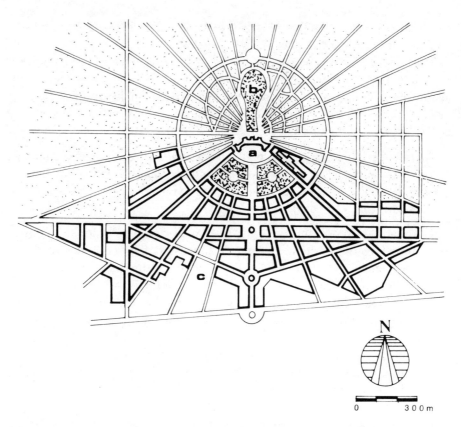

FIGURE 2.7 **18th-Century Karlsruhe, Germany**
This is an example of the Renaissance city as an object of design, using straight and diagonal boulevards leading to focal points, in this case, the palace (a) and the royal gardens
(b). The remainder of the town (c) had a modified gridiron street pattern.

printed and widely available throughout Europe. Even though few were
built, fortified cities influenced the modifications made to existing cities and
were no doubt responsible for ideas incorporated into the plans for several
entirely new ones that have since become major cities: St. Petersburg in
Russia, Mannheim in Germany, and Gothenburg in Sweden.

The Imprint of the Renaissance in the Americas

It was during the Renaissance, often called the Age of Discovery, that the
systematic exploration and settlement of the Americas began. The initial
European settlements were cast in the mould of city forms conceived in

the home countries of the explorers and settlers. Defence of territorial claims was paramount at first, and the earliest settlements adopted the patterns of fortified towns in Europe with a wall and citadel or main battery. Within the walls one finds the Renaissance street patterns and public squares. The plan for Louisbourg, Nova Scotia, (see Figure 3.2) provides an excellent illustration of the early French conception of new town-building in the New World. New Amsterdam, the original Dutch settlement at New York, was also built on similar principles.

The Spanish, the first and most assiduous colonizers, approached the planning of towns according to a set of written rules entitled *The Laws of the Indies* (sometimes called "America's first planning legislation"),[17] which covered everything from the selection of sites, the building of ramparts, and the specifications for the main plaza, to the location of principal streets and important buildings, and the size of lots. The physical form of the Spanish towns was similar to that of the bastides, widely used in Europe.

The gridiron arrangement chosen by the French for Montreal, which faces on and parallels the St. Lawrence River, also followed the bastide model and is said to have influenced such other French outposts in the Mississippi Valley as St. Louis, Mobile, and New Orleans.[18] The influence of Renaissance planning ideas through English settlement in North America is best seen in the towns established from New York to Georgia. These towns employed the gridiron layout of streets combined with public squares, following the pattern set by the new, fashionable residential districts of English cities in the mid-17th century.[19]

Two important examples, the plans for Philadelphia (Figure 2.8) in 1682 and Savannah in 1735, carry forth the concept for an entire city. The plan William Penn chose for Philadelphia was a gridiron of streets in which the two major streets crossed near the centre and formed a public square, and in which each quadrant had its own square. James Oglethorpe's plan for Savannah made more refined use of the Georgian square by providing one in each ward of 40 houses; the wards were bounded by roads of the main gridiron and can be likened in concept to the "superblocks" used in 20th-century planning. A notable exception to the rectangular layout for English settlements is Francis Nicholson's plan for Annapolis, Maryland. With its two great circles, imposing squares, and radiating streets, this 1718 plan was obviously inspired by the French Baroque designers. Such a design would not be emulated in North America until the famous plan for Washington, another three-quarters of a century later.

The last direct Renaissance influence on North American cities came from the plan Major Pierre Charles L'Enfant prepared for Washington in 1791 (Figure 2.9). L'Enfant was a French emigré engineer and artist who

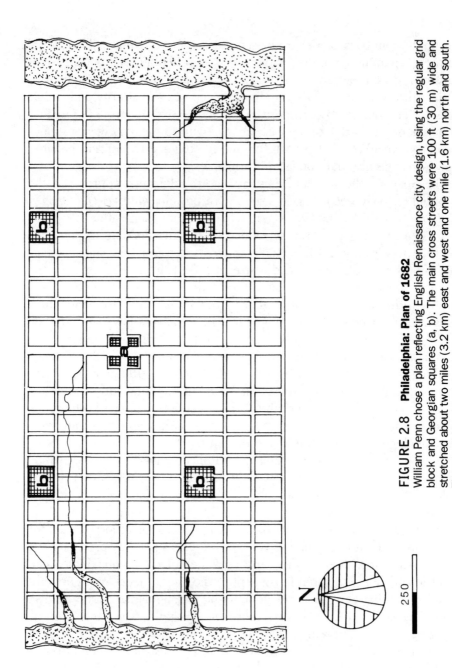

FIGURE 2.8 **Philadelphia: Plan of 1682**
William Penn chose a plan reflecting English Renaissance city design, using the regular grid block and Georgian squares (a, b). The main cross streets were 100 ft (30 m) wide and stretched about two miles (3.2 km) east and west and one mile (1.6 km) north and south. The central square (a) was 4 ha in size.

served in the Revolutionary Army under George Washington, and who had grown up at the court of Versailles. In remarkably short order, estimated at less than six months, he developed an adaptation of baroque monumental vistas, city squares, and diagonal streets superimposed on a grid of local streets. Despite such mundane impediments as awkward intersections and building lots (caused by the radial avenues crossing the local grid), the plan is noteworthy for its grand scale and its assiduous application of Baroque concepts to an entire city. Plans for several other cities employing a similar radial-grid pattern—Detroit, Buffalo, and Indianapolis—followed shortly thereafter, but only small parts of them were ever completed.

The L'Enfant plan nearly did not come to fruition. Its implementation depended on the sale of private building lots to pay the costs of the new public buildings, avenues, and squares. Washington went through a long and fitful period when land either did not sell, or was not built upon, or,

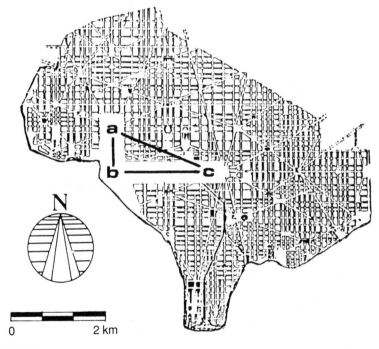

FIGURE 2.9   **L'Enfant's Plan for Washington, D.C., 1791**
Pierre L'Enfant adopted the French Renaissance traditions for his grand plan for the government buildings and monuments of Washington. A system of radial streets focuses on important points and is superimposed on a gridiron. His "federal triangle" links (a) the President's (White) House, (b) the Washington Monument, and (c) the Congressional (Capitol) Building.

when built upon, encroached on public areas. Construction had even taken place on the Mall linking the Capitol and the Washington Monument, and a railway was authorized to cross it as well. For much of the 19th century, Washington was referred to as "a plan without a city."

In contrast to city development in baroque Europe, the communities of North America were promoted as places where colonists would have a large measure of freedom to develop their own land. Thus, the control that rulers of European states were able to impose over civic structures in home cities did not exist to the same degree in their colonies. Even the power of the U.S. federal government to implement the L'Enfant plan was constrained compared to Napoleon's authorizing that the boulevards of Paris be built, which occurred at about the same time in history. While Renaissance designs could be brought to North America, they could not always be achieved.

ENDNOTES

1. An excellent background on the issues surrounding city-building throughout history is found in James W. Vance, *The Continuing City* (Baltimore: Johns Hopkins University Press, 1990), 24ff.
2. Hans Blumenfeld, "Form and Function in Urban Communities," in Hans Blumenfeld, *The Modern Metropolis*, edited by Paul D. Spreiregen (Montreal: Harvest House, 1967), 4.
3. F. Haverfield, *Ancient Town Planning* (Oxford: Clarendon Press, 1913), 25.
4. Steen Eiler Rasmussen, *Towns and Buildings* (Cambridge, Mass.: M.I.T. Press, 1949), 8.
5. Thomas Adams, *Outline of Town and City Planning* (New York: Russell Sage Foundation, 1935), 47.
6. Francis Violich, *Cities of Latin America* (New York: Reinhold Publishing, 1944), 22ff.
7. Robert W. McCabe, "Shops and Shopping in Ancient Rome," *Plan Canada* 19 (September–December 1979), 183–199.
8. *Ibid.*
9. Rasmussen, *Towns and Buildings,* 8.
10. Blumenfeld, "Form and Function," 24.
11. Vance, *Continuing City.*
12. A.E.J. Morris, *History of Urban Form* (New York: John Wiley, 1979), 66.
13. Vance, *Continuing City,* 200ff.
14. Morris, *History of Urban Form,* 125.
15. *Ibid.,* 125ff.

16. Lewis Mumford, *The City in History* (New York: Harcourt Brace and World, 1968), 367.

17. John Reps, *Town Planning in Frontier America* (Princeton, N.J.: Princeton University Press, 1969), 41.

18. *Ibid.,* 82.

19. Vance, *Continuing City,* 234ff.

Chapter 3 Physical Foundations of Canadian Communities

Cities do not grow—all of them are planned.

Thomas Adams, 1922

The foundations of Canadian communities are an accumulation of **planning** decisions made when it was necessary to choose their sites and the layouts of their streets. While these initial building blocks varied depending upon the founders and the era, the form given when establishing communities can be found in today's pattern, even though most places are vastly enlarged.

In the latter part of the 19th century, the new technologies of transportation and industry fostered rapid urban growth. The decisions of such large landowners as the railway companies and the federal government also affected the early form and character of many Canadian communities.

Increasingly, with the start of the 20th century, formal planning concepts began to influence the form that communities took. An emerging planning profession began to codify and apply its ideas, many of which continue to be employed. In turn, the vast expansion of Canadian cities after World War II, conditioned in so many ways by the automobile, made new demands on a community's land, both at the centre and on the outskirts, and brought new dimensions to city form.

Thus, in their relatively short history, most Canadian communities have evolved out of a variety of needs and influences. Our communities are a collage of planning decisions made at different times in the past for all or part of the community. These foundations may not always suit the needs of present-day communities, but they cannot be ignored in new plans. This chapter examines those factors in the foundation of Canadian communities that condition a large part of current planning efforts.

FORMS OF FRONTIER COMMUNITIES

Decisions made when the country was first being settled provide the foundations for much of today's urban development in Canada. The locations and the layouts used in the fortresses, trading posts, and railway towns are still prominent features in their present city forms. Moreover, all but a few of the places that have become cities were developed initially on the basis of a plan. From the towns of the French regime of the St. Lawrence and of the British in the Maritimes, to those established later in Ontario, British Columbia, and the Prairies, plans were usually made before or at the building of a community. A brief survey will help show the forms that characterized the early community plans as each region came to be settled.

French Canada

The earliest planned communities in Canada were those established by the French in the early 17th century. Three on the St. Lawrence River have become major cities today: Quebec City (1608), Trois-Rivières (1634), and Montreal (1642). Quebec and Montreal are the most distinctive. Quebec's Old City has the character of a medieval organic growth town. That of Montreal is more like a planted town or bastide the town form developed for setting new territories in France.[1] Their patterns are informal, having developed according to the evolving needs of the community.

Quebec's Lower Town, built by Champlain on a narrow river terrace, assumed a generally rectilinear pattern of narrow streets in which one block was left open for a public square, Place Royale, onto which fronted the town's church. The Upper Town developed outward from the fort and the cathedral. The *place d'armes* in front of the governor's fort gave an orientation to one set of rectangular housing blocks, while the *grande place* in front of the cathedral provided a different orientation to another set of housing blocks. Housing development and fortifications expanded hand in hand as the Upper Town grew, with the walls, in the 1720s, reaching the extent we see today. In the late 17th century, in an attempt to give some overall order, two parallel streets were run through the town, each to a main gate in the wall.[2]

Montreal's Old City was laid out in a more regular form than Quebec's. It is shaped, as a visitor in 1721 remarked, like a "long rectangle."[3] It extends about 1 km along the face of a ridge that slopes down to the St. Lawrence River. Walls eventually enclosed the town, but these are now gone. In 1672, two major streets that ran the length of the settlement were surveyed. Other streets, running up the hill between the two main streets, were not regularly spaced. The resulting pattern is an irregular, but now picturesque, gridiron, with many of the original public squares still remaining. Recently discovered manuscripts suggest that Montreal's original plan also may have derived from Champlain.[4]

The most interesting of the early French community plans, and among the few truly original Canadian plans, are those for three resettlement villages 10 km northwest of Quebec, which were laid out by Jean Talon in 1667. In an effort to settle the rural population in villages (as in France) rather than in long, narrow lots strung out along the St. Lawrence, Talon developed three villages: Charlesbourg, Bourg Royal (Figure 3.1), and L'Auvergne. The village design is based on the idea of farm lots radiating out from a central square surrounded by a road, on the outside of which would be located the village church, flour mill, shops, etc. Each village was about 2.5 km on a side, and the central square, called the *traite-quarre,* about 275 m on a side.[5] A main road was projected to bisect the area in each direction to link up with the other towns. There were 10 farms of 35 *arpents* (about 14 ha) in each quadrant. Charlesbourg is now part of the urbanized area of metropolitan Quebec, but its radial pattern can still be discerned.

Louisbourg (Figure 3.2), the imposing fortress town on Cape Breton Island, is another major example of French community design, but here the form and concept is completely "imported." French army engineers constructed a fortified city in the traditions of Sebastian Vauban, who had refined the concepts of European city defence in the new era of cannons and gunpowder. There were four major bastions, 5 km of ramparts, many demi-bastions, and outworks surrounding the town. It was meant for 4,000 persons and was laid out as a regular gridiron. The town lasted a scant 40 years; its fortifications were demolished by the British in 1760. The restoration of Louisbourg according to its original plan, which is now nearly complete, will provide the best example of a late-Renaissance fortified town outside Europe.

Atlantic Canada

St. John's, Newfoundland is the oldest community in Canada and, possibly, in North America. In 1583, Sir Humphrey Gilbert formally established the British claim to the area, although it is reputed already to have had a permanent village for several decades. No plan exists for the founding of St. John's; it seems rather to have evolved from its beginnings as a fishing village oriented to the shoreline. The pattern which emerged gradually for the town, and which still dominates the city's central area, was of two streets that parallel the irregular curve of the shore. One, near the water's edge and called Lower Path, is now the main business street, Water Street;

FIGURE 3.1   **The First Canadian Planned Towns, 1667**

Jean Talon's radial plan (right) for three villages north of Quebec City: Charlesbourg, Bourg Royal, and L'Auvergne. A central square at the intersection of roads to neighbouring villages was reserved for a church, cemetery, and flour mill. Settlers' houses were arranged around the square on each of the 40 triangular farms. Each village was about 6 km^2. The recent aerial photo (below) clearly shows the original radial pattern in two of these towns. Both are now part of the Quebec Urban Community. *Sources:* Commission of Conservation (plan) and National Air Photo Library.

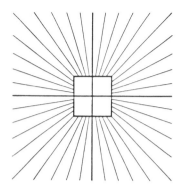

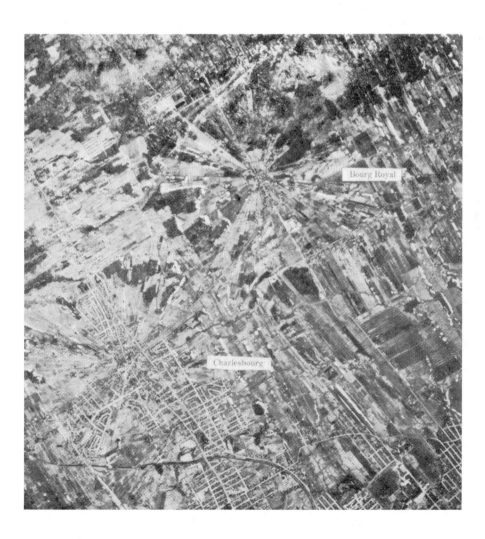

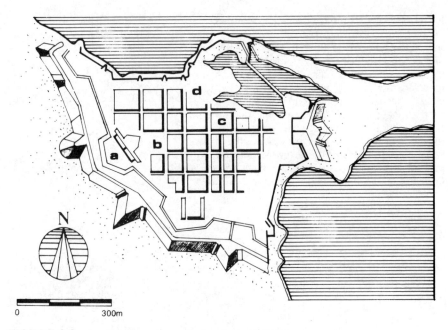

FIGURE 3.2   **Louisbourg, Cape Breton Island, 1720**
This French fortress town for 4,000 combined the Renaissance gridiron street pattern and the fortifications designed for the era of cannons and gunpowder. It is currently being restored. *Key:* (a) main bastion, (b) square, (c) hospital, (d) market.

the other, further up the slope and called Upper Path, is also a major street today.

When the British began to establish permanent settlement in the Atlantic region in the mid-18th century, communities were developed according to plans. These were almost invariably a regular gridiron, rectangular in shape, and carefully surveyed. Typically, British colonial towns of this period were laid out relative to a survey baseline along the harbour but sufficiently inland to provide an uninterrupted street on which other street lines could be established. This was the fashion in the original town sites for Charlottetown (1768) (Figure 3.3), Saint John (1783), and even on the steep hillsides of Lunenberg (1753) and Halifax. These plans allowed space for a church, a governor's residence, barracks and parade ground, cemetery, and warehouses, and were usually surrounded by a palisade. In the 1749 plan for Halifax, which was Britain's primary North Atlantic naval station, five bastions were located on the perimeter of the town. The central bastion remains today on Citadel Hill overlooking downtown and the harbour.

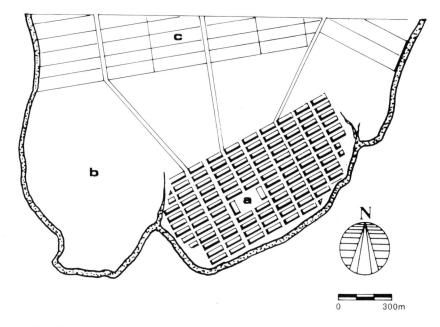

FIGURE 3.3 **Charlottetown, 1768**
The first British colonial towns in Canada featured a regular gridiron of blocks divided into individual building lots for settlers. The grid typically started from a survey baseline along the harbour. *Key:* (a) central square, (b) common, (c) farm lots.

Although the early plans for towns in this region generally follow the simplest of surveyor's layouts, they were based on the notion of providing a pool of relatively equal building sites. This would attract settlers from Europe, many of whom would not normally be able to have their own land. The gridiron pattern of streets and lots fills this function most effectively and would come to be the most widely used city form as Canada spread westward in the 18th and 19th centuries.

One other plan merits attention. In 1785, the Governor of Cape Breton, a well-known cartographer, Colonel des Barres, prepared a plan for Sydney that is undoubtedly derived from the forms of Georgian England.[6] It is not a little reminiscent of the plan for Annapolis, Maryland, with circular plazas and axial streets. Actually, the des Barres plan was a regional plan in that five satellite communities were envisioned outside Sydney and linked by boulevards radiated from the central circular plaza; each satellite was also to have its own circular plaza. Little is known about the intent of this plan and little of it was ever completed.

Upper Canada

Settlement of what is now Ontario began in the years following the American Revolutionary War. There were ambitious plans for the development of this unsettled area, which included a system of townships each averaging 100 square miles (260 km^2) and each containing a town site. The towns were to be a mile square (2.59 km^2) divided into one-acre (0.4 ha) "town lots" and were to include space for streets, church, market, and defence works. A large military reserve of land was surrounded by the town, which was surrounded, in turn, by a grid of 10 ha "park lots" and 80 ha "farm lots."

Although the concept of "mile square" towns appears to have been contemplated on maps prepared in Britain, such as the original plan for Toronto (Figure 3.4), none of the five major towns that were first developed—Kingston, Toronto, London, Hamilton, and Ottawa—followed this design. Kingston was first surveyed for a town adjacent to the small military garrison in 1784, and followed the more pragmatic gridiron pattern that was being used in towns in the Maritimes at about the same time.

Kingston's gridiron was "bent" to better follow the shoreline of Lake Ontario. The triangular space between the two grids was reserved for public uses: a market, church, jail, and battery. Other land was reserved for gardens, a hospital, and a school, while large parcels on the outskirts were granted to the clergy, members of government, and other prominent people. This approach to town layout is the same as that of other major places developed around 1800 in Ontario. The original survey lines, moreover, continue to this day to provide the basis of expansion. Today's arterial streets in Metropolitan Toronto were the original road allowances that bounded groups of five 80 ha farm lots in Simcoe's 1793 survey.

The early Ontario gridiron town plans had no aesthetic pretensions. Their aims were primarily functional: to provide for orderly development, for the equitable distribution of land, and for basic public land needs. Whatever character they achieved came from the natural site and the architectural quality of buildings constructed by the residents. There were, however, two community plans that broke with this colonial tradition: those for Guelph (Figure 3.5) in 1827 and Goderich in 1829. These two towns were to anchor the development scheme of the Canada Land Company, a private British company that had purchased the rights to settle 400,000 ha of land, the Huron Tract, in western Ontario. Plans for both these places, usually credited to John Galt, adopted the idea of a radial pattern of streets converging on a town market.

Guelph was arranged in a fan shape outward from a market beside a river; Goderich was arranged around an octagonal central market square.

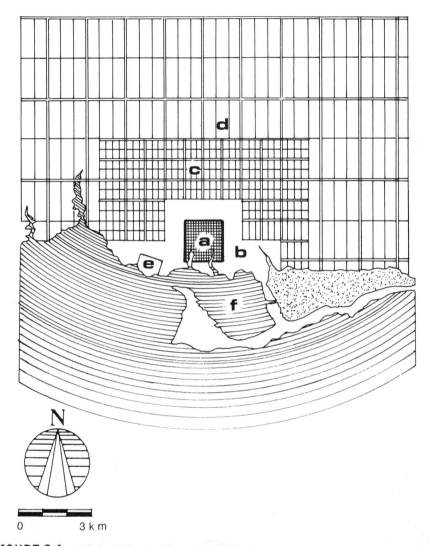

FIGURE 3.4   **Original Plan for Toronto, 1788**
Called the "mile square" plan for the central town grid (a), which was one mile on each side; it designated five public squares and a wide surrounding common (b). This part of the plan was never implemented, but the subdivision of medium-sized "park lots" (c) and the larger farms (d) did materialize. The old Garrison Reserve (e) to the west of the town became Canada's first public park in 1848. A less ambitious town grew up beside the well-protected harbour (f).

As in Renaissance designs, a gridiron was used for local streets. John Galt is known to have been influenced by the town-planning approaches used by the Holland Company, which acquired rights to develop upper New

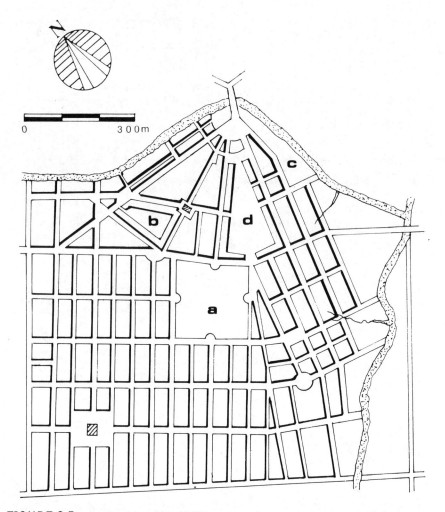

FIGURE 3.5 **Guelph, Ontario, 1827**
Planned by John Galt for the Canada Company to encourage settlement in western Ontario,
Guelph shows the influence of the radial street pattern used in the plan for Washington,
D.C. *Key:* (a) church, (b) cemetery, (c) government area, (d) market.

York state.[7] The latter development was supervised by Joseph Ellicott,
whose brother had succeeded L'Enfant as the planner for Washington.
Thus, the plans for Guelph and Goderich are descended more from the
L'Enfant concept than from Georgian England.[8] Other towns subsequently developed in the Huron Tract reverted to a common gridiron.

Western Canada

The growth of cities and towns in western Canada is, by and large, a product of national expansion rather than of colonial development from Europe.[9] There were, of course, some pre-Confederation antecedents. Many places owe their choice of site to an early fur trading post, such as Edmonton, Winnipeg, and Victoria. And British Army engineers around 1860 laid out gridiron town sites for several communities in British Columbia, including New Westminster and Vancouver, while that region was still a British colony. However, it was the establishment of railway links with eastern Canada, especially in the 1880s, that gave the stimulus to widespread town development throughout western Canada.

In barely 20 years, from 1871 to 1891, almost all the places that have become major cities and towns were laid out in conjunction with the advance of the transcontinental railroad and its branches. Very often laid out by railway engineers, the plans followed a common gridiron, whether for small communities or large and regardless of the topography of the site. These were plans for the sale and distribution of land. To draw again from Blumenfeld: "The right angle and straight line, convenient for the division of land, are equally convenient for the erection of buildings, [and] for the laying of pipes and rails."[10] The gridiron also suited the ebullient and egalitarian spirit that characterized the settlement of western Canada: ample land, equal parcels, similarity of sites. These traits also prevailed with regard to gridiron patterns employed in earlier city development in eastern Canada.

Seemingly, the gridiron is unconstrained as the basis for a town plan. It does not depend on the location of an important church, a fort, or marketplace for its beginnings. But it does depend on the ownership of land in the grid and, crucial to western Canada's communities, on where the railway station and freight yards are situated. Since the railway companies could choose from the land that was granted them as an incentive to build in the West anywhere along their routes, they chose much of their land where they planned to build railway stations and could benefit from the sale of town lots.

The initial town sites for Saskatoon, Regina, Calgary, and Vancouver did not coincide with the railway terminus. In these cities, it was the railroad's gridiron town site that became the dominant commercial centre and the location for public buildings. In Edmonton, the presence of a 1,200 ha tract of land, granted to the Hudson's Bay Company immediately west of the original town site, influenced the development of the central district of that city. Winnipeg's pattern owes much to the routes followed by fur traders

FIGURE 3.6   Impact of Railways on the Centre of the City: Toronto, 1870
The advent of railways was associated with manufacturing and commercial development, which were in the centre of most cities by the late 19th century. The marshalling yards for freight trains consumed large amounts of city space and in port cities, like Toronto and Vancouver, cut off the harbour from the rest of the city and hampered its use by citizens. *Source:* Metropolitan Toronto Library.

north and south along the Red River and west along the Assiniboine, and to the long, narrow Métis farm lots that fronted on the rivers. Nevertheless, in western communities, regardless of rivers or rival town sites, the overall gridiron gradually reconciled many differences, and often the original survey lines still govern the direction of land development. This is true for places that gained city status early, for more recent cities, and for most small towns.

NINETEENTH-CENTURY URBAN INFLUENCES

Railways, Streetcars, and Urban Form

The cities of western Canada began in the so-called Railway Era, but communities in eastern Canada were also significantly affected by the intro-

duction of railways. The location of the passenger station was important to communities both east and west; but more important over the long run was the location of the marshalling yards and freight terminals, for they consumed large amounts of space. The freight yards and terminals were usually adjacent to the passenger station and, hence, next to the downtown area. In addition, the coming of railways to Canadian communities coincided with extensive industrialization in the country. Industrial firms were encouraged to locate near the freight terminals or along rail lines.

Railroad development, while undoubtedly a boon to the economic development of communities, strongly affected the pattern of their growth. Typically, the railway passenger station "anchored" one side of the downtown commercial area, and on the other were the freight yards and industrial area and, frequently, the port. Housing development spread out from this core, but not evenly, for the freight yards proved to be both a physical and psychological barrier to residential growth.

Housing for the more affluent population was located away from the rail lines and industrial areas. Housing for poorer segments of the population was left to the land adjacent to industry and railways. The large, generally linear area occupied by freight yards and industries was also difficult for city development to cross without expensive underpasses or bridges. In inland cities, when development did succeed in leapfrogging the railway it often resulted in the establishment of lower-income residential districts on, so to speak, "the other side of the tracks." In cities with harbours, the railway-industrial development usually spread along the waterfront, creating a barrier between the community and its natural marine asset (Figure 3.6).

Since the 1950s, a number of changes (such as in the location of industries and modes of urban transportation) have caused the obsolescence of downtown railway freight facilities. In many cities, these large, centrally located sites are the object of redevelopment planning exercises to recapture area for downtown development, as in Saskatoon, Vancouver, Calgary, and Toronto. As the major landowners, the railway companies are once again helping to define the nature of downtown areas.

The street railway was also introduced to Canadian communities in the late 19th century. This form of rail transport, especially after electrification, dramatically influenced the pattern of residential development. Prior to street railways both the dependence on foot travel and poor roads tended to limit development to within 1.6 km of the central area. In the 1870s, the horse-drawn trolley permitted development to occur up to 5 km from downtown and the jobs of the central industrial area. The electrification of streetcars around 1890 saw the extension of lines 10 km and more from downtown stores and jobs. The norm was usually a half-hour trip—a norm that persists in North American communities a century later.

The streetcar lines followed streets that radiated outward from the central area of the community and were a great stimulus for land development adjacent to those routes. As a result, the overall pattern of the city assumed a fingerlike shape along transit routes. The oldest housing outside the central area is found in areas served earliest by streetcar lines. Very often this was accompanied by a strip of retail and commercial establishments that served these extended new neighbourhoods. Almost always the gridiron formed the base of development; it was simply extended as the streetcar lines were built. In many U.S. cities of the time, the radial form of development was spread well beyond the outer terminals of the streetcars by the advent of commuter railroads as much as 40 to 50 km from the main downtown. Canadian cities were not nearly so large or affluent, and thus did not achieve vast suburbanization so early (Figure 3.7).

The Beginnings of Public Parks

Many of today's major public parks in Canadian cities came into existence in the 19th century. As important as these parks are to a city's pattern and its quality of life, most were not part of the initial planning of our

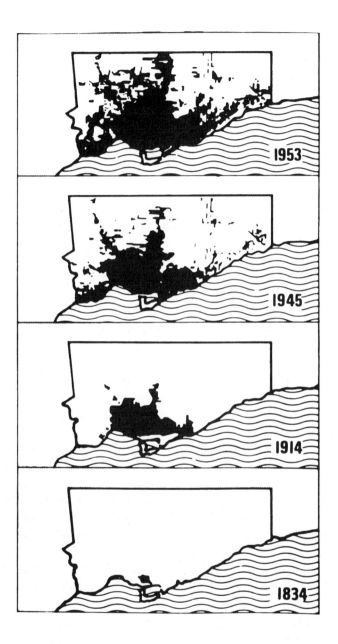

FIGURE 3.7   **Effect of Transportation Modes on the Form of the City**
Toronto's form of growth relates to the dominant mode of transportation prevailing at the time. The city of 1914 with electrified streetcars is not only 20 times larger than in horse- and foot-traffic times, but also shows the growth adjacent to the radial streetcar routes, which is even more exaggerated by 1945. However, within less than a decade, the prolif- eration of the private automobile made for a much more dispersed form. *Source:* Metropolitan Toronto Planning Department.

communities. The first plans for communities in eastern Canada provided for market squares, church squares, and military parade squares, but not public recreation areas; plans for western communities usually provided for neither squares nor parks. In part, this perspective was also shared in European cities of the 18th and 19th centuries. The idea of space being set aside for public recreation through the support of the local government first took hold in Britain in the 1840s.

Canada's first public parks to be supported by municipal funding were established less than a decade after those in Britain and around the same time as those in U.S. cities.[11] A major stimulus was the transfer of land reserves held by the central government, usually for military purposes, to the local government. The Garrison Reserve (now Exhibition Park) in Toronto came into existence this way in 1848, as did Kingston's City Park in 1852, Hamilton's Gore Park in the same year, Halifax's Point Pleasant Park in 1866, the Toronto Islands in 1867, London's Victoria Park in 1869, Montreal's Isle St. Hélène (the site of Expo 67) in 1874, and Vancouver's Stanley Park in 1886. All of these park areas were on the periphery of their respective communities at the time. There was no concept of neighbourhood parks until around the turn of the century, when various provinces introduced legislation to promote local parks.

As Toronto's parks chairman said in 1859, public parks offered "breathing spaces where citizens might stroll, drive, or sit to enjoy the open air."[12] The outlook reflected a desire to create a natural setting, often along with an appreciation of horticulture. The Public Garden in Halifax is an example of the latter; Mount Royal Park in Montreal an example of the former. Mount Royal Park, purchased by the city in 1872, is also significant among Canadian urban parks because its basic layout was by Frederick Law Olmsted, who had designed Central Park in New York City. He urged Montreal to "bring out the latent loveliness of [the] mountain beauty" and retain the wilderness and sense of seclusion."[13] Olmsted went on to prepare plans for parks at Niagara Falls, for Stanley Park in Vancouver, and for Rockwood Park in Saint John. A Canadian protégé of Olmsted was Frederick Todd, who designed the linked parks along the Avon River in Stratford, Ontario, City Park in Kingston, and Assiniboine Park in Winnipeg. As a key component in the planning of communities, these park projects represent the first major efforts by communities themselves to shape and give character to their physical environment. Large public parks modified and humanized the development patterns.

It is important to note that as Canadian communities moved into the 20th century, certain features of their physical form were already well established, as were the directions for their future growth. The factors influencing these patterns and plans were private land development, transportation technology, and public parks. The gridiron pattern was almost ubiquitous by this time, but it was not for the purpose of creating a particular urban environment. It was simply to facilitate laying out streets and building on new land. Moreover, as cities grew larger, the new rail technology highlighted new forms for urban areas as a whole. City districts were subordinated to emerging concepts of the metropolis.

THE EMERGENCE OF MODERN PLAN CONCEPTS

The rapid industrialization occurring in the 19th century (beginning around 1800 in Britain, 1840 in the U.S., and 1880 in Canada) centred on cities and brought with it new people, new wealth, and new problems. The growth of population in London, England, from 1,000,000 in 1800 to 7,000,000 in 1900 is often cited as the benchmark for rapid urban growth in this period. But just as dramatic was Toronto's experience as its population grew from just over 56,000 in 1871 to nearly 522,000 only 50 years later. At first, no cities on either side of the Atlantic were able to cope with the demand for housing, the need for transportation, and the provision of elemental water supply and sewage disposal services. Later, when technology and social conscience caught up with these needs, the result was cities that might best be described as "cluttered": smoky industrial districts, unpaved roads, mean and crowded working-class housing, half-finished suburbs, and a plethora of new electric poles and overhead cables.

During the late 19th and early 20th centuries, most large Canadian communities were assuming the physical form they would have until the great metropolitan expansion of the 1950s. But, increasingly, the emerging physical patterns of cities prompted concerns not unlike those receiving attention in Britain and the United States at the same time.[14] In response to these concerns, there emerged a coterie of professionals who gradually codified their ideas and experience about the best physical form for communities. The Canadian planning profession developed at this time and, with its British and American counterparts, generated a rich array of planning concepts, which continue to be drawn upon as heavily as those from any other area.

The planning concerns for the burgeoning cities of the turn of the century were rooted in two different perceptions of city problems. One viewed the major problem as the **deterioration of living conditions;** the other viewed it as the **deterioration of the appearance of cities.** From each sprang a different concept of the physical form that might best produce better communities. Out of the concern over living conditions came the notion of Garden Cities, wholly new communities designed to allow new patterns of living in less congested surroundings. Out of the concern over the appearance of cities came the notion of City Beautiful, the redesign of major streets and public areas in existing cities. Adherents of each approach often became part of competing planning movements. The imprint of each is to be found in Canadian community planning of the first half of this century. In turn, each approach evolved into more refined planning ideas that tended to meld the original concepts into those such as Garden Suburbs, the Neighbourhood Unit, and Greenbelt Towns (Figure 3.8). The legacy of each is examined below.

The Garden City Concept

In today's terminology, the **Garden City** would be called either a "satellite town" or "new town." Like its modern versions, the Garden City concept aimed at affecting the physical form of communities in two ways: first, it would disperse the population and industry of a large city into smaller concentrations, and second, it would create community living environments in the new setting more amenable than those of the city. That is, it was a concept for the form both of the metropolitan region and of the local community.

Ebenezer Howard, the British originator of the Garden City idea in 1898, was not an architect or surveyor but a court reporter and, as one biographer emphasizes, an inventor.[15] He presented his ideas for new towns as general diagrams rather than as plans for a particular community

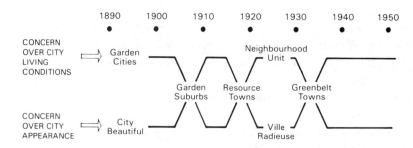

FIGURE 3.8   **Evolution of Community-Planning Concepts from 1890 to 1950**
Modern community planning grew out of two concerns: first, the deterioration of living conditions, and second, the ugly appearance of cities and towns. As planning concepts evolved, they have tended to meld these social and design concerns in their approaches.

and location (Figure 3.9). The main dimensions of Howard's Garden City were:

1. A population of about 30,000;
2. A built-up town of 1,000 acres (400 ha);
3. An agricultural greenbelt of 5,000 acres (2,000 ha) surrounding the town;
4. Provision of land for industry and commerce to supply employment to the residents:
5. An arrangement of land uses to promote convenience and reduce conflict; and
6. A means of rapid communication between the central city and the Garden City (see Figure 3.9).

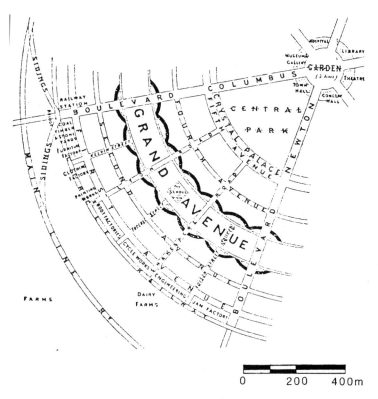

FIGURE 3.9   **Arrangement of Land Uses in Ebenezer Howard's Garden City, 1898**
The Centre and One Ward (neighbourhood) shown in Howard's diagram illustrate the concentric arrangement of land uses, with public uses and a park at the centre moving progressively outward with rings of housing, and, lastly, industry on the periphery, with farms or forests beyond.

An important feature of the Garden City's development was that all the land, including the greenbelt, would be owned by a single entity and held in trust for both investors and the residents.

In the Garden City that Howard visualized, each house would have its own garden, each neighbourhood its own area for schools, playgrounds, gardens, and churches, and the whole town its surrounding "garden" or agricultural estate, as Howard termed it. There would be a strong town centre with a town hall, concert and lecture hall, theatre, library, museum, and hospital, as well as a large public garden and ample room for shops. Each neighbourhood ("ward") would be bounded by major avenues and would house about one-sixth of the population, or about 5,000 people, in individual or group housing and be only about 1.5 km in greatest extent. An innovative, but often overlooked, part of Howard's concept was for an internal "belt of green" 130 m wide, a Grand Avenue (three times wider than University Avenue in Toronto), to separate the functional elements of the community. The concept of an internal greenbelt that would divide the area for factories, warehouses, and so on from the residential area has yet to be realized. In short, Howard outlined a "balanced community" for the modern era that, it should be noted, took into account both rail and automobile transportation.

Howard's ideas were turned into reality with the building of two Garden Cities north of London. The first was Letchworth, about 56 km north of London, which was designed by Barry Parker and Raymond Unwin and started in 1903. It has now reached close to its intended population. The second, Welwyn, was started personally by Howard in 1919 about 27 km from London. Associated with the building of Letchworth was Thomas Adams, who was secretary of the group of investors who initiated the first Garden City. A decade later, Adams came to Canada as the Town Planning Advisor to the Canadian Commission of Conservation. Although Adams did not plan any Garden Cities in Canada, undoubtedly his involvement with this early and important planning concept influenced his approach to the many dozens of Canadian communities that sought his advice. Indeed, the significance of the Garden City concept is not so much that towns would be built to a prescribed form but rather to demonstrate, as Adams remarked 30 years after Letchworth, "the advantage of planning communities in all their features from the beginning"[16] (see Figure 3.13).

The City Beautiful Movement

In 1893, Chicago hosted the World's Columbian Exposition. The design of the grounds and buildings of this fair is credited with stimulating a surge of concern for the design of cities in North America over the ensuing 40 years. On a site on the shores of Lake Michigan, selected and laid out by Frederick Law Olmsted, two Chicago architects, John Root and Daniel Burnham, conceived of a setting of buildings, avenues, statues, canals, and lagoons in true baroque fashion. Planning historian Mel Scott calls it a "temporary wonderland of grand perspectives and cross axes ... shimmering lagoons and monumental palaces ... an enthralling amalgam of classic Greece, imperial Rome, and Bourbon Paris."[17]

The need for the beautification of cities had been stirring in the United States for at least two decades before the Chicago World's Fair. It showed up in municipal art societies and in the attention given to both private and public landscape architecture, notably in the development of public parks. The Chicago fair strengthened this aesthetic effort by providing design principles that could (and subsequently did) govern the design of city halls, public libraries, banks, railroad stations, civic centres, malls, boulevards, and university campuses. Burnham was involved with the refurbishing of L'Enfant's plan for Washington in 1902, and, over the next few years, in preparing plans for San Francisco, Cleveland, and Chicago. His 1908 plan for Chicago is considered the benchmark of City Beautiful plans, containing as it did schemes for new diagonal avenues, civic plazas, public buildings, and a series of parks along the lakeshore. The latter are often portrayed, but little mentioned today is the inclusion of proposals for a network of highways for the entire metropolitan region of some 10,000 km^2 and a chain of forest preserves and parkways on the periphery.

The impact of the Chicago exposition was not lost on Canadian architects, engineers, and surveyors (who would soon make up the fledgling planning profession). They, too, were active in campaigning against the squalor and the ugly environment that were developing in Canadian communities in the period of rapid urbanization prior to World War I. Montreal architect A.T. Taylor complained (in 1893) after viewing the fair:

> The average modern city is not planned—like topsy, it just grows, and we are only allowed to touch with the finger of beauty a spot here and there. One longs for the days of Pericles or Caesar, or even those of the First Empire, when cities were laid out with beauty and effect, and were exquisite settings for noble gems of architecture.[18]

The Renaissance design principles of symmetry, coherence, and monumentality were revived by the Chicago fair, and Canadian "planners" promoted them widely with governments, chambers of commerce, and corporations.

In 1906, the first city-wide planning proposal in Canada to emanate from City Beautiful approaches was undertaken for Toronto by the Ontario Association of Architects and the Toronto Guild of Civic Art. It contained plans for a series of diagonal streets and a system of parks connected by parkways. Based on similar principles were the plans made for Berlin (now Kitchener) by Charles Leavitt in 1914 (Figure 3.10), and the 1915 plan for Ottawa and Hull jointly prepared by Edward Bennett, Daniel Burnham's associate on the Chicago plan, and Canadian Arthur Bunnell, whose name would recur in connection with planning in Canada through the next several decades.

The achievement of civic grandeur was an aim of the City Beautiful idiom in planning. This was often, in plans of civic centres, expressed with monumental public buildings grouped around a public square and a broad tree-lined avenue leading to it (Figure 3.11). Two of the most famous Canadian civic centre plans of this period (neither were built) were one for Calgary proposed by British architect Thomas Mawson in 1914 and one for Vancouver proposed by American planner Harland Bartholomew in 1929. Canadian planner Horace Seymour collaborated on the latter plan and also included City Beautiful elements in other plans he made at the time. In 1921, another respected Canadian planner, Noulan Cauchon, prepared a plan for Hamilton's civic centre in the same tradition, and the monumental quality we now see in Toronto's University Avenue, which leads to the provincial legislative buildings, was cast in a 1929 redevelopment plan for that city. One might add to this list of City Beautiful projects the former city of Maisonneuve and the many railway stations built in a grand manner in Canadian cities in this period.

The **City Beautiful movement** is commonly described in condescending terms—as "mere adornment," as having failed to address the "real problems" of city housing and sanitation, as extravagant. A number of important factors are missed in these debates. First, the classic mode that characterized many of the architecture and design concepts was the design style of the time, and it was a style that favoured adornment of buildings and public places. Second, the design style was rooted in powerful aesthetic principles that had endured from Renaissance times: symmetry, coherence, perspective, and monumentality. When it came to designing cities at this time, even those not professing City Beautiful tenets used design elements that drew upon these principles. Ebenezer Howard had his Grand Avenue and radial streets leading to the town centre; Thomas Adams' plan for several resource towns employed a central tree-lined boulevard around which to organize the community. As recently as 1979, the plan for a new civic centre in Calgary was criticized on the same

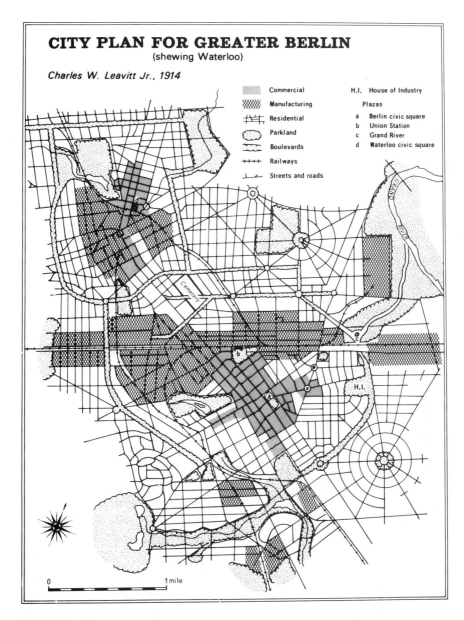

CITY PLAN FOR GREATER BERLIN
(shewing Waterloo)

Charles W. Leavitt Jr., 1914

	Commercial	H.I.	House of Industry
	Manufacturing		Plazas
	Residential	a	Berlin civic square
	Parkland	b	Union Station
	Boulevards	c	Grand River
	Railways	d	Waterloo civic square
	Streets and roads		

0   1 mile

FIGURE 3.10   City Beautiful Plan for Greater Berlin (Kitchener and Waterloo), 1914

This plan by American planner Charles Leavitt, Jr. employs all the City Beautiful design devices: diagonal avenues leading to city squares, circular streets, and parkways. Kitchener was named Berlin prior to World War I. *Source:* E. Bloomfield.

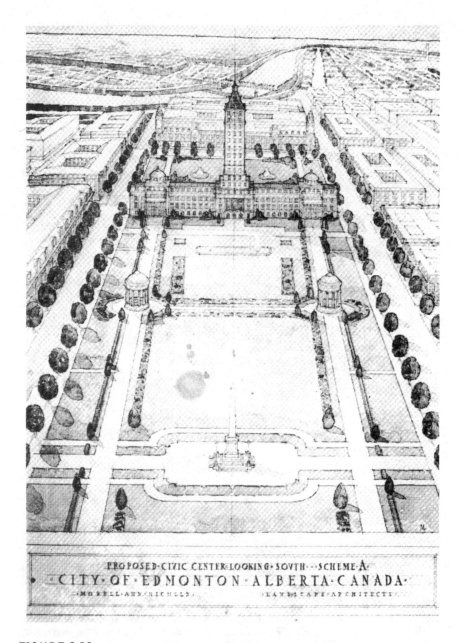

FIGURE 3.11 **Proposed Civic Centre for Edmonton, 1915**
A typical proposal for a grandiose civic centre, similar to those in other Canadian cities in this period. The aim of such City Beautiful designs was to bring a sense of civic grandeur to otherwise mundane cities. Edmonton had barely 40,000 people at the time. *Source:* Metropolitan Toronto Library.

grounds as Mawson's City Beautiful centre half a century earlier. Third, regardless of design style, City Beautiful planners had correctly identified most of the main elements of a community's physical form with which a planner needed to work: the street pattern, the public buildings, and the parks—the elements under public control.

The Garden Suburb

A hybrid of Garden City and City Beautiful approaches was the **Garden Suburb,** so called because it employed the generous residential environment of the newly developed Letchworth Garden City and was usually located just beyond the built-up urban area. Further, as with City Beautiful ideas, it broke with the standard gridiron pattern of streets, often termed, at the time, the "monotonous grid."

The forerunner of the Garden Suburb approach is Hampstead Garden Suburb in London, England, which was designed by Raymond Unwin, co-designer of Letchworth. Its curving streets fitted to the topography, and its parks and open space gave the inspiration for dozens of such residential areas across North America as well as Europe. The notable Garden Suburb projects in Canada are Shaughnessy Heights in Vancouver (Figure 3.12), Mount Royal in Calgary, Rosedale and Forest Hill in Toronto, Rockliffe in Ottawa, and Ville-Mont-Royal in Montreal. All of these were begun before World War I; many of them were built on land owned by the Canadian Pacific Railway. The designers were usually major landscape architecture firms from the United States, and there is reason to believe many of the designers were directly influenced by the work of Olmsted and Unwin.

Clearly, the Garden Suburb was never intended to provide housing for the mass of people in the community. Its generous—even by today's standards—design features meant high prices were attached to the building lots. Yet high design standards have proved a crucial factor in the persistence of such areas as Shaughnessy and Ville-Mont-Royal as favoured residential districts for nearly three-quarters of a century while many adjacent areas have deteriorated. Finally, the Garden Suburb approach provided the stimulus to later community designers of resource towns and metropolitan suburbs alike in Canada. One case of special note is Thomas Adams' plan for the rebuilding of the Richmond District in Halifax, an area devastated by an enormous munitions ship explosion in 1917. The district originally had a common gridiron pattern, even though it was on a steep hillside. Adams' proposed curving streets conformed to the topography, and his plan was largely applied in the reconstruction.[19]

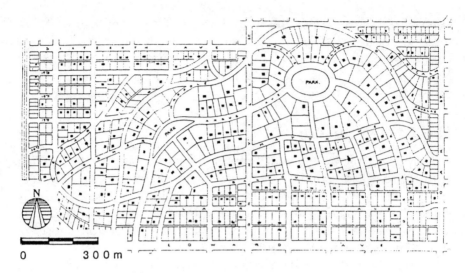

FIGURE 3.12   A Garden Suburb: Shaughnessy Heights, Vancouver, 1908
The planners of the first Garden City, Unwin and Parker, popularized this form of street lay-out in planning new suburbs. It was used in the design of such districts for wealthy Canadian homeowners as Mount Royal in Calgary, Forest Hill in Toronto, and Ville-Mont-Royal in Montreal, as well as his one in Vancouver. The gridiron was discarded in favour of curving streets, which respected the usually hilly topography.

Planned Communities for Resource Development

Paralleling the expansion of Canada's cities in the early part of the 20th century was the development of dozens of new towns on the resource frontier of the country. The planning of these settlements ranged in sophistication from a simple grid survey appended to the site for the mine, mill, or smelter, to conscious attempts to create attractive, healthful communities. Possibly the first such planned resource town was Nanaimo, British Columbia, with an interesting "cobweb" street design (dating from about 1880) of radials and circumferentials. In 1904, a plan of grandiose proportions was prepared for Prince Rupert, also in British Columbia, by prominent U.S. landscape architects. Its two main avenues and its circles, crescents, and public sites were meant to be the centre of a city of 100,000 rivalling Vancouver for Pacific trade.[20] Although this dream was not realized, the original planned layout is still evident in the present community. On a more modest scale, but just as elaborate, were the plans for three pulp and paper mill towns: Iroquois Falls (1915) and Kapuskasing (1921) in Ontario and Temiskaming (1917) in Quebec.

The plan for Temiskaming (Figure 3.13) is noteworthy both because it was designed by Thomas Adams and because it shows the influence of

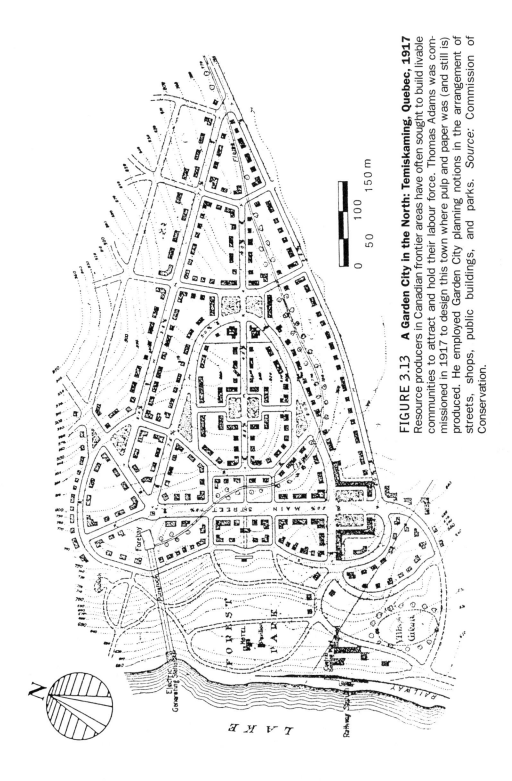

FIGURE 3.13   A Garden City in the North: Temiskaming, Quebec, 1917
Resource producers in Canadian frontier areas have often sought to build livable communities to attract and hold their labour force. Thomas Adams was commissioned in 1917 to design this town where pulp and paper was (and still is) produced. He employed Garden City planning notions in the arrangement of streets, shops, public buildings, and parks. *Source:* Commission of Conservation.

Garden City planning principles. The resource frontier town, of course, gave the opportunity of planning for an entire community from the ground up and employing such ideas as the greenbelt, the separation of conflicting uses, street patterns fitting the contour of the land, and ample land for housing. These towns could demonstrate the importance of careful, over-all planning that planning efforts in already built-up cities couldn't achieve. Thomas Adams said, in reference to his plan for Temiskaming:

> The object of such plans should be to provide healthy conditions for the workers in the factories and the mills, together with convenience of arrange-ment to secure the most efficient methods of carrying on the industry, and not merely blind conformity to meaningless division of lines of a rectangular (gridiron) division.[21]

That Adams could prepare and have such plans accepted clearly indi-cates how readily planning ideas were accepted by the corporations for whom the towns were being built. Some companies actually sent repre-sentatives to Britain and other parts of Europe to study model towns that various industrialists had built in order to obtain for their employees hous-ing more desirable than that available in the congested Industrial Revolution cities.[22]

Favourite model towns for these visits included Bourneville, built near Birmingham by George Cadbury in 1879, and Port Sunlight, built near Liverpool by Lever Brothers in 1886. Both places had played host to early conferences of the Garden City Association. These intellectual connections have continued in the planning of many dozen resource development towns, mostly in the Canadian north, right up to the present day in such communities as Leaf Rapids, Manitoba, and Fermont, Quebec.

The Neighbourhood Unit

Around 1920, with better living conditions as their objective, city planners began to search for a workable unit of human scale around which housing and community services could be organized and designed. This search cul-minated in 1929 with the ideas of architect Clarence Perry for a **neigh-bourhood unit**.[23] Against a backdrop of increasing automobile usage—and auto-related deaths and injuries—Perry proposed a way both to insu-late residential areas from traffic and to link the social needs of families to their environment. His concept was for residential areas to be organized in units of about 64 ha, or sufficiently large to "house enough people to require one elementary school." The exact shape was not specified, but it was expected to provide an area that had only about 500 m walking dis-tance for young children to the neighbourhood school at the centre. Main streets would bound the area, not pass through it. Total population would be 5,000 to 6,000 people, or about 1,500 families.

Despite charges that spatial units would not actually encompass, much less promote, a cohesive social environment, Perry's plan has nevertheless been widely used. Community plans in Canada, the United States, and Europe have repeatedly used the neighbourhood unit notion in a variety of formats to structure the residential portion of the city. Suggested populations for units have ranged across plans from 3,000 to 12,000, but the essential characteristics of a school-oriented, traffic-insulated area has persisted. The neighbourhood unit became probably one of the strongest physical organizing principles in modern community plans. Its outcome is readily seen when one flies over almost any Canadian city.

The Radiant City

The neighbourhood unit, a restrained, unaffected approach to urban development, contrasts starkly with the concepts developed by the French architect Le Corbusier in the 1920s. Instead of small clusters of mostly single-family houses, each with its neighbourhood park, Le Corbusier envisioned in his Radiant City *(Ville Radieuse)* concept the city as a huge park in which 60-storey buildings in zigzag form were woven across landscaped space (Figure 3.14). Hardly more than 5% of the ground would be covered, and many buildings constructed on stilts would allow the park space to flow right underneath. Le Corbusier was enamoured of skyscrapers and the possibilities they gave for "concentrating" the population without "congesting" them.[24] His concept had people living right in a park at very high densities—3,000 persons per hectare—but also promised to save them considerable time in horizontal travel compared to a low-density, spread-out city.

Le Corbusier's schemes departed dramatically from the cities known in either Europe or America, and aimed to take advantage of the new technology of building tall structures to alleviate the ills of the old cities. He prepared sample plans for many major cities in the 1920s and 1930s. While none of these were built as he envisioned, his influence was immense, and the idea of the high-rise building sitting in a park, a common view to most city dwellers today, is due to Le Corbusier (albeit not at the densities he proposed).

Greenbelt Towns

A third major planning concept during the period between the world wars was expressed in the "new town" plans of U.S. planners Henry Wright and

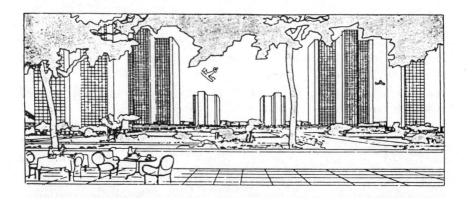

FIGURE 3.14 **Le Corbusier's View of the Contemporary City, 1922**
In Le Corbusier's eyes, modern technology allowed cities to avoid congestion and to enjoy open space at their very centres. Tall towers are arranged within a park-like setting, with very little of the ground area covered by buildings (above). His concepts are still very influential, as is evident in the 1979 proposals for Calgary's downtown (below). *Sources:* Le Corbusier Foundation (top); Calgary Planning Department.

Clarence Stein. Heavily influenced by the Garden City approach of Ebenezer Howard and Raymond Unwin, they persuaded a private corporation to undertake such a venture on the undeveloped edge of New York

City, in New Jersey. The first town was called Radburn and was, according to Stein, "not a Garden City as Howard saw it," but rather one planned for a society entering "the Motor Age."[25] Begun in 1928 and planned to grow to a population of 25,000, Radburn pioneered new design relations between houses, roads, paths, gardens, parks, blocks, and neighbourhoods.

The main elements of the Radburn plan were:

1. **The superblock**, an area of 12–20 ha with major roads on the perimeter so that through traffic would not intrude into housing groups;
2. **Specialized roads** that would allow different traffic needs, from service vehicles for houses to through truck traffic, to proceed efficiently and with minimum impact on the community;
3. **Separation of pedestrian and automobile** by a system of walkways in different places and at different levels where they cross;
4. **Houses turned around** facing gardens and parks instead of streets, with the latter becoming mainly service lanes for clusters of houses; and
5. **Parks as the backbone** of the neighbourhood, with open space left in the centre of superblocks and joined from one to the other in a continuous park.[26]

In the Depression period of the 1930s, the U.S. government sponsored several more towns of the Radburn type. They were called Greenbelt Towns, and three of the four that were planned were built, although they never reached the size of Radburn. Clarence Stein left his mark in Canada in his 1951 plan for the aluminum smelting town of Kitimat, British Columbia, which embodies the concepts that he developed in the building of Radburn. And, of course, there is hardly a metropolitan suburb planned since the end of World War II, from Fraserview in Vancouver to Churchill Park in St. John's, that does not embody the principles of Wright and Stein to a high degree.

PLANNING FOR THE EXPLODING METROPOLIS

Between 1941 and 1951, Canadian urban centres grew by three million people, or an astounding 51%. But even more noteworthy is that 83% of this growth, or 2.5 million people, occurred in places with populations over 50,000. In 1941, there were only 8 cities with populations over 100,000, but by 1951 there were 15 such places. Another five million were added to Canada's urban population in the succeeding decade—1951 to 1961—and two-thirds of this went to the largest cities. The trends were the same in the United States and Europe. Urban growth of this scale and rapidity had never before been experienced.

The term **exploding metropolis**[27] aptly captured the state of affairs of the two decades following World War II. Cities grew in population, expanded their boundaries, and increased in density (with taller buildings usually at the centre) and area (with more houses and factories on the out-skirts). Three forces combined to produce the metropolitan environments we are familiar with today. First, there were population forces due to (1) the migration of people from rural areas to cities; (2) people emigrating to Canada from abroad, most of whom went to the larger cities; and (3) a dra-matic increase in the natural growth of the population, which we subse-quently came to know as the "baby boom." Second, there were economic forces not only because of the nation's economy continuing to expand and produce jobs and rising incomes for the new and old populations of cities, but also because of the pent-up demand for housing and other urban accoutrements for the 15 years of depression and war. The third force, and in many ways the most momentous in its effect on the form of cities, was the vast expansion in automobile use.

These three forces intertwined to reshape the metropolis. The need for housing and facilities enlarged metropolitan areas. Increased affluence led to a great variety of living environments. And metropolitan residents began providing their own transportation by auto rather than relying on public transit. Although we now seem accustomed to large, spreading cities, the tenor of the 1950s regarding these changes is caught in the following quo-tation:

> Of all the forces reshaping the American metropolis, the most powerful and insistent are those rooted in changing modes of transportation. The changes are so big and obvious that it is easy to forget how remarkable they are. The streetcar has all but disappeared, the bus is proving an inept substitute, com-muter rail service deteriorates, subways get dirtier, and new expressways pour more and more automobiles into the centre of town.[28]

These writers might well have added that more and more automobiles were pouring into the outskirts of cities because that is where the growing populations could be housed most easily, and it is also where the old pub-lic transportation systems did not usually reach, or service well if they did.

The reshaping of cities that occurred in the two decades immediately following World War II affected the physical planning of communities in several ways. One effect was the way in which community planners broad-ened their perspective to encompass the enlarged scale and interdependency of the various parts of the metropolis. Another effect came through the need to accommodate many more automobiles and the introduction of new types of development catering to an auto-oriented society. Before examining these, it is useful to note what was happening to housing development at this time.

Urban Form in the Suburbs

Most of the new housing to accommodate the expanded city populations was provided in the suburbs. And most of this was low-density development of mainly one- and two-family houses and, occasionally, low-rise apartments. The physical form of a great deal of this residential development showed the influence of Perry's and Stein's ideas for planning neighbourhoods. Public planners and private developers alike embraced the principles of insulating neighbourhoods from through traffic and of providing schools and parks within walking distance.

The common gridiron was shunned and the superblock was used to structure the new residential areas. Loop streets, crescents, and cul-de-sacs became a sort of *lingua franca* of subdivision design for neighbourhoods from Whitemore Park in Regina to Calvin Park in Kingston, Ontario. Worthy of special note are three efforts at building fairly complete new communities on what were then the outskirts of cities: Don Mills and Ajax outside Toronto and Sherwood Park outside Edmonton. These "new towns" contained several neighbourhoods, district shopping facilities, and, in the case of Don Mills and Ajax, space for industries to develop. A modest greenbelt surrounded each, which would later, as urban development advanced, help provide an identity to the community within the metropolitan mass.

High-density, high-rise development in Canadian suburbs became common only after the mid-1960s, but there was an important forerunner in the previous decade: Flemingdon Park in Toronto. Widely acclaimed, this superblock of tall apartments, garden apartments, and row houses was designed by Canadian planner Macklin Hancock. Following quite faithfully Le Corbusier's concepts of "skyscrapers in a park," it would be imitated later in many cities.

Community Planning Writ Large

There was some anticipation in two of Canada's largest cities, Winnipeg and Toronto, that the post-World War II years would bring more expansion that would require planning for the entire metropolitan area. All cities had already experienced an influx of people from farms and small towns to fill jobs in wartime industries. Even without immigration from abroad, the expanded city populations would require new housing when the war ended, as almost none could be built in the 1939–1945 period. In 1943, the City of Toronto's Planning Board prepared a plan for the metropolitan area in anticipation of post-war growth, although no metropolitan governmental or planning authority existed then. In 1944, the first official metropolitan-wide planning effort was initiated in Winnipeg, and continues to the present day.

When the explosion of metropolitan development occurred, it did not take long before those involved in community planning—elected officials, professional planners, and citizens—began to realize the cities were quickly coming to be made up of several constituent communities. The downtown of the central city was no longer the only important centre of activity. Indeed, most of the residential development was going on in the suburbs, and industry was also dispersing to suburban locations. Planning required a **metropolitan view** that could grasp not only the increased size of the urban community but also the need to achieve a balance between the parts, especially between the central city and the suburbs.

By the early 1950s, there were metropolitan-wide planning programs under way from Victoria to St. John's. Although designated by different names—metropolitan, regional, area, or district planning agencies—their task was the same. They sought to guide growth of housing areas and public utilities in a balanced, efficient way, to provide for accessibility to all parts by improving transportation, and to provide for such basic amenities as parks for all citizens. Metropolitan planning, as it will be discussed in a later chapter, obliges a different view of an urban area than does community planning. It views each community simply as a part of a larger community, and the planning within this view is of developing those facilities and amenities that are important to the area as a whole.

The two most important metropolitan decisions concerned expressways and metropolitan parks. These were important because they were large, dominant users of space; they could cut a community in half or provide a boundary for it. The debate around such planning issues, especially expressways, is an indication of their importance at all levels of the metropolitan community.

Accommodating the Car

In an aerial photograph of any Canadian metropolitan area, the most prominent feature of the development will, in all likelihood, be an expressway (Figure 3.15). These massive highways are a testament to the commitment made in the early post-war years to accommodate automotive trans-

FIGURE 3.15   **Impact of Expressways on the Metropolitan Landscape: Longueuil, Quebec**
These massive modern facilities significantly revised the physical structure of Canadian cities in their effort to accommodate automotive transportation. *Source:* Courtesy of the National Film Board of Canada.

portation in metropolitan communities. In the first 10 years after World War II, automobile registrations doubled. One must add to this the even greater increase in the use of trucks to move goods and services in and around metropolitan areas in order to get the full sense of the need governments were facing to accommodate automotive traffic. Expressways, it was hoped, would relieve downtown congestion as well as facilitate movement among the housing and industrial areas that had moved to the outskirts. Because of the large amount of land they required, the cost they entailed in building, and their barrier-like character in the urban landscape, once the commitment was made to construct an expressway the physical structure of the urban area was significantly revised.

An outgrowth of the widespread use of automotive transportation was two auto-oriented facilities that also shaped the post-war city: the shopping centre and the industrial park. Both of these facilities, now commonplace in the fabric of Canadian communities of all sizes, signalled a reorientation of major community functions away from a single dominant centre. As trucks came to surpass railways in the movement of freight, manufacturing plants and warehouses were freed from central locations. Many enterprises

Planning Issue 3.1

EATON'S STORE CLOSINGS WILL HURT CITY CORES
Civic officials fear impact of vacancies

Toronto—Plans by Eaton's to close or sell 31 of its 85 stores will have a devastating effect on already suffering downtown districts in many communities across Canada, civic officials say.

"I don't think we can hide from the fact that Eaton's is the only department store that we have in downtown Peterborough, and so as a result it [the possible closing] would have a very adverse effect," said Jack Doris, mayor of Peterborough, Ont., who is hopeful that a new tenant can be found for the store in his city.

Rick Brotosik, the mayor Brandon, said going to the Eaton's store has been a family outing for the city's residents ever since the store opened in 1924.

"Eaton's is downtown Brandon," he said. "There is history oozing out of every brick. It would be a major, major factor if it should close."

In Winnipeg, civic officials are searching for ways to save the downtown Eaton's store which has been part of the city's heritage for almost a century.

"There was a time when one in three Winnipeggers worked at Eaton's," said Mayor Susan Thompson, who began her working career as a sales clerk in the store's dress department in 1968.

Nearly half of the stores on T. Eaton Co. Ltd.'s "review list" are located in downtown districts. Analysts say that's not surprising, and it helps explain why the company lost $200-million in the past two years and is now insolvent.

"Eaton's, more than any of its competitors, focused on downtown locations when the trend in North America as a whole, and Canada in particular, was toward suburban locations," said John Winter, a retail consultant in Toronto.

The downtown malls were a flop for a number of reasons. Many had only one anchor—Eaton's—which is a fatal flaw because a good mall requires at least two anchors so customers will flow from one end to the other.

Another problem with downtown malls is parking. Women,

in particular, don't feel safe parking in a dark, underground lot and prefer to shop in the suburbs where lots are well-lit and there are plenty of people around, Mr. Winter said.

"It was one of the more unfortunate decisions the chain took to anchor so many downtown projects."

Among the failures are downtown malls in four Ontario cities—Sarnia, Brantford, Thunder Bay and Guelph, some civic leaders say.

The malls were built in the 1970s and 1980s, with Eaton's as the flagship store and with the help of a $52-million Ontario government loan program designed to help cities revitalize their downtowns.

The program "was a total failure," said Chris Friel, mayor of Brantford. "Our mall hasn't been doing well for some time."

Eaton's is now threatening to pull out of all four malls. Meanwhile, the four cities still owe the province about $25-million on the loans that helped build them. ...

Mr. Winter said landlords may have trouble filling all the vacant downtown space across the country once Eaton's leaves.

"It was a dramatic attempt to keep the downtown the centre of it all," Mr. Winter said of the construction of the malls. But "the great downtown social experiment failed."

Source: Excerpted from Paul Waldie and John Heinzl, *The Globe and Mail,* March 14, 1997, A1. Reprinted with permission from *The Globe and Mail.*

that moved to suburban locations may have desired less congested surroundings in order to facilitate truck service, or may have wanted to take advantage of new single-storey modes of operation. Communities wishing to improve the image of industrial areas as ill-kept, congested, and noxious were, at the same time, promoting the siting of industries in park-like situations. Hence, the advent of industrial parks.

Major shopping facilities in pre-1950 cities were also tied to downtown areas for receipt of goods for sale and because, up to that time, most personal transportation focused on downtown, especially public transit. When the automobile's widespread availability favoured the development of suburbs beyond the reach of public transit, it meant that stores and businesses not only had a market but could also take advantage of truck transport of goods. Thus, shopping centres came to be major features of the physical organization of an urban community catering to the preference for personal transportation for shopping trips. This injected a new set of relationships into community planning, because shopping centres need both a large amount of space and ease of automobile access for a large surrounding area.

With metropolitan planning, new spatial dimensions were added to the planning outlook, which took into account the physical form of the entire urban area. The planning for such metropolitan-wide facilities as expressways, shopping centres, parks, hospitals, and airports affected the future form of both the metropolis and any constituent community. Some attempts were made to generate planning concepts encompassing all levels of the metropolitan area, notably the satellite town plan for London and the "finger plan" for Copenhagen. Implementation of plans of this scale are very difficult, however. The net result has been that community planning since 1945 has very often been a task of blending the physical forms appropriate to the community level, such as the neighbourhood, with those appropriate to the larger urban area, such as the expressway. (See Chapter 11 for a full discussion of metropolitan planning in Canada.)

Implications of the Accumulated Foundations

Those involved in planning a Canadian community today are legatees of planning decisions and planning ideas of the past. Whether these be the relatively recent acquisitions for accommodating automotive traffic, such as the shopping centre, or decisions from the distant past, such as the federal land granted for a park, a number of factors may be discerned from this review of the physical foundations of Canadian communities. Future planners of our communities are almost certain to encounter them:

1. The first is that physical forms and spatial patterns of communities are remarkably persistent once established. In part, this is due to the permanence of the structures and the desire of owners to perpetuate their investment. This is just as true for public buildings and facilities as for private ones. And, in part, it is due to the fact that, once located in a community, certain functions—the downtown, the transportation terminal, institutional and cultural centres—also become important to the community's social, economic, and physical foundations, and are not easily relocated.
2. A second point is that, regardless of community size or age of development, there are a number of common land-use components to be planned for in the physical fabric of the community. Community planning always has to provide for living areas, working (industry, shopping, business) areas, transportation, and public facilities. The design of

these individual components and their arrangement in an overall pattern is probably the essential community planning task.

3. This leads to a third point about the location of new development in a community. In its early stages, everything in a community can be grouped close around a single centre. But as a community grows, a crucial planning decision must be made: is new development to be accommodated near the centre or on the outer edge? With each successive surge of new development this question will be raised. A good many of the planning ideas examined in this chapter were attempts to answer it at various times in the past.

4. One final point is that the physical planning foundations are, in large part, a response to social and economic problems. It is sometimes argued that early planners saw the problems of the city as capable of simple solution by building a new physical environment. And, certainly, the plans for Garden Cities and neighbourhood units did have this bias. This should not be unexpected, since our understanding of social and economic problems of the city has been meagre until recent decades.

One of the major advances in community planning has been to approach planning issues in a more balanced way. The next chapter traces the evolution of community social problems and the response of community planners.

ENDNOTES

1. James W. Vance, *The Continuing City* (Baltimore: Johns Hopkins University Press, 1990), 200ff.

2. Peter Moogk, *Building a House in New France* (Toronto: McClelland and Stewart, 1971), 14.

3. As quoted in *ibid*. This is in reference to the settlement that evolved to the north of the original French village of Ville Marie.

4. John Reps, *Town Planning in Frontier America* (Princeton, N.J.: Princeton University Press, 1969), 82.

5. E. Deville, "Radial Hamlet Settlement Schemes," *Plan Canada* 15 (March 1975), 44 (reprinted from *Conservation of Life*, April 1918).

6. Michael Hugo-Brunt, "The Origin of Colonial Settlements in the Maritimes," in *Planning the Canadian Environment*, edited by L.O. Gertler, (Montreal: Harvest House, 1968), 42–83.

7. Clarence Karr, *The Canada Land Company: The Early Years* (Ottawa: Ontario Historical Society, 1974), Research Publication No. 3, 24ff.

8. Reps, *Town Planning* 350, makes a similar point regarding the origins of the radial pattern of Buffalo, New York, which was laid out for the Holland Company by Ellicott.

9. Larry D. McCann and Peter J. Smith, "Canada Becomes Urban: Cities and Urbanization in Historical Perspective," in Trudi Bunting and Pierre Filion, eds., *Canadian Cities in Transition* (Toronto: Oxford University Press, 1991), 69–99.

10. Hans Blumenfeld, *The Modern Metropolis* (Montreal: Harvest House, 1967), 27.

11. J.R. Wright, *Urban Parks in Ontario, Part II: The Public Park Movement, 1860–1914* (Ottawa, 1984). The author provided the stimulus for this section.

12. As quoted in Elsie Marie McFarland, *The Development of Public Recreation in Canada* (Toronto: Canadian Parks/Recreation Association, 1974), 14.

13. Frederick Law Olmsted, *Mount Royal* (New York: G.P. Putnam's Sons, 1881), 64.

14. For an example of the breadth of concerns, see Paul Rutherford, ed., *Saving the Canadian City: The First Phase, 1880–1920* (Toronto: University of Toronto Press, 1974).

15. F.J. Osborn makes the point in his "Preface" to Ebenezer Howard, *Garden Cities of Tomorrow* (London: Faber and Faber, 1946).

16. Thomas Adams, *Outline of Town and City Planning* (New York: Russell Sage Foundation, 1935), 275.

17. Mel Scott, *American City Planning Since 1890* (Berkeley: University of California Press, 1969), 33.

18. As quoted in Walter Van Nus, "The Fate of City Beautiful Thought in Canada, 1893–1930," in G.A. Stelter and A. Artibise, eds., *The Canadian City: Essays in Urban History* (Toronto: Macmillan, 1979), 162–185.

19. John Weaver, "Reconstruction of the Richmond District in Halifax," *Plan Canada* 16 (March 1976), 36–47.

20. Nigel Richardson, "A Tale of Two Cities," in L.O. Gertler, ed., *Planning the Canadian Environment* (Montreal: Harvest House, 1968), 269–284.

21. Thomas Adams, *Rural Planning and Development* (Ottawa: Commission of Conservation, 1917), 66.

22. Institute of Local Government, Queen's University, *Single-Enterprise Communities in Canada* (Kingston, 1953), A Report to Central Mortgage and Housing Corporation, 24.

23. Clarence Perry, "The Neighbourhood Unit," in *Regional Survey of New York and Its Environs,* Vol. 7 (New York, 1929).

24. Arthur B. Gallion. *The Urban Pattern* (New York: Van Nostrand, 1950), 376.

25. Clarence Stein, *Toward New Towns for America* (New York: Reinhold, 1957), 19.

26. *Ibid.*, 39ff.

27. The Editors of Fortune, *The Exploding Metropolis* (New York: Doubleday, 1958).

28. *Ibid.*, 53.

Chapter 4 **Establishing the Social Agenda for Community Planning**

The development of [Canadian] towns has been chaotic, and tens of thousands of so-called houses have been thrown together, which must, sooner or later, be condemned for sanitary reasons. As for town planning, there has been none.

Dr. Charles A. Hodgetts, 1912

Modern community planning, which dates from about 1950, is a distinctive social function. It is a widely accepted public activity that aims to improve the quality of daily life in our cities, towns, and regions. Any such social function does not come into being either quickly or independently of its context. There has first to be the acknowledgement of a problem that affects community well-being, and then a desire to find a solution to it. This depends, of course, on a sufficient body of people being convinced that community planning can contribute significantly to the welfare and prosperity of city and town dwellers.

The ideas for new physical forms for communities and for alterations to existing forms, as traced in the foregoing chapter, represent more or less technical solutions that the proponents of community planning feel will meet the social needs of a community. Thus, when community planning gains acceptance in any community of any size, it is a marriage of the technical and the social. We know this to be the case now, but how and why did the two come together initially? And how has this affected the outlook of community planning and the matters to which it is addressed? This chapter examines these questions in order to reveal the important non-physical roots of community planning in Canada, including the array of participants who emerged to play a part in modern community planning.

Community planning as we know it today responds to a community's needs as expressed (usually) through the municipal council, but this has not always been the case. Local self-government is a relatively new phenomenon in Canada, and the planning function in local government even newer. The genesis of Canadian community planning began, however, early in the 19th century, when problems associated with urban growth first became a concern. Then, as towns began to grow in size, to develop community identity, and to gain some experience in governing their own affairs, planning and building for community needs gradually assumed the relevance they have today. Nevertheless, the problems that communities wrestled with in the 19th century still constitute important items on the "agenda" for planners through to the present time.

EARLY PROBLEMS OF URBAN GROWTH IN CANADA

Canadian towns began to grow into cities as a result of the general industrial and commercial vigour of the 19th century. Canada was able to share in the supply of raw materials demanded by the burgeoning industrial structure of Europe, especially Britain. This meant economic expansion, population growth, and physical development for Canadian communities. The population in British North America between 1815 and 1865 grew from 0.5 million to 3.5 million people. Although most people still lived in the countryside, the major towns started to grow into cities in this period: Toronto grew from little more than 1,000 people to about 50,000; Montreal grew from 15,000 to 110,000; and Kingston grew from 6,000 to 17,000.

But sharing in the benefits of the Industrial Revolution also brought a share of the burdens. In particular, the problems of rapid urbanization that began to afflict British communities in conjunction with the Industrial Revolution soon had counterparts in Canada's towns and cities. Here are descriptions of two urban situations in the first half of the 19th century:

> Stagnant pools of water, green as leek, and emitting deadly exhalations, are to be met with in every corner of the town—yards and cellars send forth a stench from rotten vegetables sufficient almost of itself to produce a plague and the state of the bay, from which a large proportion of inhabitants are supplied with water, is horrible.[1]

> In many houses there is scarcely any ventilation; dunghills lie in the vicinity of the dwellings; and from the extremely defective sewerage, filth of every kind accumulates.[2]

The first of these strikingly similar passages describes conditions in the new colonial town of York in 1832, which would be renamed Toronto two years later. The second describes Glasgow, Scotland, in 1840.

Disease

Sanitary deficiencies were common in towns and cities of the time on both sides of the Atlantic and were a source of public concern. Moreover, those problems defied easy solution throughout most of the 19th century. There was inadequate technical understanding about the construction of a public sewer system. It was also not understood how subsoil conditions might allow outdoor privies to contaminate wells for drinking water, and it was considered normal that individual houses and businesses should provide their own water supply and waste disposal. Combine these factors with both the lack of public resources to construct sanitary and water supply systems and the lack of authority to compel private property owners to connect to such systems, and one has the setting for tragedy.

Virulent disease often spread within and between communities in 19th-century Canada. Cholera, carried by immigrants from the British Isles, spread in 1832 from near Quebec City all the way to London, Ontario, and up the Ottawa Valley in a matter of two months. And there were several more cholera epidemics over the ensuing years. Typhus hit many cities, including Ottawa and Kingston, in 1847; this epidemic helped spur on public health measures by provincial governments.

Although the public and governmental concern was there, the knowledge about the origin and spread of disease was not. Until the 1870s, when microbes were first isolated as the causes of many diseases, the prevailing wisdom (sometimes referred to as the "filth theory") attributed disease to the accumulation of wastes, human and otherwise; it was commonly believed that the air was poisonous in the vicinity of accumulated wastes, for example. Impure water was also thought to cause disease, but it was not understood until near the end of the century that waterborne microbes might contaminate a community's water supply.

Water Supply

Efforts to bring piped water to all buildings and then to secure sources of pure water were very protracted in many communities. It took Winnipeg from 1882, when it started a public water and sewer system, until 1906 to pass a by-law requiring all buildings to be connected.[3] Ottawa began a public water system in 1872, after debating it from 1855, but it was 1915 before a pure supply was obtained.[4] It took serious typhoid outbreaks in both

FIGURE 4.1   **Canadian Slum Housing, 1912**
Wooden tenements in an eastern Canadian city, showing crowded rear lots, a narrow entrance from the street, and flimsy construction. Rear lots were seldom served by water and sewerage. *Source:* City of Toronto Archives SC 244-1.

these cities to resolve the problem of water and sewer services; the same sort of impetus was needed in many other cities (Figure 4.1).

The immediacy of the problems of disease and pollution was associated in people's minds with the growth of towns and cities. Slowly but surely it became clear that the solutions to these problems required community-wide action. So compelling became this concern that, well into the 20th century, obtaining "healthful conditions" was a prime objective of those who propounded community-planning remedies for towns and cities.

Fire

Another cornerstone for community planning came out of the concern over public safety from fire. Large fires were all too common in Canadian communities throughout the 19th century (Figure 4.2). The extent of this menace can be seen in the following list of major conflagrations in larger Canadian cities:

FIGURE 4.2 **Fires in Early Cities: Toronto, 1904**
Frequent major fires occurred in Canadian cities before the introduction of adequate public water supply systems and firefighting equipment in the early years of this century. *Source:* City of Toronto Archives SC 244–679.

Halifax	1750, 1861
Saint John	1837, 1841, 1845, 1877
Fredericton	1825
Quebec	1815, 1834, 1845, 1862, 1865, 1866, 1876
Montreal	1765, 1768, 1803, 1849, 1852, 1901
Kingston	1847, 1854, 1857, 1890
Toronto	1849, 1890, 1895, 1904
Ottawa	1874, 1900, 1903
Vancouver	1888
New Westminster	1898
Victoria	1904[5]

The control of fire in towns and cities, however, was difficult for two reasons. First, the technology of firefighting was still rudimentary, lacking the necessary vehicles, hoses, etc., and the fire hydrants that had yet to be invented. Second, and even after equipment for firefighting was available, most Canadian communities lacked ample supplies of water. There are many reports of fires raging out of control because of either insufficient water or inadequate water pressure. Thus, the public's concerns both over health and over fire losses centred to a high degree on the supply of water.

The frequent loss of buildings in fires was also causing fire insurance rates to climb dramatically in this period. Local businesses became increas-

ingly worried over the waste and the cost of fires, which, in turn, prompted concern over the ways in which cities and towns were being built and maintained. In particular, the quality of building construction came in for scrutiny: were buildings safe for their occupants? Would they deter the spread of fire to other buildings? These questions, considered straightforward today, were in the past not deemed appropriate: the construction of buildings was the private business of the builder or owner. As late as 1920, no province had a uniform building code that set standards for fire safety and other hazards, and municipal building inspection practices were also relatively new. The threat of fire is no longer the concern in city-building that it once was, but the issue of civic safety is no less present. Natural disasters such as floods and earthquakes are ever-present dangers to communities, as the floods in the Saguenay region of Quebec and in Manitoba in the mid-1990s attest. These latter kinds of concerns have spawned a sub-discipline within community planning called "disaster planning."[6]

Slums

As Canadian cities grew more populous in the latter part of the 19th century, attention turned increasingly to the quality of housing. The new populations in cities came almost entirely from Europe, and most of these were poor people. It was known that cholera epidemics were attributable to newly arrived immigrants. It was also observed that many immigrant workers lived in crowded, unsanitary, rudimentary dwellings. Tenuous and often unfair assumptions were made that the poor and their neighbourhoods

were the prime sources of disease and fire (not to speak of moral degradation). As one writer notes, "bad plumbing and crowded housing were more
easily fixed on as the culprit in the spread of disease and crime than the
complete framework of poverty."[7]

It should not be thought that there were not slums in Canadian cities of
this period. A penetrating study by Herbert Ames of a working-class district in Montreal in 1896 provides details of housing conditions.[8] In the
area, 2 or 3 km^2 just to the east of Windsor Station, over 37,000 people
lived in 8,300 tenement-type apartments. These densities of, respectively,
14,300 persons per square kilometre and 33 dwelling units per hectare are
not extremely high by the standards of today's high-density housing projects. However, the conditions Ames observed in Montreal were for an
entire district, not just a housing project, and most of the buildings were
only two and three storeys high! Along with the narrow streets and almost
no open public space, the result was very high density by any standards.
Further, one-half of the dwellings had outdoor privies. Ames notes that
some other wards in Montreal had densities two and three times higher
than the area he studied. (See Figure 9.1.)

Although data on early housing conditions are fragmentary, it seems
clear that other Canadian communities suffered similar problems. In
Winnipeg, for example, in 1884 the overall density of population in the
built-up area was close to 4,000 per square kilometre.[9] By 1900, about one-
half of Winnipeg's houses still had outdoor privies; add to this the wide
spread use of horses for transportation and the need to dispose of animal
wastes. The density of development just after mid-century (1860) in
Toronto had already reached over 4,800 per square kilometre.[10] There was
concern over Toronto slums from as early as 1873; and in 1884, the Toronto
Tenement Building Association was established to build houses and apartments with "modern conveniences and sanitary appliances" for working-
class populations. These overall density figures are, of course, for the entire
city, but the poor usually lived in neighbourhoods at two and three times
the average density.

Thus, slum conditions developed early in most Canadian communities;
those that grew faster and larger developed slum districts. The factors were
usually the same: poor people, attracted to the prospect of jobs, who
obtained low-paying jobs if any, who were unable to afford very good housing, and who were offered small, insubstantial dwellings with inadequate
sanitation. The consequent crowding often led to illness and social tension.
By the end of the century, efforts were under way in many cities to deal
with slum conditions through public health measures, improved building
practices and codes, and even new housing specifically for workers.

CONTRIBUTIONS OF THE 19TH-CENTURY IDEALIST PLANNERS

During the first half of the 19th century in Europe, the congestion, squalor, and filth in cities had made the lives of the lower class unbearable and threatened the quality of life for the other sections of society. The persistence of these conditions led to many proposals to create new urban environments. Philanthropic efforts from the ruling class, political initiatives from radicals and socialists, and ideas from utopian thinkers all combined to suggest ways to intervene in the deplorable physical conditions. And, importantly, they all carried their own ideals and values about the conduct of community life as well. Many of these ideals remain firmly embedded in approaches to community planning today.

Robert Owen and the Utopians

In the period following the Napoleonic Wars, there was considerable intellectual ferment over the structure of society and the nature of community. The Industrial Revolution broke down the centuries-old connection between the town and countryside. Many thinkers of this time began to suggest the establishment of new forms of communities carefully planned to contain the best of both a town and a farm.

One such scheme was that of Robert Owen, a rich English industrialist, who presented a plan for a cooperative community combining industry and agriculture. His proposal for New Lanark in 1816 was for a settlement of 1,200 people covering about 480 ha of agricultural land. Dwellings were grouped around a large open square, three sides of which would be taken up by residences for couples and children of less than three years of age; the fourth side would contain the young people's dormitories, the infirmary, and guest accommodation. The central area would have such public buildings as schools, a library, a communal restaurant, and clubs, along with other areas for recreation. Around the perimeter would be gardens, farm buildings, and industrial units. To complement his physical plan, Owen proposed a cooperative community structure with much emphasis on education and on blending work in the factory with study and leisure.

Owen did not succeed in gaining support from authorities to build prototypes of his new town in Britain. He tried to develop a similar community in the United States in 1825, New Harmony, Indiana, but had to give that up in a few years. Despite these disappointments, Owen's ideas were very influential. His **parallelogram system,** named for the rectangular form of the town he propounded, came to be widely known, much cited, and imitated.

Charles Fourier, a French utopian writer of the same era, proposed a community of about 1,600 people carefully chosen according to their ages who would be housed in a single building, the Phalanstery, surrounded by over 2 km² of land. All accommodation would be communal in order to concentrate human relationships and achieve the "universal harmony" he propounded. The connection with the pastoral landscape is also important, as planning historian Leonardo Benevolo notes about Fourier's plan:

> The land shall be provided with a fine stream of water, it shall be intersected by hills and adapted to varied cultivation; it should be contiguous with a forest and not far removed from a large city, but sufficiently so to escape intruders.[11]

Between 1830 and 1850, there were at least 50 attempts to create Phalansteries in different countries, among them France, Russia, and the United States. Later in the century, a French admirer of Fourier's ideas, Godin, adapted the idea to the city and industrial production. His proposals for Familistery promoted the family unit with its own apartment, but with communal amenities; a workers' cooperative would control the housing and the factory. Cabet was another source of French utopian thought. He proposed a city, called Icaria, of metropolitan scale, in contrast to the village-sized ideal communities of his compatriots. Cabet conceived of a city organized under a program of total communism; its physical form would separate traffic from pedestrian walkways, put factories on the outskirts, and have two circumferential boulevards. A prototype of Icaria was begun in Illinois in 1849 by Cabet and several hundred followers, but never grew very large.

Two British ideal town plans of the mid-19th century sought to bring order to chaotic city environments through the design of the physical form alone and did not attempt to restructure social relations. Hygeia, planned by Benjamin Richardson, and Victoria, by John Buckingham (Figure 4.3), both insisted on the need for fresh air, light, and water, and on a regular and uniform design to bring order to the lives of city dwellers. Buckingham's plan is the best known for its series of concentric squares, each containing rows of buildings for houses, workshops, etc. Public buildings were at the centre, as were the houses for the wealthiest inhabitants; factories and other industrial activities were located away from the centre. It was in many ways a plan to help achieve efficient production for factories and provide full employment and amicable surroundings for workers.

Although most of these ideal towns were never built, the efforts of the idealists were important in the development of planning concepts in two

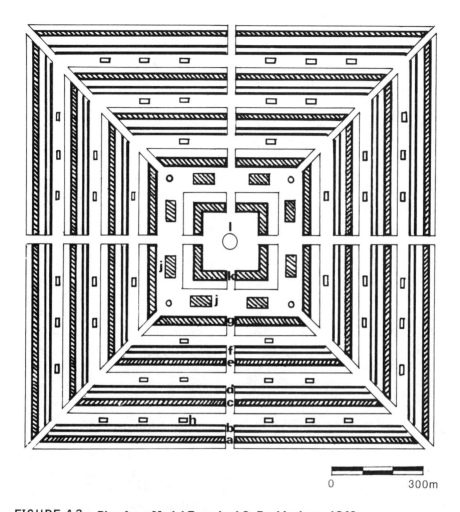

FIGURE 4.3   **Plan for a Model Town by J.S. Buckingham, 1849**
A proposed city for 10,000 people, Victoria, in the English countryside. The ideal of the village community where principles of social cooperation could be practised underlay many such plans. Roughly one mile (1.6 km) on a side, it comprised parallel rows of housing (a, c, e, g) graded to serve people of various incomes with the poorest living at the perimeter. Covered galleries (b, d, f) for workshops and retail stores allowed easy access to work and social contacts in all weather. At the centre were major public buildings (j), mansions (k), and a square (l); schools (h) were widely distributed.

ways. On the one hand, they are the first attempts at community planning that consider not only the physical form but also the sources of employment and the social structure of the inhabitants. On the other hand, they represent the beginning of the development of technical and geometric skills applied to community planning. The widespread enthusiasm garnered by these proposals indicates the increasing willingness of people to accept technical professional advice in improving communities.

Model Industrial Towns

The proposals of the utopians, in stressing the connection between improved living conditions for industrial workers and social harmony, stimulated many industrial owners in the second half of the 19th century to build "model" communities. The aims were more paternalistic than philanthropic, concerned as they were with enhancing workers' efficiency. Nevertheless, the plans for model communities provided further evidence of the ability to conceive technical solutions to some of the urban problems of the time. In 1846, the industrial village of Bessbrook was begun for linen mill workers near Newry, Ireland. In 1853, Titus Salt started building Saltaire, a model town for 3,000 people, the workers at his textile mill near Bradford in England. Similar communities were built in France, Belgium, Holland, and Italy. The Krupp family of industrialists built four workers' settlements around Essen in Germany between 1863 and 1875.

Several new British industrial towns built toward the end of the 19th century are also worthy of note. Bourneville, near Birmingham, was built by chocolate manufacturer George Cadbury in 1879. Residential areas were broken into groups through the use of intervening parks and playgrounds; the land on which the town was built was deeded to the community and has remained under town ownership to this day. Cocoa manufacturer Joseph Rowntree built Earswick near York in 1905; it, too, was made a community trust. The architects Barry Parker and Raymond Unwin planned Earswick as they had Port Sunlight for Lever Brothers in 1886. In these towns, Parker and Unwin began to design housing areas in large blocks with their own interior gardens and play spaces. Housing closely associated with open space served to provide the fresh air, light, and natural surroundings that were so often missing in cities of the Industrial Revolution; these social values are mirrored in the design of post-World War II subdivisions right across Canada.

Patrick Geddes

One of the most important 19th-century contributors to planning ideas that are still cogent today is Patrick Geddes. Born in 1854, Geddes trained as a botanist with Thomas Huxley and thereby gained his enduring interest in ecological principles. His concern over the abysmal living conditions in British cities led him to try and apply these principles to the organization of cities. His means for doing this were pragmatic, intellectual, and professional. In the 1880s, he moved into one of Edinburgh's filthiest slum tenements and proceeded to renovate it as a way of helping the inhabitants to see how they could improve their own living quarters. In 1892, he established his Outlook Tower, a tall medieval-style structure in Edinburgh, that allowed one to view the city—and, in traversing up to the outlook, to view an exhibition of Geddes' ideas about the interrelationships of social, economic, and physical features of a city.

As one biographer has said, "Geddes cannot be limited to a single discipline or profession, he must be described in a hyphenated manner, as a planner-teacher-sociologist-political economist-botanist-activist."[12] Because of these prodigious interests, Geddes brought a new approach to the task of community planning. He appreciated that human life and its individual and collective environments, both natural and manufactured, are all intertwined, and that improving cities means understanding them and planning for that reality rather than substituting another urban form. Geddes was a practical idealist:

> Eutopia, then, lies in the city around us: and it must be planned and realised, here or nowhere, by us as its citizens—each a citizen of both the actual and the ideal city seen increasingly as one.[13]

Geddes pioneered his ideas through various forms—exhibitions, lectures, writing—and through planning practices. In the early part of the 20th century, Geddes practised planning in Britain and in India. He saw community planning, in many ways, as a learning experience, both for the community and the planner. Geddes is often credited with the dictum, "No plan before survey." He stressed the importance of knowing a town's geography, history, economy, social conditions, and means of transportation and communication. Not only was he the first planner to specify what should be in the "town survey" but he also advocated that its results—maps, charts, photographs, etc.—be put on public display. This "civic exhibition," as he called it, would help citizens and officials to appreciate both the current problems and the future prosperity of planning for them. Canadian planner Kent Gerecke cites Geddes' "integrative linking" as perhaps the contribution most missing from today's planning.[14]

Geddes was among the first to give thoughtful consideration to what came to be called "urban renewal" in the 1950s. He saw no merit in bulldozing slum areas to the ground because the displaced people would simply be forced to relocate. His concept of **conservative surgery** required that efforts be made to remove as few buildings as possible and to repair and modify existing structures. Human disruption would thus be minimized, and the physical fabric of the city maintained. Geddes was also the first to recognize that as cities spread out they often grew together into a "connurbation." He cautioned against the effects on the natural land-scape, agricultural resources, and rural communities that would result from simply letting cities grow outward. Patrick Geddes is truly the first regional planner (see also Chapter 11).

THE PIONEERING OF COMMUNITY PLANNING IN CANADA, 1890–1930

As communities in the 19th century tackled the problems of disease, pure water supplies, fire, sanitation, and slums, their experience gave rise to two important realizations. First, it became evident that these problems resulted somehow from the growth and development of cities. Second, and more slowly, came the realization that the solutions to these problems lay in better coordination, regulation, and physical arrangement of the overall development of cities.

The milieu of 19th-century urban problems and the approaches taken to solve them constitute the foundation for modern community planning in Canada. The issues of public health, fire safety, and adequate housing became the first social goals of community planning, the top items on the agenda, as a town-planning movement emerged just after the beginning of this century. These issues would be found, time and again, enshrined in the preambles of planning legislation proclaiming that the by-law or plan was aimed at "improving the health, safety, and public welfare" of the com-munity.

The period 1890–1930 saw the pioneering of the ideas and practice of community planning in Canada. In general, it consisted of communities taking some halting steps to assume responsibility for their planning prob-lems and to draw upon technical and professional assistance in this regard. It was a turbulent period, with further dramatic growth of cities and advances in transportation, which brought new problems. Nevertheless, this period is among the most important in the evolution of community planning. Within it we see the development of the first locally sponsored plans in Kitchener and Toronto, the pioneering work of the Commission of Conservation, and the emergence of a planning profession. The vitality of this period was an outgrowth of vigorous public debate, as we shall see below.

Pioneer Public Movements

Four areas of public concern about city and town development had gathered considerable momentum as the 19th century came to an end in Canada. Three of these grew out of substantive issues that have already been identified: public health, conservation of resources, and inadequate housing for the poor. A fourth grew out of a widespread dismay over the capabilities of local government officials to deal adequately with the needs of a community.

Around each of these concerns there had developed, by the beginning of the 20th century, an active movement among members of the public, various professions, the newspapers, and many public officials who lobbied for the mitigation of urban problems. Often the concern focused on a special interest organization. There was, of course, overlap in the interests of each; indeed, as can happen in a small country, many of the same people were involved in two or more of these crusades for improvement in Canadian city life.

The community-(town-) planning movement came out of the confluence of these four streams of concern during the first dozen years of the 20th century. The proponents of each shared many objectives, but they also brought with them to community planning differences in values, professional outlook, and skills, and jurisdictional focus. Each came to form a part of the amalgam of social objectives that characterize community planning.

The Public Health Movement

Public health advocates campaigned throughout the second half of the 19th century for better public water supplies and sewer systems and for the eradication of slums. Various arguments were invoked over the years, from the waste of precious lives to the moral decay caused by slum conditions to the economic cost of sickness of industrial workers. The appeal for reforms was to the community's interest in caring for its members, but progress was slow when it required local governments either to make expenditures or to regulate private property.

Efforts were also made to establish regulatory structures rooted in statutes at the provincial and national levels. The first provincial Board of Health was set up in Ontario in 1883 and headed by Dr. Peter Bryce, a vigorous supporter of better health measures at the community level. He was also responsible for establishing better systems for recording vital statistics, which could be used to substantiate the needs in public health. Bryce moved to Ottawa in 1904 to become the Chief Medical Officer under the federal government's new National Health Act. Several more provinces also passed public health acts in this same period.

Dr. Charles Hodgetts, who succeeded Bryce at the Ontario Health Board, mounted a strenuous campaign for the improvement of housing. Toward this end, he advocated the use of town-planning techniques he had witnessed in Europe. Toronto's Medical Officer of Health (MOH), Dr. Charles Hastings, argued equally vigorously for better building standards and sanitary and water systems in this same period, as did Winnipeg's MOH:

> [We must] ensure that every place occupied as a dwelling unit within the City—no matter how humble it may be—is perfectly sanitary and a fit and proper place in which to bring up Winnipeg's most valuable asset—her children.[15]

This strong role of the local MOH in city development continues to the present time in most provinces.

The Housing Reform Movement

Those in the public health movement were among the first to try and arouse public concern over housing conditions, especially for the poor. They urged sanitary improvements and reductions in density. The initial arguments were humanitarian in nature, and as broader support was sought, they were augmented later with the plea that poor housing promoted disease and caused major costs for the nation's businesses.

Industrialists and businessmen joined the debate over housing in the 1890s. From their perspective, poor housing, which facilitated disease among workers, also led to absenteeism and lowered productivity. Moreover, much of the poor housing occupied by workers was expensive, and high rents usually meant pressure for more wages, the industrialists unabashedly stated.[16] But obtaining better housing for workers was difficult. With the dramatic growth of Canadian cities in the early part of the 20th century, the cost of suburban land was pushed up and inner-city land prices stayed high as downtown areas burgeoned.

Municipally provided (public) housing was considered but did not receive much support until the 1920s. Tenant cooperatives were also proposed following the urgings of Henry Vivian, a British MP who toured Canada in 1910 to promote the idea of a partnership of tenants subscribing the capital for a housing development. The most notable such project was *Cité Jardin* in Rosemont. Also in Montreal, industrialist Herbert Ames built a model tenement project called **Diamond Court** soon after the turn of the century to demonstrate how low-income housing could be improved.

Limited-dividend housing (providing a fixed rate of return on the investment) built with private capital was favoured mostly by affluent members of the community. It tapped their philanthropic spirit and reduced any "socialist" tendencies to have the municipality provide housing. A popular phrase of the time was Thomas Roden's "philanthropy and five percent," which referred to the dividend that investors would receive in building worker housing. In 1907, Roden helped form the Toronto Housing Company, which eventually built several hundred dwellings.

The Toronto Housing Company experience is important in several ways. First, there was public involvement in the projects, for although the company was started by private investors, its bonds were guaranteed up to 85% by the city government. Ontario passed legislation allowing this in 1913, following the lead of Nova Scotia, which included the option in its 1912 Town Planning Act (the second in the country). Second, the projects were designed as row houses surrounding ample courtyards in the tradition of Hampstead Garden Suburb housing (Figure 4.4). In this way, both high density and amenity were achieved, and to this day, the projects retain a distinctive, pleasing character.

Further, organizers of the company, most notably G. Frank Beer and Sir Edmund Osler, were also prominent in arguing for community-wide planning. They campaigned widely to provide playgrounds and better transportation, as well as to reduce the congestion of the population. Beer, in his remarks to the 1914 conference of the Commission of Conservation in Ottawa, linked "city planning" to conservation: "The conservation of life and desirable living conditions … are inseparable."[17]

The Conservation Movement

The turn of the century gave rise to the recognition among the industrialized countries that industrial processes were consuming natural resources at an alarming rate, often leaving in their wake waste and pollution. The persistence of these problems in city and country alike led to strong national initiatives in the field of conservation of resources. It will be remembered that this was the era in which the wilderness lands of the Rocky Mountains were urged to be secured for national parks (in both Canada and the U.S.).

In 1909, following the lead of the United States but going even further, Canada established a Commission for the Conservation of Natural Resources. Winnipeg lawyer and federal Cabinet minister Clifford Sifton was made chairman of the **Commission of Conservation,** as it came to be called. The commission concerned itself with many resources questions: lands, forests, minerals, fisheries, game and fur-bearing animals, waters

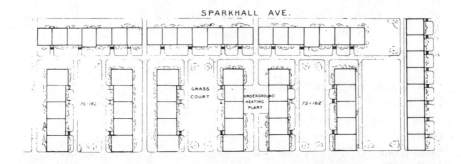

FIGURE 4.4   **Housing Project for Workers: Toronto, 1913**
Plan and sketch view of a housing development for working-class families. The Toronto Housing Company (a limited-dividend corporation) built the project, which is still in use. There were 204 "cottage flats" (one- to four-bedroom row houses). *Source:* Commission of Conservation, 1914.

and waterpower. Somewhat unique was the commission's commitment, from the outset, to human resources. Dr. Charles Hodgetts was one of the first to be appointed to the permanent staff as the Advisor on Public Health. In his years with the commission, he would often echo the maxim: "Population is our most valuable national resource."[18]

Through their commitment to the health of the population, the commission urged the improvement of housing and initiatives in community

Planning Issue 4.1

DIRTY HARBOUR, DIRTY FIGHT!

Can 400 million dollars buy a clean harbour when environmentalists say it can be done for less?

by Bob LeDrew

Halifax has a sick harbour. Every day, 100 million litres of what is euphemistically called 'grey water' is flushed into the harbour—as much waste as the oil lost from the Brear tanker in Scotland, every day. The problem is nothing new—human beings have a tendency to fill the nearest body of water with wastes from human feces to chemical byproducts, whether the place is Halifax or Hiroshima. But the proposal to clean up Halifax Harbour is running into opposition from environmentalists and from the governments that are funding its advocates.

The solution, according to Halifax Harbour Cleanup Inc. (HHCI), is to build a sewage treatment plant (STP) on a manmade island off McNab's Island, in Halifax Harbour, that will handle most of the wastes and perform what is called "primary treatment"—a process that uses screens and tanks to remove the solid material from the wastes. The plant will also, according to

HHCI president Paul Calda, incinerate the solid material collected (sludge) to create a form of oil to be used in road building. ...

Calda has little patience for the project's critics. In the past, he has called them "amateurs" proposing a dog's breakfast of untried and impractical technologies. Calda says that the cleanup can't wait for ideal solutions. "The mitigating measures we are proposing to take will hopefully minimize or lessen the adverse impacts on neighbourhoods, on the harbour, on land."...

Howard Epstein likes to be specific as well. ... His executive director's office (more a space, really) at the Ecology Action Centre overlooks the harbour from the third floor of Veith House, a former orphanage in the working-class North End that is now home to a miscellany of groups from international-development agencies to the EAC, a non-profit citizens' environmental group.

The Ecology Action Centre is one of five groups that have formed a coalition to work as watchdog on the cleanup. The groups, representing taxpayers, 'Friends of McNab's Island,' and environmentalists, have all sorts of criticisms of the project, from its technology to its site.

McNab's Island as a site upsets many. Although HHCI's Calda says the island's lack of population was a minor factor in its selection, all admit that the not-in-my-back-yard syndrome was neatly circumvented by picking a deserted island. "So now it's in everybody's front yard," Epstein says.

Critics say that the island has massive potential as an urban park and large historic resources that the STP will destroy. Not surprisingly, HHCI says that the man-made island will prevent any problem with park development or historic value.

Epstein drinks coffee from a chipped cup and talks about the criticisms with arguments he had made time and again. "Here are the major flaws as I see it with what they've proposed. First it's on McNab's Island. Number two, putting it on McNab's Island increases the cost by an order of $50-million or more. The third is that there's just one treatment plant, and that doesn't make sense, particularly for people who live on the Halifax mainland area. In order to join that up requires tunnelling under the Northwest Arm, which is hugely expensive. Next is oil from sludge. They don't yet know whether they'll be able to sell the stuff at the end. The other problem is that their proposal does not address the removal of toxics at source. ... The final of what I can think of is that they're building a one-pipe system."

Epstein says that there are simple and complex solutions to the cleanup that HHCI refuses to acknowledge. "One solution might be a system that involves a very long pipe and diffuser that goes out past McNab's Island, rather than a treatment plant of any sort. Now that would require two things: elimination of toxics at source, and a screening device to remove solids that people might throw down." This idea, which is now being considered in Victoria, B.C., depends on the natural action of sea water to disperse the waste and kill the bacteria. ...

"Our point of view is that we would like to stop polluting the harbour, but we think that half a billion dollars is too much to pay for it. The problem is that they've completely screwed up—they're just wildly out of control on the money side."

As the debate rages—the environmental assessment and review has pushed the project back by at least two years, the criticisms continue, and the project has exceeded its original $195-million price tag by $203-million—Calda says the best thing to be done is just to move ahead. "The project is not something which just happened in the last two or three years, it's been seriously talked about and studied and money spent on for 25 years. And I think, through the public opinion surveys, we found that the public is being slightly distrustful about the real intentions—is it a study project, to be studied forever or is it something for real? And we have the feeling that people want it to be for real."

But so far, the only thing that is real is the money that's been spent, the deserted island, and the fouled harbour.

Bob LeDrew is a freelance writer with Writer's Block Productions in Halifax.

Source: Excerpted from Bob LeDrew, Green City, "Dirty Harbour, Dirty Fight!" *City Magazine* 14 (Spring 1993), 41–42. Published with permission of *New City Magazine* (formerly *City Magazine*).

planning. Hodgetts, in his report to the commission in 1912, showed that he was fully aware of the scope of planning for an entire community. He set down the "essentials of town planning" in very sophisticated terms:

> The questions involved are more numerous and complicated than the mere building of a house. The various constituent parts of a modern town have to be considered and arranged in such a manner that they will form an harmonious whole … a plan for town extension contemplates and provides for the development of the whole of every urban, suburban, and rural area that may be built on within from thirty to fifty years.[19]

By the beginning of World War I, the commission's involvement with community planning had become very extensive, as will be seen in subsequent sections. Three aspects of its early work, however, deserve special mention. One of the commission's undertakings was to draft a model "Town Planning Act for Canada," which it hoped each province might adopt in order to promote local planning. Lt.-Col. Jeffery Burland, a member of the commission from Montreal and an advocate of improvements in worker housing, was a central figure in this effort, which, though controversial, would prove to be very influential. Another commission endeavour was to host the National City Planning Conference at its sixth convention in Toronto in 1914. These annual meetings were already well-established gatherings where planners from North America and Europe exchanged ideas. Thomas Adams, a prominent British planner who had been associated with the Garden City movement, came to the attention of the commission in this way. In its third major move, the commission hired Adams as its Town Planning Advisor in 1914.

By promoting community planning, the commission provided a national forum sponsored by the federal government which, undoubtedly, meant a quicker, wider dissemination of planning ideas than would have otherwise occurred in such a large and sparsely settled country. By giving Thomas Adams the central role in this endeavour, it highlighted the role of the professional in the planning of communities and by linking up community planning with the resources sector, it helped incorporate in planning the general economic values espoused by the commission. Clifford Sifton revealed these views at the 1914 convention:

> People must appreciate the idea that town planning is not born with the intent of spending money, it is simply not a new kind of extravagance, but is conceived with the idea of preventing extravagance and preventing waste and getting good value for the money which is expended.[20]

The Civic Reform Movement

The final major influence on community planning in its beginning days was a widespread movement to improve the quality of local government. There were three fairly distinct areas of concern at various times: social welfare of city dwellers, public ownership of basic utilities, and the efficiency of local government. The issues ranged from procrastination and technical incompetence to graft of municipalities, and sometimes all three.

The earliest concerns had to do with such social problems as disease, poverty, crime, and poor housing. These efforts gained considerable momentum in the 1880s, aided by new popular newspapers like *The Montreal Star, The Ottawa Journal,* and *The Vancouver News-Advertiser,* and by reform-minded clergymen like Winnipeg's J.S. Woodsworth. Their approaches, although motivated by a mixture of humanitarianism and professional and business self-interest, were characterized by the use of statistics, the advocacy of government regulation, and the promotion of the use of experts and professionals.

The second stream of civic reform concerned the provision of municipal utilities. The waterworks, street railways, and electric power and telephone systems had been developed largely by private interests on franchises offered by municipal councils on "extremely generous terms to the entrepreneurs."[21] However, as growth pressures mounted, the services were often found wanting, contracts were not being met, there were instances of influence peddling, and private utilities were often reluctant to expand into new suburban areas. Moreover, civic leaders, who were mostly drawn from the business community, wished to appear progressive and willing to have industry in their communities. As the Mayor of Medicine Hat said at the time, "Municipal ownership (of utilities) and industrial progress go hand in hand."[22]

Guelph purchased its gas works and electric power system in 1893; Edmonton had a publicly owned power system in 1902, and similar efforts can be cited from coast to coast. But the progressive-looking municipal utilities were, not infrequently, a mixed blessing: sprawl was increased when premature land development was served; operating surpluses were not always forthcoming; and inept administration was not uncommon. Despite these difficulties, the move to municipal ownership established, from then on, the rights and the responsibilities of communities to provide community-wide services.

The third target of the urban reformers was urban government itself, for, in the headlong rush for growth, problems did arise from hasty development, and civic leaders were often self-serving. Then, too, the scale and rapidity of urbanization in this period was unprecedented, much of the technology was new, and local government was relatively inexperienced. As a result of these factors, civic government structures were blamed for inefficiency. Reformers sought to reduce the power of city councils and their committees and substitute special boards and commissions. These, it was contended, could administer the various functions that communities needed to handle their growth—waterworks, transportation, parks, police, schools, libraries—more efficiently because they would not be subject to political pressures. Eventually, the planning function was also accorded this same semi-independent status in local affairs.

The attempts to separate politics from the administration of public services did not always result in increased efficiency. It also had two other long-term effects on the planning and governing of communities. First, it led to a proliferation of agencies, each responsible for a separate function and not having to coordinate their activities with those of either the city government or other bodies. Second, because the special bodies needed to develop special skills, they fostered the use of experts in the solution of urban problems. The special boards and commissions tended to acquire considerable discretionary powers and vested these in professionals and administrators.

The various urban reform movements helped Canadian communities to cope more rationally with expansion, to ensure more stability in the provision of services, and to maintain a degree of humanitarian concern for the less fortunate of their citizens. But they also initiated much more complex means of local government, which necessitated the cooperation and coordination of many bodies. This situation remains a source of frustration for community planning in many urban areas to this day.

The Impact of 20th-Century Urban Problems

Even as the various reform movements were winning support from the public and stimulating governments to institute community planning measures to help solve problems that had troubled cities for several decades, the 20th century presented new problems. The first dozen years of this century constituted a period of unparalleled prosperity, from the wheat fields of Saskatchewan to the wharves of Vancouver and Saint John. Immigrants poured into Canada ostensibly "to open up the West," but most of them ended up in the nation's cities. Urban-based industries thrived on the new inexpensive labour supply. In addition, technological solutions provided cities with both below-ground (water and sewerage) and above-ground (electric lines, paved roads) services fairly rapidly and inexpensively. Probably most important in this period, however, was the advent of powered urban rail transportation—the electric streetcar and the commuter railroad—and slightly later the self-propelled bus.

Problems of Excessive Subdivision
Cities were growing fast; the growth could mostly be coped with, and growth was considered good. Indeed, urban growth was so highly considered that it was pursued through aggressive "boosterism." Ample supplies of land were also deemed essential to accommodate the hoped-for growth. No thorough study has ever been made of the amount of land that was subdivided in anticipation of urban growth in the decade or so before World War I. However, it is possible to glean its extent in several cities from concerned accounts of the problems such subdivision subsequently raised. Here are a few examples comparing the population just prior to 1914 with the population that could be accommodated on the already subdivided land:

Calgary	50,000/770,000
Ottawa-Hull	123,000/1,600,000
Edmonton	40,000/500,000
Saskatoon	12,000/750,000
Vancouver	115,000/750,000

Abetting this surge in land speculation were dramatic increases in the coverage of street railways. Figures for Toronto and Vancouver convey something of the picture that was occurring in other cities. In 1880, Toronto had 30 km of street railways, and only 10 years later had 110 km; while Vancouver went from 26 km in 1900 to 165 km by 1914. The impact of such expansion can be appreciated from the fact that each linear kilometre of streetcar line could serve about 2 km^2 of residential land or, in pre-1914 densities, potentially 10,000 persons. Not until the automobile freeways of the 1950s would Canadian cities again witness such an impact on their scale.

And like the freeways later, the streetcar lines brought potential development but, frequently, not actual building. Land was surveyed by the hundreds of hectares, and subdivision plats were registered in land titles offices. There were, of course, not enough people heading for Canada's cities to come close, in most cases, to absorbing the amount of new building lots. Severe problems arose for cities in the short run because of the premature subdivision. As Walter Van Nus notes:

> A developer's desire to extract the maximum number of lots ... often led him to ignore the location and/or width of projected or existing streets nearby, if by doing so he could squeeze more lots out of the property.[23]

This lack of simple coordination of the extensions to cities often required, at a later time, expensive road relocation by the municipalities. In addition, the subdivision development was usually scattered, and this meant extra costs in providing such municipal services as water and sewer lines, roads, sidewalks, and street lighting. Because intervening undeveloped land did not pay its share of the servicing costs, the taxes had to be raised from the new building lots. Frequently the land that came into actual development was unsuitable for building—topographically too steep, many rock outcroppings, poorly drained—and this not only led to immediate problems for communities but often was also a source of problems many decades later.

Cities that espoused growth found themselves on the horns of a dilemma many times—a dilemma that, as we shall see, spilled over into planning outlooks. First, however, were the enormous costs of servicing the new suburbs that municipalities faced. Those that demurred in making these expenditures might find the building going to an adjacent municipality. Second, people seeking a building lot were finding land values and taxes much higher along streetcar routes and accordingly sought land beyond the end of the streetcar line. This tended to spread the costs further afield, but not necessarily the benefits. Third, most cities were faced with large housing shortages, which the mere subdivision of land on the fringe did little to alleviate. Land prices and rents rose sharply in Canadian cities in the several years before World War I, especially in and around downtown areas. Poor people and manufacturing firms traditionally located near the centre suffered most. Many firms moved to suburban locations, not infrequently followed by the shacktowns of their workers.

New Dimensions to Urban Problems

These new urban problems had several significant impacts for the then-fledgling planning profession and would continue to affect the outlook of all those involved with community planning right to the present.[24]

Land Subdivision. The first is the importance of legally subdividing a larger piece of property into house lots or other small parcels of land. The new pieces of property acquire independent status, and the community is obliged to honour this whenever they should be built upon. A community's development pattern and quality is thereby constrained even though the timing and character of what gets built is not specified. On the one hand, there are such technical aspects as road alignment, drainage, lot size, and ease of providing water and sewer lines in which the community has a rightful interest with respect to the subdivision of private land. On the other hand, there is the issue of the degree to which a community should intervene in the development of privately owned property. The unprecedented scale of pre-1914 subdivision brought home the importance of this process even to the extent of generating preventive legislation in several provinces.

The Land Developer. Second, the act of subdividing land in a speculative way involved a relatively new actor in the planning and development of communities—the land developer. In the beginning stages of most Canadian cities, land was distributed by grants to corporations, institutions, and privileged individuals who, in turn, provided building lots as they were needed. However, the surge of growth just before and just after 1900 created a demand for city land so large that it attracted many more people and groups to seek profit in providing space for newcomers.

Such old land grantees as the Canadian Pacific Railway, the British American Land Company, and the Hudson's Bay Company became more aggressive in their efforts, often to the extent of influencing the location of new municipal development. On a smaller scale, but equally pervasive, were a coterie of individual landowners (large and small), their agents, and brokers all anxious to share in the potential profit of the new growth. This was the period for the beginning of a "real estate industry."

The views of land development interests, the real estate industry, and homeowners all focused upon **the primacy of private property.** Their concerns held sway in most municipal councils at that time, much as they seem to do today. The economic slump of 1913 and for nearly a decade thereafter had the effect of imprinting on municipal consciousness the other side of the case for unfettered land development—the protection of land values. This dichotomous issue would continue to concern and exasperate community planners from then on.

Efficiency.   The third important impact of the burgeoning development in the early 20th century was to lodge firmly the issue of the efficiency of physical development. Thus, the emerging planning profession, just as it was being accepted into municipal affairs, was faced with the issue of how to manage large-scale, rapid land development. The tendency of planners to prepare physical designs for new development seemed often to be out of tune with the vigorous, widely supported process of land speculation. Planners began to promote planning as a means of obtaining efficiency in city development. It has been remarked that, at about this time, between 1910 and 1920, the "City Efficient" began to replace the "City Beautiful" as the focus of planning.[25] However, both notions contained compelling values and compete for attention on planning agendas to the present day.

The Emergence of a Planning Profession

Socially desirable activities are usually undertaken by persons who possess the requisite technical skills and also espouse the same values as the community or the larger society. We usually refer to these people as professionals in their field: e.g., doctors, lawyers, firemen, architects, engineers. In the professionals, a community vests the responsibility of identifying and advising on the solutions to its important problems. Increasingly, communities in the first two decades of the 20th century sought the advice and skills of town planners, as was noted briefly in Chapter 3.

By the end of World War I, those persons who practised town planning in Canada numbered over 100, and they undertook to form a professional organization to promote wider involvement of communities in community planning. In January 1919, they formed a Town Planning Club preparatory to establishing a formal institute. In May of the same year, the **Town Planning Institute of Canada** (TPIC) was formed, with 117 members and branches in four cities: Ottawa, Toronto, Winnipeg, and Vancouver. The organization exists to this day under the name Canadian Institute of Planners, and has several thousand members.

The TPIC received its charter in 1919, the culmination of a decade or more of vigorous persuasion and practical demonstration of the merits of community planning. The efforts of Hodgetts, Adams, Cauchon, and a score of others had borne fruit. They could now consolidate not only the acceptance of planning ideas in Canada, but also the identification of Canadians possessing the necessary technical skills to carry out planning ideas. Indeed, by 1919 all but two of the provinces had passed substantial planning statutes, and Canadian planners had helped in drafting them. Cities across the country now sought the assistance of planners, both from Canada and abroad, in civic centre plans, suburban extensions, and park planning.

The skills of these 100 or so new "town planners" included those of several traditional professions. In fact, the constitution of the TPIC originally set out that membership was limited to architects, engineers, landscape architects, surveyors, sculptors, artists, and sociologists. Lawyers could seek associate membership. This array of professional skills reveals a good deal about how planners saw the task of planning: a concern for building design, physical layout, the natural environment, civic design, social factors, and legal and administrative processes.

The names of a few of these pioneer Canadian planners should be acknowledged, at least in passing, because of the importance of their groundwork in the modern planning of many of our cities. Among them were architects Percy Nobbs of Montreal and J.P. Hynes of Toronto; engineers Noulan Cauchon, Horace Seymour, and J.M. Kitchen of Ottawa, A.G. Dalzell of Vancouver, W.A. Webb of Regina, and James Ewing and R.S. Lea of Montreal; landscape architect Howard Dunnington-Grubb of Toronto; and E. Deville, the Surveyor-General of Canada.

Thomas Adams

The person who did the most to establish the substance and credibility of the professional side of planning in the first quarter of the 20th century was, of course, Thomas Adams. Born in 1871 in Edinburgh, Adams began by studying law but is referred to variously as a journalist, as a surveyor, and, in the initial roster of the TPIC, as a landscape architect. This may well be a measure of his various talents and interests. In any case, he was acquainted with Patrick Geddes and the latter's work in Edinburgh, and also with Ebenezer Howard and the Garden City movement. For six years, Adams was secretary of the company that undertook to build the first Garden City at Letchworth. He was instrumental in promoting passage of the benchmark 1909 Housing and Town Planning Act in Britain, and was subsequently selected to organize the Local Government Board, which was to oversee municipal compliance with the new act. He was a founder and the first president of the British Town Planning Institute in 1914; half a dozen years later he became the first president of the Town Planning

Institute of Canada. As one of his biographers, planner Alan Armstrong, notes, "On his arrival here he was already well-known as an eloquent author and speaker on the Garden City movement, on agricultural land use and on housing and town planning aspects of local government."[26]

Thomas Adams was enticed to Canada by Clifford Sifton to assume the high-profile post of Town Planning Advisor to the Conservation Commission of Canada. This post allowed Adams access to the highest government circles in Ottawa and in the provinces, since senior provincial ministers sat on the commission. It allowed him flexibility for travel, of which he never seemed to tire, in order to address groups in government and in business and the public-at-large in communities from coast to coast to persuade them of the virtues of planning. It offered him a platform as a writer both in the commission's excellent journal, *Conservation of Life,* and in numerous other magazines. Thomas Adams stayed with the commission until it was summarily abolished by the government of Arthur Meighen in 1921. He continued as a consultant in Canada until 1923 and then was appointed to a new trend-setting planning venture as Director of the Regional Plan of New York and Environs.

Developing a Canadian Planning Outlook

However striking his personal achievements, Thomas Adams' importance to the development of community planning in Canada rests in the basic philosophy that he brought to his Canadian endeavours, and in how he defined, and helped others to define, an approach to planning Canadian communities. In philosophy, Thomas Adams espoused a view similar to those of the 19th-century utilitarian reformers. The latter, like John Stuart Mill and Jeremy Bentham, championed the notion that *the aim of society should be to produce the greatest good for the greatest number.* In planning terms, this might translate into a community not having to bear the burden of traffic congestion caused by faulty street layouts in private development projects. Or it might also justify a community providing adequate sanitary facilities for all inhabitants, so that the costs of disease need not be borne by others through epidemics.

The utilitarian ethic embodied a number of principles that affected planning outlooks profoundly. There is first the notion of *social progress,* carried out with public consensus about achieving it. A second principle is an emphasis on the *application of reason* to determine solutions to social problems that will lead to progress. A third is the acceptance of *government intervention* to achieve the public good if the weight of objective evidence suggests that course of action. The utilitarian outlook provided a rationalization of planners' views about the need to clear slum areas and to ensure proper suburban extensions to cities. It also provided the logical underpinning for the planning objectives of promoting *order and efficiency* in the development of communities. A Canadian planner-historian characterizes the early 20th-century planner's view as follows:

> By creating well-planned urban environments, happy and healthy homes would be made available to working families, constructive social intercourse would be facilitated, the economic and social efficiency of the nation would be enhanced, and the general happiness would be increased.[27]

One finds this view widely espoused by Adams and his planning colleagues in Canada in the 1920s, possibly most succinctly on the masthead of the *Journal of Town Planning Institute of Canada:*

> Town planning may be defined as the scientific and orderly disposition of land and buildings in use and development with a view to obviating congestion and securing economic and social efficiency, health and well-being in urban and rural communities.

There are three fundamental aspects to the outlook of the early Canadian planners that, although not much discussed today, are no less a part of the intellectual makeup of contemporary Canadian planners:

1. The main concerns were with the functioning of the city rather than with its beauty, and the approach was rational (i.e., "scientific").
2. The emphasis was on social well-being, that is, on the community as a whole as exemplified in Adams' dictum that "town planning includes every aspect of civic life and civic growth."[28]
3. There was the belief that technical solutions to planning problems could be found, and that planners were equipped to supply them.

The first two of these foundation stones distinguished Canadian planners from their U.S. and British counterparts. The broad social view of responsibility for community health and housing is derived from the British; the functional view of arranging streets, utilities, and the use of zoning is distinctively American. The Canadian planners shunned City Beautiful approaches, and possibly as a consequence did not develop concepts of overall community design, even though this would have coincided with their city-wide social concerns. They did, however, succeed in building a legislative base for the planning of communities—by the mid-1920s all provinces had fairly comprehensive planning legislation. The latter in itself represents a tremendous accomplishment in public persuasion by a relatively small group of people. It also represents a choice on the part of Canadian planning professionals to concentrate their approach on administrative and legislative processes, borrowing broad planning statutes from the British and local zoning laws from the United States.

Lastly, the acceptance of a planning profession in Canada meant that community planning was moving out of the phase of being a "cause" propounded by a "movement." It was beginning to be legitimized and institutionalized. This new phase necessitated allocating the responsibility for finding solutions to planning problems and protecting the social values of planning. It also put in planners' hands the opportunity to develop, evolve, and mould the social values of planning. Thereafter, the development of planning ideas became bound up with the outlook of the planning professionals. These people became important actors in the planning process, for they, in many ways, had invented it.

THE ELABORATION OF PLANNERS' IDEAS AND IDEALS, 1930–1955

Throughout most of the 1920s, a great deal of the efforts devoted to planning went into coping with a resurgence in land subdivision in suburban areas. Often this consisted of the filling in of areas that were subdivided prior to World War I and whose development had been cut short by the slump of 1913. Planners found themselves busy preparing plans for subdivision and preaching the need for land-use regulations, especially for zoning. The cities of Vancouver and Ottawa, most notably, were persuaded to prepare city-wide zoning ordinances in the mid-1920s. **Zoning** is an approach to specifying the kinds of uses and things that would be appropriate in the various zones, or districts, of the city. The origin and legislative bases of zoning will be discussed in the next chapter.

The advocacy of zoning posed something of a dilemma for Canadian planners. It first of all constrained them in their efforts to have communities prepare comprehensive plans for their future, and then it seems to have absorbed attention that might have gone to new ideas in planning. In the United States in the 1920s, for example, proposals were being made to raze blighted areas and provide new, publicly assisted housing for the poor. These efforts came to be known as **slum clearance** and **public housing.** They received only modest attention in Canada at the time among planners and concerned citizens. Two other important planning ideas of the 1920s that stirred little interest in Canada were **integrated resource planning for regions,** especially for water resources, and **regional planning for urban and rural areas.** This is not to say that these ideas were not appreciated in Canada, but the full extent of that appreciation was not to come until two decades or more later.

With the onset of the Great Depression of the 1930s, community planning lost a great deal of momentum in Canada. Many promising efforts in planning were halted, such as the closing of Alberta's Provincial Planning Office in 1930, to which Horace Seymour had been appointed only two years earlier. By contrast, in the United States the concepts of public housing and regional planning became cornerstones in the Roosevelt New Deal programs for coping with the Depression. Planning ideas and the planning profession were, thus, nurtured in the United States in those troubled times. The fact that there was only one city in Canada— Toronto—that by the end of World War II had a formal planning department and that fewer than two dozen towns had zoning by-laws and plans (most of them well outdated by then) indicates the state of community planning in Canada.

Renewed Interest in Housing and City Rebuilding

Several important items on the planning agenda for the post-World War II period were set forth in 1944 by a special committee established to advise the federal government. A subcommittee of the Advisory Committee on Reconstruction (the Curtis Committee) dealing with housing and planning matters noted extensive "congestion, deterioration, misuse and blight" in Canadian communities.[29] It recommended broad-scale housing programs to accommodate the backlog of housing demands caused by the Depression and the war, new housing to meet projected population growth, and the renewal of over 100,000 dwellings in the older parts of cities. It also urged on governments of all levels the need for comprehensive community planning, including the establishment of a federal Town Planning Bureau, a program of public education, and professional training programs for planners at universities. Out of the idea for a Town Planning Bureau came the **Central** (now **Canada**) **Mortgage and Housing Corporation** (CMHC), which subsequently fostered community and university planning education programs, as well as housing and planning research, and undertook the provision of housing for the poor and programs of urban renewal.

Such ideas did not originate entirely from the federal committee; many had been germinating for a decade or more. The need to deal with slum housing conditions was actively pursued throughout the 1930s by a cadre of socially minded architects, social workers, planners, and citizens. "The Housing Centre" was established at the University of Toronto by Humphrey Carver, later to assume charge of education and research activities at CMHC, and professors Harry Cassidy and Eric Arthur.[30] In 1939, in Toronto, this group encouraged people from across Canada to hold a national housing conference on the problems of slum housing: among the participants were George Mooney of the Canadian Federation of Mayors and Municipalities, planner Horace Seymour, Vancouver city councillor Grace MacInnis, Nova Scotian S.H. Prince, and Leonard Marsh, who would later be the principal draftsman of the 1944 federal committee's report on housing and planning. This conference clearly demonstrated the wide support for what Carver called "social housing" or, simply, the concept that government should be responsible for the provision of adequate housing for all Canadians regardless of income.

The results of these efforts emerged after the war in the form of several major public housing projects. The first of these was Regent Park North in Toronto in 1948, an 18 ha project built on land obtained by levelling slum housing. This was followed by two other major projects: the Jeanne Mance project in Montreal and Mulgrave Park in Halifax. It is important to notice that the approach to redeveloping older areas was clearance and rebuilding. This bulldozer approach would, by 1960, come under severe criticism and be replaced by measures for "rehabilitation and conservation" in the urban renewal process. Nevertheless, these early efforts were thoughtful and well-intentioned demonstrations of the importance accorded city rebuilding by all levels of government. They were based on thorough studies, usually done by planners, and integrated with city-wide planning efforts.

Developing a Role for Citizens

The Curtis Committee strongly recommended involving citizens in the planning of their own communities. The approach suggested would today be considered paternalistic: i.e., "to struggle against public inertia," "people will accept and support what they can understand." It was, however, a new initiative in Canadian community planning. There had, of course, been various citizen movements to lobby for civic needs in public health, housing, local government organization, and beautification; even groups of property owners (ratepayers) protested planning measures prior to this time. But they did not play a continuing role within the planning process. What was envisioned were citizen groups that could be "educated" and energized to support the proposals of the planners. For example, the Toronto Citizens' Housing and Planning Association, led by Harold Clark, which had been organized in 1944, was very instrumental in securing the Regent Park slum clearance project.

The recommendations of the Curtis Committee were embodied in the 1944 version of the National Housing Act and called upon CMHC to promote public interest in planning. The outcome of this was the formation of the **Community Planning Association of Canada** (CPAC) in 1946. It was a national organization, with provincial and local branches, that was largely underwritten by CMHC. For 30 years, the CPAC provided a forum in which citizens, planners, and politicians could discuss the needs of Canadian communities. Although, as Carver notes, "CPAC did not evolve into an instrument of local activism,"[31] as did later citizen efforts, it did provide a springboard for many good ideas and for individuals to become knowledgeable about planning and to participate vigorously inside and outside CPAC. No little credit for this is due to Alan Armstrong, the association's director for the first decade and the editor of their influential journal, *Community Planning Review.*

In many ways, it was the very success of the CPAC in raising public awareness of community planning that led to the local activism of the 1960s, which came to overshadow the national group's more conciliatory approach. CPAC's sponsor, CMHC, moreover was paradoxically to bear the brunt of many citizen group attacks for its bulldozer approach to urban renewal. Such communities as Ingleside in Calgary, Trefann Court in Toronto, and Quinpool Road in Halifax were well aware by then what good planning meant when they confronted City Hall. They also knew that it meant involving the community, just as Alan Armstrong's first editorial in the *Community Planning Review* had stated:

> Planning as here conceived means discovering first of all how the community wants to live and move, and only thereafter delineating the physical outlines fit and acceptable for those purposes.[32]

While the structure of the CPAC was not able to sustain the 1960s concerns over preserving neighbourhoods, the legitimacy given to citizen involvement by the CPAC was firmly rooted.

THE VALUES OF PLANNING

Community planning has gained acceptance because it provides reasonable solutions to the problems of cities and towns, and because those solutions promote the general aims of the community and society—that is, community planning comes to embody values that, while specific to its efforts, are consonant with the community's values. The values of planning also change over time with changing community concerns, as this chapter has shown. Usually the range of values broadens as the complex world of our modern communities reveals more concerns and more effects of our planning solutions. And within the array of values, the emphasis, or importance, shifts as the community places different priorities on its various concerns. For example, slum conditions are not so great a concern today as environmental conditions. It is not that housing **equity** for the poor has been discarded as a value but that it has been replaced by **conservation** as a priority in many communities.

Such shifts in value rankings may take place in some segments of the community but not in others. Poor neighbourhoods may see heritage preservation as a restraint on the jobs that go with new construction, while the more affluent may advocate the historic values. Some communities in a metropolitan area may wish to limit their own growth and, thus, fight highway extensions that other communities need for their growth. Value conflicts usually occur when there are transitions in community thinking about growth and change and insufficient political leadership to find a consensus on the values that should prevail. In these situations, there may not be an agreed-upon social agenda to inform planning decisions. This may be a strong signal either that a plan is needed or that an existing one needs revision.

The planning process requires that value positions be examined and debated. The result is usually a hierarchy of long-term value orientations for the community. In general, the set of value orientations that is adopted (as goals and objectives) to shape the social agenda will be drawn from an already well-established field. Listed below are those values that are part of the ethos of planning and that reflect long-standing concerns, some centuries old, in community building. They are listed in alphabetical order so as not to convey any sense of priority.[33] That is up to the community to determine when making its plans. The final part of book deals with this important topic by presenting the approaches of various participants in the community-planning process.

Beauty/Orderliness.   This is probably the planning value with the deepest roots. The search for the "ideal" physical environment goes back to ancient times, but whenever the search is renewed, even in present-day suburbs, it involves a desire to order the environment so that it meets community needs and reflects community ideals. Planners must cope with two elements in rendering this value: (1) public beauty must satisfy public taste; and (2) the choices about the environment are very long-lasting. As the current interest in heritage planning shows, a community may lose its delight in its previous environment only to have those tastes change again. But even long-lasting environments may change in the meantime.

Comprehensiveness.   Planning is concerned with long-run consequences, both of the decisions made in building communities and of the side effects of decisions. Thus, the planner will attempt to comprehend, as much as the knowledge and skills of the time will allow, the outcomes or results of a proposed plan, in terms of (1) how well the development will perform in the future, along with any problems it might generate; and (2) how others outside the immediate locale or group of participants might be affected. Applying the value of comprehensiveness does not imply the making of a comprehensive plan for a community, a nearly impossible task.

Conservation of Resources.   This value owes its recognition to Patrick Geddes, who was not only concerned about indiscriminate uses of such natural resources as water, land, and forests but also of housing and open spaces within cities. The Commission of Conservation nurtured this concern among Canadians. A modern version of this same value is in the concern shown over environmental degradation in, for example, the strip mining of coal in southeastern British Columbia, the pollution of the Great Lakes, and acid rain. The new term **bioregionalism,** which the Crombie Commission used in its proposals for the Toronto waterfront, conveys much the same value.[34] A planning issue that arises very often is the juxtaposition of long-term environmental consequences against short-term economic gains of resource projects.

Democratic Participation.   The principle of working at planning decisions through the organs of democratic local government, and occasionally through plebiscites of the citizenry, is long-lived. Much more recent is the acceptance that all people in the community have the right to participate in public decisions. No other local government activity generates more issues of concern to citizens than does planning, and of necessity, citizen participation in planning comes in many forms. Public meetings, opinion surveys, and advisory committees are some of the formal ways to obtain participation, but the spontaneous reaction of the public against planning and development proposals must also be accommodated. Another side of this value is the democratic responsibility to consult the public regardless of potential conflict. Usually the more widespread the participation the better the planning decision.

Efficiency.   The value of efficiency expresses itself in many ways in community planning. Efficiency leads planners to oppose premature subdivision of land because of the uneconomic demands for public utilities, and it also leads citizens to oppose projects that would depress surrounding land values. Efficiency is most often expressed in economic terms, but it is also of concern in functional arrangements in communities, such as in the best pattern of roads to distribute traffic and in the location of schools and parks.

Equity.   Social equity did not receive easy admission to the values of planning in our highly individualistic society, which often wishes to believe that there are no impediments to human achievement. Public planning encounters such built-in inequities as differences in housing quality, neighbourhood services, and access to jobs. The increasing cultural diversity of cities has introduced further areas of concern about equity. Public planners must not only try to eliminate old inequities but must also avoid the creation of new ones. This value is most frequently in competition with efficiency.

Health/Safety.   This combined value is one of the cornerstones of modern community planning. Concerns over clean water, clean air, and safe surroundings are often expressed now as environmental concerns rather than as fears over epidemics. But the support systems for large concentrations of population are still apprehended to be fragile with regard to disease, fire, crime, injury, and natural disasters. On the positive side are concerns over the provision of services and facilities that aid self-development and allow the less fortunate access to them as well. The recent "Healthy Communities" movement is further evidence of this value.[35]

Rational Decision Making.   A direct outgrowth of the professional planners' roots in utilitarian philosophy is the great faith placed in reason as a means to determine solutions to community-planning problems. Planning also grew up at the time of civic reform movements that stressed the use of rational administrative and management approaches to local government. As planning has evolved, its methods have become focused on providing information and conducting logical analyses in order to evaluate planning proposals. With increased citizen participation, the planner's reasoning has often been shown to reflect a particular rationale that could be at odds with others' analyses.

TOWARD A SOCIAL AGENDA

This chapter has sought to demonstrate that community planning does not grow independently of the context of problems of urban life or of the range of possible solutions that are perceived by people, experts, and institutions. The general agenda for community planning is an accumulation of concerns derived from continuing experience with city-building. But the agenda for any particular period of time will reflect the concerns important at the time, as well as the availability of acceptable means to deal with them. The same is true for any particular community: it will have its *own* agenda of planning concerns.

This does not mean that the social agenda for planning a community is formed on a random basis. The accumulated knowledge about planning and building communities, the values of planning, the availability of professional planners, and the concerns of accepted participants all constrain the planning agenda. Matters that are unique to a community may be added, but they will have to contend with the "standard" items for attention. Further, the degree of consideration that any item, old or new, is given will depend a good deal on the resolution of several recurring planning issues:

1. **How much should the community intervene?** Even if the community has the right to intervene, as is usually the case, this issue raises many ideological differences over such matters as private property rights and the role of the public sector.
2. **What makes long-term benefits better than short-term gains?** The dilemma is to establish a plan for the future that is also a help in making decisions today.
3. **Whose interests shall prevail, the neighbourhood's or the community's?** While we all know about the interdependence of parts of a community, often the connections are more intellectual than real—but not always. In many ways, this is the metropolitan area's planning problem "writ small."

Thus, the social agenda is always evolving, just as a community is an evolving entity. A community plan can give both form and perspective to the agenda. It helps to make issues and values visible.

ENDNOTES

1. As quoted in Charles M. Godfrey, *The Cholera Epidemics in Upper Canada 1832–1866* (Toronto: Secombe House, 1968), 20.
2. As quoted in William Ashworth, *The Genesis of Modern British Town Planning* (London: Routledge and Kegan Paul, 1954), 49.
3. Alan Artibise, *Winnipeg, A Social History of Urban Growth, 1874–1914* (Montreal: McGill-Queen's University Press, 1975), 232ff.
4. John H. Taylor, "Fire, Disease and Water in Ottawa," *Urban History Review* 8 (June 1979), 7–37.
5. J. Grove Smith, *Fire Waste in Canada* (Ottawa: Commission of Conservation, 1918), 277–289.
6. John Whittow, "Disaster Impact and the Built Environment," *Built Environment* 21, no. 2/3 (1996), 81–88.

7. Shirley Spragge, "A Confluence of Interests: Housing and Reform in Toronto, 1900–1920," in A. Artibise and G. Stelter, eds., *The Usable Urban Past* (Toronto: Carleton Library, 1979), 247–267.

8. Herbert B. Ames, *The City Below the Hill* (Montreal: Bishop Engraving, 1897), 27–47.

9. Artibise, *Winnipeg*, 150ff.

10. Peter G. Goheen, *Victorian Toronto 1850 to 1900* (Chicago: University of Chicago, Department of Geography, 1970), Research Paper 127, 84.

11. As quoted in Leonardo Benevolo, *The Origins of Modern Town Planning* (London: Routledge and Kegan Paul, 1967), 59.

12. Marshall Stalley, ed., *Patrick Geddes: Spokesman for Man and the Environment* (New Brunswick, N.J.: Rutgers University Press, 1972), xiii.

13. As quoted in Stalley, *Patrick Geddes*, 112.

14. Kent Gerecke, "Patrick Geddes, a Message for Today!" *City Magazine* 10:3 (Winter 1988), 27–35.

15. Canada, Commission of Conservation, *Report of the Third Annual Meeting* (1912), 141.

16. Cf. Thomas Roden, "The Housing of Workingmen," *Industrial Canada* 5, no.7 (1907).

17. G. Frank Beer, "A Plea for City Planning Organization," in *Report of the Fifth Annual Meeting*, Commission of Conservation (1914), 108–116.

18. As quoted in Alan H. Armstrong, "Thomas Adams and the Commission of Conservation," in L.O. Gertler, ed., *Planning the Canadian Environment* (Montreal: Harvest House, 1968), 17–35.

19. C.A. Hodgetts, "Housing and Town Planning," in *Report of the Third Annual Meeting*, Commission of Conservation (1912), 136.

20. Clifford Sifton, "National Conference on City Planning," in *Report of the Sixth Annual Meeting*, Commission of Conservation (1915), 243.

21. Paul Rutherford, "Tomorrow's Metropolis: The Urban Reform Movement in Canada, 1880–1920," in G. Stelter and A. Artibise, eds., *The Canadian City* (Toronto: Macmillan, 1979), 368–392.

22. As quoted in John C. Weaver, "Tomorrow's Metropolis Revisited: A Critical Assessment of Urban Reform in Canada, 1890–1920," in Stelter and Artibise, *Canadian City*, 393–418.

23. Walter Van Nus, "The Fate of City Beautiful Thought in Canada, 1893–1930," in Stelter and Artibise, *Canadian City*, 162–185.

24. Godfrey L. Spragge, "Canadian Planners' Goals: Deep Roots and Fuzzy Thinking," *Canadian Public Administration* (Summer 1975), 216–234.

25. Walter Van Nus, "Toward the City Efficient: The Theory and Practice of Zoning, 1919–1939," in Artibise and Stelter, *Usable Urban Past*, 226–246.

26. Armstrong, "Thomas Adams," 28.

27. P.J. Smith, "The Principle of Utility and the Origins of Planning Legislation in Alberta, 1912–1975," in Artibise and Stelter, *Usable Urban Past,* 196–225.

28. Thomas Adams, "What Town Planning Really Means," *The Canadian Municipal Journal* 10 (July 1914).

29. Canada, Advisory Committee on Reconstruction, IV. *Housing and Community Planning* (Ottawa: King's Printer, 1944), Report of the Subcommittee, 161.

30. The flavour of this period in Canadian housing and planning is superbly described by one of the pioneers, Humphrey Carver, in his *Compassionate Landscape* (Toronto: University of Toronto Press, 1975), especially 49–57.

31. *Ibid.,* 90.

32. "Editorial," *Community Planning Review* 1, no. 1 (1951).

33. This listing of planning values has drawn heavily on "The Values of the City Planner," in Frank S. So et al., eds., *The Practice of Local Government Planning* (Washington: International City Management Association, 1979), 7–21.

34. Canada, Royal Commission on the Future of the Toronto Waterfront, *Watershed* (Ottawa, 1990).

35. David Witty, "Healthy Communities: ACIP Initiative," *Plan Canada,* Special Edition (July 1994), 113–116.

Chapter 5　The Evolving Institutional Perspective

No one man, no board, no council, no developer, plans or builds, alone, a whole community.

James B. Milner, 1962

———————————

The challenge contained in Professor Milner's remark, which opens this chapter, is to grasp not only that there are diverse interests involved in planning and building communities but also that these interests must be appropriately orchestrated to achieve community ends. In general, the way groups of people "orchestrate" their various aims, decisions, and behaviour is through their institutions. That is, they agree, usually after repeated good and bad experience, to provide the means that can sanction, mediate, or adjudicate among contending interests. In the realm of community planning, for example, it became obvious in the 19th century that disease, regardless of its origin, could affect all members of a community. Thus, steps were gradually taken to give governments the authority to provide public utilities, to write laws and enforce them, and to vest responsibility in a Medical Officer of Health (MOH) to oversee future public health needs. The institution of the MOH still plays a prominent role in land-planning decisions in all provinces.

Today, the many decisions that constitute the development process for a community are screened, evaluated, and reconciled by an elaborate set of local and provincial government planning institutions. The evolution of these institutions—the municipal plans, the public meetings, the various by-laws, the appeal bodies, and so forth—has also helped in shaping community planning in Canada. Among developed, urbanized societies the social agenda for planning may not differ much, but the way in which issues are taken up and resolved does differ. The planning institutions we employ are responsible for that. But how and why did we come to use the planning institutions that we seem so accustomed to today? This chapter explores

the development of the main institutions for community planning in
Canada through to the early-1950s, those institutions that form the foundation for today's planning.

SOCIAL TENDENCIES AFFECTING LAND DEVELOPMENT

The institutions of community planning stem from a variety of sources in
society. There are the perennial problems of siting private buildings and
deciding how they are to be used after they are built. The social conscience
of the nation may be energized to deal with debilitating social and physical
conditions. Immigration and urbanization will call for guidance. And
vested property interests may see the need for protection from encroachment. As each in its turn vies to constrain and direct the approach to building communities, it encounters the institutions and conventional practices
already in place. Institutions are notoriously hard to dislodge, for the institutional environment for community planning at any particular time is an
accumulation of society's past responses.

Perennial Problems of Land Use

About 60% of the land in any town or city is developed for private purposes, for residences and commercial activities such as stores. Traditionally,
lands designated for private purposes are built upon by private interests to
their own designs. The perennial problem in the building and rebuilding of
communities is how to achieve consistency among all these private decisions to use and build upon land so that, in aggregate, the results promote
community values. There are two basic aspects to this problem. The first is
to prevent the activities on one property from causing damage to neighbouring properties. The second is to prevent buildings and their activities
from encroaching on streets and thereby restricting the right-of-way of
others.

Historians seem fond of citing the difficulties of past generations in finding a solution to these problems, perhaps because they know that these difficulties continue to plague us. Morris cites Julius Caesar's legislation
requiring the use of tiles as roof material and a stipulated space between
buildings to prevent the spread of fires.[1] This legislation was amended soon
after to allow common walls ("party-walls") between buildings. And
Haverfield notes the difficulty of maintaining a regular street alignment,
which was decreed by autocratic rulers of ancient cities.[2]

Several peculiarly Canadian examples are provided by Moogk in describing the buildings of dwellings in 17th-century Quebec. Frontenac is quoted as saying, in 1672, "that a very grave error has been committed in allowing private individuals to build houses according to their own fancy and without order."[3] He subsequently forbade, in Quebec, construction that was not authorized or in conformity with street alignments. Further laws for the maintenance of thoroughfares in towns were passed in 1685, 1686, 1689, 1727, and 1735, but according to Moogk there is little evidence of prosecution for violations. The width of Montreal streets was set in 1688 at 30 *pieds;* however, the actual widths ranged between 18 and 24 *pieds,* depending on where private buildings were placed. In the planning of Louisbourg, the French administrators had hoped to reserve the quayside for fishermen, but merchants and tavernkeepers already located there succeeded in resisting this plan. And prospective home builders in New France were warned by a popular writer of the time to select a site "removed from the dwellings of craftsmen whose trades entail great noise."

These homely examples convey the ever-present dichotomy of rights and responsibilities of citizens and the community as a whole. Gradually, over several hundred years, institutions and principles evolved to meet these concerns, and they are still being adapted to meet the new needs of society. English common law is the institution that provides foundations for resolving many basic land-use issues between property owners and the community. (In Quebec, French civil law provided the foundation; although different principles applied initially, the later demands of a complex urban society have led to a similar approach in land-use problems.) The common-law traditions that are most pertinent are those dealing with property rights and the "law of nuisance." The first defines the limits a property owner must observe in relation to the interests of the community. The second defines the limits on the use a property owner may make of his or her land in relation to adjoining property owners.

Property Rights

There is a long-standing misconception that common law gives unfettered use of land to those holding it. Indeed, as Lane points out, the history of common law refutes the suggestion "that there *ever* existed *any absolute right* on the part of the citizen to the land which he holds."[4] Private persons are not, therefore, land *owners* but "very privileged tenants" of "the Sovereign." Under the 1982 Canadian Constitution, Parliament, which represents the nation as a whole, is the "Sovereign." Consequently, the nation as the only true landowner can, as Lane says, "demand reasonable land use on the part of its citizen-tenants." Herein lies the basis for

Canadian communities to constrain, through regulation, the uses made of all land in the community.

Sometimes, this argument is made from the point of view of a bundle of rights that go with landownership. The community may retain certain rights in the bundle, such as to establish roads, or just retain the option to exercise certain rights, such as to expropriate land to provide a school if one is required. The citizen property holder receives, in return, a guarantee of access to public roads and a legally defined piece of property free from the encroachment of others. With regard to the latter, we have enshrined various conventions of land tenure in our laws and provided such institutional arrangements as systems for recording land transactions and land titles. These are constantly evolving institutions; among the most recent adaptations are those that allow for condominium land tenure. When planning issues involve questions of private property rights, as they so often do, these institutions are invoked.

The Law of Nuisance

This principle of common law derives from the need to settle disputes between individual landowners wherein the use of a neighbouring parcel of land is considered annoying or harmful. The law of nuisance has been said to be the earliest attempt at land-use control.[5] The multiplication of cases over several centuries provided the precedents to deal with what is now called "incompatible" land uses, first on an individual basis, then on a community basis.

The law of nuisance in regard to land-use issues is grounded in the notion that one's equity in a property should not be impaired by the uses carried on by neighbours. Typical cases are noxious odours from a factory in the vicinity, or undue noise from a dog kennel, or the traffic generated by a funeral home in a residential area. Although the law of nuisance began with disputes between individuals, the accumulation of these cases and the advent of new and larger land uses led to its extension to cover public nuisances. For example, industrialization brought factories that spewed smoke and ash over entire residential districts. Urbanization meant that people lived on small pieces of property, and in the early days of many cities, they still desired to keep for food purposes such animals as cows, pigs, and chickens. The operation of a hand laundry that required heated water in large quantities could be a fire hazard in a residential area; many such laundries were the source of major city fires. In more recent times, the law of nuisance has been the basis for dealing with many problems of pollution of the natural environment. This is a special variant on the principle of a land use being harmful to others, first, because the harm or injury may not be immediate, and second, because the harm may also be to the medium (water, air) in which the pollutant is carried.

Implicit in the examples used above is the ability to predict the outcome of juxtaposing certain land uses or of allowing a certain quality of construction. Today we would call such predicting **land-use impact.** The ability to predict, or generalize, about the deleterious effects of the use of land and buildings provides the foundation for the regulation of land uses. Both accumulated experience and the knowledge of professionals may contribute to the prediction that, for example, certain classes of uses should be separated from one another, either in different buildings or in different locations. This is the basis of the various public regulations, which began to emerge toward the end of the 19th century, concerning public health matters and building standards (particularly in regard to fire safety).

The concept of **zoning** used in community planning is also based on the premise of being able to predict the most compatible arrays of land uses in various zones, or districts, in a city. This is simply the geographical extension of the law of nuisance from a few adjacent properties to cover neighbourhoods and districts. Zoning was variously justified in its early days as securing proper sanitary conditions or protecting land values, both of which aims had connections to the law of nuisance. This institutional basis is important to remember, for in the Canadian context no further constitutional justification is required for zoning, as is the case in the United States. We shall return to this matter later.

Responses to Early Urban Problems

Canada's first major urban boom occurred in the two decades before World War I. It exacerbated the problems of disease, slums, fire safety, and transportation that were already in evidence. It also accelerated the search for solutions and thereby promoted institutional changes of long duration. For during this period of crises in city-building, a crucial ideological issue had to be resolved. The boom reflected the ethos of economic progress for many while bringing debilitating circumstances for others. In whose interest should reforms be made? The view that came to prevail, to quote historian John Weaver, was that "civic resources should assist the endeavours of those who do most for the material growth of the community, namely business and real estate interests."[6]

Although the early 20th-century cities in Canada did not suffer the alarming epidemics of half a century earlier, there were serious health problems. Water and sewer services, still rudimentary at best, were strained by population growth, and the food and milk supplies for city dwellers were often of uncertain purity. Many health problems were attributable to the unsanitary housing conditions under which most new urban immigrants had to live. It was common, however, to attribute the cause to the customs of "foreigners" rather than to the slum conditions. But since disease affected the wealthy as well as the poor, action was eventually taken. Public health laws were passed to try and ensure pure water supplies, to eliminate slum dwellings, and to provide for the purity of milk and other foods.

Bureaucratic structures were established to enforce building codes and conduct inspections of food and water. The office of the Medical Officer of Health was established in this period and wielded considerable power owing not only to the public health legislation but also to the status accorded medical practitioners. Building inspectors were appointed and building departments were established in many communities. Frequently, the new "experts" were paternalistic and authoritarian in their approach. The thrust of the new prohibitive measures was not social reform but enhancement of those with an interest in continued growth and expansion. The 1909 Manitoba Tenement Act may well have been framed with the fear of contagious disease in mind, but as Weaver notes, it was enforced as if its prime concern were the protection of property values.[7]

Another response to urban problems at the beginning of this century was the direct involvement of elite groups in the planning of cities. This took two forms. "Civic Improvement Associations" sprang up in many places in the decade from 1900 to 1910. (Later they were promoted by the Commission of Conservation in communities where they did not exist.) They often took on themselves the task of preparing a city plan, as with the Toronto Guild of Civic Art, or of urging the city government to prepare one, as in the case of Kitchener.[8] The other form of involvement was by such varied interest groups as boards of trade, chambers of commerce, the Canadian Club, and social and professional associations of architects and engineers. These groups sponsored lectures by prominent persons in planning and municipal government—Thomas Adams was a favourite speaker—and actively lobbied for civic improvements, especially visual enhancement of their city.

There are two facets of this private-sector interest in planning. First, it clearly served the interests of property owners. Their advocacy of visual order, efficient transportation, and, later, municipal reform was in the interest of protecting property values and promoting new opportunities for land development. Second, and more significant, is the strong role that property and business interests assumed for themselves in community planning and local government affairs. This "proprietary interest," so to speak, seemed to translate, over ensuing decades, almost into a right to membership on planning boards, municipal councils, and other local boards and commissions. Indeed, the formation of semi-independent local government agencies came largely at their behest. The assumption that such boards and commissions could become more effective by using the skills of persons from the business community has had an enduring impact on local government and its planning activities.

THE ESTABLISHMENT OF A LOCAL GOVERNMENT SYSTEM

Community planning as we know it today is conducted mostly within the structure and outlook of local (municipal) government. The development of the local government arrangements we now see about us is, thus, central to the development of community planning. Local government structures provide the primary institutional context for planning by a community. Further, the process of establishing local government for communities, an arduous process at times, resulted in a particular view of the powers and prerogatives available to local governments. An understanding of the derivation of these views goes a long way toward appreciating the outlook of community planning.

There is, of course, no uniform or comprehensive "system" of local government throughout Canada, as tends to be the case in Great Britain or France. Each province, under our federal system, establishes its own arrangements. Although there are some differences in local governments, the process of development has had many similarities from province to province. For one thing, each province evolved, through a lengthy period of settlement, from a situation of sparse communities to one of sophisticated urban centres. For another, there was a progression of settlement such that provinces learned from those that had an earlier need for local government. As Plunkett and Betts conclude, "by the beginning of the 20th century, all ten provinces in Canada had established essentially similar systems of local government."[9] The beginnings of community planning thus coincided with the achievement of local government institutions on a broad basis in Canada. There are precursors to this, however, in the 19th century and earlier, which are also important and will be discussed first.

Precursors of Local Government

For the first 225 years of European settlement in what is now Canada, until the 1830s, few communities had anything resembling local government.

This institution literally had to be invented. But why was it sought? The answer is that any clustering of people to form a community will generate needs that are common to the setting, and some way must be found to satisfy these needs. In the early period of settlement, the needs are usually quite rudimentary. Roads and streets, a quay or dock may be needed, as well as a school and the means to fight fires. Some of these needs require construction, some require organization, and some continue to evolve into the indefinite future. All require resources—money, time, labour.

Deciding upon the needs of a community is relatively easy. Deciding upon how to mobilize the necessary resources is more difficult because it involves reconciling viewpoints on how *best* to provide for community needs. Much of the history of local government institutions in Canada is concerned with determining the best way to structure the decision-making process: who should be involved? how much power should they have?

The earliest settlements were under French or British colonial rule, and the power to govern did not lie in community hands. However, there are many instances in which the early settlers felt that neither the governments in Europe nor the colonial administrators adequately perceived the needs of their communities. Efforts to promote local self-rule began in Quebec communities in the mid-1600s. Citizens elected a few representatives to discuss with the French governor the needs of the communities. These efforts were short-lived because the central government disapproved, and it was not until the early 1800s that further steps were taken to allow municipal institutions in Quebec. The settlers of the Maritime provinces and Upper Canada (Ontario) were mainly from the newly independent United States. They brought experience of local government with them, and soon sought a voice in their community's affairs; but there was little response from the British colonial governments, with one notable exception. Saint John's 5,000 settlers from New England obtained a municipal charter in 1785, the first in Canada. It was 47 years before the second was issued.

Some communities in the British colonies had local government in the form of the courts of quarter session. This ancient institution consisted essentially of "magistrates" appointed by the colony's governor who attended court in each district four times a year for both judicial and legislative purposes. They were responsible for maintaining order and settling minor lawsuits, but they could also establish regulations for moving animals, license various businesses, and appoint minor officials to maintain roads.[10] Counties were delineated at this time, and a large centre within each served as the seat of the courts of quarter session. These occasional and centrally controlled mechanisms were not acclaimed by all settlers.

Many, especially in Ontario, wanted locally elected councils empowered to deal with community needs. In 1812, the citizens of Kingston agitated for a charter that would allow a municipal council to pass its own by-laws and regulations.[11]

Various changes were made to meet these challenges. Local magistrates were appointed to administer "police towns," but this proved no more satisfactory than quarter sessions. The Public School Act in Ontario in 1816 —the first such act—proved a breakthrough, however, as it allowed a community to erect a school, hire a teacher, and elect school trustees to raise taxes and administer the school. Not only did this confer the right of local election; it also established the still-prevailing separation of education from other local functions in a community. In the 1830s and 1840s, local efforts to form municipalities began to succeed. Brockville was the first in Ontario in 1832, followed by York (Toronto), Kingston, and Hamilton; in Quebec, Montreal and Quebec City obtained charters in 1832; and in the Maritimes, Halifax was incorporated in 1841, Fredericton in 1848.

The Emergence of Local Government

During the 1840s, considerable effort was made to develop a sound system of local government in both Upper and Lower Canada. Ontario's Municipal Act of 1849, often referred to as the Baldwin Act after its originator, proved to be workable and enduring. Its format was for two classes of local government: (1) cities, towns, and villages for urban communities, and townships for rural communities; and (2) counties that comprised the local municipalities. Sources of tax revenue were specified, as were the form of elections and the composition of local councils and their duties. With the exception of new local government arrangements designed for large urban complexes, local government forms are not substantially different today than those specified in the early acts.

Two important contextual elements in the development of local government in Canada concern the provincial government's role. The first derives from the fact that, except for the three Prairie provinces, all the others began as colonies governed from abroad. The tendency of British colonial administration was for strong central control. If municipal institutions were allowed, the central government would ultimately be responsible, a model still found in Britain. Thus, as the Canadian provinces were emerging, there was only grudging acceptance of local self-rule. Self-rule was, and continues to be, hemmed in by various provincial audits, mandatory approvals, and supervision of local affairs. Witness, for example, the Ontario government's imposed amalgamation of the six metropolitan Toronto municipalities in 1997.

The second element derives from this strong provincial role. It concerns the constitutional setting for local government that was established in the British North America (BNA) Act of 1867. That original constitution did not establish the right of communities to a local government, but only specified that the responsibility for establishing municipal institutions lay with the provincial governments. Section 92 of the BNA Act defines this prerogative. (The 1982 Constitution carries forward the same section.) It is common to find municipalities referred to as "creatures" of the provincial government. While this superior role of the province is true in other federal states such as the United States and Australia, in Canada what is significant is the alacrity with which provincial governments perform their role. The development both of local government and, subsequently, of community-planning institutions bears this stamp of paternalism from the province.

The local government systems that were created by the provinces in the last half of the 19th century were limited in their roles and in their sources of revenue. Local governments were conceived in the need to provide to residences and places of business such services as roads, water, and fire protection. This is often described as "providing services to property." In turn, local governments were restricted to taxes applied to property for their revenue. It is not too difficult to appreciate how this constraint has forced municipalities to emphasize property ownership in their by-laws and regulations, as well as how it colours their outlook on the community. As a consequence, property owners and those who would develop even more property came to feel that their demands on the local government were deserving of attention. They, after all, were the primary source of municipal revenues. Lastly, municipalities were limited in their ability to provide social services. Education, health, and welfare services were prerogatives retained by the province, to be delegated—if at all—to such special agencies at the local level as school boards.

The Reform Epidemic

The beginning decades of local government were not auspicious. Inexperience with locally run institutions, combined with a bias toward property ownership and owners, was responsible for many cases of inefficiency, uneconomic practices, and even corruption. By the turn of the century, with the dramatic upsurge in urban development, many local governments appeared unable to cope with the new demands. They were faced with responsibilities for traffic control, parks, housing, and community planning, the extent of which had not been contemplated by those who framed the various municipal acts. Intermunicipal problems arose in transportation, water supply, and protective services because residences spread into suburbs. And financial resources were often strained to the limit when large bond issues were needed to finance public works projects.

A municipal reform movement arose primarily from within the business and professional communities as these conditions affected their interests. They contended that a local government's main task was to provide services efficiently and economically. City growth translated for them into technical problems in engineering and fiscal management. Goldwin Smith, prominent among those involved in the reform movement in Toronto at the turn of the century, stated: "A city is simply a densely populated district in need of a specially skilled administration."[12] Good government for a municipality was thus cast in terms of a business management model. This became a powerful viewpoint, and one that persists today in local government circles.

The reformers were also generally suspicious of popularly elected local governments (even though, until recent decades, only property owners could vote in most civic elections). They argued for boards and commissions with specific functions to perform and with appointed membership. Ostensibly, the intention was, as Vancouver's Mayor Bethune said at the time, to attract "the services of bright able men who have not the time to serve on Council."[13] Thus, across the country there was a spate of such agencies formed, with elected representatives often excluded from serving. Montreal acquired a Park Commission, Vancouver a Water Works Commission, and Fort William-Port Arthur (Thunder Bay) a Public Utilities Commission. These joined school boards, library boards, and police commissions in a plethora of quasi-autonomous bodies, most of which had independent budgets and their own technical professional staff.

The Residue of Reform

Civic administration was transformed in the 1890–1920 period in both substance and structure. Local government was limited to a role of "providing services to property," while matters involving economic development and what we now call the "quality of life" were assigned to parallel local agencies. Furthermore, the parallel—usually non-elected—boards and commissions developed their own constituencies and also proved durable institutions.

Municipal government was weakened by the reform epidemic. Not only was its competence questioned but it also failed to provide for broad public discussion on community issues. Municipal administration was favoured over municipal political debate; councillors often became preoccupied with administrative details, and administrators with policy making. This rather introverted view of municipal government effectively excluded participation by the public, while according to special interests in business and the property industry, as well as administrators, the "right" to run the local government. The quality of municipal administration improved over the next 30 years (1920–1950). However, when the public came to demand a voice in the big new development decisions after World War II, local governments were generally unprepared.

In addition to the fragmentation of local responsibilities and the introverted approach of municipal councils, most provinces introduced various "overseer" methods for controlling municipal activities. These took two forms. On the one hand, departments or ministries of municipal affairs were established to provide for consistency in the day-to-day operation of the municipalities the provinces had created. Guidelines and legislation covered financial affairs, administrative practices, and legal foundations, many of which required regular reports to the provincial ministry. On the other hand, many provinces established quasi-judicial tribunals for the purpose of reviewing such municipal activities as by-laws to borrow capital. Examples are the Municipal Board in Manitoba, the Quebec Municipal Commission, the Local Authorities Board in Alberta, and the Ontario Municipal Board. These boards deal with individual municipalities on an issue-by-issue basis, frequently as a form of appeal body against decisions made by municipalities. In recent decades, such boards have handled appeals in community-planning matters.

The various supervisory methods used by the provinces with respect to their municipalities made for a master-servant relationship between the two. Although established when local governments were struggling with new problems, this supervision has, if anything, increased. As a result, local autonomy is limited in considerable measure, not the least in its planning efforts.

THE ESTABLISHMENT OF COMMUNITY-PLANNING INSTITUTIONS

The development of ideas about the aims of planning and about its practice coincided with turn-of-the-century efforts to restructure local government. Indeed, there is a great deal of interdependence between the two processes. On the one hand, the emergence of planning concepts and professional skills provided a solution to the haphazard development over which there was much complaint. On the other hand, the civic reform movement generated for governing communities new structures that were necessary if a new function of local government—community was to be carried out. Thus, the emerging institutions of community planning were coloured by the then-current outlook on local government, as well as by the constitutional setting in which local government exists. We shall deal with each of these in turn.

The Social and Political Context

In many ways, community planning became a handmaiden to the interests promoting civic reform. Planning was seen to embody many of the same values reformers sought for local government—technical rationality, efficiency, and order. This was especially so for the business and professional elites who dominated the civic reform movement. It became commonplace for these interests to champion planning either through existing organizations, such as boards of trade, or through new groups. Kitchener (then Berlin), Ontario, had its Civic Association, Calgary and Edmonton had the Alberta Housing and Town Planning Association, and Montreal had its City Improvement League. Some groups actually sponsored the preparation of a plan for the community and then urged its implementation on the municipal government. Another approach was to urge the city government to establish an independent planning committee for the purpose of preparing a plan. Notable instances of the latter approach were the Civic Improvement Committee, appointed in 1909 by Toronto's city council, the Calgary City Planning Commission and the Winnipeg Town Planning Commission, both established in 1911, and the Regina Town Planning Committee of 1913. These committees lasted only a few years.

The initial efforts to link action in community planning to the local government thus follow the model favoured by the civic reformers, that is, the establishment of a body outside the direct control of elected officials. This approach was propounded for U.S. communities in the same era of local planning. In contrast, British communities adopted the approach of appointing a planning committee from the membership of municipal councils. The rationale for the semi-independent planning committee in Canada was the same as for other structural changes of local government proposed at the time: (1) it would keep "politics" out of planning, and (2) community planning was essentially a technical task that could be better achieved by a small group devoted to it. Usually unstated was the reason that a special-purpose planning body would probably direct its efforts more narrowly to the primary interest of community planning—the development of private property. This would, of course, be in the interests of the business and property groups who promoted planning so vigorously at the time.

Regardless of the precise reasons, the concept of semi-independent planning bodies for community planning prevailed in Canada. Various names were used for them. In the West they tended to be called by the U.S. name, "planning commissions," while in the East they were more likely called "planning boards" or "advisory planning committees." Where necessary, the provinces passed legislation permitting such bodies to be established. The primary function of the new agencies for community planning was to prepare a plan, or "town planning scheme" as they were then called, for the community. In larger cities, the agency might have its own staff, but more likely it employed consultants. The plan would then be passed on to the municipal government to be implemented through regulations and public works expenditures.

This institutional format for community planning had two advantages: the ability to prepare the community's plan free from the continuing political debate, and the more direct involvement of members of the community in the planning. As with every institution, there were usually costs to bear for the advantages achieved, and the semi-independent status for planning was not excepted. In the first place, unlike other special-purpose bodies favoured at this time—harbour commissions, park boards, transit authorities, etc.—the planning agency did not operate any facilities; it could only advise the municipality. The municipality alone had the powers necessary to intervene in the development of private property or to create streets or to build the needed public facilities. A second dilemma was that the recommendations of an advisory planning agency would have even less direct bearing on the actions of new operating agencies than it would on municipal operations. A third issue concerns the element of participation by the public. Although the semi-independent planning agency represented a form of populism, or direct democracy, it fell outside the community-wide forum of municipal council. The views expressed there may have reflected only limited interests in the community, such as those of downtown merchants or the residents of a well-to-do neighbourhood, that had to be reconciled with the interests of the larger community.

In other words, the institution of the special-purpose planning agency created tensions within the local government structure. This was not necessarily a bad thing and often contributed to innovative thinking, as we shall see in later chapters. It did, however, represent a paradox not recognized by the civic reformers: that the attempt to keep community planning at arm's length from the political arena in many ways heightened the connection between the two. As Milner was to comment sagely 50 years later:

> Planning boards do not exist to take planning out of politics. In a democracy, planning is a political activity. ... A planning board gives advice—I hope

honest advice. It should not be too concerned whether the council takes the advice or not. This is council's business.[14]

The Constitutional Setting and the First Planning Acts

Many of the powers necessary for a municipality to prepare a plan did not exist in this early period of planning. For a plan to have statutory power over all properties in a community, the sanction of the province as the sovereign body was required. If public works expenditures were envisioned to secure the plan's objectives, or if land-use regulations were considered desirable to achieve the plan, the legal authority would need to be obtained from the province. This is because there is a convention in Canada that a municipality may not do anything that its province has not empowered it to do.

The need for planning enabling legislation at the provincial level was recognized early in this century. In a period of less than 12 months, starting in the spring of 1912, four provinces passed substantial pieces of planning legislation that would enable a municipality to prepare and/or carry out a plan. New Brunswick was first in April 1912, followed by Nova Scotia, Ontario, and Alberta. Within about a decade, four other provinces enacted similar legislation. No explanation has been put forward for this profusion of provincial action in regard to community planning. It is especially interesting since, except for Ontario, most provinces had few cities, and these were not large in any case.

There were a number of factors that probably influenced the provinces to enact planning legislation. For one, there was considerable subdivision of land in suburban areas and often chaotic development of it. For another, the Commission of Conservation strongly promoted such legislation, especially through the efforts of, first, Charles Hodgetts and then Thomas Adams; the premiers of both New Brunswick and Alberta sat on the commission. (Indeed, Premier Arthur Sifton of Alberta was the older brother of the commission's chairman.)[15] Other likely influences were the planning efforts in Great Britain and the United States, which received extensive publicity, in particular the national Housing and Town Planning Act in Britain in 1909. And probably as important as any factor was the desire of Canadian governments to appear progressive.

The British Housing and Town Planning Act of 1909 provided the model for the first Canadian provincial planning legislation. The early Canadian acts shared three things in common with the British act. First, the planning was confined to land in suburban or fringe areas that had the prospect for development. Built-up portions of cities were initially excluded. Second, if public plans adversely affected private property, the owners could claim compensation. (Both of these provisions are evidence of the great reluctance at the time to intervene in private property development.) Third, all planning would be subject to close scrutiny by central government authorities. This provision is still a fundamental part of Canadian planning institutions: most planning actions by communities cannot take effect until after approval by the province or its agencies. More than anything else, this distinguished planning practice in Canada from that in the United States.

The early Canadian planning acts were not simply duplicates of the British act. Some variations were made to suit the Canadian approach, and several of these have endured to the present time. It will be helpful to elaborate five basic components of these 1912–1913 planning acts.

1. The Scope of Planning

Three acts (Nova Scotia, New Brunswick, and Alberta) permitted municipalities to prepare "town planning schemes," and specified the aspects of the community that the plan should cover. To quote from the New Brunswick act:

> A town planning scheme may be prepared ... with the general object of securing suitable provision for traffic, proper sanitary conditions, amenity and convenience in connection with the laying out of streets and the use of the land and of any neighbouring lands for building or other purposes.[16]

Plans were thus envisioned to encompass quite broad features of the physical environment. However, they were to apply only to "land which is in the course of development, or is likely to be used for building purposes," that is, to suburban extensions to communities. Provision was allowed for the province to authorize the inclusion of adjacent built-up land that might be affected by the plan. This limit to the area covered by plans was considered unsatisfactory by many, and within a decade plans were being made for entire communities.

Municipalities were allowed considerable scope in carrying out plans. They could purchase properties needed to implement the plan, say for a park or a street extension, using powers of expropriation. They could also make expenditures for such public works as water and sewer systems to put a plan into effect, but were required to specify in the plan how they planned to obtain these funds; we now call this a "capital improvements budget." There was also provision for a municipality to remove any building that contravened a plan and to complete any work of a private developer that would delay the plan's coming into effect. All three planning acts envisioned the province drawing up regulations for formulating and carrying out a plan. In particular, these regulations were expected to allow communities to control the density of development and the mixture of land uses—that is, what came to be called **zoning.** No such regulations were forthcoming until later years.

The planning legislation enacted in Ontario in 1912 allowed much less scope. The City and Suburbs Plans Act was simply to control the subdivision of suburban land by private interests. It applied only to those cities with a population of at least 50,000 and covered the area within 8 km of the city. All plans for subdivision of land in such locales had to be submitted to a provincial government agency for approval. Consideration of plans was limited to the number and width of streets, the location of streets, and the size and form of lots. Minimum street widths were specified at one **chain** (66 ft or 20 m).

2. Role of the Province

All four pieces of planning legislation included a strong role for the province in the planning process, although the form differed in each case. To quote the Alberta planning act: "A town-planning scheme prepared or adopted by a local authority shall not have effect unless approved by written order of the Minister."[17] This power of ministerial approval also included the power to amend a local plan to suit provincial government standards. In Nova Scotia and New Brunswick, the provincial authority in planning lay with the Cabinet (or the Lieutenant-Governor-in-Council, as provincial legislation usually refers to it). In Ontario, the approving body was the Ontario Railway and Municipal Board (now called the Ontario Municipal Board). In Alberta, it was the Minister of Municipal Affairs who approved of local plans, Alberta being one of the first provinces to establish a provincial department to support and supervise its local governments.

Such departments became common later in all provinces. Typically, its minister was charged with reviewing and approving plans of municipalities. Of course, it was not the minister's personal task, but rather that of the ministerial staff. Provincial planning legislation has changed very little since then in regard to central government scrutiny. Now, with the volume of local planning so large, provincial staffs have grown to sizable proportions.

3. Local Planning Structure

In both the New Brunswick and Alberta planning acts, provision was made for municipalities to appoint a planning commission to undertake the local planning effort. To quote the New Brunswick act again: "For the purpose of preparing a town planning scheme and carrying the same into effect, a local authority ... may appoint a commission of not less than five or more than ten members."[18] Neither province's legislation required that the format of the **semi-independent commission** be used; it was one option. However, when the Nova Scotia act was revised in 1915, it required that a town-planning board be established in every municipality. It also specified the membership: the mayor, two other members of council, and at least two ratepayers.[19]

The creation of a separate board for making and carrying out a local plan was intensively discussed at the international meeting of planners held in Toronto in 1914. It seems clear, especially from the comments of Charles Hodgetts, that the reform mood permeating North America in regard to local government was the main reason for this feature in an otherwise British-style act. Hodgetts said, "It is proposed to remove the important matters in connection with town planning out of the hands of our municipal councils. ... I may say, after twenty-seven odd years of public experience, I am not impressed with the achievements or capabilities of 'town councils.'"[20]

4. Effects on Private Property

In essence, provincial planning legislation involves delegating some provincial powers concerning property rights to a municipality. Given the strong belief in the sanctity of private property and individual enterprise, these were powers the provinces gave up reluctantly, and only then with safeguards in place. The provisions for approval or rejection of local plans that the province held were one way of restraining municipalities from extending community rights over private interests. The acts also allowed a property owner to claim compensation "whose property is injuriously affected by the making of a town planning scheme," to quote the phrase in the Nova Scotia, New Brunswick, and Alberta acts.

There was also a counterpart to the compensation provision included in these early acts. It allowed a municipality to claim up to one-half of any increase in the value of a property beneficially affected by a plan. Planners had argued from the time of Ebenezer Howard and the first Garden Cities that proper planning could enhance the value of property. Thomas Adams was particularly forceful on this point, both before and after he came to Canada. He and others contended that this **betterment of property,** as it came to be called, was due to public efforts, and any rise in the value of a property because of a public plan should thus be shared with the community. It is not clear whether any of the three provinces ever published the necessary regulations on the workings of compensation and betterment. In any case, these concepts have proved difficult to define and do not appear in present-day planning acts.

The compensation/betterment notion cuts to the heart of the issue concerning the extent of public vs. private property rights. While a private property owner may be able fairly easily to determine "injury" to his or her property, it is notoriously difficult to determine the extent to which a property's value may have been increased by a plan. A major difference is that the injury to a property is usually apparent when the plan is being implemented, whereas an increase in a property's value that is due to a plan may not materialize for many years. These early planning acts thus recognized some prior rights for municipalities by deeming that compensation could not be claimed if the provisions of the plan were for the purpose of "securing the amenity of the area." These included provisions which might "prescribe the space about buildings or limit the number of buildings to be erected, or prescribe the height or character of buildings."[21] This clause is the precursor for allowing zoning controls over height and lot coverage, although at the time (ca. 1912) the provisions could be applied only to specific areas for which plans were submitted.

5. Land for Parks

The Alberta Town Planning Act of 1913 took one further important step. It allowed the municipality to acquire up to 5% of a new subdivision area for park purposes at no cost to itself.[22] This is called **compulsory dedication** and is the same kind of requirement made of land developers who must provide road access to the building lots they create and then deed the road allowance to the municipality.

It is clear that residences deserve road access as a matter of rights, but how, in a new subdivision, is the simple amenity of a park to be provided except from the land that would normally be subdivided for houses? Further, there is the question of who should pay for the new park land. Alberta legislators took the approach that those benefiting from the park most directly—the developers who could offer a higher-quality subdivision and the homebuyers whose property values would more likely be sustained—should bear the cost. They may also have been influenced by the converse of this principle: that the community as a whole should not have to bear the cost of acquiring land later, the value of which could be much higher. Thus, the Alberta planning act was especially perceptive and its requirements were modest—the equivalent of only one building lot in every 20. It took over three decades, however, before this ground-breaking step was followed in other provincial planning acts.

The Development of Planning Tools

The first planning acts established the formal milieu for community planning, but they did not assure the preparation of plans or their implementation.

In large part, this was because support for the idea of planning advanced faster than the refinement of the tools to carry it out. There were very few professional planners available in the first few decades of this century. There was also relatively little experience anywhere, at the time, with carrying out planning under government sanction. Canada cannot be said to have lagged in supporting planning: 1909 is the date both of the first British planning act and of the first North American planning conference in Boston; by 1912, three provincial planning acts had been passed in Canada, and in 1914, the sixth planning conference was held in Toronto. The first comprehensive zoning by-law was that of New York City in 1916. Thus, the tools that Canada's planners would need to use were still being "invented" as the formal machinery of planning was being assembled.

It is important to grasp that the planning of cities and towns by the communities themselves under the aegis of the local government was virtually untried until the last decade of the 19th century. The prototypes that existed for those who wished to create healthful, efficient, and amenable communities, whether Garden Cities, model industrial villages, socialist utopias, or Garden Suburbs, differed in three significant ways from ordinary communities. First, and most vital, was that the area to be planned was under the control of a single owner or agency. Second, the object was to build a new community from the ground up rather than rebuild an existing one. And third, most of the planners' precedents did not conceive of coping with continued large-scale growth of cities and towns. Therefore, planning tools had not yet been devised for communities with multiple property-owners whose interests must be reconciled through self-governing institutions.

From this distance in time, it is possible to specify the planning matters for which the planners struggled to devise acceptable tools:

1. **Planning policy for the entire community.** Some way is needed to define the quality and direction of development for the entire community for some future period. This includes the prospects for existing built-up areas as well as for vacant areas. It also includes both public and private development efforts.
2. **A framework for guiding private development.** Since the bulk of the land in the community is privately owned and will be developed by private interests, some ways must be found to achieve development that is consistent with the aims of overall policy. The approach for development on vacant land will likely differ from that for already built-up areas.
3. **A framework for public capital investment.** Since the community must provide support services for private development as well as public

facilities, some means are needed to allocate public funds that will achieve the aims of the overall policy.

Today, we would think of the above tasks, respectively, as preparing the community plan, formulating the land-use and subdivision regulations, and preparing the capital improvements program. But the meagre experience available to planners in the first decades of this century made these formidable tasks. Let us examine the first two of these briefly for the dilemmas they posed and their eventual development.

The Community Plan

The earliest planning acts empowered a municipality to prepare a **town-planning scheme**. However, such a scheme was not meant to be a plan for a town. It was more like what has come to be called a **subdivision plan**, showing the layout of streets, building lots, open spaces, and public utilities for a new residential suburb. These are typically submitted by a private developer or public agency desiring to open up a parcel of vacant land. But how would a community's plan be structured to cover a multiplicity of such subdivision plans where, moreover, much of the land would not be developed until far into the future? And how would it integrate the new development with already built-up areas, with needed transportation links between all parts of the community, and with the infrastructure of services and facilities? Clearly, a community plan could not be as specific as a town-planning scheme.

The 1912 Ontario City and Suburbs Plans Act refers to communities having a "general plan" into which a town-planning scheme might fit. This concept is repeated in the much-expanded Planning and Development Act, which Ontario passed in 1917. It gives the following definition:

> Such a plan shall show all existing highways and widening, extension or relocation of the same which may be deemed advisable, and also all proposed highways, parkways, boulevards, parks, play grounds and other public grounds or public improvements, and shall be certified by an Ontario land surveyor.[23]

Although this definition still emphasizes the rationalization of road patterns, the act represents a major departure: it distinguished the general plan from the detailed subdivision plan.

The fact is that there was very little experience anywhere 70 or 80 years ago in preparing a broad-based community plan. The most notable early Canadian plan of this general type did not appear until 1915. It is included in the report of the Federal Plan Commission, which was charged with preparing a plan for Ottawa and Hull.[24] Indeed, it is called a general plan and presents proposals in map form for various land-use districts, for future population expansion, and for streets, parks, and waterways. Accompanying these plans are analyses of population density, land use, industrial employment, and public transit. This plan is very modern in its approach and not too dissimilar to those that would be common five decades later. A second notable example is the 1923 plan prepared for the adjacent cities of Kitchener and Waterloo, Ontario, by Thomas Adams and Horace Seymour. It is also supported by extensive analyses of traffic, land use, and population, and includes a "skeleton plan" for the region.

An examination of both the Ottawa and Kitchener plans, however, reveals a dilemma that affected the development of planning tools. Whereas nowadays the acknowledged approach is first to prepare an overall community plan and then to devise the regulations, by-laws, and other instruments to attain the goals of the plan, the reverse seems to be proposed in both these historic documents; that is, the community plan's role was seen as providing support for land-use regulations. The newly revised Nova Scotia Town Planning Act of 1915 and Ontario legislation in 1917 also formalized this bias. The difficulties that municipalities had experienced earlier in securing compliance of property owners with health and building codes probably account for this emphasis on regulations for planning.

The dilemma caused by linking the power to plan so closely to the power to regulate, as in many early planning efforts, has several sides. One to which we have already alluded is that the distinctive roles of plans and regulations—the former to provide long-term objectives and the latter to provide continuing compliance with objectives—are confused. Moreover, there is the matter of the relative importance of each to the aims of community planning. Our present-day logic holds that we should first prepare the overall plan within which we can regulate individual properties so as to achieve the plan's objectives. Another side of the dilemma is that, while the general plan instrument should be clearly differentiated and should precede (or underlie) the regulations, the two must operate hand in hand.

Two provincial planning acts of the 1920s, the 1925 British Columbia act and the 1929 Alberta act, made significant departures in regard to the situation described above. First, they clearly distinguished the roles of the community plan and the zoning by-law. Second, they permitted them to be used independently. The 1929 Plan and Zoning By-law for Vancouver, prepared by the Harland Bartholomew firm of St. Louis, with Horace Seymour as their resident planner, is exemplary. Indeed, Seymour credits his experience in B.C. with helping in the revisions he drafted for the Alberta act when he served as the chief planner for that province.

Unfortunately, the tendency for local governments to want to handle their development problems directly rather than just provide guidelines for others led to the widespread adoption of zoning by-laws without corresponding community plans. In the 1930s in Alberta, 26 municipalities used the new planning act and passed zoning by-laws, and a further 31 followed suit in the 1940s; most had never adopted a community plan.[25] In Ontario in 1971, it was found that 544 municipalities had enacted a zoning by-law, while only 356 had adopted community plans.

In summary, by 1930 planning legislation accorded the general plan for the community, often called the **official plan,** a role different from that of planning regulations. It was considered to be a superior role, but in practice the opposite often seemed the case. Nevertheless, the desirability of a municipality having a plan was formally acknowledged. Later planning acts attempted various ways of promoting the preparation of community plans, for example, requiring conformity of all by-laws and public works with the overall plan. Lastly, the various planning acts usually defined the content of municipal plans in very broad terms. However, the practice of linking the plan to the control over the subdivision of land, the construction of public facilities, the layout of streets, and the designation of land-use districts leaves little doubt that its primary purpose was for the physical and spatial development of a community.

Land-Use Regulation

In the early part of the century, it became clear that civic improvements by public authorities could not ensure that private land, which made up the largest part of cities and towns, would be developed to high standards. It was further realized that private land development fell into two general categories: that occurring on tracts of vacant land and that occurring on individual parcels of land within built-up areas. These two needs spawned their own land-use controls—subdivision control and zoning. In general, there is a sequence to these two controls: zoning applies to land after it is subdivided. We shall discuss them here in that order.

1. Subdivision Control.   The need for subdivision control became insistent in the decade preceding World War I with the dramatic suburbanization of Canadian communities. The relatively simple tasks of earlier times of transfering ownership and registering deeds for individual parcels of land were complicated by the land boom; as well, the long-term consequences for the community as a whole were becoming obvious. The subdivision of tracts of land carries with it the aim of transferring ownership and thus requires that all new owners be accorded the institutional protection of their land titles. This is the side of subdivision control that pertains to private property rights, but there are planning implications as well.

When tracts of urban land are subdivided, it is usually for the purpose of creating numerous new parcels of land. Thus, land subdivision generates many new landowners whose compliance with various development standards will need to be sought. Further, the process of dividing up the land may not be connected with immediate building upon, or even sale of, the land. Frequently, subdivision precedes actual urban development by a considerable period of time. From its perspective, the community must know the obligations it might face to service the new parcels of land as well as the consistency of the new layout with adjacent tracts. Also important is the time at which development is expected to occur. The main concerns are for street layouts, open space provisions, drainage, and the size and shape of building lots.

Although many thousands of hectares had been subdivided around Canadian cities and towns before subdivision controls were instituted, the requirement that plans for new subdivisions be submitted has had long-term benefits. It established the right of the community (and the province) to review plans for development on private land. In later land booms, especially during the late 1920s and the post-World War II period, the administration of subdivisions became the central planning activity for many municipalities. The subdivision process is now usually accorded a separate section in provincial planning acts, and elaborate systems of checking subdivision plans have been set up in provincial ministries.

2. Zoning.   The planning instrument that deals with the land uses and the physical form of development on individual parcels of privately owned land is called zoning. It deals, essentially, with (a) the *use* that may be made of a parcel of land, (b) the *coverage* of the parcel by structures, and (c) the *height* of buildings. Long before zoning, there were regulations dealing with these factors in order to assure public health, structural safety, and fire prevention. What distinguishes zoning regulations is the application of use/coverage/height standards by districts or areas within a city. The outlook of early planners in Canada in regard to zoning is captured in the following extract from the recommendations for the 1915 plan for Ottawa and Hull:

> … that the authorities take steps to segregate industry into certain areas, to control the districts devoted to business and light industry, to control and protect the residential districts and to control the height of buildings.[26]

The first efforts at city-wide districting are credited to German cities in the 1890s.[27] They were based on the experience that similar land uses tended to congregate in common districts and also that dissimilar uses had a disturbing effect on one another when mixed together. The separation of nuisance uses was the prime aim of early zoning. As can be seen in the plan for Ottawa and Hull, several different land-use districts were envisioned. Prior to this, attempts had been made simply to separate residential from non-residential uses within cities, the earliest Canadian by-law being enacted in 1903 in London, Ontario. The City of Toronto's 1904 by-law to control "the location, erection, and use of buildings for laundries, butcher shops, stores and manufactories" in effect excluded them from residential districts. Through Ontario legislation enacted in 1912, the exclusion of "apartment and tenement houses" from residential districts was also allowed in large cities.

In Toronto, as in other cities, the various health, safety, and occupancy regulations were usually enacted on a district-by-district basis. While this procedure commended itself for being flexible and responsive to the needs of individual districts, it was also complicated to administer and, not infrequently, subject to inequities between areas. Some areas were not regulated at all or only partially, and these often turned out to be the areas where poor people lived as tenants. Planners began to urge comprehensive zoning by-laws that would provide not only greater uniformity of application of regulations but also a city-wide view on private development consistent with the view of the community plan. As it turned out, this was no easy task.

The districting of a city according to specified land uses is a double-edged sword as far as those with development interests in a city are concerned. Since zoning usually respects the kinds of uses and buildings already in a district, existing owners, or those with the desire to develop land in a like manner, will have their investments justified. Those with aspirations to build differently from existing uses, whether with real intentions or simply because they want to have free rein on the use of their property, will be restrained. Planners, seeking a position that would reconcile these two outlooks, choose the argument that zoning will stabilize and protect land values. It will provide much more certainty for landowners about what they can expect to be built in their areas and for municipal governments about what expenditures they will have to make for services, as well as the tax revenues they might receive.

This was a strong argument, but it was usually grudgingly received, first, because there was little immediate experience in most places, and second, because it depended on the current prospects of the land market. If property prospects were not good or if they had been erratic, acceptance of zoning was usually facilitated. In buoyant situations, such as the mid-1920s, it could take several years for all the interests to agree on the final version of a zoning ordinance.[28]

Related to the reluctant response to early zoning is the criticism levelled in later years over the exclusionary approach that many zoning by-laws took. There were instances of zoning being used to exclude some classes of people from certain areas by excluding the commercial uses with which those classes were associated. Immigrant groups were often blatantly discriminated against in this way because, for example, they usually chose to live in the same building as their place of business.[29] The other more common form of exclusion was to separate types of dwelling units into different zones. Thus, two- and three-family dwellings would be excluded from single-family zones, and apartment buildings (or tenements) would be allowed only in yet another zone because renters were considered less stable than homeowners. And further discrimination might also have been made between low- and high-income homeowners by requiring houses to be built on larger, and thus more costly, lots in areas where the well-to-do wished, as Milner noted, "to prevent intruders from spoiling an already established area."[30] In fairness, while zoning does involve separating incompatible land uses, its over-zealous application is not inherent in this planning tool. Indeed, approaches to zoning change as times change and as planning experience accumulates. For instance, the mixing of different residential types with retail and commercial uses is now considered desirable.

There are two fundamental problems with zoning with which we shall end this discussion. The first is the dilemma between protecting existing land uses and promoting the planning future land uses. Zoning by-laws often seek, in Levin's terms, "to create those elements in the physical environment which the community finds desirable where they do not exist,"[31] e.g., achieving larger setbacks of houses in newly subdivided areas. In other words, zoning seeks also to protect future land uses and values. This gives zoning a dynamic role, but one that it cannot easily play because it is a legislative tool that must be uniformly applied. It must not be seen to be too easily changed.

The second difficulty of zoning has to do with its administration. Although the intent is that all the properties in a zone be treated equally under the by-law, physical conditions affecting the land in a zone may make this impossible. The topography of an area may render some parcels of land difficult to build upon and still maintain the legal size of yard, for example. Or an old street pattern may have left an awkward shape of building lot. In such situations, the by-law is generally regarded as causing an "undue hardship" on a property, and mechanisms have been devised to allow a property owner to seek a variance from the provisions of the by-law.

Most planning acts have recognized this contingency from very early days. These requests are heard today by a locally appointed appeal body called a Zoning Board of Appeal or Committee of Adjustment, depending on the part of the country one is in. Such appeals are meant only for minor changes to the by-law and not, say, to changes in land use. The latter would require an amendment to the by-law, and that usually can be done by the planning board and council only after scrutiny of the implications for the community plan.

REJUVENATION OF PLANNING INSTITUTIONS

Immediately following World War II, Canada's cities and towns were involved in a third major land and building boom. This one far exceeded those that had occurred prior to World War I and in the latter half of the 1920s, especially given the foregoing 15 years of depression and war when little building took place. In metropolitan areas, between 1945 and 1950, the housing stock increased between 10% and 20%. In this period for example, 11,000 new dwellings were built in Winnipeg, 3,000 in Halifax, 21,000 in Vancouver, and 31,000 in Montreal.[32] For the first time, scores of municipalities began to consider the need for community planning, and many more began to reconsider their previous planning policies and regulations. It was in this period, as noted in the previous chapter, that the Curtis Report re-established the need for community planning, which resulted in the emergence of two new national institutions in the planning realm: the Central (now Canada) Mortgage and Housing Corporation (CMHC) and the Community Planning Association of Canada.

Several provinces refurbished their planning acts in the post-1945 period, the most notable being the Ontario Planning Act of 1946. The latter legislation did not so much invent new planning approaches as consolidate the concepts and experience gained previously, such as from Alberta, and establish a clear and workable framework for municipal land-use planning. The act's framework is still largely intact today and has been much copied by the other provinces. Its main features provide for (1) the creation of planning units, usually one or more municipalities; (2) preparing, adopting, and approving "official plans," as well as specifying the legal effect of these statutory plans; (3) a system of subdivision control; (4) the delegation of powers to municipalities to enact zoning by-laws; (5) a quasijudicial appeal procedure with respect to municipal planning decisions; (6) a plan-making body composed of citizens—the planning board—to advise municipal council; and (7) involvement and education of the public through public meetings at various points in the planning process.

The spate of planning activity that occurred in the two decades after World War II is amply illustrated by Ontario's experience. In 1946, only 36 municipalities had established themselves as planning areas, only 1 municipality had an official plan, and only 1 had a comprehensive zoning by-law. Within a decade, 200 more communities were in planning areas, 57 had official plans, and 48 had zoning by-laws. By 1965, over half of the municipalities were in planning areas and 75% of the province's population were covered by official plans in effect in municipalities. And in each of the decades, 1946–1955 and 1956–1965, almost 10,000 subdivision plans were processed as nearly three million people were added to the Ontario population.[33]

New Planning Tools

There were two planning tools added to the repertoire of those involved in community planning during the 1950s. The first of these, **urban renewal,** emerged in recognition of the fact that a large portion of the buildings in Canadian communities were half a century old or older. CMHC reported in 1956 that almost 900,000 housing units were of this vintage and, furthermore, that one-tenth of all housing was in need of major repairs.[34] "Blighted" conditions, as they were called, could also be found among old factory and warehouse buildings, many of which were being abandoned for sites in suburban industrial parks. The central parts of many cities, which were also the oldest sections, suffered most from physical deterioration. It was in an effort to restore the commercial attractiveness of downtown areas and not lose the investment they represented that urban renewal approaches were instituted. Hoping to eliminate substandard housing, the federal government established a program for financing slum clearance projects. Just as the name suggests, dilapidated housing would be bulldozed. Residents of the area would be re-housed in public housing projects (a companion program to urban renewal), sometimes on the same site. Occasionally, however, the newly razed area was considered more valuable as a place for new commercial development, and the displaced residents were forced to move to public housing in another district or to crowd in with friends or neighbours if they did not want to leave their neighbourhood.

Urban renewal became very unpopular. Although new programs of rehabilitation and conservation of deteriorating buildings were initiated, urban renewal was phased out in the mid-1960s. It did, however, embody

Planning Issue 5.1

THE FORKS MACHINE ROLLS ON!

Over the past two years there has been a struggle going on in Winnipeg between a public developer and the citizens of Winnipeg. The issue is how should the Forks lands—some one hundred acres of the CN East Yards at the historic downtown junction of the Red and Assiniboine Rivers now brought into the public sphere through rail-line relocation—be used. The key fact is that these lands are the most important unprotected historic lands in North America with existing archaeological finds dating back over 6,000 years.

The public outcry against the surprise development projects (marina, German cultural centre, new CBC building, hotel and arena—more than enough developer projects to completely build over this historic site) has been such that the Planning Committee of City Council have held public hearings on the Forks and have come up with a seventeen recommendation report on *New Directions for the Forks*. These recommendations call for a freeze on all development, creation of a truly participative process for the new direction, confirmation of

Aboriginal Heritage as the No. 1 priority for the site, a downplaying of private sector development, creation of a new vision to include *sanctuary, celebration, rediscovery of both our ancient and recent history, mother earth, native ancestors and a stage for performing*, and a restructuring of the Forks Corporation. This report will be considered by Council in September.

Blithely ignoring all this public concern over development at the Forks, the Corporation and the Provincial Recreation officials held an Information Session on July 24th to announce a 6 million dollar Visitor Centre for the Forks. With only three days notice to the public, and to their own committee members as well, the architectural consultants Marshall, Macklin and Monaghan of Toronto, put forward a high-tech centre with video walls, laser walk, time capsule and featuring a space flight simulator. The audience of about 25 were aghast. It was clearly the wrong idea, on the wrong site, and with the wrong process. A long time resident of the area expressed with great emotion that this does not relate to any meaning of these lands, a management consultant called the proposal a travesty—there is no reconciliation between the meeting place idea for the Forks and non-people space capsule proposal. The Director of the Manitoba Museum of Man and Nature (situated some five blocks away) said it will only compete with the museum to the detriment of both, and everyone was shocked by the process.

In response to the unanimous rejection of their idea, Bill Barbaza, provincial director of tourism said, "we have deliberately not stacked this meeting." Regarding the process, Nick Diakiw, CEO of the Forks Renewal Corporation, said they would put a proposal call out on their idea in 10 days, and when the proposals are in we can have another information session. The Forks Renewal Corporation, a Federal/Provincial/City creation, continues to move into new levels of deafness and arrogance.

Comments overheard at the meeting were, "if we need such a Tourist Centre, it should go right downtown not on the Forks," "in all my worst imaginings I could not have seen them make it this bad," and city councillor Al Golden asked, "the public are saying slow down, what do we have to do to stop this?"

There are two realities in this conflict. One, the public is pleased with the Forks' lands being opened up, the market, and Parks Canada's National Historic Park at the Forks, but they want development to stop, and take the time to make careful future plans with real public input. Two, the developer (FRC) wants to bully plans through believing that in the end the public will approve its hotel, condominiums, tourist centre, office buildings, wave pool, multi-plex sports complex including a new arena for the Jets, parking garages, and uni-cultural centre.

Kent Gerecke is a member of Greening the Forks, a citizen's committee dedicated to preserving the Forks as a historic and cultural park.

Source: Excerpted from Kent Gerecke, "The Forks Machine Rolls On!" *City Magazine* 11 (Summer 1990), 9–10. Published with permission of *New City Magazine* (formerly *City Magazine*).

some important concepts for community planning. In the first place, its focus on the need to rebuild cities complemented the planning concerns with new development on the fringes. In the second place, it established the need for the involvement of senior levels of government to facilitate such action, especially in its financing. Urban renewal programs instituted the idea of "shared cost" approaches in community planning where, for example, the cost of a site designated for urban renewal would be shared 50% by the federal government, 25% by the provincial government, and 25% by the municipality. Another feature was the requirement that the municipality have a community plan that takes into account the future use and role of redevelopment areas. One finds these principles in use today in various new programs for renewing communities.

The second significant addition to planning tools in the 1950s was the concept of **development control.** This is an extension of the power municipalities have to undertake zoning and involves, essentially, the administrative review of plans for new development in already built-up areas. Under normal zoning regulations, as long as developers adhere to the provisions for land use, height, and lot coverage, there is no stipulation that they reveal their plans for a vacant or redeveloped site. Thus, whether a building will "fit" into an area in terms of its scale, its appearance, and its traffic entrances and exits may often not be known until the building is completed. In rapidly growing downtown areas in the 1950s, this caused planners many problems. They therefore adopted the largely British method of requiring development plans to be submitted for scrutiny before construction could begin. In this way, not only might the community be saved trouble but the developer might also be alerted to more attractive alternatives. This kind of "hands on" approach in planning has become increasingly common as planners seek ways to obtain better-quality physical surroundings.

Growth of the Planning Profession

In 1951, there were fewer than 30 professional planners employed in public planning agencies in Canada, and it is likely that no more than twice that number comprised all the planners in the country, including private consultants.[35] There were over 300 professional planners by 1961, and twice that many again by 1967. And, by the latter date, almost all municipalities with a population over 25,000 had their own professional planning staffs, nine provinces had planners on staff, and there were nearly 100 private consulting firms of planners.

This demand for trained planners could be met in three ways. The first was to shift people who had been associated with planning and development as engineers, architects, and landscape architects into full-time planning jobs. The second way was to recruit from other countries, primarily Great Britain; CMHC obtained much of its early staffing in this way, many of whom subsequently went on to public and private agencies. The third way was to recruit from professional planning education programs in

Canada. The University of Manitoba established the first such program in 1951; the University of British Columbia followed in 1952 and the University of Toronto in 1956; and by 1972 there were 11 different programs. The Canadian university programs in community planning and closely associated fields were supplying almost all the staffing needs for professional planners by the beginning of the 1970s.

* * * * * *

Thus, as Canadian communities entered the contemporary period of their development (beginning roughly in 1955), there was in place a quite distinctively Canadian planning framework. The provincial planning acts, the various institutions through which planning is accomplished and adjudicated, the planning tools, and the professional staffs could truthfully be said by that time to be "made in Canada." There had, of course, been much borrowing of concepts (and personnel) from our two main influences, Great Britain and the United States, but they were gradually fashioned to suit Canadian conditions and institutions.

In the remaining parts of this book, when we describe the practice of contemporary planning and the participants in the planning process in Canada, the importance of the legacy of the formative decades will be evident. As community planning evolved, various principles learned from past experience came to be embodied in our practices. Long-standing ideals, ideas, and premises regarding the physical form of communities, the social needs of residents, and the institutional means of carrying out planning are now entwined with our contemporary views.

ENDNOTES

1. A.E.J. Morris, *History of Urban Form* (New York: Wiley, 1979), 72.
2. F. Haverfield, *Ancient Town Planning* (Oxford: Clarendon Press, 1913).
3. Peter N. Moogk, *Building a House in New France* (Toronto: McClelland and Stewart, 1977), 13–21.
4. William T. Lane, "The Common Law as a Planning Instrument," *Community Planning Review* 1 (May 1951), 68–69. Italics added.
5. J.B. Milner, ed., *Community Planning: A Casebook on Law and Administration* (Toronto: University of Toronto Press, 1963), 3.
6. John C. Weaver, *Shaping the Canadian City: Essays on Urban Politics and Policy, 1890–1920*, The Institute of Public Administration of Canada, Monograph No. 1 (1977), 40.
7. *Ibid.*, 32.

8. Elizabeth Bloomfield, "Town Planning Efforts in Kitchener-Waterloo, 1912–1925," *Urban History Review* 9 (June 1980), 3–48.

9. T.J. Plunkett and G.M. Betts, *The Management of Canadian Urban Government* (Kingston: Queen's University Institute of Local Government, 1978), 58.

10. *Ibid.,* 48.

11. *Ibid.,* 50.

12. As quoted in Weaver, *Shaping the Canadian City,* 72.

13. *Ibid.,* 70.

14. J.B. Milner, "The Statutory Role of the Planning Board," *Community Planning Review* 12, no. 3 (1962), 16–18.

15. P.J. Smith, "The Principle of Utility and the Origins of Planning Legislation in Alberta, 1912–1975," in A. Artibise and G. Stelter, eds., *The Usable Urban Past,* Carleton Library No. 119 (Toronto: Macmillan, 1979), 196–225.

16. New Brunswick, *An Act Relating to Town Planning,* Chap. 19, 2 Geo. V, 1912, Sect. 1(I).

17. Alberta, *An Act Relating to Town Planning,* Statutes of Alberta, Chap. 18, 1913, Sect. 1(6).

18. New Brunswick, *An Act Relating to Town Planning,* 2(2).

19. Nova Scotia, *Town Planning Act,* 1915, 2(3).

20. Canada, Commission of Conservation, *Report of the Sixth Annual Meeting* (1915), 271.

21. Cf. New Brunswick, *An Act Relating to Town Planning,* and Alberta, *An Act Relating to Town Planning,* 6(2).

22. Alberta, *An Act Relating to Town Planning.*

23. For a full discussion of this act, see J. David Hulchanski, "The Evolution of Ontario's Early Urban Land Use Regulations, 1900–1920," a paper presented to the Canadian-American Comparative Urban History Conference, Guelph, 1982.

24. Canada, Federal Plan Commission, *Report of the Federal Plan Commission on a General Plan for the Cities of Ottawa and Hull* (1915).

25. J. David Hulchanski, *The Origins of Urban Land Use Planning in Alberta, 1900–1945,* University of Toronto, Centre for Urban and Community Studies, Research Paper 119 (1981).

26. Federal Plan Commission, *Report,* 46.

27. Thomas H. Logan, "The Americanization of German Zoning," *Journal of the American Institute of Planners* 42 (October 1976), 377–385.

28. John C. Weaver, "The Property Industry and Land Use Controls: The Vancouver Experience, 1910–1945," *Plan Canada* 19 (September –December. 1979), 211–225.

29. *Ibid.*

30. J.B. Milner, *Development Control* (Toronto: Ontario Law Reform Commission, 1969), 12.
31. Earl Levin, "Zoning in Canada," *Community Planning Review* 7 (June 1957), 85–87.
32. Albert Rose, *Problems of Canadian City Growth* (Ottawa: Community Planning Association of Canada, 1950).
33. Ontario Economic Council, *Subject to Approval* (Toronto, 1973), 50.
34. Canada, Central Mortgage and Housing Corporation, *Housing and Urban Growth in Canada* (Ottawa, 1956), 9.
35. Gerald Hodge, *The Supply and Demand for Planners in Canada, 1961–1981* (Ottawa: CMHC, 1972), 17.

PART 2 · The Practice of Community Planning

DEVELOPMENT CONCEPT

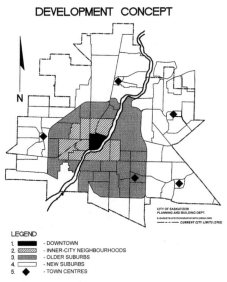

LEGEND

1. ■■■ - DOWNTOWN
2. ▨▨▨ - INNER-CITY NEIGHBOURHOODS
3. ▦▦▦ - OLDER SUBURBS
4. ☐ - NEW SUBURBS
5. ◆ - TOWN CENTRES

Reprinted by permission of Randy Grauer, Senior Planner, City of Saskatoon.

INTRODUCTION

When planning for communities goes beyond ideal conceptions, social concerns, or public outcry, a mode of planning is required to deal with the substance of environments and the processes of institutions. Progressively, modes of practice develop, tools are invented, and regularized processes are established. Contemporary community planning in Canada has well-developed modes such that practices differ little in form and content from one part of the country to the other. The focus is on the physical environment. The tools of municipal plans, zoning, and subdivision regulation are the standard media of implementation. And the steps in plan-making are now well established in legislation.

Chapter 6   Focus on the Physical Environment

Planners ... when driven to the wall to define their special field of competence tend to fall back on land use planning.

Hans Blumenfeld, 1962

What is it that community planners plan? The practice of planning and the demands made on planners in the last two decades give the impression of diverse concerns, interests, and focus: policy planning, impact analysis, growth management, social planning, economic development, etc. The diffusion of planners' competence is, however, more apparent than real. The focus is, and always has been, on the physical environment of cities and towns. As the Alberta ministry responsible for community planning reiterated in 1978, the concern is with "the forces [that] influence the physical shape of communities."[1]

At first glance, this may seem straightforward enough until we realize that professional planners talk in terms of **land-use planning**. This is a kind of planning for the physical environment that gives a sharper focus to the endeavour we call community planning. For it is in the nature of an institution to distinguish its activities and the responsibilities of its practitioners from those of other institutions. Thus, planning is not architecture, or engineering, or the practice of law. Moreover, a good deal of the defining is done by the professional practitioners in the field as they carry forward the aims they and the community have for the activity. In this chapter, we shall identify the basic dimensions of the physical environment with which community planning is concerned. The ways in which planners view the physical environment, both for analyzing and understanding it and for preparing plans, will also be described. In other words, we shall see how community planning's view of the physical environment is circumscribed and, in addition, how other interests view it.

THE PHYSICAL ENVIRONMENT OF COMMUNITIES

One can distinguish the physical environment of communities from that, say, of an agricultural area by the prevalence of structures and other forms of development of the ground space for activities of people. The focus for community planning is, thus, on what is sometimes called the "man-made" or "built" environment. In common terms, this comprises the houses, parks, industrial plants, institutions, stores and offices, streets and highways, and other transportation facilities. All of these elements, directly or indirectly, involve the existing and prospective use of land, both from a public and private point of view.

One of the main tasks of community planning is to arrive at an understanding of how the various physical elements function, the amount of land they require, and their relations with one another. Planners thus seek to identify typical patterns and trends in the use of the ground space of the community. In order to do this, they must understand how to organize their observations of the elements in the community environment. Community land use can best be understood by separating it into three basic— and interrelated—components: (1) physical *facilities*, (2) *activities* of people that use space, and (3) the *functions* that the land serves. In addition, there are three main dimensions that aid in determining land-use patterns and trends: the location, the intensity, and the amount of land required. The understanding thus obtained makes it possible to predict the land-use patterns that may be expected to develop if certain planning proposals are made for new development or redevelopment of the ground space of a community. But before discussing planning proposals, we must establish more precisely the nature of the three main components of the physical environment of communities.

Components of Community Land Use

One of the important characteristics of a city, Jane Jacobs reminded us, is its diversity, and nowhere is this more apparent than on a city's streets.[2] Here we see many uses of the land, even on a sedate residential street: e.g., houses of various kinds, possibly some with separate garages; sidewalks, maybe with children walking on their way to school; the road, probably with some cars parked at the side and other cars or bicycles passing along it; delivery trucks, street trees, and even a neighbourhood park possibly in view.

In this commonplace scene, we encounter instances of each of the three components of community land use. There are physical facilities and features (houses, garages, sidewalks, street trees, the road, a park). There are activities that are both in view (the children walking to school, the delivery of goods, people moving on bicycles and in cars) and carried on inside structures (people residing in houses, cars being stored in garages). The physical features we see have one or more purposes or functions (the houses function as residences, the sidewalks to provide a path for walking, and the roads to provide a path for wheeled vehicles and to store vehicles).

Planners have formulated a variety of ways of classifying the observations they make about land uses. The most highly regarded methods use the three components—facilities, activities, and functions—and permit rigorous measurements to be made in each category.[3] These would usually be done for each parcel of land in the community. The accumulation of such data allows the planner to determine, as Guttenberg points out, "how much space and what kind of facilities a community will need for activities in order to perform its functions at a certain level."[4] These components, in more formal terms, can be analysed as follows:

1. **Facilities:** a description of the physical alterations made to parcels of land and public rights-of-way, especially buildings and other structural features. The type of building (e.g., detached house, office building) needs to be noted because this will indicate the form and quantity of indoor space available to users. Non-building constructions (e.g., pavement, power poles, recreation equipment) may also need to be recorded.

2. **Activities:** a description of what actually takes place on parcels of land and in public spaces. This involves observing of the various users and the form their use takes, usually focusing on the relationships of people obtaining goods and services and the mode of transportation involved. Thus, a house is normally for residential activities, a firehall for protection activities, a parking lot for vehicle parking activities.

3. **Functions:** a description of the basic purpose of an enterprise or establishment located on a parcel of land. Individuals, families, firms, and institutions use a specific location for places of residence, business, government, or assembly, and it is these latter purposes that need to be noted.

Planners have not always been assiduous in the classification of land uses in communities. It is not uncommon to find a set of categories such as the following:

Residential	Industrial	Roads
• one-family	• light	
• multi-family	• heavy	
Commercial	Public	
• retail	• school	
• offices	• recreation	

There are several inconsistencies in such a list: the categories "residential," "commercial," and "industrial" specify the *function* of a piece of land while "public" denotes *ownership* and "roads" refers to a *facility*. And within categories there are references both to facilities (such as "school" and "offices") and to functions (such as "retail" and "recreation"). The industrial category, on the other hand, distinguishes types of activities between firms. Our ability to understand the physical environment of communities is hindered by such classifications.

There are several other characteristics that enter into the description of land use in a community, although they are normally secondary to those above. Such physical characteristics as **slope, drainage, bearing capacity,** and **view** may play a part in determining the use for the land. In considering the stock of land in a community, we may also wish to distinguish that which is developed from that which is undeveloped. The latter category would provide an indication of space that might be available for future development. Also often included in land-use analyses are the **performance characteristics** of the activities on the land. Some activities generate a lot of traffic, some are carried on mostly in the daytime, others are nighttime activities or have peaks of activity at certain hours, and some may generate noise or odour. These characteristics are important because, although initiated by the land use on one parcel of land, they may spill over onto adjoining parcels or even affect a whole neighbourhood. As such, activity characteristics often enter into many planning issues regarding the appropriate location of land uses.

Relations among Land Uses

One classifies land uses rigorously for more than just theoretical reasons. The physical environments of communities are complex, and we must be able to penetrate that complexity in order, for example, to assess the impact of changes that may result from new development. Figure 6.1 (a, b, and c) illustrates two aspects of this complexity. The photographs show how the land-use components may be related to one another at any single location as well as how land uses at different locations are related, especially by roadways.

First, take the common situation of a parcel of residential land with a single-family house on it. The road (a facility) provides for the access to the lot and house (another facility), while the sidewalk (a facility) provides space for children to walk and to play (an activity). Analogous relationships can be seen in any shopping plaza between the store buildings, the parking lot, the walkways, shoppers, drivers, etc. One other important aspect needs to be noted: the multiplicity of activities and/or functions that various

FIGURE 6.1   **Basic Uses of Land in Communities**
Three activities occupy most of the land in use in a typical community: residences (top),
commerce or business (above), and industry (right). The remainder is used for roads that
connect these activities to one another, and for open space. *Sources:* Canapress (top); City
of Calgary Planning Department (bottom); G. Hodge (right).

physical facilities are required to accommodate. The road in front of a store may provide for customer access, for storing customers' and employees' cars, and for facilitating deliveries to the store. The store building may, at different times, house different establishments: a store, office, repair shop, even a residence. Thus, not only are the land-use components interrelated, but also the relationships may change. Through all this, the facilities may change little if at all. Physical facilities have a high degree of permanence among the various land-use components, a fact that planners must be aware of. Many planning issues centre around whether present facilities should be changed to accommodate new activities and functions, i.e., roads widened, old buildings demolished, etc.

The second important aspect involves how land uses in one part of a community are related to and affect land uses in other parts. Households need to make purchases of food and other goods and thus create the need for access to stores. If that access is in the form of automobiles, the stores, which depend upon customers, may provide a parking lot. The workers at factories, offices, and stores tend to come from households located in many different parts of the city or town. And the factories, offices, and stores will likely receive their supplies from warehouses and producers in yet other locations. The various facilities associated with transportation in our communities—roads, sidewalks, streetcar lines, bus stops—are the visible evidence of these necessary connections. Under the ground are utility lines, which also allow different facilities and activities to take place at a wide variety of locations.

There is also a third set of planning issues resulting from the fact that various facilities are distributed differently. Houses, stores selling daily needs, and elementary schools are usually widely distributed, whereas factories, department stores, and auditoriums are not. The last often tend to be concentrated in one or a few areas. Yet facilities must be provided for their interconnection and care must be taken over whether a change in one land use will affect changes in another at a different location, as for example in the case of shutting down a neighbourhood elementary school. If a community is experiencing growth, a major planning issue is where the new concentrations of stores, factories, or offices should go—or if they should simply be added to previous concentrations.

Land Use at Different Scales

From the discussion above, one may infer the need to observe and analyze land uses over several differently sized areas. These start with the **individual parcel of land**, such as a house and lot or the property devoted to a shopping centre, apartment complex, or public building. At the next scale are **districts** where similar sets of land uses occur, as in a residential neighbourhood, a central business district, or an industrial park. At the level of the single parcel of land, the land use is described in detail; at the district level, the dominant land use is usually the basis of the description. When we view an **entire community,** the land use is usually described by groupings of districts (e.g., residential areas) or groupings of uses (e.g., local commercial areas, regional shopping centres). At the **regional level**, the description of land use may simply distinguish between urban areas, agricultural areas, open spaces, etc.

To put this another way, the planner may need to be concerned at several different levels with physical environments. Even though logically connected—parcels make up districts which make up communities which make up cities and so on—each of these physical environments is seen differently in terms of land use. There is, however, a progression of concern with the three land-use components as one moves from the parcel to the city level. When the subject is development or redevelopment of a single parcel, the planning issues tend to centre on the physical facility or improvements to be placed on the site: what type of building? how big will it be? what will it look like? There will also be concerns over the activities on the site and in the immediate vicinity of the parcel in question: will there be a lot of traffic? noise? will it block the sun? As one moves to district-level planning, there is less concern with structures and physical appearance and more with patterns of activities. Of special interest are those patterns associated with pedestrian movements and auto traffic andthose associated with such district-wide facilities as schools, playgrounds, and shopping areas.

As the planning focus moves to the city level, the land-use component dealing with function or purpose of a facility becomes most important. Indeed, at this level and at metropolitan and regional scales, the concern is only with broad land-use purposes, such as those of a special district like the downtown, and with facilities that serve the entire area, like an airport or regional park.

These differing approaches to the physical environment of cities and towns come to be reflected in the plans that are prepared for the various levels of land use. On the one hand, this is a logical ordering of the concerns of planners. Types of structures and the impacts of their activities on adjoining properties are properly the concern at the level of site planning, and the effective functioning of a downtown area the proper concern at the level of city planning. On the other hand, the inherent logic does not prevent reverberations from the planning at one level right across all other levels. The most vivid examples in recent Canadian planning, as in other countries, are the urban expressways that uproot neighbourhoods in order to connect downtown with other major facilities. But also confounding is when one neighbourhood resists tall apartments, only to have that demand shift elsewhere in the city.

In conclusion, the physical environment must accommodate a great variety of activities and purposes. Some have very localized impacts and others might affect an entire region. Moreover, the structures and surface improvements have a great deal of permanence. The latter tend to be either adapted or extended, but seldom removed, when new development needs to be accommodated. There are, therefore, many points of potential conflict among the components of land use at any level of the community, as well as between levels. A good deal of the effort put into community planning involves trying to foresee conflicts between land uses, or **incompatibilities** as they are often called. Many such situations arise when two quite normal land uses wish to use the same ground space in the community. Hans Blumenfeld's description of the conflict between the two functions of the ordinary street is apt:

> Throughout history the streets and squares of human settlements have served as a common living room for the occupants of adjacent buildings, and often for others as well. ... This function has been and still is generally

compatible with their basic function of providing access to the adjacent properties for goods as well as for persons. … But when many goods and persons move, they transform streets into arteries and squares into nodes. Noise, smells, and danger intrude into the living room.[5]

In this sort of instance, we seek though community planning ways of eliminating the conflict, or at least minimizing it to acceptable levels.

HOW PLANNERS VIEW THE PHYSICAL ENVIRONMENT

It is the job of the professional planner to understand to the greatest extent possible the workings of the community physical environment, for, as we have noted before, a great deal of planning centres around two issues: (1) the **spatial impact** on the physical environment of proposals for new development or of changes in existing development; and (2) the **spatial coordination** of the various functions and activities that constitute the physical environment. In order to make sense out of the complexity of the physical environment of a community, the planner must find ways, literally, to "measure" the important features and relationships in that environment. The three basic components devised to classify land uses—facilities, activities, and functions—constitute one such measuring tool. To achieve a more complete picture of the community environment, additional dimensions and concepts are required, to which we now turn.

Dimensions of the Community Environment

The basic land-use components provide the means for analyzing the physical environment on individual parcels of land in a city or town, as well as indicating the functional relations between parcels. The planner is, however, primarily involved with planning for much more than one parcel, such as for neighbourhoods, districts, or the entire community. This requires that the planner be able to obtain measurements of the larger physical environment. Since the larger scale is an aggregation of the land use on single parcels of land, the planner will need to be able to sum the observations and to make comparisons between single land uses.

There are four dimensions that provide the planner with most of the information needed about the community environment. These are amount, intensity, spatial distribution, and location.

1. Amount

With this dimension, the fundamental question of "how much?" may be broached, i.e., how much land is involved, how many dwelling units, how much traffic, how much commercial space, how much school population, etc.? It can be seen from these representative questions that the planner may be interested in land, dwelling units, traffic, people, and functional space. Whether one or several of these variables are involved will depend upon the size of the area and how comprehensive the planning is to be.

2. Intensity

With this dimension, the fundamental question of "how does this compare?" may be applied to a development proposal. The answer will determine differences either with development one is already familiar with or with some planning standards. In general, the measures used are in the form of ratios, e.g., persons/hectare, persons/dwelling unit, dwelling units/hectare, floor space/lot area, employees/hectare, autos/household.

3. Spatial Distribution

With this dimension, the degree of concentration of facilities, people, and activities may be reckoned. On the one hand, the concern may be with facilities (e.g., parks, schools) and services (e.g., shopping plazas) being available to people more or less equitably. On the other hand, the concern may be with overconcentration of facilities (e.g., apartment buildings, stores, public buildings), which may lead to various public utilities and transportation modes being overtaxed. The planner often talks about accessibility and congestion in relation to this dimension.

4. Location

With this dimension, the planner is concerned primarily with the "relative" location of facilities, especially those of community-wide interest or district-wide interest. That is, it is a concern with how facilities relate to each other, e.g., homes to local schools and parks, major shopping areas to the road network, industrial plants to shipping facilities.

Patterns in the Community Environment

As planners have observed, measured, and analyzed the land uses in many different community situations, they have discerned certain patterns and relationships. Many of these, such as the amount of land commonly devoted to roads or the spatial distribution of elementary schools, provide ready guidelines in understanding the layout of the community. Observations about the intensity of various land uses, such as those related to different sizes of dwellings, provide the basis for the important concept of **density,** which is used in reference to commercial and industrial land uses as well. Functional relations, or linkages as they are often called, between major land uses and districts have generated the concept of **accessibility** as well as the notion of the **separation of traffic.** Many of these are so well established as to be used by planners as principles and standards in planning communities. Since they are the *lingua franca* of professional planners, it is essential that other participants in community planning also have a grasp of them.

Land-Use Requirements

When the land in urban communities is tabulated according to seven major urban functions, it is typically found distributed in the proportions shown in Figure 6.2. These land-use shares are derived from communities in the Vancouver Metropolitan Area, but are quite typical of other Canadian communities. When communities differ in land use, the difference usually appears in the increase of land required for institutions (e.g., Kingston, Ontario), or in the generous provision of parks (e.g., Edmonton), or in the large amount of industry (e.g., Trois-Rivières).

Urban Function	Percentage of Total Area
Residential	51.2
Commercial	2.4
Industrial	8.2
Institutional	7.8
Transportation/Utilities	4.3
Recreation/Open space	5.5
Streets	20.6
Total urban uses	100.0

FIGURE 6.2   **Land-Use Shares of Major Urban Functions**

The terrain can also affect the types of land uses that are present: a hilly community will probably have few industries but a greater share of residences, for example, while a community that is a transportation terminal will probably attract a greater than average share of industry, commerce, and transport land uses. Communities may also vary in the quality of residences constituting the residential sector, depending upon the income bracket to which their housing market caters. And where two communities are adjacent, one may contain the bulk of the living areas while the other contains the working areas because of where the municipal boundaries have been struck.

Two facets of the data in Figure 6.2 are worth noting. The first is that three land uses that are normally in private ownership—residential, commercial, and industrial—constitute nearly two-thirds of the community. The second is that one-fifth of the community's space is required for streets and roads (and in some communities this share is one-quarter or more). The latter, when combined with parks and some institutional uses of land, constitute the ground space of the community over which the local government has *direct* control, i.e., only about 30% of the total community area.

Functional Arrangements

In order to plan comprehensively for a community, whether for the entire community or only a portion of it, it is necessary to have an integrated view of it. This means moving beyond simple land-use composition and obtaining a picture of how the community functions. Drawing upon the knowledge that has accumulated about cities and towns, the planner identifies several basic tendencies about how communities function that pertain to the needs of planning.

The first of these is to conceive of the community as composed of a number of major functional areas that reflect basic human activities. The planner may see the community at its most fundamental level to be made up of **living areas, working areas,** and **community facilities** all linked together by a **circulation system**. The category of working areas may be elaborated to distinguish between those providing goods and services to residents—commercial areas—and those involved in the processing and distribution of goods—industrial areas. This simple concept of the functioning parts of the community contains the essential elements with which the planner is concerned; that is, people must have places to live and to work, and these normally function best when separated from one another. The circulation system will provide for the necessary interconnections between living areas and working areas and also for access to community facilities. These four functional elements are focused upon in virtually every community plan.

The more detailed functioning of a city or town requires further elaboration of the general functional elements. For example, some community facilities are provided for the community as a whole, such as a civic auditorium or a general hospital, while others serve only small parts, such as a local park or an elementary school. The same is true for commercial facilities and also for streets and highways. The planner thus sees **hierarchical arrangements** within the broad functional areas of the community. Since, for the most part, they seem to work to the community's benefit, the planner tends to adopt a hierarchical principle when planning for the distribution of various public and commercial facilities and in the designation of streets. There is ample justification for this from two points of view. First, it streamlines services and makes the best use of funds for public investments. Second, it allows districts—residential, commercial, or industrial—to serve their primary purposes as living, working, or shopping areas effectively without undue impingement from other functions.

Density and Space Needs

One of the greatest concerns about city-building in the late 19th and early 20th centuries was over **congestion**: too many people, too little space between buildings, too much traffic. The consequences for health and safety had been amply demonstrated (see Chapter 3), and much of the effort in community planning since then has been devoted to avoiding congestion in its various forms. Intensity of land use is, as we noted earlier, one of the main dimensions planners employ in measuring the adequacy of planning proposals. Since congestion is simply the too-intense use of a community's ground space, planners sought indicators that would show when land uses would be approaching congested conditions in order to avoid them. The most widely used indicators are those relating to density.

As planners define it, **density** means the number of land uses or land users on a specified unit of ground space in the community, usually per hectare. The most common density indicators are used in regard to residential development: the number of persons/hectare or the number of dwelling units/hectare. There are analogous density measures for industrial and commercial areas, such as the number of employees/hectare. The appeal of the density measure is that it readily links the available land, structures, and activities in a community that need space. Thus, by knowing the type of development that is proposed, say the construction of a certain number of single-family detached houses, the amount of land that will be required can be calculated by knowing the density at which such housing is normally built. Or, if a certain number of apartment units were proposed on a site, it could be ascertained whether this would result in an acceptable density.

In the latter examples, the density measure would be dwelling units/hectare, and its application carries with it the knowledge of the type and intensity of such dwellings under average circumstances. It also carries with it, implicitly, some norm of acceptable and/or desirable density for the type of dwelling. Indeed, there is now widespread agreement among builders and planners about the density of dwellings that will contribute to an amenable community environment. Figure 6.3 describes the densities that typically result when different kinds of housing are built.

Dwelling unit densities start, of course, from population densities: each dwelling unit is accommodation for a household. The number of people in households and the composition of household populations differ within a community. This generates the need for different kinds of accommodation. Families with young children tend to prefer housing that has direct ground access and are most often found in low-density housing or row housing.

The average household size of these families is highest among normal household types and is commonly found to average 3.5 persons. Medium and high-density housing usually accommodates an older population: young adult couples, families with teenagers, elderly couples, single-person households both young and old. In these accommodations, the household size tends to average 2.5 persons or less. It follows that the planner can estimate the various kinds of housing needs for a community by knowing the composition of the population and therefore the types of services and facilities that will be needed in the various housing areas. Thus, low-density areas with children need schools and playgrounds within easy access, while high-density areas that generate more traffic need easy access to major roads, and so on. Examples of the physical outcome of housing at different densities are shown in Figure 6.4.

Two other aspects of density deserve special attention. First, Figure 6.3 expresses the data in terms of **net density.** This refers to the number of

Density	Housing Type	Building Height in Storeys	Dwellings per Net Hectare	Persons per Net Hectare
Low	One-family detached	1–2	12–17	43–48
	Two-family	1–2	19–29	48–84
Medium	Row house, garden apartment	2–3	24–48	72–144
	Walk-up apartment	3–4	48–96	120–192
High	Multi-family	5–10	96–192	192–360
	Multi-family	10–16	192–240	360–480
	Multi-family	over 16	240–960	480–1,680

FIGURE 6.3   **Typical Densities (Net) of Different Forms of Housing**

FIGURE 6.4   **Styles of Housing Comprising Different Densities**
The single-family detached house (top) dominates *low*-density districts; townhouses (above) provide housing at *medium* density; and taller apartment buildings (right) create *high*-density living areas. *Sources:* G. Hodge (top); CMHC (above, right.)

dwelling units or people being accommodated on the residential building sites and does not include public roads or other community or commercial land uses. There is another useful measure of density that planners employ in estimating broad-scale land requirements, **gross density**; this includes all land uses in the community and is usually expressed in terms of persons per square kilometre. Canadian communities tend to have gross densities of 3,000 to 4,500 persons per square kilometre, depending upon their age and size. Newer and smaller communities usually have lower densities, with the converse being true for older and larger communities. This raises a second issue about differences in density. There are not only differences because of the size and age of a community, but also because of the style of building that is acceptable in the community. For example, 125 dwelling units per hectare is considered high density in Kingston, Ontario, and is the maximum normally allowed, whereas densities several times higher are considered acceptable in other cities. The density indicator is thus used not only in determining housing and land requirements, but also in assessing the compatibility of proposed development with the existing physical form of the community.

Before leaving the topic of density, the reader should consider the simple diagrams in Figure 6.5 (a, b and c). Since density is most often invoked when there is a proposal that would enlarge the accommodations provided in the community, the figure shows the two basic ways in which density may increase.

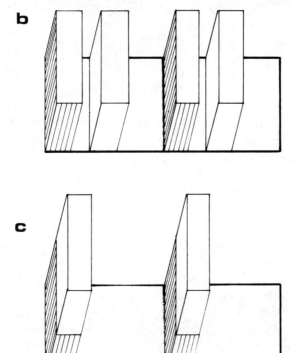

FIGURE 6.5 **Relations between Residential Growth and Density of Development**

a. *Horizontal Growth:* Total area increased; height and coverage unchanged. No change in density.

b. *Infill Growth:* Coverage doubled; area and height unchanged. Density doubles.

c. *Vertical Growth:* Height doubled; area and coverage unchanged. Density doubles.

Source: Adapted from Hans Blumenfeld, "The Conflict between the Two Functions of the Street," *Contact* 13, nos. 2/3 (1981), 11–15.

Planning Issue 6.1

MONSTER HOUSES TAMED

Vancouver city council fought back at monster houses Tuesday, approving a package of by-law amendments to restrict their size and appearance.

The amendments were drafted by city planners after two public hearings at which more than 50 delegations expressed concern about the bloated five- and six-bedroom boxes that have angered many Vancouverites, particularly those on the west side.

"This has been quite a lengthy process," said Ald. George Puil, who moved the amendments. "Council can't stand still on this issue. We have tried to apply Band-Aid effects, but neighborhoods are still quite concerned."

When given final reading by council, the new by-law will

• Limit the height of single-family houses to 9.1 metres, or 10.6 with the planning director's permission.
• Discourage double-height entryways and rooms.
• Minimize bulkiness of houses.
• Limit floor-to-ceiling heights to 3.6 metres.
• Discourage demolition of older houses.
• Speed applications for permits for renovations and additions.
• Establish a committee of designers, architects, builders, and planners to report to council so it can deal more effectively with such neighbourhood concerns as views, neighbourliness and streetscapes.

Council asked the director of planning to report back on ways to maintain backyards so big houses don't overlook and overshadow neighbors, but it decided not to put restrictions on exterior finishes.

Source: "City moves to tame monster houses," *The Vancouver Sun*, April 4, 1990.

Bulk of Buildings

Closely associated with the idea of density is the concept of **bulk.** As Figure 6.5 shows, the density on a site may increase by increasing the height of a building, covering a larger portion of the site with a building, or both. In general, the larger the site area that a building covers the bulkier it will be, not only in actuality but also in our visual impression of the building. Bulk is thus a measure of the actual **volume** of a building (its height times its coverage). But it involves aesthetic considerations as well as land-use and economic realities.

First, aesthetic considerations: refer to the standards of taste and appearance by which members of a community assess the bulkiness of buildings. A community that has no very tall buildings, such as Saint John, may want to limit the height of new buildings; a community that has lots of open space, such as Saskatoon, may want to limit the coverage of buildings on a site. In Vancouver, where the mountain vista is treasured by most, the bulk of downtown buildings has been a subject of planning debate for more than a decade. Zoning by-laws always contain in their bulk regulations the aesthetic concerns of citizens. (See Planning Issue 6.1.)

Second, the bulk of a building also has land-use implications. The bulkier the building, in general, the greater the number of activities associated with it—that is, more dwelling units, commercial establishments, etc., will be located there. The planner is aware that more intense use of a site may put pressure on public services and facilities such as sewer lines, roads, and schools. In addition, the bulk of the building will affect the amount of ground space that might be needed on the site for access, for parking, and simply for open space for the occupants of the building. Bulky buildings may affect the light and air available, both to occupants and to people on adjacent properties. Tall buildings may shade lower buildings and nearby properties from the sun, an issue that has become prominent in regard to the installation of solar energy units.

Third, the economics of building are directly associated with the matter of building bulk. The value of the land, the economical size of the establishment, and the costs of building all enter into the original proposal made by those wishing to develop a site. Take a simple case: apartment buildings more than three storeys tall usually require the installation of an elevator, but it is normally not economical to build at less than six storeys in order to recover the extra cost of installing an elevator. Thus, the taller building imposes the need for the land to accommodate twice the number of apartment units. How can this extra bulk be accommodated? There are similar versions of this trade-off argument for all types of structures built for commercial purposes in a city or town. An analogous issue pertaining to residential structures arose recently with the advent of "big houses" ("megahouses") in the new house market. (This issue is discussed further in Chapter 9.)

Planners have devised an index of building bulk called the **Floor Area Ratio** (FAR)—sometimes called the Floor Space Ratio (FSR) or Floor Space Index (FSI)—in order to respond to the various aesthetic, planning, and economic interests in these matters. The FAR relates the floor area of a building to the area of the site. An FAR of 1.0 is the equivalent of a one-storey building covering the entire lot. (In the case of buildings for commercial purposes, it is assumed that the owner is entitled to use 100% of the site.) A one-storey building may not suit the owner, who may wish, for example, to provide parking, so a 1.0 FAR might be translated into a two-storey building covering only half the site, or a three-storey building covering one-third of the site, and so on. At some point, the builder may find it economically unfeasible to build taller, or the community may find only certain heights of buildings acceptable. On the latter point, there appear to be community norms on downtown building bulk. For example, in Toronto an FAR of 12.0 is acceptable, but in Vancouver an FAR of 6.0 is considered the limit. Most smaller cities seem to prefer an FAR of 3.0.

The Floor Area Ratio is used to determine more than just the acceptable levels of building bulk. There may be setback requirements from the front, back, and side lot lines, parking space requirements, and in some cases, requirements to provide recreation space and landscaping. Each of these will reduce the amount of the lot that can be built upon at ground level, thereby forcing the building to be made taller. The FAR may also be used to obtain more open space at ground level than that normally required. In parts of cities where land costs are very high (as in many downtown areas and at key intersections) and where the economics of development demand the intense use of a site, a higher than normal FAR may be offered as a bonus in return for providing extra open space at ground level. The widespread appearance since the 1950s of plazas and sitting spaces in areas with tall office buildings and hotels is evidence of the workings of this incentive system.

A more recent method that planners use to manipulate the bulk of buildings is called **Transfer of Development Rights** (TDR). This technique allows the building bulk permitted on one site to be used on another site. For example, planners may feel that the full attainment of the bulk permitted by the zoning regulations for a particular site will produce a building that is not suited to its surroundings. Negotiations may be undertaken to have the building's developer build on another site that does not normally permit such bulk. Developers themselves may offer to forgo bulky development on one site in order to obtain greater bulk on a site they favour more. Through the TDR, communities may be able to obtain open space, more amenable streetscapes, greater concentration of development, and so on.

Linkages and Accessibility

In the planner's view, the community environment is a set of living and working areas, each occupying a specific part of the ground space, and community facilities distributed at various locations. Implicit in this view is the notion that interaction must be facilitated among them. Essentially, this means there must be the means of circulation available so that individuals, households, firms, and institutions that are, of necessity, separated from one another may be in contact. In this view of the physical environment, the planner focuses on the patterns of interactions between people, firms, and institutions. Although there is a great deal of individuality and complexity in these interactions, important patterns may be discerned in the fairly repetitive routines that people or organizations follow when engaging in activities in the community.

Some activities are regularly patterned, such as the daily journey to work or regular food marketing; some are casual or infrequent, as in partaking of entertainment activities and visits for medical care. Commercial firms and public institutions have comparable patterns: they receive supplies, make deliveries, and are the destination for employees and clients. A commonplace example is the daily pattern of children, teachers, and other staff travelling to their local school. The planner thinks of these interactions in terms of **linkages** and seeks to accommodate them, both by arranging a suitable pattern of land uses and by providing an appropriate transportation network.

An early step in community planning for land use is the consideration of which activities need to be linked and how close this access ought to be. Another consideration is the various means of transportation that are likely to be used. Accumulated experience in these matters indicates that closeness of access is more appropriately measured in terms of time and cost rather than pure distance, especially if the linkage must be made by automobile or public transit. Where access is usually achieved on foot, such as to local schools, parks, and shopping areas, distance is the limiting factor. The table in Figure 6.6 shows the time and distance standards that planners have found which will provide a high level of convenience for most residents (probably 85% or more) in most urban communities.[6]

Every linkage is, of course, accomplished by some form of transportation, and the planner must be cognizant of the modes of travel that might be used for different linkages. For some time now, perhaps since the planning of the model industrial villages 100 years ago, planners have recognized the incompatibility of wheeled and foot traffic in many situations. The response has been to try and find ways to separate modes of travel: most simply, sidewalks are provided as well as roadways, or exclusive footpaths may be used, as in the designs for greenbelt towns. Nowadays bikeways and entire pedestrian shopping precincts may be set aside. Another facet of planning for traffic separation was recognized when automobiles came into widespread use in the 1920s. The auto could not only travel

Destination	Time-Distance
Place of work	20 to 30 min
Central business district	30 to 40 min
Local shopping centre	0.8 km or 10 min
Elementary school	0.8 km
High school	1.6 km or 20 min
Playgrounds and local parks	0.8 km
Major park or conservation area	30 to 45 min
Commercial deliveries	30 to 60 min

FIGURE 6.6   **Standards of Accessibility to Selected Urban Land Uses and Facilities**
Source: F. Stuart Chapin Jr., *Urban Land Use Planning,* 2nd ed. (Champaign-Urbana: University of Illinois Press, 1964), 376. Copyright 1965 by the Board of Trustees of the University of Illinois. Used with the permission of the University of Illinois Press.

much faster than all other modes; it could also cover greater distances. Yet the auto holds no advantage unless it is allowed to move expeditiously. Areas not originally designed for such traffic may thus suffer through having to accommodate it. Community plans have therefore come to incorporate areas where the land use is intended to separate automobiles from living and working areas.

Planners' Principles of Community Land Use

There has developed out of about a century of planning thought, analysis, and practical experience a number of principles that guide planners in arranging land uses in a community. These principles, which are usually implicit in advice that planners offer rather than stated outright, have been accepted as desirable goals by builders, architects, engineers, and the general public. Although not heralded, their importance in the actions that give form to the community environment should not be minimized. The basic ones are listed here:

1. Land uses with different activity characteristics may have to be separated from one another to allow for their effective functioning.
2. The pattern of land uses should provide for the integration of all functions and areas.
3. The circulation system should reflect the land-use pattern.
4. Social cohesion should be promoted by providing the opportunity for the proximity of home, employment centres, shopping opportunities, recreation areas, and schools.

5. Residential areas should be attractive and well drained, and have variety in their design.

6. Housing should be provided in a range of types to suit the income structure of the community.

7. Commercial and service areas should be concentrated to provide both convenience and efficiency.

8. Modes of traffic with differing characteristics should be separated from one another.

9. The downtown area should be considered the social and business heart of the community.

This list of planning principles may be added to or modified as conditions and tastes change in a community. Indeed, the first principles above, about separating and uses, has been gradually changing as the benefits of mixed-use development are recognized, especially in larger cities. In effect, two tendencies are at work to modify these basic principles. The first is the realization that many of these principles emanate from earlier planning concepts that are now considered too rigid (such as the separation of uses). The second tendency is to establish new planning principles as new issues arise such as for waterfront planning, environmental pollution, energy conservation, or affordable housing.

TYPES OF PLANS FOR THE PHYSICAL ENVIRONMENT

In planning for a community's physical environment, a planner will almost certainly be called upon to prepare or assess several different types of plans. There are four basic possibilities: first, the planning approach may focus on development for already built-up areas or for undeveloped land. The types of plans that may have to be considered are subdivision plans, redevelopment plans, site plans, and project plans, either singly or in combination. The second possibility is that one or more component districts of a community—the central business district, residential neighbourhoods, waterfronts—may warrant special consideration. Third, plans may be made for the main functional elements of a community: the transportation network, the park system, community facilities, or housing. Fourth, and most important, is a comprehensive plan for the community as a whole, comprising all the previous elements and concerns.

This discussion will focus on the comprehensive community plan first. Although called by various names—the Official Plan in Ontario, the

General Municipal Plan in Alberta, for example—it is the cornerstone of local planning throughout Canada. Following this discussion, we will examine the types of plans that have emerged in regard to specific problems and areas. It will become evident that the context for these latter plans is the comprehensive community plan. The primary basis of judgement of a specific area or functional plan is the contribution it makes to attainment of the overall community plan.

The Comprehensive Community Plan

A comprehensive plan for a city or town is a 20th-century planning concept. Its underlying premise is that of a long-range plan (possibly for 20 years or more) for the overall physical development of the community, which can be used to guide both public and private development efforts. Since developments in the physical environment concern housing, the location and functioning of industry and commerce, and community services and amenities, the community plan also serves to help organize and direct social, economic, and political forces in the community in a rational and productive manner. This adds further to the notion of its comprehensiveness. It is usually the only such broad-based plan a community ever has.

The community plan, if it is to be comprehensive and long-range, will of necessity be a *general* plan. The plan deals with all the essential physical developments in the community environment but usually not in detail. It is not intended to be a blueprint document, but one that presents the major proposals for future physical development. Thus, it uses a limited number of very broad land-use categories, shows only major transportation routes and public facilities, and provides only a general picture of the locations and sizes of major facilities and districts in the city or town. The aim is to provide a guide, both graphically and verbally, to all the major elements in the community physical environment and the desired relationships between them. The general map included in the 1965 plan for the City of Regina illustrates the approach described here (Figure 6.7).

The focus of the community plan is on the main issues in physical development and the major proposals for future development. This is primarily to help direct discussion and debate in the community so as to arrive at agreement on policies and proposals that affect not only the overall functioning of the community but also the content of plans for specific areas and projects. Every plan is also a mixture of the general and the specific. Some elements in a community are so prominent—a civic centre, the main thoroughfare, a large institution, the downtown—that they cannot and should not be cloaked in generalities. What the plan will probably highlight is their relationship with other parts of the community. Some elements may

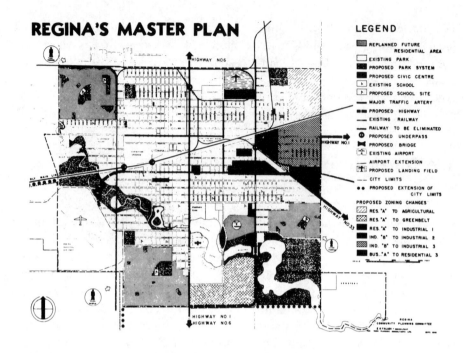

FIGURE 6.7 **Comprehensive Community Plan Map**
The main city-wide facilities and land uses are shown on this plan map for Regina by well-known Canadian planner Dr. Eugenio Faludi. *Source:* City of Regina.

be areas of special importance to the community's future form and character, e.g., a waterfront area, a district of historic buildings, special vistas, a greenbelt. The community plan may contain distinct sections devoted to these special areas.

Functional Plans

Some elements of a community's physical structure may be so important to the overall functioning as to require more elaboration than is possible within the community comprehensive plan. The two most common elements to which this applies are (1) transportation and circulation systems and (2) parks and recreation facilities. These occupy large and strategic portions of a community's ground space, demand considerable public investment, and are complex functions in and of themselves. Thus, separate functional plans are frequently prepared subsequent to the publication of the community plan, or sometimes they are drawn up in order to update the outlook of a comprehensive plan that is already in use.

A functional plan usually provides proposals at all levels of detail. A general concept plan is provided to encompass the main proposals and projects (such as a new bridge or conservation area), but there will also be detailed proposals for the location of facilities and, often, the acquisition of land by public authorities. Functional plans may be prepared by departments within the local government that are responsible for the particular function or, in some cases, by public agencies established outside of the local government to carry out the function.

Special-Area Plans

There are special areas in almost every community that will require, or perhaps deserve, more detailed planning. The central business district (CBD) is the area most commonly singled out for special planning consideration. This stems from the fact that it is the key to a community's vitality, both economically and culturally. The CBD often provides residents and visitors with the strongest visual image of a community; it represents the most dominant concentration of land values and investment in property, as well as providing a locus for social transactions. As such, the CBD needs to be continually maintained and renovated in order to function effectively. It is also a complex area requiring detailed planning analysis and design.

CBD plans tend to focus on three aspects of the downtown area. The first is the functional arrangement of land use, for most downtowns accommodate several functions: retail shopping, financial and business services, entertainment, and government institutions. In larger communities, these functions may occupy discrete, but usually overlapping, parts of downtown. The second aspect is transportation and parking, for the downtown tends to contain those functions to which the entire community needs access. The third is the three-dimensional character—the urban design—of downtown. Concern is shown in CBD plans for the heights of buildings, prominent views, walkway systems, squares and open space, mall boulevards, and street furnishings. Concerns over aesthetics and architecture are usually greater in CBD plans than in any other physical plan.

Other districts may also merit special planning attention in a community depending upon the historical and geographical circumstances. Seaport communities, often concerned over the demise of shipping and industry, prepare plans for revitalization of harbour areas, as did Halifax. In communities with clusters of historic buildings, such as the Old Town portions of Montreal and Victoria, there may be an impetus to plan for the conservation and upgrading of these areas. The future of inner-city neighbourhoods may also stimulate special-area planning, as the example from Calgary shows

(Figure 6.8). Again, as with CBD plans, these special-area plans are normally framed within the context of the comprehensive plan and they, too, pay particular attention to detailed functional arrangements of land use, transportation, and visual design.

Land Development Plans

Planners prepare or evaluate two types of plans dealing with new development of the ground space of a community. One is the **subdivision plan**, which involves dividing a large parcel of usually vacant land into numerous building lots. This is most commonly done for residential development, but may also be used in industrial and commercial development. The other is the **site plan**, which involves development on a single parcel of land that is usually either vacant or about to be made vacant by the razing of existing structures.

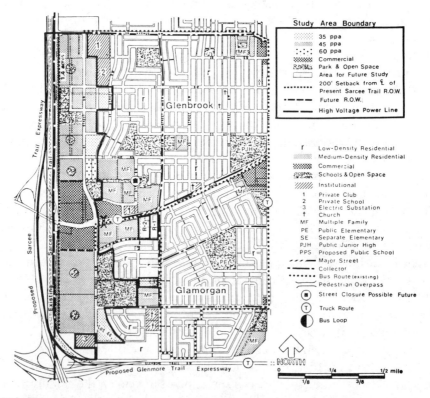

FIGURE 6.8　**Special-Area Plan for a Residential District**
In order to provide a more detailed view of land uses, traffic, and facilities in different districts, special-area (or secondary) plans are prepared. This one is for several Calgary neighbourhoods. *Source:* City of Calgary.

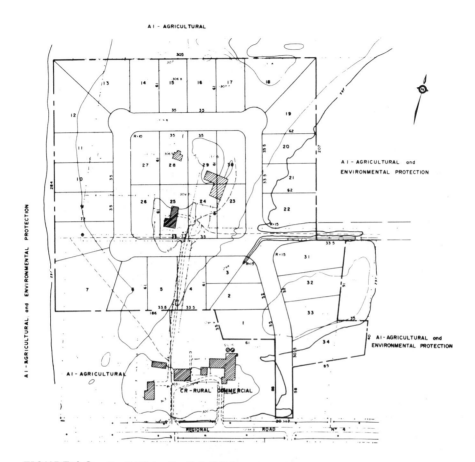

FIGURE 6.9   **Draft Plan of a Subdivision**

Before land can be subdivided and built upon, a plan must be submitted and approved showing the arrangement of lots, the alignment of streets, and the uses of land. *Source:* Canada Mortgage and Housing Corporation, Residential Site Development Advisory Document (1981), 24.

A subdivision plan, in contrast to the general land-use plans referred to above, is a precise plan. It must show exactly the proposed property lines, street system, water and sewer lines, and topographic changes to the site. The proposed Ontario subdivision in Figure 6.9 illustrates such a plan. The reason for the detail is that, upon completion, the municipality assumes responsibility for the subdivision as an additional part of the community. Thus, careful scrutiny is given to subdivision plans so as to avoid such problems as those identified by the Ontario government for its municipalities:

> Water pipes, sewers and roads might have to be run through vacant land to reach scattered subdivisions, thus increasing their length and the cost of services to the public.

Subdivisions laid out on hilly ground could have street patterns that ignore the slopes. This also increases costs, makes them difficult to maintain and more hazardous in cold weather.

Others, laid out in poorly drained soil and provided with septic tanks and well water, become health hazards when the septic tanks pollute the wells or when the septic tank beds are subject to flooding.[7]

Subdivision plans must also indicate areas set aside for parks, schools, and any other such public facilities as walkways, churches, and shopping areas. In a number of provinces, it is required that the subdivider deed 5% of the subdivision to the municipality for park use. However, before all these details are considered, the subdivision plan is examined for its conformity with the aims of the comprehensive plan and the requirements of the zoning regulations for the area in question.

A site plan refers to the proposed land-use arrangements for, normally, a single parcel of land. It is usually prepared by the proponent of a development (not necessarily the owner of the property) for one or more new

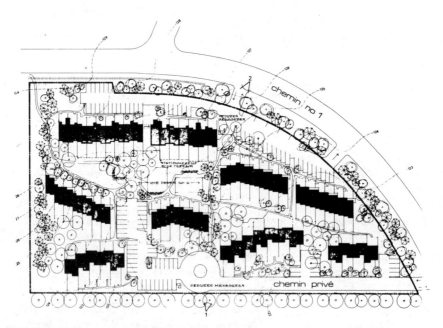

FIGURE 6.10   **Site Plan for a Housing Project**
The precise location of buildings and arrangement of open space are shown on a site plan for a housing project. The plan usually refers to a single parcel of land. Such plans are often required when building permits and development control agreements are being sought.
Source: Boucher & Fafard, Architectes, Laval, Quebec.

buildings or for making substantial changes to existing buildings. A site plan is a precise, blueprint-type plan that is concerned with the placement of buildings and the connections linking the site to the street system and to public services. All non-building types of facilities such as parking lots, recreation areas, and interior roads must also be included on a site plan, as must any topographic aspects that might affect drainage. Figure 6.10 illustrates a typical site plan.

Increasingly, site plans are required to be submitted so that they can be scrutinized for their consistency with community objectives. Aesthetic and functional considerations are also taken into account in this nearly final phase of land-use planning. In Ontario, this process is called **site plan control**; elsewhere the term **development control** is often used to refer to the same local vetting of developers' site plans.

OTHER VIEWS OF THE PHYSICAL ENVIRONMENT

As Seen by Other Professions

Planning for the physical environment of a community will elicit views other than those of the planner. The lawyer, architect, and engineer, each of whom plays a substantial role in the planning and development of communities, express different concerns, not to mention the more recent and important view of the environmental specialists. Each of these participants contributes his or her view to the planning process and thereby affects its outcome in terms of the focus of concern as well as the nature of the physical plans that are prepared.

1. The **lawyer** views the community environment as, essentially, a configuration of parcels of land, each of which has a legal description and carries a certain set of property rights. The lawyer thus seeks great precision in regard to plans affecting the parcels of land that constitute the community. Because planning proposals may have the effect of redefining property rights—limiting uses, heights, and placement of buildings, etc.—lawyers have a natural concern that planning processes be conducted properly and that prior property rights not be arbitrarily taken away. The two types of physical plans that most closely reflect the physical environment for the lawyer are the subdivision plan and the site plan because of the precision accorded to property lines. It is, however, the case that the written land-use regulations and planning policies are of much greater importance to the lawyer involved with community-planning matters.

2. The **architect**'s or urban designer's view of the community environment is mostly a three-dimensional one: that is, the architect is concerned with what can be built on the ground space of the community and what the resulting construction will look like. This concern extends from the design of individual buildings and other structures to groupings of buildings (e.g., an apartment complex), to streetscapes and the design of open spaces in the community. The architect may design subdivisions to achieve certain groupings of buildings, and is the professional who usually prepares the site plan for a project. Except with respect to special district plans and the height regulations for buildings, community plans have very little to say explicitly about the visual outcome of land development. Comprehensive plans may state a policy of wishing "to preserve the character" of, say, the downtown area, but it usually remains the prerogative of the designer to bring in the third dimension. As building aesthetics are often the subject of vigorous debate in a community, it is easy to see that visual qualities are very important in planning. They are, however, not easily resolved, impinging as they do on people's values about aesthetics, the extent of land-use control, and the nature of growth and change in the community.

3. The **engineer**'s view of the community environment is primarily functional. Thus, the engineer is concerned with how well the various physical elements function in the community—the street system and other forms of transportation, the water supply and sewerage system, the electricity and communications systems—individually and in conjunction with one another. The engineer's view is both comprehensive and detailed in regard to the community environment, but tends to be limited to providing a framework of services and streets within which land development can take place. A special concern of the engineer is the way in which natural drainage patterns may be affected by land development. It is the duty of the municipality to try and ensure that, when the surface of the land is modified in any land development, nearby properties are not affected adversely in regard to drainage. The engineer's concern is, indeed, part of the traditional concerns of community planning that were addressed in the first planning acts in Canada: the alignment of streets, the efficient extension of public utilities and drainage conditions. Subdivision plans and site plans are usually required to address these matters directly.

4. The **environmental planner** and environmental interest groups have, in recent years, brought into sharp focus concerns over the effect of planning and development decisions on the natural environment of a community. Their view encompasses the land, water, and air of the

community and the quality of each. The most pressing concerns are with the effluents generated by various land uses: sewage, other liquid effluents, smoke and fumes, noise, and solid wastes. Belatedly, it seems, we have come to know that these effluents, if they are not planned and managed properly, can be dangerous for the health and safety not only of people on neighbouring properties but of the entire community. There are also related concerns with more passive elements of the environment, such as the disturbance of areas of natural vegetation (e.g., marshes and woods) and the preservation of views. Community plans have increasingly come to respect these factors, and planners scrutinize development proposals regarding their environmental impact. However, the issues are still in many ways very technical, complex, incompletely understood, and controversial.

Emerging Views

Just as we saw the physical planning perspective evolving in previous generations as new issues and ideals emerged (see especially Chapter 4) so, too, are views of the physical environment being modified in this generation, sometimes quite dramatically. Briefly, here are some of the more prominent new views:

1. The **energy-efficient community** notion came into prominence during the energy crisis of the 1980s and prompted the examination of physical environments for opportunities to conserve energy. It involves reducing the amount of travel by residents, especially by automobile, clustering land uses, and orienting buildings to take advantage of solar heating possibilities.

2. The **healthy community** concept has (re)entered the purview of planners motivated by a much-expanded definition of health (compared to the public health movement of the past) and broad support from federal and provincial health ministries.[8] It grew out of the need to shift from traditional institutionalized health care to the more holistic approach of improving community environments so as to enable people to support each other more effectively and achieve a better overall quality of life.[9]

3. The **postmodern suburb** is a reaction to the monotony and sameness of most post-World War II suburbs and has led to a variety of ideas: creating town centres, infill schemes, and new social spaces for the enormous and diverse populations that now live there.[10] A variation on this theme, and an American term for it, involves recognizing the evolving suburb as *Edge City*.[11]

4. The **New Urbanism** is another reaction to prevailing modes of urban design, but proponents of this view seek to recreate community values such as neighbourliness through a greater mixture of land uses and physical forms that mirror small town settings, especially those of the late-Victorian era.[12] Also often involved are issues of physical sustainability.[13]

5. **Bioregionalism** considers the physical environment from the perspective of ecological principles and aims to counteract the environmental destruction caused by current city-building and other economic production. Communities and the environment are seen as integrated elements and, further, are bound up with their local regions and the "web of life", including the geology, soils, wildlife, water systems, as well as human cultures, etc.[14]

These viewpoints expand the way in which planners must view the physical environments, as well as add to the complexity of the planning task. While they contribute to a more complete view of community environments, they still tend to deal only with the outward aspects, the physical form, of a city or town.

There are two other, what one might call "interior", views that have received little attention until recently. First is the general view of city residents. In an innovative study, Hok Lin Leung, a Queen's University planner, conducted a survey to find out how Ottawa citizens perceive their city environment.[15] To them, the city has many more dimensions and is expressed in a different way than what planners usually work with. Variables of age, gender, income and workplace seem to make the difference. The second of these interior views of the city is the specific one provided by women. British planner Clara Greed points out that the "everyday life" of women involves short journeys, the need for localized facilities, access to a mixture of land uses, as well as concerns over safety and child care.[16]

Traditional planning practices and tools have barely begun to acknowledge these emerging needs and concerns, much less incorporate them into the comprehensive community plan. That process will need to become more inclusive, a topic we will discuss more fully in succeeding chapters.

All of these viewpoints could come into play in the planning of a contemporary community. They undoubtedly add to the complexity of the planning task, but they also contribute to a more complete view of the community environment. Their integration will be facilitated by the framework provided by the comprehensive community plan; this once again underlines the important coordinating role of the community plan.

ENDNOTES

1. Alberta, Department of Municipal Affairs, *Planning in Alberta: A Guide and Directory* (Edmonton, 1978), 1.
2. Jane Jacobs, *The Death and Life of Great American Cities* (New York: Random House, 1961).
3. Cf. Albert Z. Guttenberg, "A Multiple Land Use Classification System," *Journal of the American Institute of Planners* (August 1959),143–150; and Gerald Hodge and Robert McCabe, eds., "Land Use Classification and Coding in Canada: An Appraisal," *Plan Canada* (June 1968), 1–28.
4. Guttenberg, "Multiple Land Use."
5. Hans Blumenfeld, "The Conflict between the Two Functions of the Street," *Contact* 13, no. 2/3 (1981), 11–15.
6. F. Stuart Chapin Jr., *Urban Land Use Planning*, 2nd ed. (Champaign-Urbana: University of Illinois Press, 1964), 376ff.
7. Ontario, Department of Municipal Affairs, *Three Steps to Tomorrow* (Toronto, 1972), 44.
8. Cf. Brijesh Mathier, "Community Planning and the New Public Health," *Plan Canada* 29, no. 4 (July 1989), 35–44.
9. David Witty, "Healthy Communities," *City Magazine* 12, no. 4 (Fall 1991), 20–23.
10. John Sewell, *The Shape of the City* (Toronto: University of Toronto Press, 1993).
11. Joel Garreau, *Edge City: Life on the New Frontier* (New York: Doubleday, 1991).
12. Andres Duany et al., *Towns and Town-making Principles* (Cambridge, MA: Harvard University Press, 1991); and James Howard Kunstler, *Home from Nowhere* (New York: Simon and Schuster, 1996).
13. Sym van der Ryn and Peter Calthorpe, *Sustainable Communities: A New Design Synthesis for Cities, Suburbs and Towns* (San Francisco: Sierra Club Books, 1986).
14. Kirkpatrick Sale, "Bioregionalism—A New Way to Treat the Land," *The Ecologist* 14, no. 4 (1984), 167–173.
15. Hok Lin Leung, *City Images: An Internal View* (Kingston, Ont.: Ronald P. Frye and Co., 1992), 271ff.
16. Clara Greed, "Promise or Progress: Women in Planning," *Built Environment* 22, no. 1 (1996), 9–21. Other useful references are Leonie Sandercock and Ann Forsyth, "A Gender Agenda: New Directions for Planning Theory," *Journal of the American Planning Association* 58 (Winter 1992), 49–59; and Beth Moore Milroy, "Feminist Critiques of Planning for Work: Considerations for Future Planning," *Plan Canada* 31, no. 6 (November 1991), 15–22.

Chapter 7 Steps in the Plan-Making Process

In order to be able to make a plan we must be able to predict; in order to be able to predict we must know; in order to know we must develop hypotheses or theories; in order to establish theories we must obtain and classify facts; we must observe.

John Dakin, 1960

When a community sets out to make a new plan, or to amend its existing plan, it is embarking on a process with a recognized set of steps and characteristics; it embarks on what is known as the **planning process.** The plan that the community adopts is, thus, the culmination of a process. In other words, the activity of community planning comprises both a plan and a process, each of which, in its own way, is an essential element. Unlike other kinds of decision making in a community, planning is not aimed at finding a solution to a particular problem. Community planning is better characterized as preventative than as remedial in its approach to community problems. As such, it requires time for deliberation, analysis, and design, as well as for the involvement of diverse community interests; that is, there needs to be time for the process to be undertaken.

The community-planning process is, essentially, two planning processes. One is the **normative process** that a community, usually through its municipal government, undertakes to determine its needs, objectives, acceptable courses of action, and whom to involve in the deliberations regarding its plan. The other is the **technical process,** primarily followed by the professional planners, or their counterparts, of studying the community and designing the plan. Both of these processes are, in turn, based on a long-standing theoretical view or concept of what constitutes a good planning process for a community.

In this chapter, we shall describe each of these planning processes. We start, however, with the conceptual view, since it constitutes something of an ideal against which planners measure actual community-planning efforts. The normative and technical processes will be discussed in terms of both their parallels and their differences. Some significant new variations on traditional processes are introduced in a concluding section.

THE CONCEPT OF A COMMUNITY-PLANNING PROCESS

One popular analogy that is used to describe the community-planning process to those new to the idea is that it involves the same sorts of decisions that go into choosing a daily wardrobe. There are, of course, certain similarities—assessing the occasion, considering the possibilities, and making a choice between alternatives—but the community-planning process has some distinctive differences. Indeed, the community-planning process is notably different from other planning tasks—personal, corporate, or institutional—in that it involves planning for and with a community.

The community with which community planning is concerned must be perceived both as a physical community of buildings, streets, and open spaces and as a human community of individual people, groups, and social institutions. Each of these facets of community obliges special consideration in the planning process. On the one hand, the physical community is the substance of the community-planning process. The types of buildings that are built, their location, and their relation to one another and to streets and open space are the outcome of the process. The inherent permanence of physical structures means that the choices made by community planners are long-range in nature; the results of city-building, as we noted in the opening chapters, persist long into the future. Furthermore, the physical community is never completely built: it grows, ages, deteriorates, and is transformed by successive development projects. It also comprises unique districts and neighbourhoods, each of which has its own integrity and which, in combination, constitute the character and image that belongs to the particular community. In the terms used by planners, the planning for a community must comprehend both the parts and the whole of the city; that is, it must be comprehensive in its outlook.

The human community, on the other hand, is the recipient of the outcome of the planning process, as well as the proponent in that process. People initiate, manage, deliberate upon, and decide on the results of the planning process. Thus, the diverse values, objectives, and interests that are inherent in any community become part of the process. This diversity ensures that community planning must deal with a multiplicity of objectives, and this alone differentiates the process from that of most other planning efforts. Whether it be the planning of a daily wardrobe, the production schedule of a manufacturing plant, the deployment of military weapons, or the fund-raising strategy of a charitable organization, the objectives are clear-cut and limited in number. Often only one main objective motivates such efforts.

The frequent calls for community planning to employ the practices of business corporations, or those used in such major engineering and scientific triumphs as space exploration, fail to recognize the diversity of objectives with which community planning contends. The competition for attention to various goals that this implies requires the process to select the courses of action reasonably, not capriciously: that is, the community planner not only must take into account all of the important ends of the whole community, but must also maximize the attainment of those ends that are considered most important. What developed in community planning to meet these criteria is called the **rational-comprehensive planning process.** It is simply a logical decision-making process suited to the diverse needs of communities in their plan-making efforts.

The Rational-Comprehensive Process

Up until the 1950s, the process of community planning was much less systematic than it is today. In its earliest days, it was practised in traditional (architectural) design terms, with the aim of producing aesthetically pleasing and efficient layouts. In turn, the public health and housing reform movements provided planning with an extensive set of statutory controls. This led increasingly to intervention in land development and use in order to minimize negative effects that the actions of one land user had upon the interests of others. As we discussed in Chapter 5, planners then put more and more stress on community planning as a tool for achieving efficiency in city-building.

The "efficient" use of land in a city carries with it the assumption that the planner can demonstrate attainment of this aim. Further, the idea of efficiency is a rational concept. Increasingly, traditional planning approaches were found to be deficient in their rationality; they were found often to be aesthetically, politically, or administratively arbitrary. The functioning of cities was not understood, and little thought was given to the process of formulating land-use policies in a pluralistic society.

The foremost attempt at systematizing the community-planning approach was formulated by the U.S. planners Meyerson and Banfield in the early 1950s. The rational-comprehensive approach, as it has since been called, contends that a planner would be acting rationally by following three general steps: (1) to consider all the possible courses of action; (2) to identify and evaluate all of the consequences following from the adoption of each alternative; and (3) to select the alternative that would most likely achieve the community's most valued objectives.[1] Although this process has had its critics, it still remains the general basis for community-planning practice today. It is, of course, greatly simplified in these three steps and deserves to be more fully elaborated.

Canadian planner Ira Robinson melds the initial formulation of Meyerson and Banfield with the adaptations suggested by later planning thinkers and comes up with the following five steps:[2]

1. Identify the problem or problems to be solved, the needs to be met, the opportunities to be seized upon, and the goals of the community to be pursued, and translate the broad goals into measurable operational criteria.
2. Design alternative solutions or courses of action (plans, policies, programs) to solve the problems and/or fulfil the needs, opportunities, or goals, and predict the consequences and effectiveness of each alternative.
3. Compare and evaluate the alternatives with each other and with the predicted consequences of unplanned development, and choose, or help the decision maker or decision-making body to choose, that alternative whose probable consequences would be preferable.
4. Develop a plan of action for effectuating or implementing the alternative selected, including budgets, project schedules, regulatory measures, and the like.
5. Maintain the plan on a current and up-to-date basis, based on feedback and review of information to adjust steps 1 through 4 above.

This concept of the planning process is sometimes called **synoptic** in that it provides for all the principal parts of the community, physical and social, to be brought into the picture. Another term, more common today, that captures the same spirit of planning is **holistic**. This view has venerable roots, drawing as it does upon the work of Patrick Geddes around the beginning of this century. Geddes put great stress on being able to see, to know, and to appreciate the basic facets of any community before making plans for it. His view always encompassed the people, the geography, and the economy of the community, and he advised planners "that survey and diagnosis must precede treatment."[3] Just as important to Geddes was that the knowledge and appreciation of the community obtained by the planners should be shared with the community.

Thus, the community-planning process is not only a logical process for decision making; it is also a participatory process. It obliges the planner and the policy maker to keep all the items of a proposal for change—a new shopping centre, for example—and the issues that enter into their analyses and deliberations clearly in view. And the community, for its part, can and should become closely involved in vetting both the knowledge from the surveys and the issues raised in the decision making. The ideal of Geddes has not always been promoted assiduously by planners. But it stands, nevertheless, at the foundation of our modern plan-making processes for Canadian communities.

The Flow of the Process

The rational-comprehensive planning process appears, with its several steps, to be a sequential process, with the community moving progressively from the identification of problems to the implementation of projects. Indeed, the community traverses all those steps, as shown in Figure 7.1, but not in strict sequence. In actual practice, many of the phases are linked to preceding phases by **feedback loops** (of which a few possibilities are indicated on the diagram). These serve, in addition to helping in the essential review of the outcome of the planning process during the implementation phase, to inform and adjust the initial phases of problem identification and goal articulation.

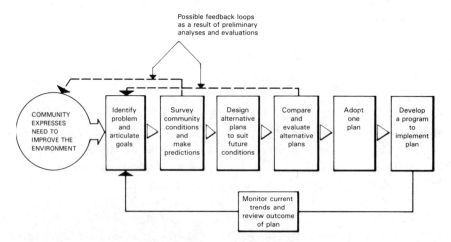

FIGURE 7.1 **General Model of the Community Planning Process**
Although the process is essentially linear, there is ample opportunity for review of decisions and choices at the various steps and for reiteration of all or part of the process.

The secondary feedback loops permit conclusions reached at one stage in the process to be re-examined, and part, or even all, of the process to be reiterated. These feedback loops allow for the difficulties encountered in forecasting and the normal debate over the outcomes of planning proposals. A community may find, for example, that the population forecasts indicate only limited growth; this would then limit the development alternatives for the community. Or it may find that alternative plans, while meeting overall community goals, are objectionable to certain neighbourhoods. This may cause a reappraisal of goals that had been decided upon earlier. Formal community-planning processes, prescribed in planning legislation, allow for some of these feedbacks in specified review phases. But mostly the evaluations, reviews, and reiteration take place informally, and the need for them is readily recognized by those community members and groups involved.

THE NORMATIVE PROCESS OF PLANNING COMMUNITY LAND USE

The actual process a community goes through in planning its land use approximates the conceptual or rational process described above, but may deviate from the sequence or accord special weight to certain steps. The main reason for this is that land-use patterns of communities stem from the outcomes of various social, economic, and political behaviour. Myriad decisions by individuals, groups, businesses, institutions, and governments are involved in the use to which the parcels of land in a community are put. Each of these "actors" behaves in the context of individual and shared values. Since there is never a perfect match of individual and community values in land use, one might say that the process of planning community land use is concerned to a large degree with determining **norms** by which the various value orientations may be reconciled. Thus, it is a normative process: it both recognizes and intervenes in the value system of community members.

It follows that the place given to the identification and articulation of goals is bound to be more prominent in actual community planning. Indeed, any steps in the process that invoke the need to define goals for the community plan or to evaluate whether the plan will attain stated goals will assume more importance and visibility the more a community plans. The technical aspects, the analyses, and the administrative requirements of the plan are less subject to community debate. Almost of necessity, then, as a community plan it may need to allow for many feedback loops in the process of refining goals and planning proposals. Let us examine briefly how the process is initiated and the arrangements that are made for its conduct in actual community settings.

The Determinants of Land Use

The planning process in a community is initiated by the actions of individuals and groups, in both the private and the public sector, who desire to occupy and/or improve some part of the community's land base. These actions range over a host of possibilities, such as the redevelopment of an old residential area into an apartment complex, the acquisition of marshland for a conservation area, and the upgrading of a local road into an arterial highway. The outcomes of these actions may not necessarily result in a desired pattern of land use from the point of view of the community. This is true for the countless other initiatives that occur regarding the location and pattern of land use.

A community-planning process is put in place, so to speak, to harmonize the various factors and forces that determine land use. The determinants of land use may be categorized into three types according to their value orientation—that is, those motivated primarily by economic values, those by social values, and those by public interest values. We shall examine each of these briefly; however, it should be noted that seldom are land-use decisions the result of only one of these determinants. Not only do the individuals and groups who participate combine all the basic values to some degree, but also many land-use decisions that affect each other evolve concurrently.

Economic Determinants

The land use of a community is influenced by economic forces operating both outside the community and within its boundaries. External economic forces are the trends and conditions in the larger economy in which the community exists. They act mainly through the demand for the goods and services supplied by the community and may affect land use in several ways. They may account for the investment in key establishments for manufacturing, commercial, or institutional use and, thus, in the buildings they use and the land they occupy. This is most obvious in a community dominated by a major manufacturing plant or public institution. These uses often require large amounts of land in strategic locations. Since the decisions regarding the future of these large establishments are made usually outside the community, they may not always reflect the wishes of residents and there may not be unanimity in the community about privileges that might be accorded these land users. Two other ways that external economic forces influence land use are in the amount and rate of land development. If the regional economy is expanding, for example, this may call for more land to be developed for houses and stores, parks and schools. Moreover, the rate at which the larger economy is operating—whether in fast growth or stagnation—will influence the rate at which land undergoes development and buildings are built upon it.

While external forces affect the composition and vitality of the economy, localized forces determine most of the land-use arrangements and the physical character of the community. This is done through the forces of supply and demand acting through the local land market. The land (or real estate) in a community may be looked on as a commodity to be bought and sold and has a value because of its potential to produce income through some future sale or development. The actual market value of land varies between parcels in the same area and between different areas in the community. Each parcel of land is unique according to its location, size, shape, form of building space, tenure, etc. And, as John Hitchcock notes, when it comes to housing, types of households differ and make different demands for housing.[4] Housing is also strongly affected in its value and usability by the activities on other parcels of land, especially those in the same vicinity. Thus, certain locations and districts come to be valued for one kind of use, such as those preferred for residential neighbourhoods, while other uses find the attributes of other areas more appealing.

In any event, land is usually owned by a large number of different persons or organizations and developed by still others, all with their own personal aims, resources, and concerns. Take, for example, the process of creating housing in a community, the largest use of urban land. It involves landowners, the homebuilding industry, brokers and facilitators, and the home buyer. All these actors are in the private sector, furthermore. If the new housing is to be built on raw land, the interrelations among these actors could resemble those shown in Figure 7.2. Most of the same actors are also involved in converting already built-up land to other uses. Depending upon the planning proposals, some part of the array of values represented by these actors will enter into the planning process. It goes without saying that they seldom coincide with one another. Thus, a critical aspect of the normative planning process is to find a balance for the diverse economic interests in community land development.

Social Determinants

Although it often seems that all land-use decisions in a community are stated in dollar terms, many are influenced primarily by social factors. There are two main ways in which social factors influence land uses: one is

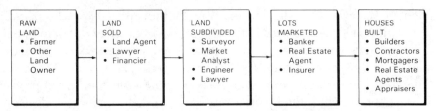

FIGURE 7.2   **Steps in the Conversion of Land to Residential Use**
In the process by which raw land is converted to use for housing, many persons and groups have an economic interest.

the social "ecology" of the patterns of residence and the other the social response to proposed changes in the community. People have strong feelings about the ways in which their community or neighbourhood is arranged and functions. These are rooted in values that, not infrequently, oppose values of economy and efficiency, as citizen protests against planning proposals show.

Among the aggregation of people who constitute a community, one finds a process in which homogeneous units cluster together. Residential districts may form through ethnic, cultural, or income compatibility of populations, and they, in turn, may choose to live away from commercial or manufacturing areas. Of course, the reverse may also happen. It is important to note that segregation of uses and districts is a continuous process of sorting the community into physically and geographically distinct parts according to values, attitudes, and social interests.

The prestige (and/or economic power) of some groups of people or firms, accordingly, leads to a hierarchy of areas in the community. Thus, some residential areas enjoy more prestige than others, and some commercial areas are more favourably located than others. The results of this sorting are not always beneficial for the living conditions and economic prospects of all residents. The tensions that this can create between areas of a community become part of the milieu of social values with which planning must frequently contend. Interest groups may be formed, such as those of ratepayers, businesses, and tenants. They may express concerns over the effects on land values and rents, but as often as not, they voice concern over continued social cohesion of the areas in which they live or do business.

During the past two decades, there has been a noticeable increase in the number of social values that community planners must take into account. This has happened, notably, with respect to three issues: (1) the quality of the natural environment, (2) the importance of the historic features of the community, and (3) the needs and concerns of women. These issues are often advocated vigorously in various land-use decision-making arenas by individual citizens and groups who may have no direct interest in the affected lands through ownership, tenancy, or proximity of residence. Each of these issues areas, thus, introduces additional values about the substance and form of communities into plan-making. Not infrequently during such deliberations, flaws are revealed in the planning process itself. Canadian women planners have noted, for example, that women and other groups tend to be excluded from involvement in the planning process because of the time of day meetings are scheduled or the lack of transportation or the unavailability of child care.[5] The community-planning process is being challenged to reconcile not only economic and social values but also differences in social values. With the increasing diversity of community populations, the latter challenge is certain to increase.

Public-Interest Determinants

Community planning not only mediates between private land-use interests; it is also an active determinant of land-use patterns on behalf of the public interest; that is, out of the values and institutions of community planning have arisen principles and standards for the location of both public and private facilities and the design of public spaces. The provision of water and sewer systems, the design and alignment of roads, and the allocation of park space are three ways in which public-interest factors control, or at least pre-condition, land-use planning. Whereas the private economic and social interests who participate in the community-planning process generally advocate on behalf of a single piece of land or a single issue (such as the environment), it is up to the community's planners to prepare plans that ensure sound, amenable development for the community as a whole.

The public interest, perhaps not surprisingly, is not based on a single entity or set of values. Although the local government of the community is usually the most important entity in this realm, other jurisdictions may also be involved. For example, the local or regional school board, the housing authority, the public utilities commission, and the provincial ministry of highways are some of the other public bodies one encounters. Each has its own mandate to interpret what is in the public-interest in land-use matters within the community. Usually, the views of these other bodies are mediated through the local government and, nominally, it is the local governmental structure—the mayor, council, planning board, planning staff—that is the focal point for implementing public interest matters in land use. Provincial statutes for planning and municipal affairs delegate this responsibility to local governments. It is largely up to the local government to decide the manner in which it will exercise this responsibility.

The Importance of Goals

The process of framing a community plan is, in large measure, a process concerned with sorting out the values and attitudes in the spheres of each of the three main determinants, and putting in place what amounts to a commitment toward future land-use decisions that encourages these interests to act in harmony. That process, as we have indicated, is normative— that is, it both recognizes and intervenes in the behaviour of community members. Moreover, community planning comprises more than sorting out differences in current viewpoints about land use. It is primarily concerned with establishing a context for the future land-use pattern to evolve. The plan that emerges from the process is a statement of community goals and aspirations for its future physical form.

One of the central notions of modern community planning is that the identification of goals is an integral part of the planning process. Such other city-building activities as engineering and architecture, or such civic policy activities as transportation and recreation, tend to begin with a limited number of goals already given. In planning, the identification of goals and the design of courses of action to achieve them tend to proceed in a symbiotic fashion.[6]

Planning, as we noted at the outset of this book, derives initially either from the need to solve problems or from the desire to achieve ambitions or aspirations. The proposed solution to a community problem carries with it a goal to be achieved. For example, the shortage of parking space that promotes the idea of a proposed parking garage in a downtown area may be seen as consistent with the goal of maintaining the vitality of the downtown area. The desire of a community to provide adequate park space for each of its neighbourhoods, conversely, carries with it the need to designate specific areas that may be used for parks, and to design those parks. Thus, goals may justify proposed solutions to problems as well as stimulate a solution. In the actual planning process, regardless of whether it is initiated by a goal or a problem, the focus alternates from one to the other as goals, designs, or project ideas are refined.[7] Indeed, one planner sees the planning process as a progressive refinement of goals into projects.[8] Or, to put this another way, the schematic presentation of the planning process shown in Figure 7.1 has as its second step "goal articulation," and it may be fairly said that the entire process is one in which goals are being articulated.

Goals are basic to the planning process and, thus, become a cornerstone of the plan for the community. A plan is sometimes referred to as a statement of goals. The importance of goals stems from the fact that they provide the rationale by which the community, through its plan, may justify what needs are to be served and also whose needs are to be served by the proposed land-use arrangements.[9] Given the likelihood of competition among land users for some locations in the community and of conflicts between the values of different interests, goals are important because they represent the resolution that has been made in such controversies. They represent choices among the various value positions. Goals, in effect, say, "When we encounter this situation we will probably act this way for these reasons."[10] In addition, goals represent both a general commitment of the community to long-term planning and a willingness to communicate these aims to all members of the community so that they may participate more effectively.

Before broaching the other important areas of the normative process, it will be helpful to sort out a few semantic difficulties. The term "goal" is used in a variety of ways in planning, along with a variety of such synonyms as aims, ends, purposes, objectives, and policies. Some distinctions should be made, in particular, between goals, objectives, and policies, because each reflects different facets of the planning process. A "goal" refers to an ideal, a condition, or a quality to be sought in the community's physical development. It might be to provide a maximum of access to the waterfront for all members of the community. Thus, a goal in community planning expresses a desirable direction for progress. An "objective" is, by contrast, something that the community seeks to attain; it is more like a target in that it can be reached. While the purpose of a goal is explicit, that of an objective tends to be implicit. For instance, to elaborate upon the waterfront example above, a community may have the objective to provide a walkway for public use along its waterfront. A "policy" may be defined as the preferred course of action to achieve an objective or goal. At its root, policy is about choices made by or on behalf of people; it is the course of action the local government thinks will be acceptable to the diverse interests of the community. Thus, in regard to its waterfront, a community's policy may be to acquire a strip along the waterfront for the purpose of constructing a public walkway. This example not only illustrates how goals, objectives, and policies form a sort of hierarchy of community intent, but also how they represent the progressive translation of general ideas into operational targets and then to actual physical projects.

The Roles of Plan-Makers

The goals one finds enshrined in a plan for a community usually seem self-evident and uncontroversial. Yet a brief pondering of the diverse community interests involved in the outcome of land-use decisions reveals the maze of controversy that frequently arises in setting objectives. One of the main reasons for making a plan is to provide a basis for debate and discussion among competing interests to resolve present and future land-use conflicts.

Traditionally, plan-making was considered primarily a technical task to be carried out by professional planners and/or by a small group of knowledgeable citizens. The goals for achieving basic health, safety, and amenity seemed then to be self-evident. Today, the decision-making processes for planning are more open and democratic, with, as a consequence, many more people involved in plan-making. As well, the issues have become more complex. Plan-makers thus face a dual problem: on the one hand, they must devise objectives and criteria that are relevant to a greater cross-section the community, while on the other hand, they must devise meaningful procedures for consultation about goals.[11]

In the Canadian community situation, it is the local or municipal government that is ultimately responsible for setting the objectives and making the plan. This means, in jurisdictional terms, the elected council of the municipality. But while there must be some ultimate plan-making authority, the issue is more complex than that. Community planning, as we have been stressing, is a process as well as a function of local government. It is a process that might be likened to a cycle of behaviour involving the following four general phases: (1) experiencing needs and wants, (2) defining goals, (3) planning alternatives, and (4) deciding and acting.[12] Since this is a process involving many individuals and groups, it is probably more realistic to see it taking the form of several successive cycles, say the form of a spiral, as the concerns of various interests are progressively resolved.

As a process occurring under community auspices, it must have a visible, identifiable pattern of roles and responsibilities. Further, as a process that involves both normative, or political, judgements and technical judgements, it requires plan-makers who can cover each aspect as well as those who can link them together.

There are three principal plan-makers in most Canadian communities and their roles correspond to the three distinct needs of the planning process: (1) to decide on the plan's goals and content, (2) to facilitate the public process, and (3) to provide technical assistance to plan-makers.

1. Deciding on the Plan.   To become the official policy of the community, the plan will need to be validated by the local governing body. This role falls to the municipal council (or its counterpart). The council is the ultimate arbiter of what is acceptable to the diverse interests within the community as well as what is in the best interest of the community. It almost goes without saying that the process of resolution at this level takes place within the "political climate" that characterizes the community. The planning policies that the council deems acceptable will reflect what is acceptable to elements within the community that wield influence. The council's role may be linked to presiding over the final cycle of community planning in which the plan is produced.

2. Facilitating the Public Process.   Prior to deciding on the plan, the process demands that there be broad public deliberation on what goes into it. In the typical Canadian community, this phase is presided over by an advisory planning body established by the local council. These advisory bodies are called planning boards in some parts of Canada and planning commissions in other parts; such bodies may simply be a standing committee of the council. They play an essential role in the community-process in examining private and public values, attitudes and preferences regarding land use and its planning. It is their task to receive, consider, and refine planning proposals and, then, to advise the council on how to proceed.

In the normal course of plan-making, the advisory board provides advice to council only after it has deliberated over the proposals made by various interests in the community, the responses of other interests (e.g., the province, a regional government), and advice from the technical staff. In this sense the advisory board links the political (i.e., normative) and technical sides of planning.

3. Providing Technical Assistance.   Planning proposals usually involve issues that require technical study and analysis. The technical sphere of planning is presided over by professional planners. For example, a proposal for a shopping centre requires an assessment of the effects of traffic on surrounding areas and road arteries, while the proposal for a subdivision near a water course requires an assessment of environmental effects. Such studies are normally carried out by the planning staff of the municipality or by consultants commissioned to assist them.

The issues and implications for the pattern of land use in a community have long since passed those of health, safety, convenience, and amenity that stimulated the increased numbers of of technical advisors in the planning process around the turn of the century. Planners must be able to grasp the way in which market forces tend to allocate and arrange land uses, the way in which cultural factors affect land-use patterns, as well as a variety of other concerns, including the natural environment, energy, housing, and heritage planning. The role of the planner, it has been said, is to provide a basis for a "*balanced* consideration of economic, socially rooted and public interest factors throughout the land-use planning process."[13] This balance is provided through systematic study of issues raised by various interests, on the one hand, and, on the other, through the design of alternative courses of action. In the latter endeavours, the planner tends to structure the planning process by directing the attention of the planning board and council to selected courses of action that respect private and community interests. This, then, involves the planner at several stages throughout the planning process.

Tensions in the Planning Process

The actual planning process a community goes through (the normative process) varies in two major ways from the rational-comprehensive model. The first is the need to designate specific groups and individuals to preside over certain steps in the process. These appointments not only carry with them specific duties and powers—as, for example, the advisory planning board—but also are composed of people with their own personal and professional backgrounds. The second has to do with the substance of the social agenda that the plan-makers are asked to consider. For example, if planning proposals are contentious, they may require several iterations of the planning decision cycle before goals are articulated clearly and discussion of alternatives can proceed. It is also common to find that results of analyses presented by the professional planner tend to throw a new light on the issues.

The community-planning process has been criticized for being too optimistic, both about our analytical capabilities and about the altruism of community members.[14] A large part of the criticism centres on the difficulty, if not impossibility, of the process being truly comprehensive. In other words, can the planners (including the planning board and council) really take into account all the parts of the community and foresee all the consequences attending upon all the alternative courses of action? There is, of course, validity in this critique, and it contributes to one of the inherent tensions in the community-planning process.

Another tension concerns the importance given to rational analysis: identifying problems, translating goals into measurable criteria, predicting consequences, and evaluating alternatives, to draw upon Robinson's terms. These all are, or could be, the subject for rigorous analysis. Indeed, as our knowledge of the functioning and growth of communities has grown in recent decades, it has become possible to carry out more sophisticated surveys and diagnoses of community ills and planning proposals alike. But an almost inevitable condition appears in the wake of scientific applications in the community-planning process: more information usually exposes further gaps in our knowledge, as well as uncertainty over our predictive powers.

FIGURE 7.3   **Protest at Burrard View School**
Inherent tensions in the planning process are exposed when neighbourhood residents dispute the decisions of planning bodies. *Source:* Photo courtesy of *North Shore News.*

Community planning, as with other public policy making, moves with difficulty from objectives to operations. This means that, having identified *which* needs are to be served, it becomes necessary to translate those into *whose* needs are to be served. If, for example, a new expressway is deemed necessary to serve the entire community, its actual location will impinge on some neighbourhoods and some groups of people in the community more than on others. (See Figure 7.3.) Here we encounter one of the most fundamental tensions in community planning—the tension between fact and values. Difficult value-based judgements must be made if the planning process is to progress toward community goals. Rational analyses, by providing relevant facts and information, bring planners to this threshold but do not carry them over it. This is because beyond facts lie preferences, and to this point, the scientific approaches to sorting out personal and group preferences are likely to be of little use to community planners. A Gallup poll approach, for instance, does not work well within a diversity of community values.

Thus, the community-planning process involves several inherent tensions. They are a reality of the process and should not be denied or obscured. The most significant of these derive from the following dichotomies encountered in planning communities:

1. **Neighbourhood/City.** The final outcome of planning (the actual projects) occurs at the neighbourhood level of a community; thus, judgements arise regarding the status of the values of people in local areas against those of the entire community. The "not-in-my-back yard" (NIMBY) syndrome is evidence of this tension (see also Chapter 15).
2. **Long range/Short range.** As the time frame increases, the degree of accuracy of predictions decreases, and further the commitment of the community for projects well into the future will compete with desires to solve immediate problems.
3. **Ameliorative/Developmental.** The nature and pace of change may either be forced on a community by external circumstances or be sought by a community to achieve a certain environmental quality; either direction is a normal source of debate.
4. **Fact/Value.** Establishing the facts of trends, conditions, and impacts relevant to planning actions is different from establishing the social objectives of what might be done through community planning.

That the rational-comprehensive model of planning contains these "soft" areas for planners and decision makers indicates the complexity of planning for communities. Moreover, the same tensions exist for any other model of the planning process that might be invoked. The process of community planning is not simple, in any case. A major advantage of the rational-comprehensive approach is that it allows a holistic process to encompass these tensions. Importantly, the community-planning process should be open and accessible to community members, so that the judgements that have to be made in regard to each of the above tensions may be reviewed and debated if necessary.

Inherent in public decisions about land use is the notion of **intervention.** Both with regard to private profit making and social interests and to other agencies with public-interest mandates, the means of intervention must be developed to resolve the tensions on behalf of the community. Such a process of resolution takes place within the "political climate" that characterizes the community. In other words, the content of the plan and the means of intervention will reflect what is acceptable to those elements in the community that wield influence. The underlying tension in the normative planning process involves the need to bring together the various interests sharing a concern, in the best interests of the community. (For a broader discussion of the process of resolving tensions, see Part Three, especially Chapter 14.)

The community plan that results from the process thus becomes a record of the deliberations of the community in regard to the achievement of its goals. The judgements made about any of the inherent tensions should reflect a community consensus, something that may not be easily achieved if the plan invokes fundamental cleavages. However, once this consensus is achieved, the plan should become a matter of public record of what was agreed upon, as well as the basis for decisions. As one U.S. planner has put it, "If we could all remember what we did and why we did it, we could do very well without a plan."[15]

TECHNICAL STEPS IN THE PLANNING PROCESS

Although the actual planning process may not follow precisely the steps of the rational-comprehensive model, it proceeds with an underlying sense of rationality. This is largely attributable to the studies and analyses that have become a standard underpinning of the various steps in the process. The professional planner, who has the obligation to bring all relevant facts to the plan-makers' attention, structures a parallel planning process. It complements the normative process and provides information for all those involved in plan-making—the planning board, the council, citizens, and groups—to understand the problem and the policy implications of the analysis.

The technical planning process has three main phases: diagnosis, prediction, and evaluation. These phases approximate the three main decision-making phases of the rational model—problem identification, design of alternative plans, and evaluation of alternatives. This may give the impression of a sequential, step-by-step process, but as with the earlier descriptions, the steps in the technical process may overlap and be repetitive. For example, it is common for the professional planner (hereafter referred to, simply, as the planner) to be asked to evaluate planning proposals submitted by developers or public agencies, thus initiating the evaluative phase. This may necessitate going back through the previous phases, or the process may be completed at this point. It should also be noted that the same phases and their studies and analyses are applicable regardless of whether the plan-making effort is for a single project or the entire community.

The material below is organized according to the sequence of basic phases in order to convey a sense of the coherence that does exist in the planning process, despite its variations. The technical planning process is based on objective studies. As planners have sought precision and clarity in their analyses, they have turned to quantitative methods and statistics. In this section, we do no more than outline these and place them within the context of plan-making as a process; for a full description, the reader should turn to texts devoted to planning analyses.[16]

Diagnostic Studies

The planning process is invoked most frequently by the desire to solve a problem in the development of a community. The goals may be the reduction of traffic congestion in the downtown area or the increase in the supply of housing for low-income families; each community has its own distinctive set of problems. Normally, the planner would initiate efforts to identify and delineate the problem—to *diagnose* it. The term is used in the same sense that a medical doctor diagnoses a patient's reported ailment—that is, he or she identifies the nature and scope of a medical problem. The planner, analogously, employs a number of diagnostic tools that will describe both the extent of the planning problem and the community context into which it fits.

Planning studies at this stage are, essentially, descriptive. The most common methods the planner will employ fall into the realms of descriptive statistics and survey research. Using the two problem examples cited above—downtown traffic congestion and housing shortages—will help to demonstrate the diagnostic approach. In the case of traffic congestion, the planner would seek data on current conditions: the volume of traffic on affected streets, evidence of delays at certain points and certain times, the degree of use of parking facilities, and possible associated problems, such as businesses affected or the effect on pedestrian flows. In the case of housing shortages, the planner would seek data on the size and composition of the current housing stock, its condition, and vacancy rate, as well as data about those people reported to need housing, including family size, composition, age, and income. In both these types of planning problems, the planner would also seek data on past conditions.

Analytical Dimensions

There are two basic sets of dimensions of planning diagnoses. The first is the **substantive,** the "what" of the study. The second is the **procedural,** the "how" of the study. The substantive dimensions comprise three main types: population, the physical environment, and the economy. All three recur throughout the various analytical phases of the planning process. In the diagnostic phase, the planner is mainly concerned with identifying who or what is involved and at what scale. The data are, thus, mostly numerical counts: the number of people, dwelling units, automobiles, jobs. Alternatively, the average value of such data may be sought, e.g., average income, years of schooling, age of dwelling. At this level of analysis, interrelationships between characteristics may also be helpful, such as persons

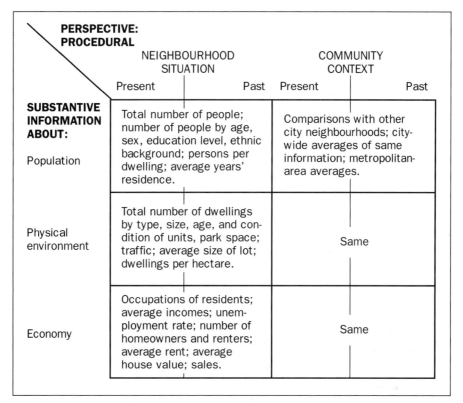

PERSPECTIVE: PROCEDURAL	NEIGHBOURHOOD SITUATION		COMMUNITY CONTEXT	
SUBSTANTIVE INFORMATION ABOUT:	Present	Past	Present	Past
Population	Total number of people; number of people by age, sex, education level, ethnic background; persons per dwelling; average years' residence.		Comparisons with other city neighbourhoods; city-wide averages of same information; metropolitan-area averages.	
Physical environment	Total number of dwellings by type, size, age, and condition of units, park space; traffic; average size of lot; dwellings per hectare.		Same	
Economy	Occupations of residents; average incomes; unemployment rate; number of homeowners and renters; average rent; average house value; sales.		Same	

FIGURE 7.4   **Types of Information Used in Neighbourhood Planning Analyses**
The planner seeks information about the population, the economic milieu, and the physical features of a neighbourhood. Data showing present conditions and past tendencies allow forecasts to be made. Information about other neighbourhoods is used to compare present conditions and future prospects.

per dwelling unit, automobiles per employee, persons per unit of land (density). Figure 7.4 indicates typical diagnostic information for a neighbourhood planning problem. If the planning focused on a commercial area or an industrial area, the information types would reflect the characteristics of such areas.

The procedural dimensions reflect how a planner thinks about a planning problem and its analysis. Specifically, integral to the planner's view is the twofold notion of the problem and its larger context, that any specific problem area is part of the surrounding community and may be affected by it, or vice versa. Even if there is no direct connection between the two, knowledge of comparable conditions in other parts of the community can aid in understanding the local situation. The planner also will want to know whether current conditions in a problem situation are stable or changing. For example, the housing in a neighbourhood may change little, but as families age, the use of such facilities as schools and parks may change. Data on past conditions are often as important as those that portray the present in diagnosing whether conditions are improving or worsening.

Data Sources

The most common source of data for diagnostic studies is the Census of Canada, especially those portions dealing with population, housing, and labour force. Every ten years, the census provides a complete set of data for each incorporated city and town; every five years, it provides a limited set of population data. The value of the census lies in its accuracy, complete coverage, and consistency. This provides a community planner with an objective baseline of information at any time, and also with the data to trace trends in information over fairly long periods. It also allows easy comparison among communities throughout the country. One can obtain data for small areas (census tracts) within a city as well.

As useful as the census is to planners, it has relatively large time spans between the publication of its findings. This can be a problem when a community is experiencing high population movements in and out, which may happen between censuses. Moreover, since the census is geared to providing nationally comparable data, it cannot cover distinctive local conditions. The planner, therefore, may need to seek other secondary data sources or to develop primary data sources within and for the community. Another source of data is the property assessment data that is collected in most parts of Canada by provincial agencies. The latter data are highly detailed, based as they are on individual properties. Sometimes quite helpful to the planner are data gathered by other local agencies—for example, planning departments, public utility departments, and school boards.

However, there is hardly a planning problem for which diagnoses or other analyses can be completed on the basis of secondary sources. Each community has unique features, as does each neighbourhood and district. To get a complete picture of a place, it is necessary to gather first-hand information and even to gain first-hand experience. The planner obtains this through field visits, observing the continuous activities and functioning of an area, perhaps at different times of the day or week or year, and speaking informally with its users. Some planners may claim that this is not objective data; however, there is simply no substitute for the personal understanding obtained "on the spot."

The formal, objective approach to such knowledge employs questionnaires and other formal surveys that record observations about an area.

These may take the form of personal interviews with users of an area or facility, such as householders who may be affected by a school closing or shoppers' who may have to deal with reduced parking in a business area. Or they may take the form of inventories of, for example, an area's traffic, a building's condition, or lot coverage. Survey research can yield high-quality information when the research instruments (e.g., a questionnaire) are constructed thoughtfully and with scientific objectivity. The design of the research instrument is, therefore, important in enabling the planner to provide more penetrating observations, as through the use of statistical analyses. There are established methods for survey research that should be used in this regard.

Increasingly, efforts are being made to combine the data obtained from various sources, with the aid of computers, and develop planning information systems. It has always been evident to planners that much useful data exist in files in other departments within the same city, in adjacent cities, and in special-purpose agencies. Nowadays, a good deal of this information is stored in computer files. With today's more flexible computers, data can often be shared. There are still difficulties in combining data from some sources owing to differences in format and dates of collection. Since most planning analyses are for small portions of the entire community, these difficulties are not insuperable and good case-by-case data bases for analysis are possible.

Predictive Studies

In the second phase of the technical planning process, the planner moves from description to prediction; that is, the planner becomes concerned both with predicting what is possible within the context of the problems and with predicting (designing) likely solutions for problems. The first of these facets is largely grounded in such analytic approaches as the prediction of future population levels or economic growth. The second, the design of solutions, goes beyond normal analytic skills and calls for the planner to synthesize the various elements in the problem situation and, possibly, combine them with new elements. One hears, not infrequently, about planning being both an art and a science. In this phase, that is quite evident, for the planner needs to link analysis and design. Because of the elusiveness of the latter, the emphasis here is on the objective analytical methods.

Analytical Approaches

In this phase, the planner draws upon methods of analysis capable of distinguishing the factors involved in the planning problem. On the substantive side, the population, economy, and land uses need to be taken into account in order to predict their outcome should conditions change in the future. The complexity associated with any of the major factors is obvious; even more complex are the relationships among them.

The methods developed to cope with this complexity draw upon the concept of systems analysis. In this view, the various parts of a problem are perceived to be linked, forming a functioning whole or **system.** A system's overall character affects the way in which the separate parts work, so that the parts cannot be adequately understood without understanding the whole. Thus, for example, a neighbourhood may be thought of as a system (more properly, a subsystem of the city system) in which the age composition of the population is linked to the need for housing, the use of schools and parks, and traffic considerations. A particular neighbourhood will also have a distinctive character, in terms of tradition, location, status of residents, etc., which affects the functioning of the various elements within it. Other parts of the city may be similarly perceived. While this approach is persuasive, it must be acknowledged that analytical methods cannot offer us a complete view of the complexity of a city system. However, partial views are available through analytical **models** (the analyst's way of replicating a system) of the economy, population growth, and the housing market, to name the main ones. The planner's tendency to think in terms of interrelationships and interdependencies allows the gaps between partial models to be identified even if not fully understood.

Because of the importance of population growth and change in a community, there is hardly a planning study that does not begin with this factor. Of a variety of methods for forecasting population, the simplest extrapolates into the future data on past population levels by graphical and mathematical means. This often provides the planner with a satisfactory overview of population tendencies. However, the planner may need to understand the role of births, deaths, migration, birth rates, age, income, or ethnicity in regard to a population change in order to plan for a particular client group, such as the elderly, an increasingly common concern. For these needs, the planner will use more extensive data and more elaborate methods. The most useful of these tools is called the **cohort-survival method,** which allows each age cohort for either sex to be forecast separately.

The future of the local economy is important because of its connection with the need for housing, public utilities, and transportation. Economic studies at the city or town level attempt to determine employment opportunities, rather than volume of business. Through the prediction of employment, the planner has a way of linking the economy of a place to the size and needs of the population. Probably the most common type of question raised in regard to a local economy would be one like this: "If we were to get that new factory with its 500 jobs, what effect would it have on the local economy?" The answer to such a question is usually approached through a **community economic base model,** or one of its variations. The foundation of these methods is to estimate the impact of the additional income brought to the community by firms that export their products to other communities and regions (which is the case with most factories). The community economic base model uses the notion of an economic multiplier to estimate the portion of the exporting factory's income that will accrue to the community and thus generate other jobs in the local economy.[17]

Of course, it is not just factories that may be considered "export industries." All forms of activities catering to tourists are almost wholly export-oriented because they serve people from other communities. The same is true for firms in the business districts and shopping centres of cities and towns: a substantial portion of their business volume is due to the purchases of people from the countryside and other communities. There are other more elaborate economic models that may be used in understanding and predicting economic impacts on communities, such as **input-output** and **industrial complex** analyses. Indeed, the tools available for economic analysis are the best developed among those the planner has available. A general note of caution is appropriate at this point, for one frequently hears dramatic multiplier effects claimed by community boosters, such as: "Every job in the tourism industry generates five other jobs in the community." It is extremely rare for new export industries to generate more than one additional job each in the community, and the ratio is often much less.

Less well developed are methods for predicting **land-use changes**. This is especially so at the detailed level of individual properties because here the reasons for land-use decisions and the responses to the decisions of others are affected by the personal outlook of those involved. Analytical approaches to land use thus favour a broader view of the community, such as predicting the amount of residential land that would be needed in light of population growth or economic expansion or the opening up of a new highway. There are also in existence useful models for predicting the impact of a new shopping centre on established businesses.[18] But, all in all, this area of analysis is underdeveloped.

Before leaving this discussion of predictive studies, we should note again that the planner's view of a community is of a linked set of factors. Therefore, by knowing about the changes in one factor, the planner can estimate the changes in another. For example, when the future population of a community is known, the proportion of the population who will be in the labour force or the number of households that compose that population can be deduced. In this way, sometimes known as a **step-down analysis,** estimates can be made of future job levels in the economy and land-use needs for business and industry. Or, stepping down from population to households, estimates can be made of residential land use. Since these relations tend to be transitive, it is also possible to employ a **step-up analysis** to estimate population from a knowledge of the number of jobs expected in the community, such as illustrated in Figure 7.5. The results of

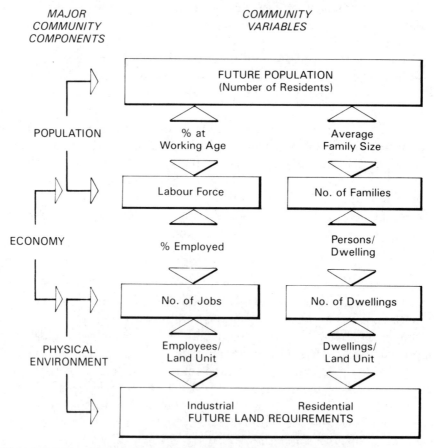

FIGURE 7.5   Chains of Reasoning Employed in Predictive Studies
Planners use the functional relationships between people, jobs, and housing to make predictions about the future population, labour force, number of dwellings, and the land required for various community uses.

such analyses are, of course, limited by the assumptions one makes about the connections between the factors.

Design Approaches

Analytical models and statistical studies will take the planner only so far in predicting possible alternatives for the future arrangement of a community's physical environment. The numerical analyses do not provide a way of combining the various elements into a physical, visual community of houses, stores, streets, parks, etc. That task falls into the realm of land-use design and it involves aesthetics. As Canadian planner Hok Lin Leung has stated, "Modern city planning is rather blind to aesthetics."[19] The concern that citizens often evince about new high-rise buildings or the removal of old trees is as much about aesthetics as anything else in planning. It often seems that today's planners are oblivious to visual and three-dimensional elements of city form and texture, with rare exceptions.[20]

It devolves on the planner to draw upon knowledge gained from experience with urban development and growth to conceive and present possible future physical designs for the community or for some part of it. The physical design task in community planning is one of combining the right physical elements into a unified whole. And what is "right" for the design is informed by (a) the goals and objectives that have been agreed upon, and (b) the results of analyses that have been undertaken. Still, it is a process of synthesis that demands capacities in the planner to "see problems in new ways, to break out of conventional boundaries of thought, to use analogy and metaphor."[21] Proponents of the **New Urbanism** are injecting design metaphors drawn from small towns into city designs.[22]

Although this discussion focuses on the spatial design of the environment, it is important to mention that the design of policies, programs, and regulations for managing community-building involves the planner in much the same process of synthesis. A program for future housing needs also involves imagining future possibilities, for example.

Design is an elusive process to describe, whether it be for planning, architecture, engineering, or the arts. Prominent U.S. planner Kevin Lynch provides some helpful touchstones for our purposes. As Lynch notes, most environmental designs are adaptations of previously used solutions.[23] Many urban forms are now applied customarily in community design, for example, the neighbourhood concept for residential areas or the layouts for local shopping plazas. Most are mere imitations of these stereotypes, but more imaginative solutions may also emerge by improving upon earlier designs. The converse of the adaptive approach is to seek optimum, or "ideal," design solutions that best satisfy the objectives for the community or the project. The design of new towns, like Kitimat, B.C., or the design of innovative housing, like the Habitat '67 project in Montreal, are usually approached in this spirit. Another approach to design may be generated out of the analysis of problems and potentialities of each location. This approach focuses on the present reality and is appropriate where the planned changes will "intrude" on an existing situation, as, for example, in the location of new arterial roads or expressways in already built-up areas. There are a number of variations on these approaches, and the planner will likely gravitate to one or another for the planning problem at hand on the basis of both professional experience and personal preference, for all designing entails a high degree of personal involvement.

In the design phase of planning, there remains the question of how to introduce possible designs into the planning process. This question arises mainly for two reasons: first, there are always numerous possible design solutions to planning problems, and second, choices among designs will be made by both planning boards and citizens. The planner may employ two general strategies: either to generate a limited set of alternatives that reflect the likely range of possibilities or to develop one reasonable possibility and refine it on the basis of verbal deliberations. The first of these strategies may be time-consuming and expensive. Sometimes the planner may have one preferred design; this may save money in the design phase if the selection is good, or incur waste if not. In actual design, some compromise is often made between these two strategies by first identifying the range of basic alternatives and then choosing one for full development. Thus, the professional planner plays a key role in structuring the process for other plan-makers through the designs for the environment, as well as through the programs he or she selects for deliberation.

Evaluative Studies

The third major phase in plan-making consists in deciding among the alternative plans that have been assembled. The planner assists the plan-makers by providing means by which the relative merits of plans can be evaluated. When a community plans, it anticipates and prepares for change. Thus, the plan that is chosen will have consequences, and the planner's evaluative studies aim to determine the nature of those consequences beforehand. There are two general concerns at this phase: how well a plan *attains* the planning goals and objectives of the community, and the *impact*, or cost, that will be incurred in going ahead with the plan. Even if only a single alternative plan is put forward for consideration, it will still need to be evaluated for its success in attaining goals and its community impact.

Impact Assessment

Impact studies have become familiar in the past decade or so, along with rising concern over the effect of new development on the natural environment. Environmental impact assessment procedures are now in widespread use, although they are not required as a matter of course in community planning in Canada as they are in the United States. Such provincial government agencies as highways departments undertake them; many large projects, such as energy projects, require them, both in southern Canada and in the Far North. The scope of environmental concerns in local planning is, if anything, increasing. For example, the British Columbia government recently passed legislation requiring local plans to take into account impacts on fish stocks and fish-spawning streams.

The **environmental impact statement** (EIS as it is often called) attempts to forecast the consequences of a project for its surrounding natural environment, including plant life, wildlife, soils, water, and air conditions. The natural interrelations and interdependencies of phenomena in the environment require that impact assessment capture the ecological interactions. The actual complexity of natural systems as understood by biologists, botanists, and zoologists has, however, defied the development of precise means of environmental impact assessment. The most common approach uses a checklist of potential effects in order to ensure that impacts are not overlooked and that those identified may be pursued in depth. More elaborate are matrix techniques that identify the interactions that occur when a project disturbs one part of the environment. The magnitude of each effect may be included in the matrix, either in absolute terms or on the basis of a rating of the expected impact.[24]

Despite their lack of precision, environmental impact techniques have an intrinsic value in identifying for plan-makers the widespread ramifications of development projects for natural systems. In one respect, this reiterates the importance of natural resource conservation and Patrick Geddes' maxim for planners of generally "no plan before survey." The concerns of environmentalists have also led in the past decade to extending the same ecological concepts into other realms of planning practice. **Social impact assessment** methods have begun to be developed to help determine the effects on people's lives, community functioning, and social and cultural traditions of possible changed conditions resulting from large projects. Such assessments are required prior to the initiation of large projects in the Far North; as well, they are becoming a more common part of the planning scene in other parts of Canada.[25] Indeed, the Environmental Assessment Act in Ontario requires impacts on social, cultural, historic, and economic "environments" to be assessed.

A form of economic impact analysis with strong roots in planning is **cost-benefit analysis.** Developed originally in the 1930s for use in river basin planning, it is now widely used in other planning endeavours. The term "cost-benefit" has become something of a generic phrase in planning to show an awareness that proposed projects carry with them costs as well as benefits and, further, that both the costs and benefits of a project often cannot be quantified into dollar terms. In water resource projects, for example, it was recognized that the costs of displacing people from their homes had many "intangible" costs, as there might also be intangible benefits from the improvements in recreation. It is not difficult to imagine analogous costs and benefits from expressway building, urban renewal, and airport development projects.

It is also not difficult to imagine that as the multitude of factors that the planner tries to take into a cost-benefit reckoning expands to include intangible (but still very real and pertinent) items, the more difficult the summation of costs and benefits becomes. Several variants of the approach have arisen, for example, limiting the reckoning to costs and revenues that can be rendered in dollar terms or broadening it to include an evaluation of effectiveness in achieving specified goals. Planning-programming-budgeting systems (PPBS) are a form of the latter, but the most pertinent to planners is the Planning Balance Sheet developed by Lichfield.[26] It mixes both "hard" and "soft" data about the plan in the effort to include measurements of all its effects. Weights are not assigned to the various impacts; rather, that type of judgement is left where it properly belongs—with the plan-makers.

Plan-Attainment Evaluation

Economic efficiency is the essential criterion of cost-benefit approaches, but planners have never regarded this as the main measure of a plan's worth. The goals and objectives decided on by the community are considered the paramount criteria for evaluation by many planners. In other words, if a plan is to help achieve a community's goals, then the worth of a plan may be looked at in terms of whether it represents progress toward those goals. In response, planners have developed "goals-achievement" evaluation methods. These methods allow plan-makers to compare complete plans without the necessity of disaggregating them as in the Planning Balance Sheet. The best known of these techniques, the **goals-achievement matrix,** was framed by planner Morris Hill[27] and emulated by many others.

The goals-achievement matrix is a way of summarizing overall performance with respect to each goal of each alternative plan. In its simplest form, the columns of the matrix represent the alternative plans or policies being considered; the rows represent the goals and objectives the community has set. Since not all goals are usually considered of equal importance, this method allows each to be weighted to reflect its importance to the community. Further, if some goals have several facets, as is often the case, then each row may be elaborated into several to capture the range of aims. The most thorough approach is to define quantitative measures, or scores, that reflect degrees of success in achieving each goal that could, in turn, be "summed." These may turn out to be only ranked scores, but this still provides a strong base of comparison.[28]

Plan evaluation is a crucial step in plan-making. Not only is it the opportunity to review a plan before its implementation, it is also the phase where an appreciation of the "whole," of the comprehensiveness of the plan, is best obtained. The plan evaluation phase should be taken as a major opportunity for plan-makers to "learn" about their community and its development and the kinds of commitments and trade-offs that are required in order to achieve a better community environment. Two of the most important tasks of the planner are to ensure that there are opportunities for evaluation for other plan-makers, and to provide the means for undertaking such assessments.

THE PLANNING PROCESS AND COMMUNITY LEARNING

Just describing the community-planning process in words, as this chapter has attempted to do, has a number of limitations that are due to the nature of the process. Explicitly, the process is rational, that is, it is promoted as a sensible, logical way to avoid chaotic decision making. The process is also complex, as it involves many decision makers and requires an understanding of elaborate human and physical systems. Less explicitly, the planning process effects change, or intervenes, among community interests on the basis of shared values and attitudes. However, one of the most confounding situations to many plan-makers, including professional planners, occurs when they put forward a planning proposal on which they have spent considerable time deliberating (including having media coverage) only to have, say, a neighbourhood group object just before it is to be adopted. This not-infrequent occurrence results when the neighbourhood perceives the outcome of the planning intervention, but does not accept the overall rationality of the scheme. It testifies to the complexity of the process of effecting change in the community environment.

Planning Issue 7.1

COMMUNITY CHANGE: WHOSE VIEW?

West Vancouver should stay the same.

That was the overwhelming opinion expressed Tuesday evening at the public hearing to consider the municipality's Official Community Plan update.

With the exceptions of West Vancouver's Chamber of Commerce, school board and local real-estate board, most of those attending the meeting at West Vancouver Secondary School showed great resistance to change. They doubted the benefits of future development above the Upper Levels Highway, and were especially unhappy with the prospect of further encroachment of higher density residential development.

The replacement of smaller, older homes with large, high-priced mansions was also lamented by residents, particularly since the older homes have enabled young families to live in West Vancouver.

Most residents concerned about upzoning came from the Ambleside and Dundarave areas where there is a mix of multiple and single-family zones.

"I'm under pressure from residents living on larger lots who want to move to more convenient locations," said planning director Steve Nicholls. "There's pressure from residents themselves, who want to demolish cottages and construct large homes because the land prices have now exceeded the value of those houses."

But the residents charged that the much talked of "pressure" was coming from developers.

Nicholls is now faced with the task of amending the community plan to reflect the concerns expressed.

"One group says it's a 'do nothing plan,' while the other thinks it proposes radical changes," said Nicholls.

Source: Excerpted from "West Vancouver residents say no to change," *North Shore News,* March 6, 1990.

In Planning Issue 7.1 we have an example that demonstrates differences between the plan-makers and the neighbourhood residents in how they learn—not only differences in the amount of time each has had to learn but differences in perception of the substance and in prevailing values as well.

It is appropriate in many ways to characterize the community-planning process as a learning process, for it is a process whereby plan-makers acquire an understanding of the problem through their perceptions of knowledge about the particular situation and of the processes of community change. Not everyone, including official plan-makers, enters the process either at the same time or with the same background and the same propensity to learn what is necessary to make a decision.

This has led to the realization, in the past decade or so, that a "more active relationship should be developed between planners and their clients."[29] Increased interaction, particularly through verbal communication, is aimed at mutual learning for both planners and clients. Mutual learning generally leads both to broader participation and a less bureaucratic style of planning. It thereby facilitates all participants in appreciating the respective positions of others in the plan-making process.[30] This includes planners' interactions with developers as well as with citizens.

An excellent example of mutual learning in practice in a Canadian suburb is described by Leung. Scarborough, Ontario, undertook negotiations with developers over its planning criteria for office and commercial development. Municipal planners learned that they could "soften" their criteria for such stipulations as Floor Area Ratios and density and still attain their planning objectives. The developers learned about the "logic of land use designation … [and] came to appreciate the need to go beyond market demand and jobs and argue their case on planning grounds as well."[31] Not least, mutual learning in this case helped to streamline the negotiation process.

In many ways, a **social learning model,** as it is often called, offers a way of resolving the dichotomy of dealing with planning problems either in a rational-comprehensive manner or in an incremental manner (i.e., each case on its own merits). The rational stance often seems naive, while the incremental stance simply seems opportunistic.

There is, however, a realistic position for plan-makers, postulated by Etzioni, that sits somewhat astride the other two directions.[32] It is called **mixed scanning** and is used widely by decision makers even if not explicitly recognized by name. It involves, first, identifying fundamental issues and values without a concern for details and specifications. Then, local detail and technical results are focused upon. The alternation of focus, from general to detail levels (e.g., from city-wide to neighbourhood levels), allows viewpoints to converge without sacrificing important aspects of either—something that often occurs when only one route is chosen. This approach also enhances the learning opportunities for all the participants in the process.

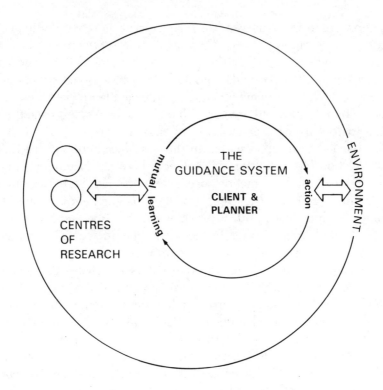

PLANNERS CONTRIBUTE

- concepts
- theory
- analysis
- processed knowledge
- new perspectives
- systematic search
  procedures

CLIENTS CONTRIBUTE

- intimate knowledge
  of context
- realistic alternatives
- norms
- priorities
- feasibility judgements
- operational details

FIGURE 7.6   **The Planning Process as a Set of Transactions**
Planners and clients (politicians, citizens, developers) each contribute to the planning
process in distinctive ways, leading to mutual learning in this conceptualization of John
Friedmann's, which he calls "transactive planning." *Source:* John Friedman, *Retracking
America* (New York: Anchor/Doubleday, 1973). Copyright © 1973 by John Friedman. Used
by permission of Doubleday, a division of Bantam Doubleday Dell Publishing Group, Inc.

Another dilemma faced by plan-makers is the disparity between the
desired cooperative process of implementing the plan and the sometimes
seemingly contrary actions taken in this regard. Again, the plan-makers
may question the wisdom of preparing a long-range comprehensive plan
compared with making separate planning decisions whose prospects for

fulfilment might be better known at the time. This dilemma has been broached by Chapin and Kaiser in their concept of a "planning and guidance system."[33] This approach aims to organize the local government's role in affecting land-use decisions, both in the public and private sectors. The local government not only has its overall plan to influence land development, but is also involved in a variety of planning actions to provide services, examine applications, regulate development, provide data, and license activities. In all these efforts, the community is "guiding" land development. The **guidance system approach** systematizes the various planning actions, policies, regulations, and investment decisions into a continuous, interpenetrating set of activities that embody the basic aims of the comprehensive land-use plan. In the next chapter, we shall examine the formal frameworks that exist for plan implementation and compare them with the integrative guidance system approach.

Community-planning learning involves plan-makers and professional planners accepting that it is natural for citizens and developers to want to be involved in planning their community. Further, it requires that citizens and others outside the formal plan-making process also be accorded the status of "clients" of the plan-makers along with those who have plan-approval powers. John Friedmann calls this style of planning "transactive planning," and Figure 7.6 shows one of his diagrams illustrating this concept.[34] The planning program of the Greater Vancouver Regional District in the early 1970s is exemplary in regard to shifting the context and style of planning in this new direction.[35] The Vancouver experience, and that from elsewhere in Canada, is gradually leading to an acceptance of the notion of mutual learning, or what now tends to be called "consensus building"[36] in community planning.

ENDNOTES

1. Martin Meyerson and Edward C. Banfield, *Politics, Planning and the Public Interest* (Glencoe, Ill.: The Free Press, 1955), esp. 312–322.

2. Ira M. Robinson, ed., *Decision-Making in Urban Planning* (Beverly Hills: Sage Publications, 1972), 27–28.

3. Patrick Geddes, *Cities in Evolution,* 3rd ed. (London: Ernest Benn, 1968), 286.

4. M.A. Qadeer, "The Nature of Urban Land," *The American Journal of Economics and Sociology* 40 (April 1981), 165–182. See also John R. Hitchcock, "The Management of Urban Canada," *Plan Canada* 25, no. 4 (December 1985), 129–136, for an excellent discussion of supply and demand for housing.

5. Penelope Gurstein, "Gender Sensitive Community Planning: A Case Study of the Planning Ourselves In Project," *Canadian Journal of Urban Research* 5, no. 2 (December 1996), 199–219.

6. One of the earliest and best discussions of planning goals is Robert C. Young, "Goals and Goal-Setting," *Journal of the American Institute of Planners* 32 (March 1966), 76–85; also helpful in this regard is Robinson, *Decision-Making in Urban Planning*, 33–41.

7. This idea is expressed well in Ian Bracken, *Urban Planning Methods* (London: Methuen, 1981), 11–35.

8. John Friedmann, "Planning as a Vocation," *Plan Canada* 6 (April 1966), 99–124.

9. Bracken, *Urban Planning Methods*, 30.

10. Frank Beal and Elizabeth Hollander, "City Development Plans," in *The Practice of Local Government Planning*, edited by Frank S. So et al. (Washington: International City Management Association, 1979), 153–182.

11. William L.C. Wheaton and Margaret F. Wheaton, "Identifying the Public Interest: Values and Goals," in Robinson, *Decision-Making*, 49–59.

12. F. Stuart Chapin, Jr., *Urban Land Use Planning*, 2nd ed. (Urbana, Ill.: The University of Illinois Press, 1965), 29ff.

13. *Ibid.*, 67.

14. A helpful review of the issues surrounding the rational-comprehensive model is found in Bracken, *Urban Planning Methods*, 11–36.

15. W.G. Roeseler, *Successful American Urban Plans* (Lexington, Mass.: D.C. Heath, 1982), xvii.

16. The most recent book on planning analyses is Richard E. Klosterman, *Community Analysis and Planning Techniques* (Savage, Md.: Rowman and Littlefield, 1990). Three earlier ones are (1) F. Stuart Chapin, Jr., and Edward J. Kaiser, *Urban Land Use Planning*, 3rd ed. (Urbana, Ill.: The University of Illinois Press, 1979); (2) Donald A. Krueckeberg and Arthur L. Silvers, *Urban Planning Analysis: Methods and Models* (New York: Wiley, 1974); (3) Bracken, *Urban Planning Methods*.

17. The foundation for this approach is found in Charles Tiebout, *The Community Economic Base* (New York: Committee for Economic Development, 1962); for a Canadian example, see Craig Davis, "Assessing the Impact of a Firm on a Small-Scale Regional Economy," *Plan Canada* 16 (1976),171–176.

18. Robert W. McCabe, *Planning Applications of Retail Models* (Toronto: Ontario Ministry of Treasury, Economics and Intergovernmental Affairs, 1974).

19. Hok Lin Leung, *Land-Use Planning Made Plain* (Kingston, Ont.: Ronald Frye, 1989), 129.

20. Cf. Allan B. Jacobs, *Looking at Cities* (Cambridge Mass.: Harvard University Press, 1985).

21. Cf. Michael Teitz in *Journal of the American Institute of Planners* 43 (July 1977), 314–317.

22. James Howard Kunstler, *Home from Nowhere* (New York: Simon and Schuster, 1996).

23. Kevin Lynch, *Site Planning*, 2nd ed. (Cambridge, Mass.: MIT Press, 1971), Chapter 12, 270–288, provides all the references used in the accompanying discussion.

24. Robert W. Burchell et al., *Development Impact Assessment Handbook* (Washington: Urban Land Institute, 1994).

25. Peter Boothroyd, "Issues in Social Impact Assessment," *Plan Canada* 18 (June 1978), 118–134.

26. Lichfield's most recent book is Nathaniel Lichfield, *Community Impact Evaluation* (London: UCL Press, 1996). An earlier book is Nathaniel Lichfield et al., *Evaluation in the Planning Process* (Oxford: Pergamon Press, 1975): on cost-benefit analysis a valuable text is E.J. Mishan, *Cost-Benefit Analysis*, 2nd ed. (London: G. Allen, 1971).

27. Morris Hill, "A Goals-Achievement Matrix for Evaluating Alternative Plans," *Journal of the American Institute of Planners* 34 (1968), 19–29; this is also reproduced in Robinson, *Decision-Making*.

28. John C. Holmes, "An Ordinal Method of Evaluation," *Urban Studies* 9 (1972), 179–191.

29. Anne Westhues, "Toward a Positive Theory of Planning," *Plan Canada* 25, no. 3 (September 1985), 97–103.

30. This approach was first advocated by Geoffrey Vickers, *The Art of Judgement: A Study of Policy Making* (London: Chapman and Hill, 1965); and Edgar Dunn, *Economic and Social Development: A Process of Social Learning* (Baltimore: Johns Hopkins University Press, 1971).

31. Hok Lin Leung, "Mutual Learning in Development Control," *Plan Canada* 27, no. 2 (April 1987), 44–55.

32. Amitai Etzioni, *The Active Society* (New York: The Free Press, 1968), 282–309.

33. Chapin and Kaiser, *Urban Land-Use Planning*, 58–65.

34. John Friedmann, *Retracking America* (New York: Anchor/Doubleday, 1973), 171–193.

35. Harry Lash, *Planning in a Human Way* (Toronto: Macmillan, for the Ministry of State for Urban Affairs, 1976).

36. Judith E. Innes, "Planning through Consensus Building," *Journal of the American Planning Association* 62, no. 4 (Autumn 1996), 460–472.

Chapter 8 The Community Plan: Its Characteristics and Role

The Master Plan is not an end but a directive. It cannot be definitive and inflexible, but must be constantly adapted to changing conditions. Such adaptations ... are to be made only with the whole scheme in mind.

Jean-Claude LaHaye, 1961

Community planning is an activity with many facets: it comprises several types of plans and a variety of processes as the effort is made to seek an improved community environment. But it is not a random set of plans and processes. It has a coherence that is provided by the comprehensive community plan. Like the keystone in a stone archway, the community plan (master plan, general plan, municipal plan, official community plan) is the fundamental component of community planning, the component that provides the *raison d'être* for detailed plans and regulations. Against the community plan are judged private development proposals, as well as decisions for public investment and regulation in regard to land use. Indeed, the latter, which include zoning by-laws and capital budgets, are often referred to as "tools" for implementing the community plan, thus indicating their interdependence with the overall plan.

Seen in this light, the community plan is more than a design for improvement of the physical environment, more than a statement of what the community wants to become. The community plan plays a distinctive role in governing a community. In this chapter, we discuss the focus of the plan, its content, whom the plan serves, and its relation to other planning tools. The aim will be to show how the community plan and the tools for its implementation, like the stones in the archway, comprise an integrated set of instruments for guiding the development of land use of a community in the direction it desires. (See Figure 8.2, page 240.)

Here, we underscore the concept of community-planning activity embedded in the planning legislation of all the provinces, an aspect to be discussed in detail in the next chapter. Suffice to say, as planning instruments have come to be enshrined in statutes, they have, in part, assumed a legal role with more precise requirements of content and specified relationships among them. For this reason alone, it is important to discuss plans and planning tools together.

THE SCOPE OF THE COMMUNITY PLAN

To describe the scope of a community plan is not a simple task because it is not a simple device. A community plan spans several important dichotomies in the life and development of a community. First, there is one concerned with *future* aims vs. *immediate* needs; next, there is one concerned with the *ideal* view vs. the *pragmatic* view; and, of course, there is the *city-wide* view vs. the *local* view. Implicit in each of these is the basic dichotomy that a community plan tries to address: the *planning* of land use vs. the *control* of physical development. This brings the community plan to a consideration of the basic values and objectives that inform the decisions of the governing body. In order to sharpen our perspective on the inherent complexity of the community plan, we should look first at the general concerns that a plan addresses.

Concerns of the Community Plan

The concerns addressed by a community plan were discussed in the preceding two chapters: that is, it defines the substantive focus in the physical environment, structures a planning viewpoint, and ultimately provides a policy instrument. These concerns are reiterated briefly here.

1. Importance of the Physical Environment

From the time the first planning acts were being framed in Canada three-quarters of a century ago, the focus of community planning has clearly been the physical environment. These acts have very often carried a statement of general aims, that they would allow a community "to plan and regulate the use and development of land for all building purposes." In other words, the focus has been on the "built" environment, both in terms of what existed in the way of houses, stores, factories, parks, schools, institutions, and roads and in the prospects for such development on vacant land.

Over the past four decades, coinciding with the growth and refinement of professional planning practice, the focus of community planning diffused to encompass other concerns. While the focal point remained the physical environment, it was realized that planning for that environment required taking into account social, economic, and financial aspects of the community. For instance, the type of people in the community, their level of affluence, their values, as well as the kind of economic development all affect the kind of built community that exists or will exist. The focus also enlarged in recent times as the possible deleterious effects of city-building on the natural environment came to be realized. Most recently, the impact on energy use of different forms and patterns of urban development are being included in the focus of community planning.

Because of this expanded perspective asked of plan-makers, it should not be assumed, as it sometimes is, that the community plan is a plan for the social, economic, natural, and energy dimensions of a community as well as for the physical environment. Not only are these other dimensions outside the direct control of local councils, it is vital to grasp the constancy and importance of the physical environment in promoting community well-being. Two pragmatic issues are central here: first, almost everything that gets built has a long life span, and second, the public investments needed for support and service involve large capital outlays and must be financed over a long period of time. The primacy of the physical environment in preparing a community plan has been reiterated firmly in deliberations over new planning legislation in several provinces.[1] This sharp focus does not preclude consideration of other dimensions of the community. Indeed, since the community's physical plan is usually the only overall plan it has, it can serve to organize and direct debate and decision making about social and economic factors in a productive and rational manner.

2. Patterns and Processes of Land Development

A community's physical environment develops on a land base that is mostly privately owned, some of which is built on and some of which is vacant. Furthermore, the physical environment is ever changing, either through the natural aging of buildings and facilities or in response to change through population and economic growth, new technology, new values and goals. A good deal of the thrust of any community plan is to promote ways in which the land base should be developed in order to respond to anticipated change in the community. The solution is usually not self-evident because the land base is owned by a large number of different persons, groups, and organizations, each with their own viewpoint of the future of their own land as well as their own aims for the community as a whole. A progression of typical questions that plan-makers must ask will help illustrate the range of concerns:

- Will change (e.g., growth) require additional land?
- Is new development best on the fringe of the community or located within already-developed sections?
- Where is vacant land available and for sale?
- Are there built-up areas that might be appropriate for redevelopment instead?
- Will redevelopment increase densities and place pressure on adjacent stable areas?
- What will be the cost to the community to provide public utilities and roads to vacant undeveloped land?
- Will growth in one section of the community lead to decline in other sections (as with a new shopping centre and the old downtown)?
- In sections of the community where stability and continuity of land use is sought, how can these sections be protected and also encouraged to renew themselves?

The above types of concerns mean that a community plan must be able to take into account the dynamics of land and building development. Further, it must provide an interface between the ideals and goals of the community and the need to manage land development activity. Land development is a vital process, sometimes in need of control. While the community plan does not directly regulate land use, it does provide the criteria—the terms of reference—for regulatory efforts. The community plan thus acts to mediate those difficult questions: which land is to be developed? where would development best be located and when? and, not least, whose land is to be developed?

3. Establishing Good Planning Principles

Experience in planning and building cities has shown that certain ways of structuring the physical environment work best. Out of this have developed planning principles (such as we referred to in Chapter 6) that guide or motivate plan-makers. They tend to reflect, in turn, the basic values of planning: health, safety, welfare, efficiency, and amenity. Planning principles are, thus, like obligations for plan-makers. The community plan ought to promote their achievement because this will help ensure a "good" community environment.

Three important planning principles have come to direct planning behaviour in a consistent way in modern communities:

1. **Appropriate land-use assignment.**   Each land use usually has distinctive locational and activity characteristics. Land uses should be spatially located where they will function most effectively and such that

they do not conflict with other uses (e.g., separating heavy industry from residences; locating shops next to transit routes).

2. **Integration of activities.**   Since the activities associated with various land uses need to be linked to one another, systems of movement of people and goods should be provided that are convenient, economical, and safe (e.g., between homes and jobs; between industry and transportation).

3. **Neighbourhood integrity.**   Residential areas should be well defined, sufficiently large to maintain their own character and values, fully protected from the hazards of major traffic routes, and have parks, schools, and stores within easy reach by walking.

It will be readily noticed that the third principle follows closely the "neighbourhood unit" concept propounded by Perry in the 1920s. Further, it tends to parallel contemporary ideas about the neighbourhood in neo-traditional planning (the New Urbanism).[2] Perhaps this illustrates how deeply such physical planning design notions have penetrated community-planning thinking. Also, the idea of respecting the integrity of residential districts is carried over into the design principles for other districts—shopping precincts, industrial parks, historic districts, waterfront areas—so that their distinctiveness and effectiveness can be promoted.

Planning principles for the physical environment are, in many ways, at the heart of a community plan. They determine the actual physical conditions under which people will live, work, shop, and play in the community. They may or may not be made explicit in a community plan, but they are, nevertheless, embedded in it and the implementing tools.

4. Coordination

There is probably no closer synonym in most people's minds for the idea of "planning" than "coordination." A good deal of the original justification for community planning was the chaos of traffic and slums in the centre of cities and the helter-skelter subdivision of land on the fringes of cities. The wisdom of developing cities in an orderly fashion—aligning street patterns of adjacent subdivisions, providing utility and transport lines at the time they are needed, providing schools and parks in residential areas—did not escape the notice of citizens. The coordination of city-building activities gave people confidence in the government's use of tax resources, added to their sense of physical well-being, and contributed to their aesthetic sense of a pleasant and well-functioning community.

Given the diversity of bodies that make decisions, in both the public and private sector, regarding the future physical environment, it is clear that there must be a means of coordination. Further, the coordination must be intentional and provide a focus of responsibility. Those plan-makers primarily involved in establishing an overview of community needs—the local council, its planning board, and planners—are not themselves the agencies that actually develop and re-develop the community. Their overall plan provides a focus: for example, the parks department or transit authority might use the plan as a guide in designing their services, or builders, land developers, and business firms can know of the community's intentions and be guided by the plan.

5. The Need for Policy

Physical development (planning) matters occupy perhaps one-half of the agenda of the average municipal council at its regular meetings. This attests to the major importance that planning matters occupy in community government. But it is also important to realize that by the time planning matters arrive on the agenda, councillors are caught in the press of other day-to-day issues and must make decisions. The existence of agreed upon policies for the physical development of the community enables councillors to judge development problems and proposals in light of ideas about the kind of community they and their citizens want rather than on grounds of expediency.

In order to deal with the array of planning concerns discussed above, it is necessary to do more than just identify them: yes, it is sensible to have a certain arrangement of land uses; yes, we should apply the best planning principles; yes, it is wise to have coordination of investment actions. But in order to provide some assurance that these concerns can be met, a commitment must be made to the community's objectives for its physical environment—that is, there must be a **public policy.** The community plan acts as an expression of this policy, as though it were stating, "In these kinds of situations, we will act in this way for these reasons." It states the community's position in advance and requires a persuasive argument before any deviation can be considered. Serious community planning demands we go beyond speculation and idealization and make a commitment to strive for goals. Effective community planning requires a plan that embodies firm commitments.

Characteristics of the Community Plan

In general, then, a community plan's main characteristics may be derived from the above set of concerns. In a phrase, *the community plan is a long-range, comprehensive, general policy guide for future physical development.* These are the essential characteristics of the plans prepared for communities, regardless of the name conferred on them by their respective provincial planning acts (official plans, general municipal plans, etc.). There are, in addition, several other characteristics that provide a linking function to such aspects as the background analyses, staging of the plan, and capital investment needs.

The first planning acts offered planners the opportunity to prepare detailed "town-planning schemes," but experience seemed to show that a broad, policy-oriented plan must precede and give direction beyond the immediate development problem. In recent years, there have been suggestions for financial plans, social plans, and now energy plans, but all these turn out to depend upon the general community plan. To reiterate, the four essential features of a community plan are:

1. **Focused upon the physical environment.** The plan should encompass the entire land (and water) base of the community and both man-made and natural features of the environment. The plan should deal explicitly with four basic physical elements of the community:

Living areas	–the areas comprising the residences of citizens;
Working areas	–the areas comprising industries, places of commerce, and other forms of economic development;
Community facilities	–the location and character of public and private facilities providing community services for both the neighbourhood and overall area; and
Circulation	–the systems and facilities needed to enable people and goods to move between living areas, working areas, and community facilities as well as between the community and its region.

2. **Long-range and forward-looking direction.** The time scale of the plan is determined by factors relevant to the particular community such as population and economic growth, the condition of structures, and the need for utilities and amenities. Importantly, modifying the existing government, building new facilities, and paying for the public infrastructure take considerable time. A common time horizon for plans is 20 years, and intermediate targets may then be set to accomplish specific projects.

3. **Comprehensive in viewpoint.** The plan should comprehend, or embrace, "all significant factors physical and non-physical, local and regional, that affect the physical growth and development of the community"[3]—that is, the plan should deal with the basic physical elements, as indicated above, as well as any other significant physical areas or features that are distinctive to the community. The viewpoint

must also be broad enough to take into account conditions and trends in the larger geographical setting of the community.

4. **General and broad-based in perspective.**   To be effective as a comprehensive instrument and as a policy guide, the plan should focus on the main concerns and issues of the community and the broad design components for its physical development. The plan is not a blueprint and should not include any details that distract from overall physical design proposals and policies. It is primarily for defining the general location, character, and extent of desirable future development against which detailed proposals may be evaluated. Some detail specification may be necessary in order to clarify the intent of policies or to provide physical images to which the community can relate.

In addition to the above four essential features of a community plan, there are several others that are included in many plans. Some plan-makers accord them an individual place within the plan report, because of their importance in linking the general physical design with the policy role of the plan as well as with related policy areas.

5. **Linked to social and economic objectives.**   Even though a community plan focuses on the physical environment, it is in many respects a vehicle for achieving social and economic objectives, at least in part. Indeed, a physical development plan that is not in accord with these objectives may be less than successful. The two most obvious subject areas where there is a strong interrelationship between physical/socioeconomic objectives are in housing[4] and in the provision of space for industry and commerce. It is vital that the process of community planning takes into account social and economic factors and that the plan clearly states social and economic objectives that can be furthered by the physical development proposals. In this way, the community plan serves to focus attention on non-physical planning goals and to point up the need for coordination in their attainment.

6. **Based on planning analyses.**   The analyses of current conditions and the forecasts of future conditions in the community form one of two cornerstones of the plan, the other being the community objectives. The analyses of population, economic base, and land use define the range of possibilities for the plan-maker. It is important that at least the main findings and the rationale behind the analyses be reported within the plan. Moreover, many of the analyses pertain to non-physical factors (e.g., population age, income, employment) and this, again, will assist in clarifying the relationships between the physical plan and social and economic factors in the community.

7. **Implemented by stages.**   In contrast to older community plans, which presented a single long-range concept, it is now common for the progression of development to be stated. This is important because not all new development areas are likely to be opened up at the same time; if development is left to disperse, it could result in costly extensions to roads and utilities to the municipality; sprawling development can be inefficient for commuters as well as for those providing commercial services. The inclusion of a staging plan clearly signals the community's intentions to land developers, homeowners, business firms, and institutions.

8. **A guide for capital improvement.**   An overall plan is done in large part to help predict and anticipate the demands for public works and other capital investments. Most plans provide a very general indication about needed investments, as, for example, when a new area is opened up for residential development and roads, utilities, parks, and schools are planned. A greater degree of specificity is, however, more helpful to the local council for scheduling capital projects. To this end, many communities prepare a Capital Improvements Program in conjunction with their overall plan. The CIP is often structured to relate to the annual budgeting process of the community and also to project several years into the future as anticipated by the community plan. Thus, it makes the stages for development proposed in the plan more realistic.

9. **A basis for community design.**   An ever-present value of planners and an expectation of citizens is that of visual beauty for the community. The community plan's proposed pattern of land uses is the base upon which the three-dimensional environment of buildings and open spaces is designed and constructed. Although community plans result in a particular community form, in recent years the design element has been notably absent from many community plans. A community design component of an overall place can be vital in communicating to citizens and developers the key built and natural features and special districts that have a particular significance for the community.

Most provincial planning acts provide only a broad hint of the plan's scope, much less its content and characteristics. The above points thus attempt a synthesis of concepts and experience that reflect planning practice in Canada. It is perhaps unwise to seek a more precise definition, for every community plan will need to respond to the aspirations and problems of its particular community setting. The community plan must ultimately persuade citizens that it reflects their best interests as well as those of future citizens. In this task of human communication, community plans take a variety of forms. There are those that convey their message in a colourful booklet, those that use a newspaper tabloid format, those that come as ponderous tomes, and those that are one-page poster plans (Figure 8.1). But, regardless of format, the most effective community plans have the scope indicated above.

THE POLICY ROLES OF THE COMMUNITY PLAN

A community plan is foremost a **policy statement** about the future physical environment. The content and scope that we have defined provide the necessary direction for its use in planning the community. But it is a document, an instrument, to be used in the realm of community government. Thus, the community plan plays a number of roles according to its uses in policy determination and implementation by the local council, planning board, and planning staff, as well as by citizens and developers. These roles call for the plan to have other more functional characteristics so that it may effectively achieve what the community wants for its future environment. The community plan must be a vehicle for both policy determination and policy implementation.

The Plan in Policy Determination

The community plan's role in policy determination is a progressive one. It begins with the preparation and initial adoption of the plan and continues through its regular review and evaluation as day-to-day physical development matters are considered. The community plan is an ultimate base of policy in its own right. It is also the basis for formulating secondary policies.

   The efforts that go into the initial adoption of the plan are the most important, for when the plan is adopted it will represent the culmination of thorough deliberation about major alternatives by many sectors of the community, as well as by the planning board and local council. Ultimately, it is the council that adopts the plan, but the deliberations that lead up to that point are vital. Usually a draft plan is made available to community members to communicate the basic ideas and alternatives. The reactions, both positive and negative, are part of a process educating the community and the council about the major issues in physical development. If this period of public learning and debate is effective, it will normally mean that the council is not later surprised by unresolved issues. Three important policy characteristics of a community plan can assist in the initial deliberations, as well as throughout the life of the plan.[5]

FIGURE 8.1   **Community Plans for All Sizes of Communities**

1. *The plan should be in a form suitable for public debate.*
2. *The plan should be available to the community.*
3. *The plan should communicate readily its proposals to the public.*

The council's adoption of the plan represents a declaration of the policies that the council intends to apply in regard to future physical development proposals. In this way, private interests may anticipate the probable reaction to proposals for development. The impact of the plan as a statement of policy is as important inside the local government framework as outside. Coordination of the actions of public officials in various city departments as well as in semi-independent commissions and boards is hereby encouraged. Lastly, the plan's policies are an important guide for judicial bodies in appeals against land-use regulations.

While it is important that community plan policies be firm and be applicable over a long period of time, a plan should not be considered immutable. Conditions in a community do not remain static, and not infrequently, new problems arise that were not anticipated when the plan was adopted. For example, trends may change in population growth or job creation, or new information may become available that affects land-use decisions, as was the case in the energy crisis of the late 1970s. Moreover, some policies may prove unworkable or unrealistic. The council should thus be willing and able to amend the community plan if the situation or conditions warrant it. Proposals for large new projects, a new airport or redevelopment of industrial areas, for instance, may trigger the need to review the compatibility of the project with the plan. Or a new transportation study may show how the road network could be refined. It is important that the plan be able to accommodate review and renewed debate. Thus, we should add a fourth characteristic to facilitate policy roles of the plan:

4. *The plan should be amendable.*

While the plan should be amendable, it should not be subject to trivial challenges, which would threaten its role as a continuous statement of policy. Moreover, frequent amendment probably indicates a lack of agreement and commitment on basic policies. If not abused, amendability of the plan is important, for it means that basic development policy can be debated and refined and the extent of community agreement broadened in the process. This also means that the plan is being consulted in regard to decisions that need to be taken. For all these reasons, there is in most provincial planning acts provision for the community plan to be reviewed on a regular basis. The Planning Act of Ontario requires a maximum of five years between regular reviews of the plan by the council. Some planners try to have their planning boards review the plan annually.

There are also a host of current topics brought before council that impinge on plan policies. These cover such matters as parking regulations, use of public parks for non-recreational activities, or the use of advertising signs in public thoroughfares. Usually, specific concerns such as these are not part of the community plan policies. However, cumulatively, as part of the day-to-day actions of a council, they may affect the community environment. The plan's effectiveness may be impaired if the decisions are not consistent with its policies. Conversely, council's actions may reveal its perception of changed conditions or outlooks, and thus the need to reconsider policies set forth in the plan.

Plan-makers seek to create a community plan that becomes an explicit part of the backdrop against which the local government and its officials make their decisions—that is, one that becomes a "working plan." In this way, its policies are in use and are frequently being tested. In this day-to-day use the policy determination role overlaps with the policy implementation role of the plan.

The Plan in Policy Implementation

The means for bringing a community plan into effect are increasingly specified in provincial planning acts. Local councils are thus required to take a number of formal steps that give legislative effect to the policies of the community plan. If land use is to be regulated by zoning, provincial planning acts require the local council to pass a zoning by-law. It is now normal to require the community to have an overall plan in place before enacting zoning regulations and, moreover, that the zoning by-law be consistent with the community plan. Provincial planning acts tend to include, in addition to zoning, such other important plan effectuation measures as sub-division controls, urban redevelopment, and site plan controls, and to specify council's role in enacting, approving, or amending proposals in these areas.

In general, there are two levels of actions that councils take in regard to plan implementation. At the first level, the matters are legislative in nature: that is, the passing of local by-laws based on the principles and policies of the plan. The two most common are for the control of land use on already-developed or developable land **zoning** and for the arrangement of new properties for development on vacant land **subdivision control.** Some provinces provide for councils to pass **development control** by-laws that would allow the community to review proposals for development on a property-by-property basis rather than on a district basis, as in zoning. And in some places, the **program for capital improvements** in the community is required to conform to the community plan. There are, in addition, detailed plans for development that a council is occasionally called upon to approve. These may include plans for downtown revitalization, streets and highways improvements, and parkland acquisition and development.

At the second level, there are many routine council decisions that arise in conjunction with implementing the by-laws that council has passed. Councils are usually required to approve proposed plans of subdivision, development control agreements, applications for rezoning, as well as public works expenditures under the capital improvement program. Other routine council decisions that may affect the plan's policies are requests for street closings, traffic regulation, transit routes, and the locations of firehalls, libraries, and schools.

Policy Perspective for the Community Plan

The perspective we have been describing for the use of the community plan is, essentially, hierarchical. The plan may be considered the keystone in an arch, as in Figure 8.2. One can see the hierarchy of control measures, the distinction between those that operate in the public and the private sectors, as well as the roles of various participants.

On the left side of the diagram are the initiatives that are taken by city officials in support of the overall plan. These may be required under the planning act in some provinces. It can also be seen that they deal progressively with specific parts of the physical environment as one moves away from the locus of the community plan. The zoning by-law usually deals with the entire community; subdivision control is applied to specific areas within the community; and the capital improvements program specifies individual projects. Further, as the general concerns shift toward the specific, the involvement in decision making shifts to an increasing array of participants. The planning board and staff have roles in formulating the zoning by-laws and subdivision controls, and additional members of the municipal staff become involved in formulating the program for capital improvements. Council is thus dependent upon the advice and actions of several levels of participants within local government circles in preparing the plan and in providing the supporting legislative framework. Note also that the initial stages of plan preparation—basic forecasts, background studies, identifying alternatives, initial designs—are usually allocated to an advisory committee or board and to professional staff. Although the board and staff are advisors to council, theirs is not a passive role. Indeed, they function more as joint participants and can influence council on the progress of planning more than any other participants, if they choose.

Referring again to the diagram, the right-hand side comprises those initiatives normally taken by individual property owners and other development interests and agencies. In other words, when a person or a corporation wishes to develop or redevelop land in the community, it is necessary to apply to the municipality. Each application to, say, rezone a property to allow a different use or to construct new buildings on vacant land represents a potential step in shaping the physical environment. The review and approval of such applications are important steps in carrying out the poli-

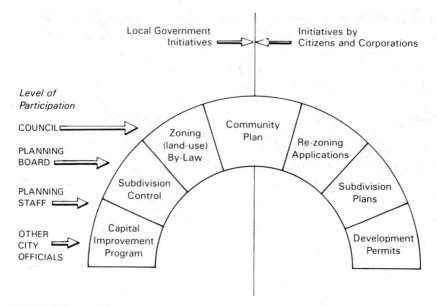

FIGURE 8.2   **Key Role of the Community Plan in Land-Use Control**
The community plan has the same position as that of a keystone in an archway. Initiatives
of both the local government and the citizens and corporations depend upon its integrity.

cies of the plan. In general, these applications have ultimately to be
approved by the council, which can determine their consistency with the
plan's policies. However, planning staff and other officials (such as building
inspectors) play crucial roles in receiving the applications and judging their
acceptability at the outset.

In summary, once a community plan is adopted, it sets in motion efforts
by various participants to implement its policies and proposals. There are,
basically, two policy streams. One is used by the council to secure *compliance* (through by-laws, budgets, regulations) with the policies it has
approved in adopting the plan. The other is used to *communicate* to others
(officials, citizens, developers) the aims and policies, the hopes and expectations, of council regarding the future physical environment. Both streams
frequently converge, as, for example, when experience shows the nature of
applications from the private sector to differ from forecasted trends, or
when budget constraints change capital spending. These may then show
the need for amending the plan. An effective community plan is one that
is put to use in the continuing development of the community. A plan that
is used to evaluate proposals for development has its own policies re-
evaluated and, if necessary, its sights reset.

THE COMMUNITY PLAN AS A LEGAL DOCUMENT

Up to this point, the need for a community plan has been discussed in terms of its worth as a guide in long-range decision making, as a commitment on the part of the community, as an instrument of education, communication, and coordination. The implication was that it is up to the community to determine the worth of preparing a community plan. Provincial planning legislation until very recently was permissive in this regard: "... a municipality *may* prepare a plan for ... ." Increasingly, provinces are requiring their local governments to prepare a plan. For example, the planning act for Alberta requires all municipalities with a population of more than 1,000 to prepare a "general municipal plan." Other provinces stipulate the need for a municipality to have an overall plan before it may exercise control over land uses.

Traditionally, plans for Canadian communities prepared under provincial legislation are legal documents. They require formal council endorsement and usually approval by the province. (Contrast this to the United States system, where community plans were until recently considered local policy initiatives and their existence a matter of local prerogative.) However, the strength of the plan as a basis for public decisions, especially for regulating private land development, was not much tested until the last two or three decades. But as land-use controls have become more prevalent, the courts have been resorted to in order to challenge the community's right to place constraints on the development of private land. Since land-use controls are almost inevitably enacted to achieve some intended form for the community environment, it became necessary to provide the courts and others with the policy rationale—the plan—on which these were based.

Another important aspect of this shift in approach is the introduction of flexible land-use control practices and instruments. Early zoning practice, largely justified because it could provide stability to neighbourhoods and land values, did not envision the dynamics of land development occasioned by the urban growth of the past several decades. In view of these pressures and needs, planners sought ways to accommodate new styles in building subdivisions, industrial parks, and office buildings, as well as the ubiquitous automobile, for example. The response was to devise means by which individual development proposals could be appraised by the planners. One avenue was to institute development controls requiring, under a local by-law, that development proposals for the siting of buildings, traffic access, and architectural qualities be submitted for review. Another avenue was planned unit development, which encouraged developers to plan their projects in conjunction with local planners. Yet another was the use of negoti-ated agreements with individual developers, commonly called **development agreements.** Zoning remained as the general framework, but it was no longer the only prescription for what might be done with properties.

These recent practices encourage diversity and innovation in develop-ment, but they also increase the problems of coordination among deci-sions, not to mention the possible arbitrariness of such decisions. Thus, the mandated plan for the entire community comes to assume a more vital role as a backdrop against which development decisions can be assessed. It is still debated whether a plan imposed by a higher level of government can be as meaningful as one generated by local needs and experience. And, certainly, many community plans produced to comply with provincial leg-islation are often complex and ponderous in language in an attempt to fore-stall legal challenges. There are, however, examples of plans for large com-munities and small that fulfil legal requirements yet offer a vigorous ren-dering of community aspirations. The crafting of a community plan requires skill and sensitivity on the part of plan-makers.

ENDNOTES

1. Cf. British Columbia, Ministry of Municipal Affairs, *The Planning Act: A Discussion Paper* (Victoria, 1980), 40.
2. Cf. Andres Duany et al., *Towns and Town-Making Principles* (Cambridge, Mass.: Harvard University Press, 1991).
3. T.J. Kent, Jr., *The Urban General Plan* (San Francisco: Chandler, 1964), 99. Much of the discussion in this section is based on the concept of a community plan posited by Kent. This influential text was reprinted in 1991 (Chicago: Planners Press, American Planning Association).
4 Provincial planning legislation in British Columbia requires Official Community Plans to include a statement of housing policy, especially regard-ing affordable housing (B.C. Municipal Act Sec. 945 2.1).
5. Kent, *Urban General Plan,* especially 119–123.

Chapter 9   Implementing the Community Plan by Land-Use Regulation

Discretion is an essential element of planning. Somebody has to say yes or no to a request for permission to develop land at a certain time and in a certain way.

Anthony Adamson, 1956

Up to this point, we have emphasized the importance of the community plan in the planning activity of a community. The plan provides the foundation for planning action; it is a record of what has been decided for the future community environment, of the kind of community we want. However, planning is an activity involving diverse participants and their decisions about land use. Most planners would argue that, while it is important to prepare a plan, it is equally important to design and apply appropriate *tools* for guiding the decisions of participants so that the plan is achieved or implemented. Certainly, the two are interdependent: a plan without tools for implementation is probably destined to gather dust on the shelf; such tools without a plan add up to meaningless or arbitrary regulation.

This chapter and the next examine the tools and approaches used in implementing the community plan. In many ways, the tools of planning—zoning, subdivision control, capital budgets, and so on—are very familiar. People encounter the effects of these tools more often than they come in contact with the plan itself. Not infrequently, the planning tools are seen as the end product of planning rather than its means. Further, where planning tools are also land-use regulations, they often have negative connotations in people's minds because they can be used to restrict development or change on privately owned property. Sometimes they are believed to have more power over the plan's implementation than they actually carry. It is important, therefore, to grasp the nature and capabilities of each of these planning tools.

The ways in which planners go about implementing the community plan cover more than land-use regulation. It is necessary to have ways to coordinate development in the public sector. And it is necessary to find ways to integrate the effects of all the tools. Beyond this, there is the need to keep the community abreast of, and involved in, planning policy and implementation decisions. In this chapter, we concentrate on the planning tools that are used to guide development on private land—the planner's traditional tools for land-use planning and regulation. Let us first briefly review the various tasks involved in implementing a community plan in order to establish a perspective.

THE TASKS OF PLAN IMPLEMENTATION

The ultimate task of plan-makers is to establish the conditions that will attain the goals of the plan. Those conditions derive from a combination of policy directives, legal instruments, administrative practices, and means of promoting community participation in planning. The task of plan implementation is therefore accomplished through a variety of tools and approaches. While a community plan may be given final form (at least until it needs to be amended), plan implementation is a *continuous* process. The tools of planning deal with a continuous, functioning community; they must be able to respond both to the kind and character of present-day development initiatives and to the decisions that will be made as the future unfolds.

Planning tools act as an *interface* between the policies of the plan and the aims of those who make decisions that transform the physical environment. The latter include all those who own some land within the community—the average residential homeowner, who may have no plans for developing his or her property, as well as those who are in the business of land and building development. Also included are those in public agencies who make decisions to invest public funds and construct roads, schools, parks, parking-garages, etc. Each has the potential for making decisions that could affect the future community environment.

Thus, we have to recognize, initially, two basic dimensions of the task of plan implementation:

1. **Guiding Development on Private Land.** This, in turn, breaks into two subdimensions:
   (a) presently developed areas, and
   (b) vacant or undeveloped areas.

2. Coordinating public development efforts.   (especially the coordination of capital investments).

Around these two dimensions have developed the best-known and most refined planning tools. Zoning, or "districting" as it used to be called, is the primary tool for guiding development decisions on presently developed private land. It has been supplemented in recent years by more direct controls over individual properties, variously called development control or site plan control. Subdivision control is used in guiding development on large parcels of vacant land. The municipal capital improvements program and budget are used to coordinate municipal investments in physical improvements to the environment. These familiar tools are designed for the *direct* guidance of land-use decision maker, (i.e., they may be used to constrain or limit actual development decisions); they are usually backed by statutory powers vested in the municipality by the province.

There are also tools that work to influence development decisions *indirectly*. Indeed, a good deal of planning implementation is involved with more than regulating land use. Considerable attention and time must be devoted, for example, to guiding persons who are considering development of their land and who look to officials in other municipal departments and agencies to apprise them of planning policies. There is also the need to promote the public's involvement in order to test its acceptance of plans and policies.

These latter tasks have not generated formal, institutionalized tools that planners use. Rather, *certain approaches* have emerged to help in accomplishing such tasks. These take the form of organizational arrangements for the operation of the planning function within municipal government and for obtaining public input. The approaches often differ in form from community to community (with the exception of provincially prescribed public meetings). Thus, communities develop individual planning styles to achieve the goals of the community plan.

One final point needs to be made about plan implementation and the tools associated with it. This concerns the outcome, the physical result, of decisions taken in the name of planning. The community plan is intended to encompass *all* community land-use decisions, present and future, in order to achieve some envisioned physical environment. In a planned new town, the physical results may approximate the design promoted in the overall plan. But in the typical Canadian community, change in the existing environment is not subject to such direct design. The regulations for guiding development on private land are usually invoked only when the persons or groups with interests in the land signify their intention to develop or redevelop their properties. Investment decisions by the municipality may be subject to decisions originally made by private interests, as well as subject to available financial resources.

In short, the comprehensive coverage of the community's future land use as propounded by the plan can be achieved only in part. Planning tools, whether for guiding private land development or public investment, can be utilized only in limited situations that occur over extended periods of time. There is also much latitude within the provisions of land-use regulations as to the form of building, amount of open space, or type of activity housed in a building that actually comes to be established. Similarly, a budget for public works projects cannot define their visual appearance and, sometimes, not even their location. Thus, direct public planning decisions ultimately constitute only a small part of the output of decisions affecting land use.[1] Moreover, that portion decreases as time elapses after adopting the plan. Figure 9.1 shows one way of visualizing this process.

This raises a fundamental question for plan-makers: *how to attain a future community environment that reflects the goals and designs of the overall plan?* If, as stated above, the extent of the direct effect of the plan and of planning tools is limited, then the issue must be faced in terms of the quality of the planning guidance provided. Thus, the issue becomes how to be most effective in the use of planning tools in attaining the community plan's goals and design concepts. Planners have found through experience that success in plan implementation involves attention being paid to two facets of the process: (1) assiduous application of planning tools in a manner consistent with the policies of the community plan; and (2) strategic

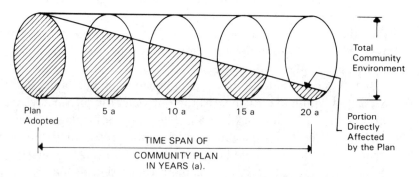

FIGURE 9.1   **Changing Role of the Community Plan in Land-Use Decisions**
Over the life span of a community plan, public planning decisions assume a smaller and smaller proportion of all the decisions affecting land use, and private initiatives stimulated by the plan increase in scope.

programming of capital investments by the community to promote the community plan. In other words, in guiding the continuous physical development of the community, planners can and do have a major influence on the outcome of the plan's initiatives by concentrating on the two facets in which they have a direct role. We shall return to this notion in the next chapter.

PLANNING TOOLS FOR ALREADY-DEVELOPED AREAS

An established city never ceases changing: buildings age, some deteriorate, new residents desire improvements to existing buildings, new activities vie for space, and so on. All such changes can have an important effect on the physical environment of the surrounding area and even of the community as a whole, depending on the nature, magnitude, and intensity of the change. It was the advent of intense industrial uses and vast areas of often squalid housing for factory workers that alerted 19th-century communities to the fact that growth can present dramatic transformations that are not always in keeping with ideals. It was in this latter context that communities began to seek ways to achieve beneficial development of the privately owned land that constituted the majority of their territory. Zoning was invented as a tool for this purpose over a century ago; it introduces the following discussion.

The developed part of a community is that portion which, in general, comprises relatively small parcels of land already built upon or that could be built upon. There are usually a small number of large parcels of land occupied by such institutions as hospitals, factories, or parks. These are part of the developed area, too. But large parcels of land in use as farms or other resource extraction, or those that are simply vacant and not divided into small parcels, are not considered developed land. The latter type is usually found on the fringe of the community and may, indeed, become developed in the future, but its future use is still to be determined at the time of its subdivision into smaller parcels. Here again is another distinction that should be kept in mind when considering such planning tools as zoning: these tools are designed for land for which the intended use is already determined. The first of these to be examined is **zoning,** followed by a complementary tool, **development control** (site plan control); the **redevelopment plan** rounds out the discussion.

Zoning

Origins and Nature

Zoning grew out of the general observation about city development that similar uses tend to congregate in areas separate from other uses. Further, when congregated in their distinctive areas, the land uses and activities—industry, commerce, residences—seem to perform their respective functions more effectively than when intermingled. German town planners in the latter half of the 19th century employed these observations to devise ways of organizing the growth of industrial cities to ensure efficiency for the factories and amenability for the workers' housing.[2] Municipalities in all countries experiencing industrialization in this period, including Canada, sought to regulate the siting of buildings and the provision of basic services for safety and health reasons. The German approach was to differentiate the regulations according to the needs of the uses located in (or planned for) their respective *districts*. The practice became known as "districting" and, later, as "zoning," especially in the United States and Canada.

Besides observing the functional differences in land use (e.g., many industries have noxious effluents, commercial areas generate a lot of traffic, etc.), early planners also perceived aesthetic differences among land-use districts: the height of buildings, the space between them, their setback from the road, the road pattern that best suited the use. Not least, early planners did not fail to notice that differences between land uses reflected differences in *density* of land use. In residential districts, there were differences, for example, in the number of dwellings on each parcel of land, as reflected in the height and bulk of buildings, the size of dwelling units, and the amount of open space around them. Analogous observations were made in regard to industrial and commercial land uses and their structures. In short, districting principles lent themselves to consideration of physical design of communities to achieve the arrangements and densities of land uses a community might prefer.

As important as anything about zoning, and something that probably accounts for its longevity among planning tools, is its simultaneous applicability to individual properties and large areas. When zoning was established, it was a major departure in the exercise of statutory powers by municipalities. Previously, municipalities had used powers for enforcing safety, health, and structural standards on an individual property basis. But since land use occurs on an areal basis, it was necessary to apply regulations to all the properties in a similar area. With this sort of tool, planners were more likely to achieve consistency in the types of uses and structures constituting the physical environment of the distinctive zones or districts of development.

In North America, the first comprehensive zoning by-law was enacted by the City of New York in 1916. The first such Canadian zoning by-law was enacted in 1924 for Kitchener, Ontario, and was formulated by planners Thomas Adams and Horace Seymour.[3] A comprehensive zoning by-law established districts for the entire community. Prior to the above dates there were districting by-laws in some communities to deal selectively with heights of buildings and the location of noxious uses. For example, in 1904 Ontario cities had the right to control the location, erection, and use of buildings for laundries, butcher shops, stores, and "manufactories."[4] And there were instances of by-laws designed in a discriminatory fashion to limit the residency of specific minority groups to certain areas of the city.[5] As zoning came more widely into practice in the 1920s, it had to meet the test of court challenges, especially with regard to the principle that it must apply *universally* and *uniformly* to all properties within the areas in question. Earlier exclusionary tendencies gave way to a more general rationale of the protection of property values from dramatic shifts due to the mixing of incompatible land uses.

Zoning practice developed along the same general lines in the United States and Canada, although there are significant constitutional differences between the two countries that affect zoning. The basic difference lies in the fact that the U.S. Constitution spells out personal property rights whereas the Canadian Charter of Rights does not. In the United States, the validity (constitutionality) of zoning by-laws was not confirmed as a power available to municipalities until it had been tested by the U.S. Supreme Court.[6] In Canada, municipalities were deemed, under powers granted to the provinces under the British North America Act, to have the statutory power to regulate land use.[7] The usual concern over zoning practice in the United States is whether the by-law involves a "taking" of property rights granted to property owners. The concern in Canada is more general, that is, whether the by-law is discriminatory in pursuing the public interest. Thus, zoning by-laws in Canada can have much more scope than those in the United States. This constitutional difference has given rise in Canada to the complementary practices of development control and site plan control, which allow a municipality to specify certain land-use regulations on a property-by-property basis. More will be said of these later in this chapter.

Recent Zoning Perspectives.   It is perhaps not unexpected that a planning tool that has been around for three or four generations would acquire some critics and require some changes. Indeed, zoning has been blamed for many planning ills over the years that were due, more to its misapplication than to inherent flaws. But, like all of the planning tools described here, zoning has considerable flexibility and has been applied in a variety of ways to suit local conditions and local preferences.

Still, zoning is a simplified view of city development that sees activities located in discrete districts housed in distinctive types of structures. It generalizes the pattern of development and then categorizes the activities that take place there in terms of discrete physical forms. This has the result in many communities, especially larger ones, of reducing the diversity of activities that exist to a limited number of technical categories. The very mixture of activities that gives character to a neighbourhood may be obscured by the zoning, often because they either could not be fitted into the categories or could not even be fully perceived at the time as being compatible.[8]

Moreover, neighbourhood activities often change over time and new ones may be able to be accommodated in structures not originally meant for them (such as professional offices in old warehouses or the many new home occupations made possible through telecommuting). Or there may be completely new formats for an old activity (such as the advent of "big-box" retailing and ethnic shopping malls). We shall note, in the following sections, how planners have responded to new needs and possibilities in their zoning provisions.

Substantive Focus

Zoning has a quite precise focus. It provides a set of standards regarding (a) the *use* to which a parcel of land may be put, and (b) the *size, type,* and *placement* of buildings on that parcel. These standards are made explicit in the text of the zoning by-law according to the districts in the community to which they apply. An accompanying map, or **zoning plan** as it is sometimes called, specifies the boundaries of each zone and, thus, the properties affected by the different district regulations. The zoning by-law may also regulate the density of population from district to district by specifying the number of dwelling units allowed per building and/or the number of individuals that may occupy a dwelling unit. Most zoning by-laws contain provisions covering the external effects of activities carried on in buildings through their requirements for off-street parking and loading areas, size and placement of signs, and accessory uses and home occupations. There may be the need or desire in a community to specify land-use districts that contain distinctive local features for functional, historical, environmental, or aesthetic reasons, in which case the zoning by-law may contain provisions covering a number of special districts.

Land-Use Types and Districts.   Three basic land-use categories are usually identified in zoning by-laws: residential, commercial, and industrial. In each of these categories, there may be a series of zones depending upon the nature of the activities, the type of building, the density of development, or the lot size. A variety of residential zones may be distinguished, for example, by the number of dwelling units permitted on the lots that are typical of the zone. If large apartment buildings and large tracts of land are being developed, the zone may be defined by the number of dwelling units per hectare. Among commercial zones, the distinctions may be in terms of the service needs of people: central business, neighbourhood commercial, highway-oriented commercial, or shopping centre. For industrial zones, the differences in standards usually reflect the characteristics of the processes carried on by the firms. For example, industries using heavy machinery or emitting considerable smoke, noise, or odours would usually be in a zone separate from those whose processes had much less external impact. Similarly, those engaged in mostly the shipping, storing, and transfer of goods would likely warrant a separate zone. Figure 9.2 illustrates a typical listing of zones found in the zoning by-laws of a medium-sized city.

For each land-use zone, it is common practice to specify the uses that are permitted to locate there. This may necessitate a long list of valid uses in order to include all likely and desirable types. The following list shows the establishments permitted in the Neighbourhood Commercial Zone of the City of Kingston, Ontario:

- Retail stores
- Neighbourhood stores
- Offices for or in connection with a business or profession
- Banks or financial institutions
- Restaurants
- One-family dwellings, two-family dwellings, provided that such dwellings are located within a commercial structure
- Libraries, art galleries, or museums
- Shopping centres

A brief look at the uses permitted in the above zone indicates how, even in this rather ordinary by-law, an interesting mixture of land uses can be accommodated: dwelling places, offices, restaurants, and stores. Other communities, especially larger ones, like Toronto, Montreal, and Vancouver, have developed zoning provisions for encouraging special combinations of mixed uses, thereby considerably blunting the criticisms that zoning prevents mixing.[9]

By definition all land uses not explicitly mentioned in such a list are thereby excluded from being located within the zone. Unspecified uses already present in the zone before the by-law was enacted are usually

Classification	Predominant Land Use
R1	Single-family residential
R2	One- and two-family residential
R3	Apartment residential (medium density)
R4	High-density residential
C1	Downtown commercial
C2	Neighbourhood commercial
C3	Automobile-oriented commercial
M1	Light industrial
M2	Wholesale and transportation
M3	Heavy industrial
P	Public use (health, education, religious, administration)
R	Rural and agriculture
EN	Environmentally sensitive area

FIGURE 9.2 **Land-Use Districts in Typical Zoning By-law for a Medium-Size City**

excepted. The list of permitted uses in each zone is thus distinctive, although a small amount of overlap will undoubtedly occur between the lists of permitted uses within the sets of zones in each of the basic residential, commercial, and industrial categories. Banks and restaurants will generally be permitted in all commercial zones, for example.

The land-use zones, and the lists of permitted uses associated with each, in most instances reflect the type of uses already existing in the community. Where residential neighbourhoods, commercial areas, and industrial districts already exist and are in stable condition, the zoning regulations are formulated so as to continue those uses in their respective areas. This is the basis for the concern of some that zoning is essentially *protective* of existing uses and *restrictive* of new uses. But zoning may also be used to specify land uses in areas in the process of new growth or redevelopment from earlier uses.

A new and dramatic example of this strategy is the initiative being taken in Toronto to revitalize two old industrial districts close to downtown. The land-use provisions of the zoning regulations are being eliminated, leaving only specifications for building height and setback standards, all with the aim of attracting alternative activities to the districts.[10] In this sense, zoning may also be used in a *prospective* way.

Building Height, Bulk, and Placement.   Just as important as land use to zoning is the resulting effect of the size of buildings constructed on parcels of land along with the placement of the buildings on the parcels. For example, height controls often existed in cities long before comprehensive zoning was accepted (including in ancient Rome). Controls regulating how close to the street buildings could be placed (now called the **setback**) were also long-lived concerns in cities. Zoning by-laws gathered together these various concerns over the built environment and refined and articulated them in conjunction with land-use district aims for the community environment.

In a typical zoning by-law, one will find that each land-use zone includes specifications for the maximum height of buildings and the proportion of the parcel of land that may be built upon. From these two dimensions—height and area—the potential **bulk** of a building may be ascertained. If there are requirements for leaving space around the building, specified as setbacks from the boundary lines of the property, then the exact space within which the building may be sited on the property is identified. This exact space on the parcel combined with the allowed bulk of building defines what is sometimes called the **building envelope** (see Figure 9.3).

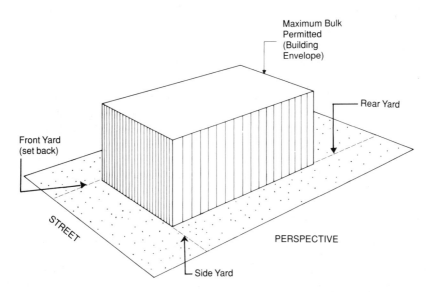

FIGURE 9.3   **Basic Dimensions for the Placement, Coverage, and Height of Structures on Building Lots**
These dimensions determine a "building envelope" and govern the bulk of buildings allowed on a site.

Within each zone there is a distinctive building envelope and buildings may be built on each parcel of land so that each building envelope is completely filled. This would be the most intense development that could occur in the zone. In practice, for a number of reasons, this intensity does not always result: for example, owners may not wish their buildings to be as tall as allowed, or may want more space around them, or may not be able to afford to build such a bulky building, or the shape of the building may be a different shape than the building envelope (as with peaked-roof houses in residential zones). Custom is also important in influencing the bulk of buildings. An owner may want his or her building to be in keeping with the bulk of buildings already existing in the district. And existing norms for building bulk, it should be noted, may be a function of long-standing zoning standards.

The chart in Figure 9.4 codifies the requirements for building height, lot coverage, and setbacks for a typical set of residential zones in a city. If one were to visit the actual districts to which they apply, it would probably be obvious that the requirements reflect the norm of existing conditions in

Residential Zone	Min. Lot Area m²	Min. Lot Width m	Max. Lot Coverage %	Front Yard m	Side Yard m	Rear Yard m	Floor Area Ratio	Max. Height m	Storeys
R1	1,000	22.5	35	10.5	4.5	9	—	10.5	3
R2	500	15	30	7.5	3	7.5	—	10.5	3
R3	330	9	40	4.5	2.5	7.5	—	10.5	3
R4	200	7.5	50	4.5	1.5	4.5	—	10.5	3
R5	1,000	15	50	6	✓	4.5	1.0	12.5	4
R6	1,500	15	50	4.5	✓	✓	1.5	25	8
R7	1,500	15	70	4.5	✓	✓	3.0	✓	✓
R8	4,000	25	100	✓	✓	✓	5.0	✓	✓

✓ Indicates variable standard to suit project.

FIGURE 9.4   Typical Building Envelope Standards for Residential Buildings in a Larger City

A zoning by-law specifies the maximum or minimum measurements for the placement, coverage, and height of buildings in each district. In an older city, it is usually necessary to accept the smaller dimensions of lots plotted before the by-law (e.g., R-3 and R-4). In larger cities, provision must be made for tall structures (e.g., R-7 and R-8), with no height limit but constrained in their bulk. New "monster homes" may require Floor Area Ratios in zones R-1 to R-4.

those districts of the city. For example, older residential districts may have smaller or more variable yard or height provisions than newer, more uniform suburban districts. Often, the more affluent residential areas will be found to have requirements for large lots and setbacks commensurate with their more spacious character. Until recently, the regulation of building bulk was confined to areas where large office or apartment buildings could be built. Nowadays in many cities, bulk regulations are being added to zoning by-laws concerned with one- and two-family residential areas. The recent trend to "big houses" (sometimes called "monster" or "mega" homes) caused consternation in many communities because neighbours felt that the new large houses changed the neighbourhood character. In effect, what was happening was that builders were now using most, if not all, of the allowable building envelope under the zoning regulations, thereby permitting monster homes to dominate the streetscape (see Figure 9.5). Municipalities in the suburbs of Vancouver have revised residential area zoning regulations by reducing the size of the building envelope and applying a Floor Area Ratio (FAR), usually around 0.3, that would limit the bulk of new dwellings.

In central commercial areas, it is common to permit building on 100% of the lot area, in recognition of owners' need to extract maximum use from the higher-value land. Larger lot coverage is usually allowed in areas where tall apartment and office buildings are located, also because of the higher value of land and buildings. However, in recent decades, in order to reduce the bulk of such buildings and also to provide usable open space for residents of apartments or for office employees, provisions are included in zoning by-laws to require more open space at ground level for every increase in height. As well, the overall height of tall buildings may be regulated according to the total area of all floors expressed as a ratio of lot area, that is, according to the Floor Area Ratio of the building. Thus, referring to Figure 9. 4, an FAR of 1.0 in an R-7 zone that limits lot coverage to 50% means that the owner could build a building of two storeys equal in floor area to the lot size, or else build a taller building, also equal in floor area to the lot size but covering less than 50% of the lot.

Since cities are always changing in their physical form, it is not uncommon to see a conventional urban activity change in its physical characteristics. Such is the case with retailing, an almost inherent urban activity. In the past decade or so, new retailing "formats," as they are called, have appeared in the form of bulky warehouse-type establishments that dwarf existing retail operations. The advent of these so-called big-box retailers has led many municipalities to revise their zoning regulations and commnuty plans to accommodate a wider mix of retail building types. The

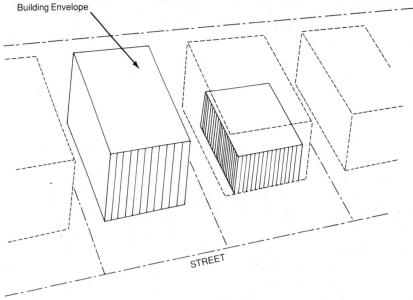

FIGURE 9.5 **The Increasing Bulk of Recent Dwellings**
New "monster homes" often dwarf older neighbouring dwellings, even though built within the same zoning regulations. The new houses take advantage of the entire building envelope. *Source:* G. Hodge.

Town of Markham in Ontario, for example, has added a "retail warehouse" designation to its zoning provisions and the City of London has revised its official plan accordingly.[11]

Density.   The intensity with which the community's land is used is a basic planning factor because it relates to the issue of congestion in the use of public facilities such as water and sewer lines, streets, parks, and so on. The specification of uses and the bulk of building on a parcel of land do not deal with the number of users of the land and buildings. This is especially crucial in residential areas where multiple-family accommodation is provided, in order to ensure that overcrowding does not occur, whether inside or outside dwellings.

Most zoning by-laws where multiple-family dwellings are common now include specific density regulations. In the community plan, density may be referred to by the number of people per unit of land area. However, the zoning by-law must be specific enough to relate to individual parcels and buildings. Density specifications in zoning by-laws may take one of two forms, or a combination of both. The first, and most common, is to specify the *maximum number of dwelling units per unit of land area* (hectares). Various multiple-residence zones may then be created corresponding to existing development patterns or following new styles and trends in the housing market. At the lower end of the scale, zones corresponding to three- and four-storey walk-up apartments may limit development to 24–48 units/ha, for example. Medium densities (96–192 units/ha) are usually related to areas in which the buildings would be taller and have elevators, but probably not exceed ten storeys. High-density zones would be for much taller buildings with densities of 240 units/ha and more. Of course, what is considered a "high" density or a "low" density is related to local conditions and tastes. (It may help to refer to Figure 6.3 on page 167.)

The second method of specifying residential density is according to the *amount of floor area included in each dwelling unit.* This is usually stated as a minimum area (in square metres) in order to ensure that adequate-size apartments are built. Such a regulation is often required in older parts of communities, either where conversion of existing buildings to apartments is likely to occur or where original lot sizes were small and on which older, smaller buildings might be cleared and new apartment buildings constructed. Such a regulation is usually combined with a limitation placed either on the height of buildings or on the number of dwelling units that may be included.

Parking/Loading.   Minimum requirements for off-street parking and loading are common in zoning by-laws. Again, the main objective is to minimize possible congestion in the public streets in the vicinity of a property that might be used more intensively, such as for multiple residences or commercial purposes. Parking standards have been developed through planning experience with various land uses. In residential areas, at least one parking space per dwelling unit is usually needed. However, in higher-density areas this may need to be higher to accommodate parking by residents and visitors. In commercial and manufacturing areas, the standards are often in terms of the number of employees on the assumption of having to provide space for those who drive their cars to work. Loading facilities located off the street are a common requirement in commercial, manufacturing, and institutional zones, with standards usually in terms of the number of square metres of the establishment.

Other Concerns of Zoning: Signs. Typically, one finds several other concerns addressed in the zoning by-laws that pertain, generally, to appearance and safety of land use. Most by-laws deal with the size, height, and location of signs on a building. Signs tend to be discouraged altogether in residential areas; in commercial areas the signs may be regulated to reduce "sign competition" and produce a particular character for the area. Signs that overhang public streets are regulated as well for safety purposes.

Accessory Buildings. Most land uses require, in addition to the principal structure, structures for parking or storage. A garage on the same lot as a single-family house is an accessory use, as is a storage shed on a commercial property and a security guards' building at a manufacturing plant. These are usually quite closely defined in the regulations for each particular zone. The implication is that these uses and structures would not be permitted in the zone without the principal use to which it is an appendage.

Home Occupations. From zoning's earliest days, communities sought to limit commercial activities in residential areas while usually allowing individuals such as music teachers, insurance agents, doctors, and hairdressers to offer services from their homes. Traffic, safety, and noise were the concerns with respect to some "home occupations," as they are usually called in zoning by-laws. Not until the last decade or so were there very many people carrying on business from their homes, but this has now dramatically changed. Both recessionary pressures and the potential of computer and other telecommunications have promoted many new home occupations right across the country, in large cities and small. For example, it is estimated that one-third of Toronto's dwellings in 1993 housed some form of business activity or home occupation.[12] This has stimulated the city to amend its zoning by-law to allow a wide range of "new" home occupations.

The exterior of the home would not be able to be changed, nor would exterior signs advertising the business be allowed; there are similar provisions in other cities.

Aesthetics. Just as zoning strives for a similarity, or compatibility, of uses within a zone, it also strives for a similarity of appearance of buildings. However, few explicit specifications of building appearance have been included in zoning by-laws, save those governing height of buildings. This is largely because zoning grew out of a notion that public intervention in private property should occur only to protect health, safety, and the general welfare of a community.

The regulation of architectural qualities of structures, of course, means being able to define aesthetic norms in legally defensible terms, something not easy to do in such a subjective area. A compromise position used in a number of cities is the designation of particular zones in which the architectural plans of structures are reviewed because the areas are considered of major importance in the "civic design" of the community. One such zone was established for Toronto's University Avenue in the 1920s in the hope of achieving a monumental character to this street leading to the provincial legislative buildings. In the 1950s, Vancouver enacted similar regulations for new structures on its West Georgia Street. The latter approaches act as a separate "zone" superimposed on the by-law's district regulations.

The difficulty of formulating aesthetic regulations on a comprehensive basis in zoning by-laws has led to several new variations. Within the jurisdiction given by development control procedures to municipalities, it is possible to request modifications to facades and exterior materials used on buildings. Because of the recent concern over historically important districts, many provinces have enacted legislation allowing the architectural quality to be closely regulated in such districts. Zoning also can aid in this as the "heritage main street" district in Markham, Ontario's by-law indicates.[13] Both these approaches serve to guide private development on a building-by-building basis in contrast to zoning by-laws, which strive to develop regulations that apply generally to all buildings and properties. It is because the ideal of comprehensive regulations has significant limits that these supplementary tools have come into existence. We turn now to a discussion of these new tools.

Development Control

Origins and Nature
Another way to regulate land use is to institute a permit system in which each property owner must apply at the time of a proposed development

change in order to have the allowable conditions established. This form of regulation is generally referred to as **development control**.

Canadian planning practice, until the 1950s, closely followed the primary mode of land-use control in the United States, that is, zoning. In the United States, the constitutional entrenchment of property rights required any by-laws that regulate land use to be applicable uniformly and universally, and not to deprive property owners of constitutionally guaranteed rights. In Canada, neither the old BNA Act nor the more recent Charter of Rights and Freedoms entrenches property rights. Thus, there is not the same legal basis in Canada for zoning or any reason to limit land-use regulation to that form of by-law.[14]

Development control approaches entered Canadian planning practice largely through the efforts of British and British-trained planners who emigrated to Canada after World War II and came to hold senior planning jobs. British planning practice never embraced zoning, preferring to leave responsibility for plan implementation in the hands of local administrators. Development control was considered particularly useful for the period during which a formal community plan was being prepared, especially in fast-growing cities. Each proposal for new development, buildings or subdivisions could be reviewed to ensure consistency with the aims of the emerging plan, and a development permit was issued as warranted. The system was widely used in western Canada from the mid-1950s, but did not enter regular planning practice in Ontario until 1970. While it began as an interim measure to be used during plan preparation, development control has become part of the routine of planning practice, in conjunction with zoning.

Substantive Focus

Development control is known by various names among the provinces: in Alberta the term is **development permit,** while in Ontario the term now used is **site plan control.** The approach is, however, similar. Development control regulation is invoked at the actual time a proposal is made to erect a new building or to significantly expand an existing one. The focus is thus on the building rather than its use. Since development control works within the context of zoning, it starts with the premise that the zoning regulations as to the use of the site and the allowable building envelope provide the basic frame of reference. The latter is usually not negotiable at this stage of regulation.

Development control is concerned with the actual placement of the building on the site (within the building envelope), the appearance of the building, its relation to surrounding buildings and areas, and its relation to streets. The following extract from the current Ontario planning act illustrates the scope of the approach one generally finds in development control. The person or group proposing the development must provide to the municipality

> plans showing the location of all buildings and structures to be erected and showing the location of all facilities and works (e.g. swimming pools, fences and walls, landscaping, walkways, outside lighting, parking areas). ... Drawings showing plan, elevation, and cross-section views for each building ... sufficient to display
> (a) the massing and conceptual design of the proposed building;
> (b) the relationship of the proposed building to adjacent buildings, streets, and exterior areas to which members of the public have access; and
> (c) the provision of interior walkways, stairs, elevators, and escalators to which members of the public have access from streets, open spaces, and interior walkways in adjacent buildings.

A development control by-law usually requires proponents of a development in specified districts to submit their application and plans for review. Many places have specified their entire community as subject to development control. The applications may be reviewed by a committee or a designated official on whose recommendation a development agreement or contract is drawn up specifying the conditions that the developer is legally bound to fulfil in the actual construction process.

The original purpose for which development control was introduced into Canadian planning—the bridging of plan-making and zoning—still exists in most provinces. In specific areas, it may be necessary or desirable to reconsider present zoning and planning policies. Development control can be invoked on a limited-term basis under what are often called "interim control by-laws," or more commonly "holding by-laws." This tool, a hybrid of zoning and development control, must specify the area, the duration of time for which the by-law applies, and the types of changes that will be allowed in that period. Usually only minor changes will be allowed according to existing zoning regulations.

The availability of development control powers opened up avenues of plan implementation beyond those envisioned for it originally. The technique enables a community's plan-makers to deal with developers and their projects on a *case-by-case* basis, rather than on the uniform basis found in zoning. Development control, then, means that a community can enter into *negotiations* with regard to each project and impose individualized conditions for it. This approach "provides and encourages flexibility and variety in development that zoning would not allow," says planning lawyer Stanley Makuch, because "different developments create different demands."[15] The advantage of planners being able to directly influence a project's outcome is very attractive. At the same time, it underlines the role of the community plan to provide guidelines for such negotiations. This discretionary approach is prominent in much of community planning today, and more will be said about it in Chapter 14.

Redevelopment Plans

In most communities, districts develop in a consistent, amenable way: buildings and uses are compatible, street patterns are regular, and the renewal of properties follows accepted norms. There are two typical instances where this fails to happen. In the first, older areas of a community deteriorate without benefit of their hoped-for rejuvenation. In the second, inadequate or incompatible development may take place in the fringe areas of communities, despite zoning regulations.

In the 1950s and 1960s, most new urban development was taking place on the edges of cities. It consisted not only of new housing and the facilities needed to support the growing populations, but also of businesses and industries relocating from their inner areas. The older parts of cities which had suffered neglect in the two decades of depression and world war were often blighted further by the exodus of firms and residents. Planning strategists argued that urban blight was becoming too extensive for the actions of the normal land market to counteract and, therefore, major public initiatives would be needed to rebuild older areas. Urban redevelopment programs were instituted, providing government funds that would enable communities to plan and carry out the rebuilding or refurbishing of large blocks of land.

There have been many versions of city-rebuilding programs, from the urban renewal of the 1950s to the neighbourhood improvement programs of the 1970s. Central to all of these was the notion of designating a specific area for redevelopment and preparing a plan for its rejuvenation. There is an essential difference between this type of planning approach and that of zoning. Under a **redevelopment plan,** the community can intervene directly in private property and, indeed, take the initiative for improvement away from the landowner by acquiring land and removing or replacing buildings. Provincial planning acts delegate this power to prepare redevelopment plans to municipalities, under the condition that the plans are conceived within the objective of the overall community plan.

Terminologies differ among planning acts: in Ontario the redevelopment plan is now called a **community improvement plan,** while in Alberta it is called an **area redevelopment plan.** The scope of a redevelopment plan is well illustrated in the purposes contained in the 1977

Alberta Planning Act. The designated-area plan may be implemented, to paraphrase the legislation, by preserving or improving land and buildings, or rehabilitating, removing, constructing, or replacing buildings, or establishing and improving public roadways, public utilities, or other services in the area. These planning prescriptions are very similar to those found in Canada's earliest planning acts, 65 years earlier. This no doubt reflects a continuing concern that some physical development may be of poor quality from its outset, and thus there is the need for public intervention to set it on a proper course.

While redevelopment plans are usually thought of in relation to older, blighted, high-density ("slum-type") areas, there is another situation for which they are appropriate. Not infrequently, land authorized for urban development does not achieve the intensity of use envisioned for it in plans and zoning by-laws. Often areas may be found on the fringe of the community that have a potential for more intensive development, such as those with scattered country residential acreages, junkyards, and strips of drive-in services of various kinds. The aim of the redevelopment plan may be to achieve more efficient and economic patterns of development for providing public utilities and roads or for aesthetic reasons, or both.

PLANNING TOOLS FOR VACANT AND UNDEVELOPED AREAS

A characteristic of the development of cities and towns is that it usually takes place on small parcels of land. These small parcels are created by splitting up large tracts of land through a formal process known as **land subdivision.** The process is formal because of the need to register and certify landownership with respect to these parcels. But the process is also part of a larger process of the economic land market—the supplying of developable parcels of land to the community. In the latter case, land subdivision is a competitive process by which each subdivider aims to attract development to his or her new parcels of land.

One of the earliest difficulties confronted by community planners was achieving satisfactory town extensions as cities and towns expanded. Canada's first planning acts recognized that the creation of new parcels of land could have adverse effects on both the nature and direction of the future development of the community. There was experience with subdivisions in which individual parcels had inadequate access from adjoining streets, streets did not align with or match the size of streets in already-developed areas, and building lots were not drained properly or even of sufficient size and shape to create a satisfactory physical environment. Since the community has the responsibility to provide public services and street access to all parcels of land, it has a direct financial interest in the proper subdivision of land for future development. It was the early planning acts that established this community interest, in order to maintain consistent standards among competing land subdividers and to create the kind of environment that was compatible with the community's aims and within the community's economic capability to maintain. Or, as a recent document from the Canada Mortgage and Housing Corporation notes, the "two central issues" are "cost and quality."[16]

Subdivision Control

The tool developed by planners in response to the above need is known generally as **subdivision control**. In essence, it consists of the authority of the community to approve any plans for splitting up land for development, to ensure that such plans meet local standards for health, safety, and convenience. In subdivision control, community approval is tied to the province's power over registration and certification of valid parcels of land for future sale. This enables planning authorities to exercise a high degree of control over the manner in which land can be used for residential building or other purposes, as well as over the time at which the land can be developed.

Provincial planning legislation vests subdivision control powers in provincial or local authorities, and sometimes in both with the municipality giving "draft" approval and the province giving "final" approval of the registered plan of a subdivision. There is usually a provision stating that registered plans are not required where only one or two small parcels are being created, or where the new parcels are too large to be sold as building lots. Provisions of the latter kind are known as "consents to a land severance" and constitute a special (and not insignificant) form of land subdivision regulation, which will be dealt with in a later section.

Subdivision control has two basic components, one substantive and the other procedural. On the substantive side, this tool attempts to obtain high-quality physical environments. It does this by subjecting plans that propose the subdivision of land to an appraisal of their content according to planning and engineering standards. On the procedural side, subdivision control operates as a monitoring process, with prescribed steps and with respect to all those public bodies having an interest in the outcome of the proposed land subdivision and subsequent development. The latter formal side is necessary because of the constraints that this scrutiny places on the ownership rights of those proposing the subdivision and of the ultimate owners of the subdivided parcels alike.

It can be seen that subdivision control is a *process* type of planning tool (in contrast to zoning, which is legislative). Subdivision control processes differ in detail from community to community and from province to province, both with respect to provincial planning institutions and concepts of subdivision standards. On the general level, the substantive and procedural components of all the provinces have much in common. We deal now with each of these components briefly, concentrating on residential subdivisions, which constitute the bulk of subdivision activities in most communities.

Subdivision Standards

Central to subdivision control is the examination of the actual design of the proposed subdivision and an appraisal of the standards used in its layout. A subdivision plan, as a Newfoundland planning manual states, "is in itself a small planning scheme."[17] It is thus scrutinized according to planning criteria pertaining to the form and density of housing, street systems, open space, and essential community services. Since a subdivision is likely to involve modification of the land surface, various engineering criteria pertaining to drainage, road construction, and the installation of public utilities are also invoked in appraising a plan of subdivision.

Most provinces, in their planning legislation, establish the general factors which a proposed plan must take into consideration. In the Ontario planning act, a plan of subdivision must indicate the legal boundaries of all parcels, the location and widths of streets, the intended use of parcels, natural features of the site, physical features such as railways and highways, and the availability of water supplies and other municipal services. Such a plan, obviously, contains a good deal of detail and must be accurately drawn; subdivision plans are usually required to be certified by a licensed land surveyor as to the boundaries of the overall site and the individual parcels. This is called the **draft plan**, since it may still undergo revisions before final approval is given. The draft plan is also required to consider subdivisions, streets, and land uses on adjoining lands, as well as any zoning or other land-use controls pertaining to the site.

In addition to these basic formal requirements of the planning legislation, most provinces and many communities have manuals or handbooks that set forth design standards for subdivisions. They are part of a continuing effort to promote good-quality subdivision design, an outcome easier to advocate than to achieve. According to a review of Ontario's nearly 25 years of experience in this area, "much contemporary subdivision design is still poor to mediocre in quality" and there is a "pervasive utilitarianism" about most subdivision planning.[18] There are two reasons for much of the lacklustre design. The first is that, as with other aspects of civic design, subdivision

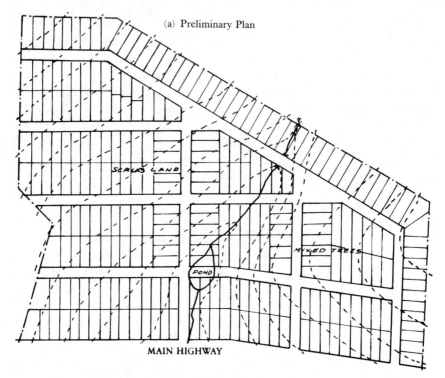

FIGURE 9.6   The Benefits of Improved Subdivision Design
In this example from Newfoundland, a Preliminary Plan (a) submitted by the developer was improved in its final version (b) by provincial planners to include substantial open spaces, lots for commercial development, and less street area and length, and, hence, to have lower costs for services and preparation that could be passed on to homebuyers. In addition, the new layout was more pleasing, promoted better drainage, and provided a greater variety of lots. *Source* (figures and table opposite): Courtesy of the Newfoundland Department of Municipal and Provincial Affairs, Urban and Rural Planning Division.

plans call for special design skills and an awareness of what constitutes a good residential environment. Such skills are unfortunately not plentiful among the surveyors, architects, engineers, and planners who lay out sub-divisions:—thus the need for guidelines and manuals. The second reason is the tendency of many subdividers to concentrate on the yield of lots from the site, often with disregard for the natural topography, amenities, and rational circulation system. Paradoxically, it can be shown that the best-designed subdivisions are also the most efficient.

An example of the value of striving for good subdivision design can be seen in a typical situation illustrated in a Newfoundland subdivision manual.[19] Figure 9.6 shows both the initial proposal and the refined subdivision

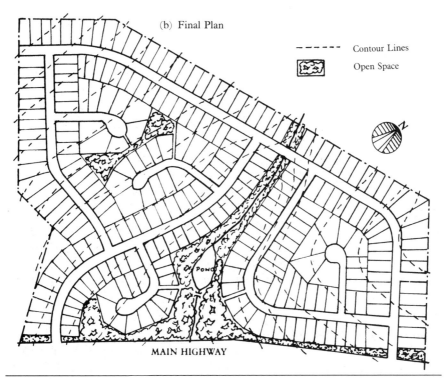

(b) Final Plan

- - - - - -   Contour Lines

Open Space

MAIN HIGHWAY

Design Factors	A. Preliminary Plan	B. Final Plan
Area	22.5 ha	22.5 ha
Residential lots	264	261
Commercial lots	0	4
Open space	0	3.2 ha
Street length	2,694 m	2,565 m
Street area	19,955 m^2	15,733 m^2

design for a tract of land abutting a main highway. On environmental grounds, the second plan provides a greater variety of lots, a more interesting layout, ample public open space, housing buffered from the highway, and respect for the topography. On economic grounds, it has a smaller length of streets to provide, lower costs for water, sewers, and street lighting, and a drainage system that respects natural features.

Other factors that will be taken into account in appraising a subdivision plan include concerns over energy conservation, access for pedestrians, and availability of public transit. Subdivision design can, for example, provide layouts that allow homes to be positioned in order to take advantage of available sunlight for passive solar energy, as well as employ natural features and vegetation to reduce the effects of adverse climatic conditions. Good subdivision design always stresses the separation of traffic modes and, in particular, the provision of exclusive routes for pedestrians. There should be direct and safe connections between dwellings and local activity centres (school, stores, library, church), and recreation areas and public transit stops. And wherever possible, pathways should have only moderate grades, so that they can be used by the elderly and those in wheelchairs. There are clearly many facets that contribute to the ultimate quality of the residential environment that will result from a subdivision plan. No simple list can possibly encompass all of them; however, a set of questions that planners use in reviewing residential proposals will provide a basic overview of concerns (see Figure 9.7). Before leaving this discussion, the reader should note that where a subdivision plan is intended to accommodate commercial or industrial uses, analogous subdivision standards are applied in appraising it.

Subdivision Application Procedures

Subdivision control is a system that prescribes the way the subdivider applies for a permit to allow a tract of land to be split up and parcels sold off. Because of legal constraints, the province defines a procedure to be followed in applying for approval of the plan for a subdivision, as well as the prerequisites for such approval. Procedures differ among provinces largely as a result of where the final authority for approving a plan is lodged. Some have reserved this power for the provincial minister in charge or for appointed officials. Others have delegated subdivision approval powers to municipalities; still others involve such intermediate-level bodies as regional planning commissions or metropolitan governments. There are, however, several common features to all subdivision control procedures:

1. **Specified process.**   In order to protect the rights of owners to subdivide their land, the process of applying for approval is specified. It indicates the form the application must take, the steps the plan's review will follow, and often the maximum amount of time the process will take.

2. **Plan circulation.**   Since a proposed subdivision of land may affect the interests and activities of a wide array of agencies, a draft plan is circulated broadly for comment and recommendation. Typically, all provincial government departments with an interest (e.g., transportation, housing, energy, agriculture, health) are asked to review a plan.

Also, public and private utilities, transportation companies, and special-purpose bodies are included in the review process, along with various departments of the local government.

3. **Conditions for approval.**   The subdivider is considered responsible for the provision of the roads, parks, and public utilities necessary to serve the subdivision. Since they ultimately come under community ownership, it is necessary to specify how they shall be paid for and the standards to which they will be built.

4. **Subdivision agreement.**   In order to ensure that the basic services are provided for the subdivision, a contract or subdivision agreement is usually required to be signed between the subdivider and the municipality and is often registered against the deed to the property. These agreements cover such matters as staging of development, provision of services, roads standards, minimum construction and material standards, conveyance of lands for parks, and demolition and removal of existing buildings.

5. **Final plan.**   The plan of subdivision is not operative until it has received final approval. Such approval is given only after any conditions imposed on the draft plan from the review process have been fulfilled and a subdivision agreement exists to secure necessary services and standards. At this point, the plan may be registered and binds all future landowners. No additional demands can be made on the developer of the land.

The subdivision plan review process is the community's opportunity to have a direct effect on the outcome of the development of a portion of its physical environment. There are, as well, two vital facets of the community's review of a plan of subdivision, regardless of whether it is the final approving authority. The first is to determine the proposal's *compatibility* with the aims and design envisioned for the area in the community's overall plan. In conjunction with this, the community reviews the plan's compliance with zoning regulations that already apply to the area, as well as the possibility that amendments to both the zoning by-law and community plan may be required to accommodate the subdivision. The second facet that the community will need to be concerned with is whether the subdivision is *premature* or not. An approved subdivision makes demands on the community's resources in that services must be provided, roads and parks maintained, etc., whenever the land is built upon and people come to live there. It is therefore in the community's interests to know the timing or staging of the actual development. In most provinces, a community can establish conditions regarding the staging of development on the site to coincide with its

---

Review Each Subdivision Plan with These Questions in Mind

Community Context
- ❑ Does the street layout conform to the existing street pattern?
- ❑ Does the plan relate well to existing community facilities?
- ❑ Does the plan conform to the policies of the community plan?
- ❑ Does the plan provide adequately for education, recreation, and shopping needs of residents?

Residential Needs
- ❑ Do the proposed dwelling types suit community needs?
- ❑ Do dwelling arrangements ensure privacy?
- ❑ Will dwellings be affected by excessive noise, dust, or fumes?
- ❑ Is the size of lots adequate for the dwellings?

Streets and Parking
- ❑ Are the grades, widths, and intersections of streets adequate?
- ❑ Are parking provisions adequate?
- ❑ Is pedestrian access separated from the street?

Public Services and Utilities
- ❑ Has drainage been carefully considered?
- ❑ Are water and sewage facilities adequate and conveniently located?
- ❑ Is street lighting adequate?

Environmental Considerations
- ❑ Does the arrangement of lots and dwellings make the best use of the climate?
- ❑ Have trees been left to stabilize the soils?
- ❑ Has provision been made so that storm-water runoff does not pollute other water bodies?
- ❑ Has the amount of paved area been minimized?

Aesthetic Considerations
- ❑ Do dwelling arrangements result in attractive streetscapes?
- ❑ Will street furniture be provided?
- ❑ Are natural features of the site incorporated in the design?

FIGURE 9.7 **Planning Checklist for Proposed Residential Subdivisions**

own plans for investments in services as well as with its desires to achieve a particular spatial pattern of development. In this sense, subdivision control becomes part of an integrated planning process, rather than being an isolated act affecting only one proponent and one area.

Consents and Severances

A special form of land subdivision, particularly for rural areas, is the severing of one or two small parcels of land from a large tract such as a farm. A subdivision plan is normally not required for this purpose, but since it is necessary to register the new parcel and convey title properly, a formal process is required. It is known as **granting consent to the land severance,** or, in popular terms, simply as a "consent" or "severance."

This process was, until recent decades, mostly used to allow farmers to create a homestead site for themselves or for a close relative also involved in the farming or other rural activity, and to create occasional lots for summer cottages. However, with the increased demand for year-round country residences and cottages after 1950, obtaining a consent became a source of income to rural landowners. It also became a source of problems for rural communities by creating scattered and ribbon development with consequent difficulties and costs of providing services and road maintenance. In recreation regions, increased severances for cottages not infrequently led to pollution of lakes. Indeed, the ills associated with excessive use of rural severances led to the popularization of the term "sprawl" to characterize development in fringe areas of cities and in rural areas.

Consents must be formally approved, often by the same approving body that processes subdivision plans. A consent is usually required to meet the same conditions as a subdivision plan with regard to dedicating land for streets, road widening, and parks. However, beyond these basic requirements, provincial planning legislation is noticeably silent on planning criteria that should be considered. Some efforts were made by local approving authorities in Ontario in the 1970s to establish criteria for consents—for example, conformity to community plans, avoidance of high-grade agricultural lands, and adequacy of waste disposal to prevent pollution of nearby waterbodies. The results can be characterized as inconsistent, even in these areas.

An Ontario report calls consents "the Achilles' heel of planning."[20] And a probe of the issue in New Brunswick cites the lack of a planning system that could provide for "suitable consideration of the overall implications" of individual land severance proposals.[21] While individual applications for a consent may be justified, it is the accumulation of consents decisions that needs to be considered. Two provinces, Quebec and British Columbia, appear to have made some headway in reducing rural consents, especially where agricultural land is concerned. B.C. established its Agricultural Land Reserves in 1973 and Quebec established its "protected areas" under its Commission de protection du territoire agricole in 1978. Although there has not been a halt to the subdivision of agricultural land as was sought by these government interventions, it is clear that it has been greatly reduced.[22]

Replotting Schemes

A special form of subdivision planning that has received much attention from planners in western Canada has to do with salvaging subdivisions that attracted little or no development. The practice is called **replotting** because it involves redesigning the street system, the pattern of building lots, and the open space of an already-existing legal subdivision. In many communities in the past, the promise of rapid growth often led to considerable subdivision of land in excess of actual growth. These subdivisions usually predated planning and subdivision control practices and, not infrequently, were inefficient and unimaginative gridiron designs bearing little relation to topographic features or existing community patterns. Many of these older, undeveloped subdivisions were in fringe areas, and as communities expanded, especially after World War II, they were found to be incompatible with present-day planning and subdivision standards.

Provisions were incorporated into planning legislation to allow communities, in effect, to redesign these old subdivisions. A replotting scheme in Alberta involves three steps.[23] First, the existing subdivision must be cancelled and all parcels consolidated. Second, a new design is formulated by the community and registered. Third, the newly subdivided land is redistributed among affected landowners. Replotting offers a number of advantages to a community: more efficient street patterns and utility service, more amenable residential settings, and tax returns from land previously under-utilized.

Condominium Subdivisions

A type of subdivision of property that is relatively new in the realm of planning is that of condominium ownership, or "strata-title" as it is called in some provinces. Essentially, it denotes conveying ownership to a housing unit without conveying title to the land on which it sits. The latter, the site, is held in common by the owners of all the dwelling units sharing the site. The typical forms of **condominiums** are row housing and apartment buildings, although recently there has also been an extension of this form of common ownership into commercial and industrial development projects. The main advantages are the sharing of common community facilities and no responsibilities for site maintenance, which is provided by a corporation formed by the owners.

Because creating a condominium project results in splitting up a larger piece of property among several owners, most provinces have developed means to ensure property rights and consideration of planning standards. Condominium legislation has been developed to cope with the special features of ownership, and existing subdivision control legislation and regulations are used to allow examination of planning implications of the project.

Condominium development may take the form of either a brand new building(s) or a transference of the single ownership of an existing building to shared ownership. The latter approach, **condominium conversion** of existing multiple-unit rental buildings, has received special attention from planners because it neither creates any additional dwelling units nor assures present residents of the continuation of their housing. While conversion is popular with owners of older apartment buildings, it has frequently proved contentious when tenants are forced to move as buildings are upgraded to attract higher-income purchasers. Elderly and/or low-income tenants are often caught in such conversions and must try to find accommodation in a rental housing market which, in many cases, is already tight. Since condominium conversion may actually reduce the stock of rental units in a community, many cities have enacted conversion policies that limit conversions where the rental vacancy rate is abnormally low and where present tenants are not going to be the subsequent condominium purchasers in the project. The experience in Montreal is a good example of the difficulties that surround this issue.[24] With over three-quarters of its households being renters, it searched for 20 years for a solution. "Benchmark" rents were finally established in 1993 so that conversions could not occur in apartment buildings with rents below this level, the purpose being to protect low-income tenants, including university and college students. Even this can produce a dilemma for municipalities that often enjoy higher tax returns from the refurbished apartments.

TOOLS FOR FINE-TUNING LAND-USE PLANNING

The main tools of land-use regulation used by planners—zoning and subdivision control—are founded on the principle of being universally and uniformly applicable in regard to the properties and the landowners in the community. In other words, the regulations that will affect the development of a property apply equally to all similar properties and are known to the owner beforehand. This means that land-use regulations are formulated in *general* terms to cover normal configurations of site, location, and property characteristics. But among the numerous parcels of land and kinds of projects to which these must apply, it is evident that not all will have the same characteristics. Moreover, the regulations may cause hardship for some owners or anomalous land-use arrangements for the community. Thus, there have developed a number of planning tools that are aimed at responding to special circumstances of properties and land uses not adequately covered by the general regulations. The most common of these tools for fine-tuning are described briefly below. In effect, they refine the impact of zoning.

Variances

Zoning by-laws cannot cover all the distinctive situations that might affect each of the parcels of land within a zone. There may be unusual conditions of topography, size, shape, and location that affect the development of a parcel in the manner envisioned in the regulations. For example, a parcel with a steep slope may not allow, without undue cost, a building to be sited to meet setback requirements, or the specific land uses applying to a property in a commercial zone may not cover a similar use that is being proposed. In order not to create situations of special hardship, planning legislation allows for adjustments in by-law provisions to be considered in regard to a *particular parcel* of land. One means of adjustment is called a **variance,** since it allows the provisions of the zoning by-law to vary from their stated terms.

Variances introduce a needed degree of flexibility in the application of a zoning by-law, which otherwise might require a formal amendment. The variance does, however, operate in a delicate area of judgement wherein it must be decided whether a *major* hardship or difficulty is created by the regulations and moreover, whether in relaxing the zoning standards there might be adverse effects on adjoining properties and the community environment. Since the variance that is allowed is expected both to create only minimal effects of surrounding properties and to convey no special advantage for the applicant, it is usually referred to as a "minor variance." Criteria defining what qualifies as minor have never been well established, which has led, at worst, to numerous abuses of the variance and, at best, to controversy over many decisions.

The granting of a variance, because it affects property rights and also involves an appeal from the requirements of legislation, is a formal process spelled out in provincial legislation. It is a process that usually devolves to the municipality in the form of a special appeal body. The names of these appeal bodies differ from province to province. In Manitoba the body is called the Variation Board, in Saskatchewan the Board of Zoning Appeal, and in Ontario the Committee of Adjustment. These bodies are usually required to give notice of the application for a variance to all property own-ers within the vicinity and to provide reasons for their decision, which is normally final and binding. In some communities, the activities of the appeal body are coordinated by the municipal planning staff, but in most no connection with local planning efforts is attempted or, possibly, even recognized.

Non-conforming Uses

A zoning by-law is essentially future-oriented, but in already developed areas, its standards are not likely to fit all uses and structures that existed before it came into effect. The concept of natural justice prevents the vio-lation of property rights that existed before the by-law was passed. Thus, there may be uses and structures that do not conform to the standards in the new regulations but that will legally be allowed to continue. It is cus-tomary to refer to them as **legal non-conforming uses**. There are actu-ally three forms of pre-existing conditions that may not conform to the current by-law. One is the *use* to which a property is put, such as a store in a residential neighbourhood; another is a *structure* that may be situated so as to not provide the required yard space; and the last is a *lot* that is smaller than would now be required.

Non-conforming-use status copes with anomalies between the standards of earlier development and those standards favoured by the community in its current by-law. However, if the community wants to achieve its new standards, then there must be a way of bringing the earlier development into conformity with them. Thus, most zoning by-laws have provisions that limit any expansion of the structure and the use to which it was being put at the time of the new by-law, as well as rebuilding in the event of the building's destruction. In this way, the aim of the community to have the non-conforming uses replaced is balanced against vested property rights. The record of non-conformities disappearing is not salutary in most cities, and there are many instances of applications to enlarge such uses. An appli-cation for a change in a non-conforming use is often handled by the same zoning appeal body that deals with variances, and the procedures are much the same.

Transfer of Development Rights

As noted earlier in this chapter, zoning defines for each property a build-ing envelope in which the owner has a right to develop a structure of a specified volume; that is, there are "development rights" for each property. Two decades ago, it began to be proposed that the community might wish to allow an owner to sell the development rights on one property to someone who owned land located in an area where the community wished to encourage development, such as in an urban renewal area. This is the notion, now widely practised in large cities, that is known as **Transfer of Development Rights** (TDR).

TDR basically shifts density potential from one area to another. It aims at benefiting three interests. One is the owner, who can sell the development rights on a parcel on which he or she cannot or does not wish to undertake further development, perhaps because there is already a satisfactory building on it. The purchaser, or transferee, of the development rights also may benefit, by obtaining sufficient additional density to make a project economically feasible. The community could benefit, sometimes doubly, by achieving development where it had been planned and by limiting development at the location from which the development rights were transferred. For example, in some cities TDR has saved historically important buildings from demolition and replacement. The process through which such transfers take place is one of negotiation between property owners and city officials. This and other forms of negotiation in the planning process will be discussed in Chapter 14.

Planned Unit Development

Many communities have included in their zoning by-laws a means by which the requirements of normal zoning districts may be modified and more innovative standards incorporated in the plan for a project. This approach, which is generally called **Planned Unit Development** (PUD), offers the developer an option to build within a set of requirements established especially for the project, rather than in strict conformity with existing regulations. The incentive for the developer in PUD may lie in achieving a few more dwelling units, in being able to mix several kinds of dwelling units and even some retail uses, or in producing a better-quality and hence more marketable project. The community, of course, also wants the better design and offers, through PUD, to relax such standards as height, yard size, lot size, and dwelling type in return for working along with the developer to achieve a mutually acceptable project that has been planned as a unit.

The most noticeable result of PUD is that more common open space is available to residents than would occur if normal zoning regulations were followed. This is often obtained by forgoing the requirements for side yards, which are usually under-used, reducing the width of lots, and allowing dwellings to be built with no intervening space. This approach is called **zero-lot-line** and offers the opportunity to stagger, cluster, and group dwellings instead of using the traditional form of subdivision with standard

Planning Issue 9.1

VANCOUVER ALLOWS TALLER BUILDINGS

Council move provides for corridors with views of mountains

VANCOUVER — The City of Vancouver has decided to trade in its stunning vistas of treetops and mountain peaks for something more inspiring: tall buildings.

After a long wait while citizen protest was measured, Vancouver city council voted overwhelmingly on Tuesday night to raise the allowable maximum height for commercial office towers in the city downtown core.

The lifting of the limit to 187 metres (roughly 60 storeys) from 135 metres was strongly opposed by some designers and urban planners and a neighbourhood whose view of the mountains could be blocked, but most citizens appeared uninterested in the issue.

Because the downtown sits on a peninsula partly surrounded by a ring of mountains, residents in many neighbourhoods are able to see over the current skyline to the slopes of the coastal rain forest and the mountains capped in snow, when it is not raining.

Existing restrictions that preserve partial "view corridors" between the downtown buildings for some communities will be preserved, according to the plan approved by the 11-member council. ... Two members voted against the plan.

The introduction of a downtown skyline that soars upward according to developers' designs instead of the current relatively flat skyline of limited-height buildings drew praise from several councillors.

"Cities have always been the greatest manufacturing accomplishment of people," councillor Gordon Price said. "In every culture ... height has been something humanity itself seems to want to engage in."...

Source: Excerpted from "Vancouver Allows Taller Buildings," *The Globe and Mail*, May 8, 1997, A4. Reprinted with permission from *The Globe and Mail*.

setbacks. There may also be noticeable savings in land costs for each dwelling, thereby providing more affordable housing. The Alberta Planning Act of 1977, for example, quite explicitly promotes PUD by permitting municipalities to apply to have an Innovative Residential Developments Area established. The success of PUD depends on negotiations between municipal staff and the developer.

View Planes

Throughout the practice of land-use regulation, there is always the need to consider the balance between the development rights conveyed to a property owner and the rights of the community, which might be impinged on by the actual development. Sometimes those latter rights may be infringed upon at some distance from the parcel being developed. A common case in point is the obstruction of views, which people in the community have traditionally enjoyed, by new tall or bulky buildings. Planners have become aware that the character of a community is very often grasped by people through the recurring views they have of landmarks, historic and significant structures, and special landscapes, and have developed legal mechanisms that specify the protection of selected views. Thus, communities can enact by-laws that limit building height and bulk in specific "view plane" or "view corridor" areas. **View planes** are three-dimensional, governing both height and breadth of view from the specified area. The case of Halifax was cited earlier; this city has moved to protect traditional views of the harbour and old parts of the city from the area of the Citadel that overlooks the harbour. In Ottawa, the National Capital Commission has regulations governing views of the Peace Tower, but has had only limited success in protecting them. Vancouver's city council recently decided to allow taller, but not bulkier, buildings in its downtown area while maintaining existing view corridors to the mountain backdrop. (See Planning Issue 9.1.)

Special Districts

Traditionally, zoning took a simple view of city development, and district classifications reflected this. Three general categories of land use were used—residential, commercial, industrial—and within these only limited numbers of subcategories. Each of the districts—whether single-family two-family, neighbourhood commercial, or light industrial—had standards for bulk, yards, and uses, standards that were the same no matter where in the city the district was located. As well, these standards ignored differences in character between one such district and another in the same category. Zoning practice now recognizes that many neighbourhoods in cities have unique characteristics or problems. Some may be historically important in the community, and some may be stable while others are not.

Special district designation, which is now a fairly standard part of zoning, is designed to cope with new and special needs in land use. One of the most common is the historic district; another is the special designation of districts in which large institutional or public uses occur (e.g., hospitals, universities, and airports); zones to protect and encourage waterfront development are also becoming common. One of the most widely used types of special district is that defined for environmentally sensitive areas, such as those subject to flooding or those having special ecological characteristics. The advent of special districts indicates not only that cities are too complex for the range of response offered by simple land-use regulations, but also that we may have new perceptions of what is important in land use.

Amendments

The outright revision of a zoning by-law, or of a community plan for that matter, can be seen as a means of adjusting to special needs and changes in the community environment. The reason for not considering revision sooner in this discussion of the myriad of adjustment tools is that it represents a more far-reaching step, involving a broader public interest. In the opinion of most people involved in conceiving and administering plans, this is a step that should not be taken lightly. Provincial legislatures require formal steps to be taken for an **amendment,** steps that are much the same as those for the original enactment of a zoning by-law or community plan.

The extra statutory hurdles in the amending process, as compared to the other forms of adjustments, reflect the need to provide security in the continuance of major commitments to planning decisions. In the case of zoning by-laws, particularly those of long standing, property owners come to rely on the district standards and have a right to expect their continuance unless a major change can be justified on planning grounds. (Indeed, it is not unreasonable to call amendments "major variances.") For the community plan, the rationale for amendment should be more substantive, such as a major change in growth patterns, the introduction of such new forms of transportation as a rapid transit line, the establishment of large, new land uses, or the disposition of the community to alter its course of development. A change in a community plan often necessitates an amendment to the community's zoning by-law, and a proposed by-law amendment may signal the need to consider a plan change. Good planning practice makes these two initiatives interdependent, and some provinces require that the implications for each be considered simultaneously. Amendments of by-laws and plan changes should be possible when the planning considerations are substantial and the community as a whole is in agreement.

Making Land-Use Regulation Effective

Land-use regulation definitely falls on the process side of planning. The various statutory controls described above are themselves not plans of desired development, but rather the means by which the community's planning objectives are linked to the development process, that is, linked to the aims, inclinations, and decisions of those individuals, firms, and organizations that may wish to develop land. Mostly, land-use regulations are intended to shape the plans of prospective developers in the private sector, but public bodies, including the community itself, are also influenced by them.

In their basic forms, like zoning and subdivision control, land-use regulations are negative in their approach. They function, essentially, to establish minimum standards for development. But while they can be effective in preventing development considered to be undesirable, these regulations are relatively powerless in obtaining desirable development. In other words, they inform the developer of what is minimally acceptable, but the actual decision to develop land at or above these standards remains with the developer. A few new approaches, such as Planned Unit Development and Transfer of Development Rights, offer *positive* incentives to developers to work with planners in return for relaxing burdensome aspects of the controls. Development control approaches are another way in which the community's planners can actively work with developers to secure the most amenable projects.

Land-use regulation is a process in which land developers respond to the standards set by community officials. In this sense, it is a reactive process for the community's planners; they must await the initiatives of the developers. Further, the community's planners in this realm are diverse. They include the professional planners on staff (or consultants), planning boards, zoning boards of appeal, the local council, regional or district planners, provincial planning ministries, as well as other government bodies and public utilities. All of these may be "actors" in one area or another of land-use regulation, depending upon the prescribed procedures. It is important to appreciate that each actor is able to influence the outcome of the planning goals of the community; in effect, each participates in implementing the community plan. Thus, the need for promoting active roles for participants to secure mutual learning (i.e., respect and appreciation) is apparent.[25]

Making land-use regulation effective in the attainment of a community's planning goals is a complex task. Coordination among the diverse actors is essential to assure that the various tools are used in a consistent fashion. The two main components of this task are (1) the presence of an overall community plan and (2) an organizational focus for planning within the community. The plan, or at least a clear statement of planning objectives, provides the benchmark against which the various actors can assess the impact of the decisions they must make. But there must also be a commitment, within the community, to the plan: there must be some person or group whose responsibility it is to uphold it. This could be the director of planning, a planning committee, the council, or some combination of all these. The approach that needs to be taken will involve both monitoring all activities in the regulation of land use (such as subdivision proposals, applications for variance, etc.) and influencing the deliberations of various bodies (through representations, analyses, etc.).

Land-use regulation, as we noted at the outset of this chapter, is only one of the major tasks involved in implementing a community plan. There are areas in which the community may operate in a more direct way, such as through its capital investments and programs, which will be described in the next chapter. However, a theme we wish to stress with regard to implementation of plans is that *the various tools are interdependent.* Concerted efforts at coordinating land-use regulation activities can enhance the efforts occurring through other tools; the reverse may also be true if coordination is weak.

ENDNOTES

1. One important planning study suggests this portion might be no higher than 10%: William L.C. Wheaton, "Public and Private Agents of Change in Urban Expansion," in M. Webber et al., *Explorations into Urban Structure* (Philadelphia: University of Pennsylvania Press, 1964), 154–196.
2. Thomas H. Logan, "The Americanization of German Zoning," *Journal of the American Institute of Planners* 42 (October 1976), 377–385.
3. Elizabeth Bloomfield, "Reshaping the Urban Landscape? Town Planning Effects in Kitchener/Waterloo, 1912–1926," in G.A. Stelter and A. Artibise, eds., *Shaping the Urban Landscape* (Ottawa: Carleton University Press, 1982), 256–303.
4. Ian MacF. Rogers, *Canadian Law of Planning and Zoning* (Toronto: Carswell, 1973), 120.
5. Cf. John C. Weaver, "The Property Industry and Land Use Controls: The Vancouver Experience, 1910–1945," *Plan Canada* 19 (September–December, 1979), 211–225.

6. Cf. Richard F. Babcock, "Zoning," in Frank S. So et al., eds., *The Practice of Local Government Planning* (Washington: International City Managers' Association, 1979), 416–444.

7. Cf. Rogers, *Canadian Law*, 119.

8. This is one of the main complaints of those promoting the New Urbanism or its variant Traditional Neighbourhood Design (TND). See such critiques as Andres Duany et al., *Towns and Town-Making Principles* (Cambridge, Mass.: Harvard University Press, 1991); and James Howard Kunstler, *Home from Nowhere* (New York: Simon and Schuster, 1996).

9. Ken Greenberg and Frank Lewinberg, "Reinventing Planning in Toronto," *Plan Canada* 36, no. 3 (May 1996), 26–27.

10. *Ibid.*

11. Brenton Toderian, "Big-Box Retailing: How Are Municipalities Reacting?" *Plan Canada* 36, no. 6 (November 1996), 25–28.

12. Alan Demb, "No Place Like Home: Legalizing Home Occupations in Toronto," *City Magazine* 14, no. 2 (Spring 1993), 8.

13. *Ibid.*

14. Earl Levin, "Zoning in Canada," *Plan Canada* 7 (June 1957), 85–90.

15. Stanley Makuch, "Planning or Blackmail?" *Plan Canada* 25, no. 1 (March 1985), 8–9.

16. Canada Mortgage and Housing Corporation, *Residential Site Development Advisory Document* (Ottawa, 1981), 2.

17. Newfoundland, Provincial Planning Office, *Residential Subdivision Design Criteria* (St. John's, 1975), i.

18. Ontario Economic Council, *Subject to Approval* (Toronto, 1973), 65–66.

19. Newfoundland, *Residential Subdivision*, 55–64.

20. Ontario Economic Council, *Subject*, 66.

21. Comay Planning Consultants et al., *A Study of Sprawl in New Brunswick* (Toronto, 1980), 96.

22. Evelyn P. Reid and Maurice Yeates, "Bill 90—An Act to Protect Agricultural Land: An Assessment of Its Success in Laprairie County Quebec," *Urban Geography* 12, no. 4 (1991), 295–309; and Christopher Bryant and Thomas Johnston, *Agriculture in the City's Countryside* (Toronto: University of Toronto Press, 1992), 137–189.

23. Alberta, Municipal Affairs, *Planning in Alberta* (Edmonton, 1978), 25–28.

24. Arnold Bennett, "Montreal Debates Condo Conversion Again," *City Magazine* 14, no. 2 (Spring 1993), 10.

25. Hok Lin Leung, "Mutual Learning in Development Control," *Plan Canada* 27, no. 2 (April 1987), 44–55.

ᵖublic Policy nitiatives in ᴐommunity ᵖlanning

ᵤish between two questions: What would we like to
ᵥe best achieve it?

Earl Levin, 1962

An examination oɪ tne present and past physical development of a community reveals a blend of private and public structures, facilities, and spaces. While private development constitutes the largest part of a community's land use, public development may be said to constitute the most strategic part of the land use. The framework of the public roads, utility lines, parks, libraries, fire stations, parking structures, and community centres articulates the form of the community. The nature, location, and timing of public development efforts are thus crucial to the outcome of the community plan. To these one should also add the planning style used by the community, which can modulate the involvement of various public and private actors in achieving the goals of the plan.

In the last chapter, the discussion centred around the planning tools that can directly guide the decisions of private land owners. Those tools constrain the choices that landowners have when they make the decision to develop or redevelop land. But the initiative remains with the landowner, and neither the effectiveness of the tool nor the nature of the development is apparent until such choices are exercised, that is, until an application for zoning or a subdivision plan is made, and until physical development actually takes place. As important as those tools are, they are essentially reactive in nature. Thus, a community that makes a decision to plan cannot count on the necessary action to be taken by landowners to make the plan come to fruition within any explicit time frame.

While plan-making is aimed at stimulating and guiding the actions of decision makers, *planning* and *action* are distinctive activities. In logical terms, planning is necessary but not sufficient to obtain a planned outcome. This dilemma has been recognized for many decades, but probably no more incisively than by American planner Martin Meyerson in his concept of the "middle-range bridge" for planning.[1] He advocated various planning tools to link the long-range aims of the community plan with the short-range perspective of most private development actions and public action programs. These would include, in particular, the budgeting and programming of the community's capital investment in facilities and land, as well as public incentive and support programs to stimulate private action and detailed plans for improving specific areas.

In this chapter, we shall explore a number of the middle-range planning tools that can allow a community's planners to take the initiative to bring planning, policy, and action closer together. Since the foundations for some planning actions may derive from provincial legislation outside the conventional planning acts, we will also examine these sources of community initiative. The overall aim of the chapter is to provide an approach by which a community can guide the various actions and initiatives needed to bring its planning aims to fruition.

LINKING PLANNING AND DEVELOPMENT AT THE LOCAL LEVEL

Each year, local public officials, both elected ones and their staffs, are in the position of making expenditures that may contribute significantly to the implementation of the community's plan. The most important of these are expenditures for physical facilities, for development incentives, and for special-project-area development. Most of these expenditures are part of the local government's annual budget. Thus, it is within the control of a municipal council to influence directly the outcome of much of its own plan. The local council usually considers the budgetary process to be the most important activity it performs, because its choices allocate the community's normally limited financial resources. However, planning and budgeting are not synonymous, and unless a deliberate effort is made to link the two activities, a lack of coordination in the use of resources can hinder the plan. There is a need to develop procedures that keep the objectives of the plan, and the efforts of planners to implement it, tied to the budgetary process. In this section, we explore methods for doing this.

Coordinating Capital Improvements

There is always a financial cost to a community in achieving its overall development plan. Even in a community that decides its future lies in maintaining the status quo, there will be upkeep and maintenance costs as facilities and streets wear out. In communities that choose to improve their physical environments, city facilities will need to be built, renewed, or upgraded to some degree. Communities that accept the growth of new subdivisions, office complexes, and other developments are destined to expand community facilities at some substantial cost to the local treasury. In each case, the question is not *whether* there will be these sorts of costs, but *when*.

The community plan, by projecting the best possible arrangement for development, determines what kind of improvements, or investments, are needed. The plan is, however, only a general guide. Development projects differ as to when they will happen, if private, and as to when they are needed, if public; the plan is not able to anticipate precisely the timing of development. Moreover, the availability of funds for public facilities and projects will determine when the community can afford to make the capital investment. Thus, as the community sets about implementing its plan, it is faced with choices as to which investments it will make from its limited capital resources, and when it will make them.

This kind of activity, which arranges the expenditures for projects according to a time schedule, is called "capital programming." A form of programming in use for over a half a century in planning is **Capital Improvements Programming** (CIP). Specifically, CIP is a means of linking physical planning with its long-term perspective and the budgeting of community expenditures with its annual perspective. The basis of CIP is the expenditure of funds for such physical facilities as roads, sewer lines, parking garages, and community centres. These sorts of projects are relatively costly as well as permanent. Because their financing is often subject to borrowing funds with long periods of amortization, the community must decide on the level of debt that it can support each year. Because physical facilities are usually long-lived and not easily changed once constructed, it is necessary to consider both the expenditure and the planning ramifications of each project.

Some definitions will help to place CIP in context:[2]

Capital Improvements Program: a schedule of proposed expenditures for public physical facilities covering a period of several years into the future.

Capital Improvements Budget: the expenditures for physical facilities to which the community is committed in the next fiscal year. This annual budget usually comprises the first year of the multi-year CIP.

Capital Improvements: new or expanded physical facilities that are relatively large, expensive, and permanent, such as streets, libraries, firehalls, and water mains.

The basic objective of CIP is "to determine that set of projects for each time period which if carried out would provide the greatest 'product' over all future time periods."[3] In order to achieve this objective, CIP involves several important subtasks that must be blended together into a viable program to guide capital expenditures. In many respects, preparing the CIP is a process like that of preparing the overall community plan. Although it deals with more details of development and its time frame is shorter, the CIP must reconcile competing ends into a composite "middle range" plan of facilities. The cost of the proposed facilities must be within the reach of the community's financial resources, and the facilities must contribute toward implementing the overall plan.

The facilities and projects that the CIP will need to consider arise out of the activities of various functional departments and agencies of the community government—the roads department, the parks department, the library board, etc. Each group will have its own set of projects that it believes will enhance the development of the community. Rarely will the community be able to afford all projects at once. Moreover, it is likely that some facilities will need to be constructed before others (e.g., roads will precede a community centre). This leads to two basic decisions about each suggested project: "(1) its importance relative to other projects, and (2) its desirable sequence relative to other projects."[4]

Steps in the CIP Process

The CIP process involves a number of formal steps conducted by a specified agency of the local government. Often it is the planning department that is assigned the role of soliciting proposals for capital improvement projects and assigning the priorities for construction. Typically, the CIP process is conducted on two different levels: a five-year program is prepared every four years, with the first year comprising the expenditures in the upcoming budget year, and the program is reviewed annually to adjust the sequence of projects should major changes occur in financial resources or community needs in the time period of the program. Changes are not encouraged in the CIP once it has been formulated. An important characteristic of the CIP is that it clearly indicates the community's investment intentions for several years ahead so that private developers and other government agencies may better program their investments.

All communities conduct the CIP process according to their own organizational arrangements. The order of steps may not exactly parallel that listed here, but at some point each step will be taken in each community.

1. **Analysis of financial resources.**   Projects in the CIP must be financed out of the community's available resources. Thus, projections of revenues and/or expenditures must determine how much money will be available in the current and subsequent years. The community will have expenditures for projects already built or authorized, usually in the form of bonds that have been issued. New projects requiring the community to borrow funds may have to wait until previous projects have been partially or completely paid. And the operating costs of new and proposed projects after they are built can affect the allocation of revenues between operating and capital budgets in the future.

2. **Requests for proposed projects.**   Each department involved in making capital expenditures in the local government is requested to submit proposals for the projects that they will require over the ensuing five years. Requests must usually conform to a format that provides the planning department (or other CTP agency) with all the necessary information, enabling it to compare the merits of each project. The basic information to be supplied includes:

   - A description of the project, its location, and when it is required;
   - The expected cost of the project and when these costs would likely be incurred (possibly over several years if the project is large);
   - The justification for the project and its relation to other projects in the same and/or other departments;
   - The status of ongoing projects;
   - The sources of funding in cases where other than local sources might be available; and
   - The priority rating in comparison to other departmental projects.

3. **Choices among functional groups.**   The essential aim of CIP is to complete the development envisioned in the community plan for a given capital outlay. There is, however, no analytic system that allows direct choices among separate projects emanating from different departments, as, say, between a new sewer, playground, or firehall. Also difficult is deciding on the projects according to specific years. It is usually recommended, first of all, to conceive of the five-year CIP as a whole and decide on those functional groups of projects that would best achieve the plan's objectives.[5] For example, projects may be grouped into such categories as transportation, residential development, industrial renewal, health care, recreation, protective choices, or whatever is appropriate for the particular plan and the planning period. Thus, some sewers or streets might be important for industrial renewal areas and others for new subdivisions.

4. **Determining the sequence of projects.** The timing of projects is central to CIP if the community's development sequence is to be both efficient and amenable. Initially, when considering the sequence of projects, it is necessary to exclude those for whose services there will not be a demand until after the five-year CIP period. Then, the projects of each functional group are organized in terms of the order in which they need to be built. At this point, only a sequence of construction, without specific dates, is shown. Some projects need to be built early because (a) they will increase the service performed by existing facilities (e.g., additional sewage treatment capacity), (b) they could cost much more if delayed (e.g., the acquisition of park space), and (c) they are strategic in influencing the form and pace of private development (e.g., the extension of water mains and arterial roads). There is, as well, the need to consider the advantage of linking such projects as sewer and street construction in order to avoid repeated road disruptions.

5. **Setting the priority of projects.** Choosing the projects to be built, and those that will not be built, is the most crucial step in the CIP process. To determine the priority of projects, it is necessary to go beyond their sequence and rate them according to their relative importance in the community's development. The first criterion is whether they can be achieved within the given capital budget. A second criterion is whether the project is specifically identified in either the comprehensive plan or some functional plan adopted by the community. Beyond these two criteria, the setting of priorities is difficult because of local preferences and political considerations. Various ranking schemes have been developed to derive a measure of the relative importance of projects.[6] The final determination of which projects should be included combines their sequence and importance positions, and starting from the most important and progressing to the least, they are placed in time sequence until all the capital resources available for the five years are exhausted.

As with all planning decisions, the CIP process has a *technical* and a *policy* side. The process described above pertains mostly to the technical side, tht is, the process undertaken by the community's staff of planners in analyzing capital needs and formulating a program. Both elected and appointed officials use their political roles to influence the CIP. Department heads tend to favour projects in their own departmental area more than city-wide issues. Elected officials often desire projects that favour particular areas or groups in the community. And often elected officials wish to keep capital commitments vague so as to be able to change their minds and respond to new needs. Thus, the relatively rational CIP process cannot be considered apart from its political aspects, which, at their best, enhance the technical judgements and make the CIP more pertinent to community needs and goals.

A newer, and closely related, middle-range planning process that some communities now employ is called **Community Strategic Planning.** Strategic planning processes, long used in business planning, have been adapted for community use. It is a more interactive method than CIP and can involve a wide array of community stakeholders to decide upon the actions and projects they wish to have their local council take. The process usually starts with developing a vision of the community, say, 10 years ahead, and then identifying the actions that need to be taken to achieve the vision, that is, developing a *strategy.* A strategic planning process can be a valuable supplement to preparing the overall community plan because it can involve citizens quite directly in the implementation of the plan. Port Colborne, Ontario, is a good example of such a process in action: according to this community, its strategic plan "has made the journey ahead much clearer."[7]

Mobilizing Development Incentives

Communities very often have financial resources available for influencing development decisions by private landowners and builders. The most common of these are in the realm of creating new housing or refurbishing old dwellings. They usually involve low-interest loans or outright grants to those who participate in the objectives of the program. The majority of funds for such programs tend to be supplied by the province or the federal government (or both), with some portion coming from local funds.

One of the most widely used incentive programs in recent years, the **Neighbourhood Improvement Program** (NIP) of the mid-1970s, can help illustrate these programs' value in community planning. Under NIP, homeowners as well as communities could receive federal funds in areas that were identified as needing upgrading in housing and community facilities. Homeowners could receive grants and loans to repair and improve their dwellings in such areas. The community could receive grants to assist in acquiring parkland, in improving streets and sewer lines, and in carrying out other activities that would promote residential renewal.

Other similar programs in use in recent years include those to promote the development of low-income housing through municipal non-profit housing corporations, to rehabilitate unused upper storeys of downtown commercial buildings for apartments, and to renovate disused industrial buildings for commercial or residential uses. These types of programs vary in the way the resources are made available. In some cases, the municipality may offer the incentives directly, while in others the community may be asked to approve the award of funds by a senior government to ensure that the use conforms to local planning objectives.

Incentive programs may be of strategic importance in stimulating private development in previously uneconomic types of uses and in parts of the city avoided by developers. Since private development and investment are relatively uncontrollable, it is important that a community be aware of incentive programs that are available. Such programs may possibly be linked with capital investments by the community itself (as was practised in NIP areas) for a more concerted effort at rejuvenating the physical environment. Thus, the order and sequence of projects in the NIP may need to be examined in light of various incentive programs for private development.

Other Statutory Tools

There are several other means by which communities can influence the quality of the physical environment. Two of the most important, expropriation and building regulations, are embedded in legislation codifying the responsibilities of communities to their residents. Communities are assigned roles, as municipalities, to provide a safe and amenable environment for all their citizens; that is, the municipality has a formal (legal) responsibility to act on behalf of the entire community to make sure that the decisions made by individual landowners not only do not impinge on their neighbours, but also serve the best interests of the entire community. Building regulations and the power of expropriation stem, respectively, from two constitutional powers that reside in the municipality: the police power and the power of eminent domain.

Building Regulations

In general, municipalities in Canada have the power to regulate the construction of buildings within their jurisdiction. The reason for this is to ensure that new buildings and the reconstruction of older buildings will not endanger the health, safety, or general welfare of the public. This power to approve building construction derives from the constitutional power (called, in legal terms, the **police power**) held by the province and delegated to the municipality. The task of the municipality, in essence, is to enforce the provincial building code that sets basic standards for construction. To accomplish this, the municipality employs building inspectors whose job it is to review plans for buildings and to issue building permits if the plans meet basic standards of the code. Building inspectors also monitor the actual construction to ensure adherence to the agreed-upon plans.

The issuance of a building permit represents, in many ways, the final step in developing a building project. It is, therefore, a crucial step for the municipality. It can at this point determine whether the construction plans for the building conform to community-planning expectations of the project. Not infrequently, building plans are found to contravene the setback and height regulations of zoning by-laws. Many communities combine a review of zoning requirements with the building inspector's review of construction plans at this stage. In a related way, the issuance of a building permit is seen as the indication that building on a site is going to proceed shortly thereafter, but there is no guarantee of this. There are usually some sites within a community on which development is preferred to occur as soon as possible. Increasingly, communities are tying the approval of zoning amendments and development agreements to either the issuance or the duration of a building permit.

Occupancy permits are often required, especially for residential projects, before use of a building can be allowed. The prime criteria at this stage are usually the meeting of fire and other safety conditions. Since zoning by-laws and/or development agreements may have required the buildings to meet other conditions, such as the provision of open space or walkways, this is another opportunity to ensure that planning conditions have also been met. To some, this may suggest undue constraint on developers and buildings, but it should be remembered that construction requires a legal, contractual arrangement with the municipality in which the steps of issuing building and occupancy permits are specified. Further, the municipality should be rigorous in taking these steps and in verifying any related planning provisions, and it need not be dilatory in its procedures,

Expropriation

From another long-lived constitutional power held by Canadian provinces—**eminent domain**—municipalities derive the power to obtain land needed for community purposes. The essence of eminent domain is that the highest property right on the use of land rests ultimately with the community. Specifically, if there are public uses of specified parcels of land that would be of more benefit than those proposed by the private owners, then the community may acquire the land. Normally, most municipalities have been delegated this power by their province, as have such other public agencies as school boards, highway departments, and public utilities.

The term used in Canada for this municipal power is **expropriation.** It is probably most often used for road-widening purposes when an existing right-of-way is not sufficient to accommodate an enlarged thoroughfare. Other instances include a community's need for park space in an already

Planning Issue 10.1

LEGACY OF URBAN RENEWAL

The former residents of the demolished community of Africville still weep while remembering how, 25 years ago, their homes and church were bulldozed and they had to load their belongings on to City of Halifax dump trucks.

Today, they want to return to live on the land that city planners once called a slum, but that was home to 400 people on the northern outskirts of Halifax along the Bedford Basin.

The destruction of the predominantly black community and the emotional upheaval caused by the plan to improve housing standards and integrate black residents into Halifax have become a symbol for blacks who say they still face widespread discrimination in Nova Scotia.

Although the city planned in the 1970s to use the Africville land for industrial expansion, little activity has taken place and most of the area where 80 homes stood is a rarely visited park.

Former resident Laura Howe remembered how the Baptist church, the centre of the community, was knocked down and how, a few weeks later, she was ordered to move.

"I was moved in a big yellow dump truck and all my possessions were just loaded on," she said. "They allowed us $500 to buy new furniture. We were called squatters and we were given $500."

The Africville residents who held deeds were paid about $12,000 for their homes.

Allan O'Brien, who was mayor of Halifax at the time of the Africville relocation, acknowledged that such a decision would not be made in 1989.

He said the politicians acted on advice of the city staff and representatives of the Africville community.

Source: Excerpted from "25 years after Africville razed, former residents long for home," *The Globe and Mail,* November 20, 1989. Reprinted with permission from *The Globe and Mail.*

built-up area or space to build a public building. When a community designates a property for public use, it must acquire it from the owner by paying a reasonable price. Usually, the price to be paid will be the current market value as judged by an independent land appraiser. Strictly speaking, the power of expropriation is used only when the public agency cannot acquire the needed property through normal purchase procedures; it then has the power to acquire the property regardless of the willingness of the owner to sell. Municipal councils tend to use their power of expropriation sparingly because of the political ramifications of taking away private property; they try instead to negotiate a purchase. Nevertheless, this power of eminent domain has a valuable place among planning tools, as it ensures acquisition of properties of strategic importance in the completion of the plan.

Targeting Special Areas and Functions

Beyond incentive programs to entice private investment to occur in response to the community plan, the community may decide to undertake specific development projects on its own. It may target a specific *area* such as downtown, an industrial area, or a waterfront whose improvement would benefit the community and attain the objectives of the plan. Or it may target a specific *function* such as the mass transit system or hospital services or parks as a strategic move to achieve the plan. The essential feature of both types of community initiative is the investment of *public funds*, sometimes accompanied by special land-use regulations, to indicate community priorities.

Special-Area Initiatives

The targeting of special areas for development offers a strategic tool for achieving planning objectives. Such targeting acknowledges two facets of city development. First, there are differences in the pace of development between various areas at different times (e.g., the suburbs growing faster than downtown). And, second, public infrastructure expenditures (for roads, parks, etc.) usually precede private investment. Thus, a substantial investment in public funds within a short period of time may be necessary to stimulate new private development or the renewal of existing uses. Two common initiatives, for business areas and waterfronts, will demonstrate the issues and the outcomes.

1. Business Area Improvement.   Plans and programs for **downtown revitalization** are the most common special-area initiatives. Most of the buildings in these areas, in both large cities and small towns, represent extensive private investment, if not the largest concentration of such capital. It is usually in the community's interest to protect this investment in order to maintain economic as well as cultural vitality of the core area. Such initiatives are normally based on a plan that details the objectives of the initiative. The plan describes the hoped-for attributes to be achieved (e.g., the street pattern, land uses, open spaces, views) and the set of public and private actions necessary for the plan's attainment (see also Chapter 6).

Often these plans are initiated through programs of financial assistance made available to communities by senior governments. Typical of these are Main Street Programs and Business Improvement Area programs for small and medium-size communities (e.g., Ladysmith, B.C., and Carbonear, Newfoundland).[8] These programs help underwrite capital investments such as new sidewalks, sewers, and streetlights and may also offer incentives to private builders and landowners to participate. Under this stimulus, the community may be able to achieve more direct, rapid, and amenable development than might normally occur. The community, in turn, is required to make a commitment to a concerted effort in budgeting its capital and organizational resources. The immediate need may be for road improvements, parking structures, public open spaces, or a civic building to give impetus to other development.

At a much larger scale are redevelopment programs for central districts of major cities such as those for the Winnipeg downtown core, *le centreville de* Trois-Rivières, and Market Square in Saint John. In the latter cases, the capital resources of both provincial and federal governments were also required. Their aims may include (as they do in the Winnipeg Core Area Initiative) the development of new housing, heritage conservation, new community facilities, the formation of local economic development corporations, retraining of core area residents, industrial modernization, and assisting the development of new commercial buildings.[9] Of similar type are programs for waterfront redevelopment (Toronto's Harbourfront and Halifax's Historic Properties) and conserving heritage areas (Montreal's Old City and Vancouver's Granville Island). The aims may differ from those found in core area programs but the means for achieving them are much the same.

2. Waterfront Enhancement. There is hardly a city in Canada that doesn't have a waterfront on a lake, river, or the ocean, and a very large proportion of them have come to realize its importance to both their heritage and their economy. Planning for waterfront redevelopment has occurred in Montreal and Windsor, in Victoria and Halifax, among others. It has often been to reclaim a neglected industrial and port area and make it functional once again for business, residence, and recreation. Canadian planner David Gordon, who worked on such plans in Toronto and studied the experience of other cities, notes that the two basic planning strategies have been historic preservation and public access, and that these are used in combination.[10]

For many cities, the waterfront is where the community began, and there is frequently a stock of older historic buildings that are worth conserving and adapting. For both the older port area (e.g., Saint John) and the waterfront scenic area (e.g., Saskatoon) public access is crucial. It is not uncommon that these areas are cut off from the city by railway lines or highways, and public initiatives can be used to link the area to existing streets and create such things as water's edge promenades and parks. The most successful waterfront projects according to Gordon focus on "the quality of the public space" in the project area.[11] In other words, public policy initiatives by way of heritage legislation and capital expenditures on streets and parks are crucial for waterfront enhancement.

Meeting Functional Needs

A community plan may aim to improve specific functions within a community. Increased traffic may need to be accommodated, sewage systems may need to be upgraded, and affordable housing may be in short supply. Such needs often occupy large portions of land and/or demand considerable public investment. They usually require a separate functional plan (see Chapter 6) showing location, land acquisition, and the disposition of capital expenditures as well as other expected outcomes of the project. The following are typical of such projects:

- **Rapid transit systems** that aim to relieve current traffic congestion in the downtown area, as with the recent ones in Calgary, Edmonton, and Vancouver;
- **Social housing projects** that provide affordable housing for the elderly and other low-income groups not normally able to compete in the economic marketplace;[12] and
- **Regional parks developments** that aim to improve recreational opportunities and protect natural environments.

To these could be added improvements to an airport, a new convention centre, college, or health care facility, or an expanded freeway system. A recent demonstration of this is the approach of the City of Calgary in planning its future transportation system. The Calgary Go-Plan is aimed at guiding capital expenditures on transportation over the next 30 years; the planning process itself is costing several millions of dollars.[13] Often, one of the outcomes from such a functional planning exercise is to bring into sharper focus larger questions about the community's future shape, This happened in Calgary: proposed transportation corridors evoked considerable public debate over the urban form, the ecological consequences, and the balance between public transit and automobile transportation and led to improvements in the plan.

The planning and programming of public projects is undertaken for three main reasons: (1) to benefit present residents, (2) to direct new development in a growing community, and (3) to attract development to a stagnant community. Typically, some combination of these reasons comes into play. A new rapid transit system, for example, may both relieve downtown auto traffic and direct new development to locales adjacent to new stations that now have improved accessibility; similarly, a new college could both benefit local residents and attract new residents and businesses.

While the functional needs of the community may be spelled out in the community plan, the actual functional plan is often prepared by agencies outside the local government that provides the funding. A provincial government department or crown corporation may be responsible for rapid transit and freeway projects, or a metropolitan government may have responsibility for regional parks, hospitals, and airports. An example of this is the siting of treatment and transfer facilities for hazardous wastes in Manitoba communities. This is handled by the provincially owned Manitoba Hazardous Waste Management Corporation (there are similar agencies in other provinces). Not unexpectedly, such projects are now being called "difficult-to-site" projects. The Manitoba agency has developed a voluntary process in working with communities to assure greater acceptance of these facilities by sharing power and decision-making responsibility. It is achieving much success.[14]

Traffic Calming

A public policy initiative found today in many Canadian communities is aimed at achieving better ways of integrating land uses, people, and various forms of traffic, especially automobile traffic. It has been given the name **traffic calming,** and in its broadest sense it seeks to make communities more livable. Although it is now part of the technical planner's approach, it got its start from citizen concerns and protests in Europe (Germany, the Netherlands, Denmark) in the 1970s and later in Australia.[15]

Three basic principles motivate traffic-calming approaches:

1. The function of streets is not to act just as a corridor for automobiles;
2. People have a right to not have their quality of life spoiled by undue traffic caused by automobile use; and
3. Trips are a means of accessing some desirable land use or activity, not an end in themselves.[16]

The thrust of these principles contrasts with the traditional planning principle of separating various forms of traffic (autos, cyclists, pedestrians) from one another and classifying roads to promote traffic safety and greater mobility. The problem with the traditional approach was that automobile traffic multiplied faster and travelled at greater speeds than had been expected with resulting increases in unsafe streets, growing air pollution and noise, and impediments for business and their customers.[17]

Traffic calming invokes public policy in regard to one of the fundamental public responsibilities in a community environment—creating and maintaining public rights-of-way. Various methods are used in traffic calming, including raising the surface of streets at intersections (traffic "bumps"), and narrowing streets with trees, traffic circles, and looping streets.[18] Usually, traffic calming is undertaken on a neighbourhood-by-neighbourhood basis upon the request of the residents. One of its most commendable aspects is that it requires planners to examine the full range of relationships of traffic and land use in planning livable communities.

Public-Private Partnerships

A fairly recent targeting approach in urban development is that of blending private resources with government policies in what are called public-private partnerships. This approach arose in response, on the one hand, to increasingly limited public financial resources and, on the other, to political pressures for the privatization of services government has previously provided. These partnerships tend to be focused on specific projects rather than on, say, downtown renewal or neighbourhood traffic calming, which we described above. One finds them used in the development of highways (such as Route 407 that skirts the Toronto metropolitan area) and recreation areas (such as the Cypress Bowl area in Vancouver's outskirts).

Almost any public facility that a government body constructed and has operated—hospitals, bridges, airports, etc.—is now being considered for such partnerships. The essential arrangement is that a private body (for-profit corporation or non-profit group) provides the capital to build or buy a facility the governmental body wishes to provide to the community or region, and the governmental body establishes the standards for its construction and regulates its operation. The private partner then gets a return on its investment usually by charging a toll to users as with the Confederation Bridge to Prince Edward Island and the Cobequid Pass toll road in Nova Scotia.

There is still considerable debate over many of these types of partnerships, ranging from concern over their social costs to the failure of governments to maintain existing "free" facilities. Some opponents cite the differential benefits for those citizens able to pay the tolls and those who can't. Others are concerned with the monopoly aspects given to private companies. Yet others claim that the cost of added pollution occasioned by, say, a toll road is not being recovered by these arrangements. Suffice to say for now, such project arrangements are often being negotiated on other grounds (e.g., the government is able to save its capital) than those established in community plans.

Some Implications of Targeting

The great advantage of targeting special areas and functional needs is that it can generate tangible results from the planning process in a relatively short span of time. But it must be remembered that such specific planning has the effect of directing the allocation of public spending (and, if successful, private investment) toward one area or project and away from others. Thus, care must be taken not to starve existing projects of public funds and opportunities for private development. As with other middle-range planning tools, special-area/project targeting requires that considerable attention be paid to integrating planning and action.

This need is especially evident in view of the diverse interests involved in realizing a refurbished downtown or rapid transit system. These include departments within a local or regional government, agencies and departments of one or more senior governments, and private development interests. Given the often substantial amounts of resources required, a city may be able to do no more than indicate the desired project or redevelopment in its community plan. The public agency that, for example, can develop a rapid transit system may opt to do the project planning itself. Or the private developer with large and/or strategic land holdings may demand concessions in zoning. In such instances, project developers rather than community planners become the ones controlling public policy on the location of facilities and the bulk of buildings. Not infrequently, relations between the development agencies and host communities sour when projects diverge from local planning norms and objectives. Nowhere is this more evident than in the Harbourfront project in Toronto, which required a federal royal commission to seek a reconciliation of local and agency planning aims.[19]

THE PUBLIC PLANNING FRAMEWORK

Community planning, as we observed right from the opening chapters, is a widely accepted public activity. This is, of course, a generalization valid for every country that adopts a planning approach to improving physical environments of cities, towns, and regions; it is not unique to Canada. Equally common are the reasons that community planning comes to be used from country to country: rampant urban growth, physical deterioration, congestion, unhealthful and unsafe conditions, inefficient activity patterns, uninspiring development, and the like. The roots of Canadian planning are similar to those of other places that have also called forth a public planning response. However, the type of public planning response, the style or practice of planning, does differ considerably from one country to another. The planning institutions and planning tools we employ are responsible for that.

This section presents an overview of the public institutions and procedures of Canadian community planning. The aim is to provide a perspective on the setting within which planning is accomplished in practice. This perspective has three facets: the statutory foundations, the formal step-by-step process of plan-making, and the structure for appeals. It is important to grasp this institutional setting, for Canadian community planning is characterized, as perhaps is the case in few other countries, by a highly structured legalistic/bureaucratic format that operates in conjunction with a rather open land market of multiple owners. It offers many opportunities for public initiatives to shape the outcome of community planning efforts that do not exist in the U.S., for example. Or, looked at from the point of view of constraints, the formal setting establishes the boundaries of planning action by both public and private actors. Examples of the setting for planning in Ontario and Alberta demonstrate the formal plan-making and plan-implementation process.

Statutory Foundations

Since the 1920s, nine of the ten Canadian provinces have had in effect substantial pieces of planning legislation. (Nowadays all provinces and the Yukon and Northwest Territories have such statutes.) These planning acts, as they may be called generically, are the foundations for land-use planning and implementation at the local government level. Planning acts are the type of statute often referred to as **enabling legislation** because they enable, or allow, a municipality to carry on a specified governing activity. Such legislation is necessary for local planning so that the powers over private property and land use residing with the province are available to the municipality, that is, are delegated to the municipality. Planning acts are mostly *permissive* in their provisions; they do not require municipalities to make plans and land-use regulations. If the community should choose to do so, the act prescribes the planning content and the procedures to be followed. Then, any local plans and planning by-laws take on much of the force of the planning act; they, too, are statutes. This is the basis for describing Canadian community planning as *statutory:* it is empowered by statute, and its output (which falls within the terms of the act) has the power of statute.

This particular statutory aspect, which has characterized Canadian community planning for over three-quarters of a century, generates a high degree of dependence on the province by local planners. The province, until recently, has been the final arbiter of community plans in all provinces and of local land-use regulations in most. Provincial planning establishments are of considerable size, and most of their activity involves overseeing local planning efforts and refining the process of planning for land development by formulating guidelines for special situations and applying the planning act. Starting about the mid-1970s, eight provinces undertook extensive revisions of their planning acts. These efforts sought to refine (sometimes called "streamline") elaborate planning legislation and supporting bureaucratic structures. Thus, local planning in Canada operates not only within a provincially generated framework; in many respects, it operates as if the province were the ultimate client and the planning act an incontestable authority. Planning acts deal normally with the following five matters:

1. The creation of planning units;
2. The establishment of organizational machinery;
3. The content, preparation, and adoption of statutory plans;
4. The format for enacting zoning, building, and housing by-laws; and
5. The system for subdividing land.

The planning act (or the applicable legislation in the province) specifies who may plan, what they may plan, and how they may plan for community planning to be statutorily correct. There are differences among provinces in the methods and the style that are used, but the general thrust remains the same. To illustrate the foundations for planning provided by a provincial planning act, let us consider those of Ontario and Alberta in terms of the five elements above.[20]

1. The creation of planning units

Alberta	Ontario

• A two-level system of planning units comprising
  1. The region
  2. The municipality
• Special arrangements for sparsely settled and resource areas.
	• An eclectic system of planning units based on the single municipality, including cities, towns, villages, townships, boroughs.
	• Regional municipalities and counties.
	• Special arrangements for northern Ontario.

Each of the above units is delegated the power to prepare plans. Powers of implementation are specified for each type of unit.

2. The establishment of organizational machinery

Alberta	Ontario
• A hierarchical system comprising: Minister of Municipal Affairs Alberta Planning Board Regional Planning Commission Municipal Planning Commission or Council Development Officer (to administer land-use by-law) Development Appeal Board	• A hierarchical system comprising: Minister of Municipal Affairs and Housing Ontario Municipal Board Regional Municipality (where created) Municipal Council Planning Advisory Committee Committee of Adjustment

Each of the above agencies is assigned specific roles and duties in the planning process.

3. The preparation of statutory plans

Alberta	Ontario
• A hierarchy of plans is specified for each municipality: Regional Plan General Municipal Plan Area Structure Plan (for a neighbourhood or district within the municipality) Area Redevelopment Plan (for a redevelopment area)	• A three-level system comprising: Official Plan for Regional Municipality or County Official Plan (for all or part of municipality) Community Improvement Plan (an area within a municipality requiring replanning or renewal)

Each of the above plans must conform to the plan directly above it in the hierarchy.

4. The enactment of land-use and building regulations

Alberta	Ontario
• A single planning instrument, the Land Use By-Law, combines features of zoning and development control. • Enactment similar to that for General Municipal Plan. • Administered by Development Officer.	• A set of planning instruments comprising: Zoning By-Law Interim Control By-Law Site Plan Control By-Law • Enactment similar to that for Official Plan. • Variances administered by Committee of Adjustment.

5. The subdivision of land

Alberta	Ontario
• Application of landowner accompanied by a Plan of Subdivision to Regional Planning Commission except within cities of Calgary and Edmonton. • Approved by Regional Plan Commission, Calgary, Edmonton, • Municipal Councils may propose replotting schemes and approve them after hearings.	• Application of landowner accompanied by a Plan of Subdivision to Minister of Municipal Affairs and Housing. • Application referred to pertinent municipality (and second-tier government when that applies). • Approval by Minister and/or specified second-tier governments.

The listing on the previous page shows that each of these planning acts provides a firm and comprehensive foundation for community planning. From one point of view, it may be too restrictive, but practice has shown that there is plenty of scope for municipalities both to be innovative in their planmaking and to meet their individual community needs.[21] Another point of view on the provincial planning acts goes back to their earliest days. Most of these acts were promulgated before any community within the respective provinces had formulated a plan. The planning acts were ahead of their time and thus in a position to promote the value of community planning.

One could say that planning acts have successfully fulfilled their role. Indeed, the pervasiveness of community planning in Canada has led to a new level of maturity among communities regarding planning such that provinces are, again, revising their planning acts. Ontario and Newfoundland, to cite just two examples, are proposing to devolve their responsibility for approving plans and by-laws onto the municipality.[22] No longer would ministerial approval be required and the province would limit itself to a review to make sure that provincial interests are protected. Not a little of the initiative for this devolution comes, of course, from reductions in the size of provincial planning staff. Nevertheless, it points to a much less paternalistic process.

Before leaving this discussion of statutory foundations for planning, it must be noted that all provinces have other pieces of major legislation that affect the substance and organization for planning. Every province has an act, usually called the Municipal Act, to cover the duties and organization of its constituent municipalities. Almost all provinces now have some form of legislation for environmental assessment and protection. Nearly as common are statutes covering the establishment of condominiums, the designation of historic buildings, the location of pits and quarries, transportation, water quality, and the use of natural resources. In British Columbia, for example, municipalities may have to deal with the provincial Agricultural Land and Forest Land Commissions in regard to the zoning and subdivision of land. And, recently, the province passed legislation requiring the care and quality of fish-spawning streams to be taken into account in local official community plans. The administration of these statutes is most often in the hands of officials from ministries other than that containing the provincial planners. As with most provincial legislation, these statues can provide opportunities for planning as well as constraints. Therefore, it is wise to be aware of the range of the provincial statutory foundations that could affect the outcome of a particular planning effort.

Formal Steps in Plan-Making

Chapter 7 discussed the process of plan-making in a normative context, that is, one that involves the refinement of community goals through a more or less rational set of steps comprising both technical studies and community participation. There are four general phases: (1) experiencing needs and wants, (2) defining goals, (3) planning alternatives, and (4) deciding and acting. But how does this general planning process translate in terms of the statutory planning framework described in the preceding section?

Planning acts, as noted, not only specify who may plan but also prescribe how they may plan. A minimum set of steps that must satisfy the statutory requirements of the act is set forth. These formal steps approximate many of the steps in the normative process. The differences lie in various technical and participatory steps undertaken in the real community setting to accommodate the social, economic, and physical conditions unique to the community. Thus, when a Canadian community plans, its normative process is articulated by planning act requirements, and its actions are punctuated by several required steps. Figure 10.1 shows the general steps required to bring a community plan into effect. These steps are much the same as those required for making amendments to a plan and for enacting and amending a zoning by-law. But, as we noted above, some provinces are eliminating the final step of provincial approval, thereby shortening the process and leaving responsibility with the community.

Drawing again upon the Alberta and Ontario approaches, there is, with but one major and one minor exception, general agreement between these two statutory processes. Each proceeds through technical steps to the preparation of a draft of the plan and the implementing by-law. At this point, in Alberta, the municipal council would give initial consideration to the plan and first reading to the by-law and then call a public hearing. In Ontario, the public hearing would be held before any council consideration of the draft plan and by-law. This is only a minor difference. Objections to the plan may, in Alberta, be made only on procedural grounds, and if so, a court will hear representations to void the by-law. In Ontario, appeals to change the plan may be made on substantive grounds by the minister, by citizens, and by government agencies. If the minister agrees that these appeals are not trivial, he or she must refer the plan to the Ontario Municipal Board for further hearings and recommendations. The next section discusses the role of appeal bodies more fully.

One facet of the normal process of plan-making that becomes evident from these descriptions is that planning decisions are the product of several bodies, not just the local council and its advisory committees. In some provinces, like Saskatchwan, the outcome of a community plan or zoning by-law or subdivision plan may be the result of modifications made at three levels: the community, the ministry, and the appeal board. Within the first two levels may be a large number of other, non-planning agencies also involved in the outcome. Within the municipality, provision is usually made to have planning proposals reviewed by all technical departments and public utility companies. At the provincial level, there is also widespread distribution of municipal planning proposals to various ministries and crown corporations. Somewhat in contrast is the rather limited role for the public in the formal process. It seems, therefore, that in light of the efforts taken to preserve the statutory basis of the plan, and of the inherent paternalism of the provinces, one would be justified in speculating on *whose plan* is represented in the final output. Among the provinces, Alberta, Ontario, B.C., and Newfoundland have evolved the formal plan-making system that most respects the integrity of locally made planning decisions.

Structures for Appeals

The statutory nature of Canadian community planning imparts a legalistic bias to many of its activities, but especially to the structures for appeals of planning decisions. Most provinces have established some form of quasi-judicial body to hear appeals from people or agencies that object to an official plan, zoning by-law, or subdivision plan. The Ontario Municipal Board has been the model for most planning appeal bodies. Its proceedings are conducted much like those of a courtroom (through the adversarial process), and its decisions have the force of law. Objectors (including citizens and citizen groups) and proponents are expected to be represented by legal counsel, although other representations may usually be heard.

In order for an appeal to proceed, a number of specific steps must be taken. First, no appeal can be made until the by-law approving the plan, zoning change, etc., has been passed by the local government body. Second, there is only a limited period of time after approval of the by-law—30 days is common—in which an appeal can be lodged. Third, the appeal body or the minister in question, depending upon the province, will decide whether the objection is trivial, in which case a hearing would prove dilatory to the planning process.

In many respects, hearings of provincial appeal boards tend to become hearings *de novo* (as lawyers call them), or brand new considerations, of the planning pros and cons. This is not only time-consuming and costly to all participants, but also may bring in planning evidence and arguments not heretofore considered by the community and its council and planning

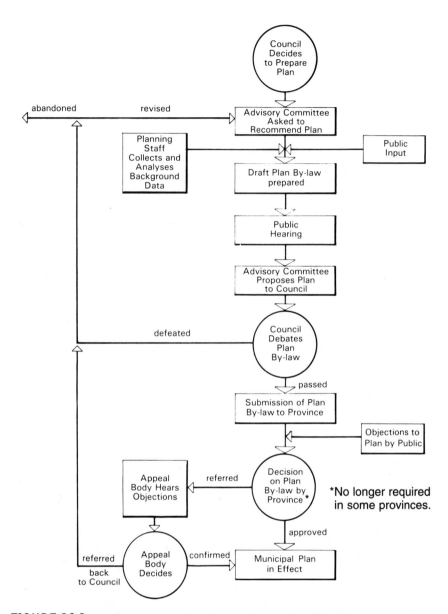

FIGURE 10.1   The Process of Plan Preparation by Municipalities
These steps apply generally to all municipalities. Some differences exist in the requirements for public input, as well as in appeal procedures from one province to another.

bodies. In recent years, limitations have been placed on some aspects of appeal body powers. Still, in the provinces where they are used, provincial appeal boards create a significant and additional avenue through which planning decisions may be made, one that is likely to be developed with its own rationale and criteria for its decisions. This means it has the potential of becoming planning for a community rather than planning by a community. This is one of the major dilemmas of the legalistic style of planning, for it must honour judicial concepts, including the right to appeal to a third party.

Not all provinces use a provincial appeal body with broad-based powers of intervention. Saskatchwan, for example, has two levels of appeal on planning matters. Each municipality with a zoning by-law is required to appoint its own Development Appeal Board to deal with appeals on plan amendments, rezoning applications, minor variances, development permits, and subdivision plans (where the local council has approval authority). Appeals of the decisions of the local appeal board may be made in many instances to the Planning Appeals Committee of the Saskatchewan Municipal Board. The latter committee must hold a public hearing on appeals made to it. The right of appeal to the courts on any planning matter also exists, but usually only if there have been procedural irregularities or disputes on points of law in previous hearings.

GUIDANCE SYSTEMS FOR PLAN IMPLEMENTATION

Mention has been made several times in this and the previous two chapters of the interdependence of the means of implementing the community plan. Sometimes, private responses to zoning regulations or housing incentives necessitate actions for public investments in making improvements in community facilities. Sometimes the reverse is true, as when public investments are made in an effort to stimulate private development. Or there may be conflicts among implementation tools, as when zoning regulations prevent innovations in housing arrangements proposed by developers in their subdivision plans. There may also be disjunctures in the timing of planning efforts, especially if they emanate from several public agencies. These situations, and many others that could be cited, point up the need for coordination of all planning actions because planning instruments have their distinctive clients, roles, and timing. Like their counterparts in a symphony orchestra, planning instruments must be orchestrated to produce a concerted effort to achieve a harmonious physical environment.

At the outset of this chapter we invoked Meyerson's notion of a "middle-range bridge" between the community plan and the public and private processes that create the form of the community physical environment. That term has been replaced in recent years with the notion of a "guidance system," but the aim is still the same. A guidance system for planning would comprise all of the means by which the local government guides land development and associated activities toward the achievement of community objectives.[23] Its role is to organize the various planning instruments such that they form a "bridge from the land use plan to the built environment."[24] But this will be a bridge comprising many strands, and the way in which these strands are interwoven will be complex. Thus, the notion of a system in which all the parts are interrelated in achieving a final outcome is appropriate.

The initial step in conceiving of a guidance system is to outline all of the types of planning instruments available to the particular community to guide land development. These include, as we have discussed, those that provide guidance by influencing or persuading both public and private sectors to take action with respect to the community goals and the potential for changes in land use. The most prominent of these instruments is, of course, the community plan. Other instruments that provide guidance are those deriving from such statutory controls as the common law of nuisance, the police power, and eminent domain, by which private land use can be directly regulated. Public expenditures in capital improvements, incentives programs, and special-area development are other ways to guide land use.

It can be seen from such an array that some planning instruments provide guidance in an explicit fashion while others are more implicit in their thrust. However, both are integral parts of a "land-use guidance system," as Chapin and Kaiser call it.[25] They distinguish these two components as decision guides and action instruments (see Figure 10.2). **Decision guides** result from planning activities that are concerned with formulating land-use policies and plans, that is, those planning outputs that aim to guide the decisions of actors in the land development process. **Action instruments** are those means by which the local government intervenes directly in the land development process, especially through regulation and investment.

There are several types of decision guides. The long-range community plan is the central one, along with other land-use policies that may be enunciated from time to time. Also a part of this component are various data that either are used in background studies for the community plan or are generated in the course of monitoring continuing conditions in the community. Many communities, for example, regularly produce statistical summaries of population, housing, land use, development activity, etc.; these summaries can assist private and public decision makers to place their investment decisions in the context of current conditions and trends. The action plans that may be made for special areas or for particular functions, along with the capital investment strategy, constitute the third major type of decision guide. Decision guides have two roles. One is to guide the formulation and use of the action instruments so that they produce a con-

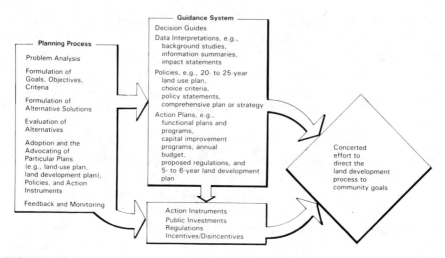

FIGURE 10.2 **A Guidance System for Land-Use Planning**
By linking the plan-making process more firmly to continuing policies, administration, and action plans, land development can be guided to attain the goals of the community plan. *Source:* Adapted from F. Stuart Chapin, Jr., and Edward J. Kaiser, *Urban Land Use Planning,* 3rd ed. (Urbana: University of Illinois Press, 1979), 60. Copyright 1979 by the Board of Trustees of the University of Illinois. Used with the permission of the University of Illinois Press.

sistent and effective outcome. The other role is to provide a policy context that informs the citizens, private developers, and public officials of the planning commitments that have been made.

Action instruments are the ways in which the local government may take action to achieve the policies, plans, and strategies encompassed by the decision guides. Capital investments are one type that contributes directly, according to the community's own criteria, to the goals of the plans, especially in the realm of community facilities and infrastructure. Public expenditures on programs for such community services as recreation, transit, and public housing also contribute to planning outcomes, while regulations on land use, as for zoning and subdivision control, restrain the nature and location of land development by private developers. Other types of action tools aimed at directing private development efforts are the various incentives and disincentives in the form of program expenditures, lot levies for utilities charged to subdividers, and flexible zoning such as the transfer of development rights and donation of park land.

Components such as these still need to be woven together to form a guidance system for the community's land use. The design of a guidance system is beyond the scope of this presentation, and in any case, it must be a result of the melding of the decision guides and action instruments that are available and appropriate to the particular community. There are, however, basic dimensions that are common to all communities: these are the content, location, timing, and agents responsible for implementation.[26] **Content** refers to such mechanisms of the guidance system as the degree of public intervention in land development, the regulative devices, public investment programs, land acquisitions, and not least, administrative procedures, such as which department will coordinate the capital improvements program. **Location** refers to the geographic areas in the community where facilities are to be located, redevelopment is to occur, utilities are to be replaced, or where housing incentives are to apply. **Timing** refers to the programming of urban development by date of implementation, as well as the pace and location of development, both private and public. **Responsible agencies** refers to the department within the local government and other such local public agencies as school boards, library boards, and public utilities that make the final decisions on facilities and programs. Lastly, one should add, the **public participation process** into which the various action instruments and decision guides fit. In the current era of consensus-building in planning, it is essential that the public be well-informed not only about planning intentions but also about the planning tools that might be used and their impacts.[27] A well-informed public could add greatly to the effectiveness of a planning guidance system.

It can be seen that designing a guidance system for land use is no small task. However, in most communities the components of the system exist; administrative and political mechanisms are likely already in place, such as a development control system and a capital improvements program. As with most other planning activities, the necessary ingredients for instituting a guidance system for planning involve, first, the will to begin and, second, the commitment to maintain the system. Further, whether the guidance system concept is used or not, there must be some way of linking the plan with the planner's tools if this last vital phase of the planning process—implementation—is to be meaningful and effective.

ENDNOTES

1. Martin Meyerson, "Building the Middle-Range Bridge for Comprehensive Planning," *Journal of the American Institute of Planners* 22 (Spring 1956), 58–64.
2. These definitions are adapted from Frank S. So, *The Practice of Local Government Planning* (Washington: International City Manager's Association, 1979), 129.

3. Robert Coughlin, "The Capital Programming Problem," *Journal of the American Institute of Planners* 26 (February 1960), 39–48.

4. *Ibid.*

5. *Ibid.*

6. So, *Practice,* 136ff.

7. Manfred Fast, "Community Can Make It Happen: Forging the Port Colborne Ontario Strategic Plan," *Small Town* 26, no. 1 (July-August 1995), 10–15.

8. Francois Leblanc, "La renaissance des centre-villes: Le programme Rues principales," *Plan Canada* 29, no. 5 (September 1989), 8–13.

9. Matthew Kiernan, "Intergovernmental Innovation: Winnipeg's Core Area Initiative," *Plan Canada* 27, no. 1 (March 1987), 23–31.

10. David L.A. Gordon, "Planning, Design and Managing Change in Urban Waterfront Redevelopment," *Town Planning Review* 67, no. 3 (1996), 261–290.

11. *Ibid.*

12. An amendment to B.C.'s planning legislation in the early 1990s now requires local government to include a policy statement on affordable housing in its official community plans.

13. Barton Reid, "Go-Plan Looking into the Future," *City Magazine* 16, no. 1 (Spring 1995), 8–10.

14. Alun Richards, "Implementing a Voluntary Process for Difficult-to-Site Projects," *Plan Canada* 36, no. 1 (January 1996), 31–32.

15. A good example from Australia is Citizens Advocating Responsible Transportation, *Traffic Calming: The Solution to Urban Traffic and a New Vision of Neighbourhood Livability* (Angrove Q. Australia, 1989).

16. *Ibid.,* 18–19.

17. As cited by Danish planner Ole Djurhuus, "Danish Planning and Design Procedures for Traffic Calming," paper presented at Cascadia Calming Symposium, Victoria, September 1995.

18. J.P. Braaksma & Associates, *Reclaiming the Streets: Setting the Stage for a Traffic Calming Policy in Ottawa,* report to the City of Ottawa, 1995, 86ff.

19. Barton Reid, "Harbourfront: Aesthetics vs. Dollars," *City Magazine* 8, nos. 3 and 4 (Fall 1986), 9–10.

20. Alberta, *The Planning Act, 1977,* Statutes of the Province of Alberta (1977), Chapter 89; and Ontario, *An Act to Revise the Planning Act,* Revised Statutes of Ontario (1983).

21. For example, for Ontario, see Llewelyn Davies Weeks Canada Ltd., *The Operation of Municipal Planning,* a report to the Planning Act Review Committee (Toronto, 1977), Background Paper No. 2; and, for Alberta, the innovative poster plans for small towns described in Chapter 12 *supra.*

22. Ontario, Commission on Planning and Development Reform in Ontartio, *New Planning in Ontario, Final Report* (Toronto, 1993); and Stan Clinton, "Changing Times: Newfoundland's Municipal Planning and Implementation Systems," *Plan Canada* 37, no. 2 (March 1997), 18–20.

23. Much of the discussion in this section is based on the guidance system concepts in F. Stuart Chapin, Jr., and Edward J. Kaiser, *Urban Land Use Planning*, 3rd ed. (Urbana: University of Illinois Press, 1979), especially 60–65 and 482–511.

24. *Ibid.*, 64.

25. *Ibid.*, 60ff.

26. *Ibid.*, 509–510.

27. Judith E. Innes, "Planning through Consensus Building: A New View of the Comprehensive Planning Ideal," *Journal of the American Planning Association* 62, no. 4 (Autumn 1996), 460–472.

Chapter 11 Regional and Metropolitan Planning in Canada

Planning has to be at a scale which is large enough to work out a strategy for growth within a setting as broad as the entire urban-centred region.

Leonard Gertler, 1966

Many planning problems have effects on areas well beyond their source. The drainage of storm water from a subdivision into a watercourse has the potential of causing pollution to areas downstream, for example; or a major sports facility in one community may generate large amounts of traffic flowing through normally quiet residential areas in another. Probably the classic example is **suburbanization,** when those who work and shop in an older central city choose to reside in a newer, lower-density community on the edge of the city. Indeed, few planning problems are confined within an individual community. The reasons stem from the interrelationships of various economic and social activities in a community and the ways in which the effects of development are transmitted through space by transportation, the flow of water, and the economy, among other factors. Thus, it is often necessary to undertake planning for areas larger than one community, areas large enough to encompass the major effects of development problems.

Patrick Geddes was perhaps the first among contemporary planners to sense the need for larger-area planning. He observed the spread of urban development in 19th-century England and coined the term "conurbation" to capture the interdependent quality of these linked cities. He also propounded the need to plan together all the features of a river basin (e.g., the land and natural features, as they are affected by agriculture or industry or water control) and the needs of a population for land for recreation and for residences. What Geddes noted was how areas are unified by either the problems of their development or by their resource base, and sometimes by both. When large areas are distinguished by certain unifying characteristics, they are called **regions.** He called for planning for regions as well as for their constituent communities.

Some of the most enduring ideas and ideals in planning are associated with regional planning. The Garden City movement, initiated by Ebenezer Howard and advanced by Thomas Adams, was not concerned exclusively with planning single new towns. It was based on a concept of how best to organize the territory around large cities, that is, to concentrate populations and provide open space between towns rather than let cities sprawl. Figure 11.1 illustrates Howard's regional ideal for the new towns and how they would be connected to the large city by railways. Another regional

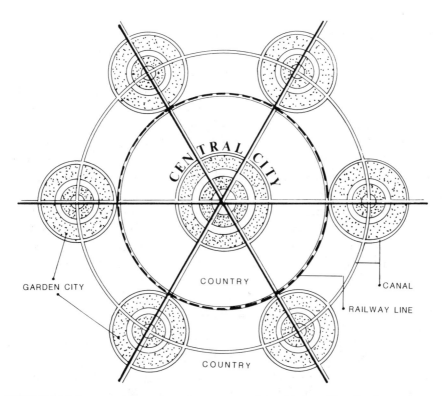

FIGURE 11.1   Ebenezer Howard's Concept of the Metropolitan Region
Howard's 1898 diagrammatic concept for satellite Garden Cities has been far-reaching. A greenbelt of farms and forests would separate all communities, but they would be interconnected by major transport routes. Metropolitan plans for London, Washington, and Vancouver owe much to this model.

planning thrust was manifest in efforts at conserving natural resources, especially in the planning of river basins. The famous Tennessee Valley planning during the 1930s in the United States is the epitome of this approach.

Planners have traditionally proposed the regional approach for two kinds of planning problems, one involving the growth and spread of cities into the countryside, the other the development and conservation of natural resources. Both concerns generated distinctive forms of regional planning; there are many examples of each in Canada. In this chapter, we shall review the nature of each type of large-area planning—regional resource planning and metropolitan-area planning—and describe Canadian experiences with each. But first it will be helpful to expand on the regional planning perspective introduced above.

THE REGIONAL PLANNING PERSPECTIVE

Planning for the physical environment is commonly talked about on two levels—city (community) planning and regional planning. Although the two are obviously complementary, each has developed in its own distinctive way. This fact stems partly from basic differences in the planning issues and objectives addressed by each, and partly from differences in jurisdictional arrangements. Of the two, city planning is the easier to define, because it is concerned with influencing urban physical development within municipal boundaries. Regional planning is concerned with many different facets of the physical environment, human as well as natural attributes, over large areas that may include city areas as well and may not have well-defined political boundaries. Indeed, the roots of regional planning have generated a different outlook from that of community planning, and it is instructive to review them.

The Roots of Regional Planning

Regional planning is a product of the intellectual and social ferment of Europe and North America in the mid- and late 19th century. It parallels in many ways the responses of the proponents of utopian communities of that period, which we have discussed in Chapter 4. Many observers of the growth and spread of cities of that time believed that the natural environment was being threatened by the demands of modern capitalist urban society. Among the most prominent were Frederick LePlay in France and, later, Patrick Geddes in Britain. They turned their attention to promoting ways to make the earth more habitable and, especially, to achieving a balance between human and natural factors. Geddes propounded his famous trinity of factors to be taken into account in spatial planning: *Folk* (the people of the region), *Work* (the economy of the region), and *Place* (the geographical dimensions of the region).[1] The interrelations among these factors not only signify the integrity of any region; to Geddes, they also provided the foundation for undertaking regional planning.

Geddes demonstrated his notions in a hypothetical geographical unit, "The Valley Section" (Figure 11.2). The Valley Section presented the spatial relations of a set of settlements each with distinctive geographical and human values. Within it are embodied two basic principles of regional planning: (1) the need to take a synoptic approach to regional problems in order to encompass the interrelationships of areas; and (2) the planning of each area in coordination with adjoining areas. Thus, the planner sees in a given region that the different factors interact such that change in one leads to changes in others. Of course, the use of a river basin to illustrate these principles made much sense, for much of human settlement has taken place in such regions, and the parts of river basins are clearly linked.

This concept of the river basin as a natural region of high order has proved to be a powerful one in planning. It spawned many efforts in river basin planning throughout the world, in the United States, Colombia, Russia, India, and even in Canada. The most dramatic and successful of these is that begun in the 1930s for the Tennessee River, a major tributary of the Mississippi River, in the south-eastern United States. This region of several thousand square kilometres was for many decades subject to major floods owing to inordinate cutting of its forests and debilitating agricultural practices that rendered its soils incapable of holding water. Since the basin overlapped several states, the U.S. federal government established a spe-

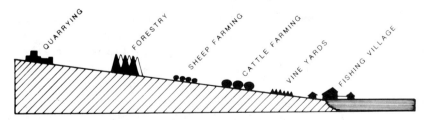

FIGURE 11.2   **The Valley Section of Patrick Geddes**
Geddes used the example of activities at different levels in a valley to emphasize the need to plan for them together. This integrated view of planning, dating from 1892, is the forerunner of modern ecosystems planning.

cial agency, the **Tennessee Valley Authority** (TVA), with the power to plan and develop the region. The TVA's mandate was to rehabilitate the region for the benefit of its inhabitants through the construction of dams, electric power generation, reforestation, promotion of improved agricultural methods, irrigation, and the building of new towns. This broad mandate was based on the same principles of the interdependence of the parts of the region that Geddes espoused. Urban historian Lewis Mumford commented as follows about the TVA:

> The Tennessee Valley project, with its fundamental policy of conservation of power resources, land, forest, soil, and stream, in the public interest, is an indication of a new approach to the problems of regional development. ... The river valley has the advantage of bringing into a common regional frame a diversified unit: this is essential to an effective civic and social life.[2]

There is more than a hint in Mumford's remarks of a strongly held philosophy about planning for human communities. For him and others who witnessed the growth and spread of large cities in the 1920s and 1930s and the consequent debilitation of resources and the environment, the region was a special place created by people interacting with their environment. The natural region could be a bulwark against massive urbanization and the standardization of culture. This regionalism—a belief in the profound connection between humankind and the territory it inhabits—has re-emerged in Canada and elsewhere in recent years under the name **bioregionalism.**[3] Many of the same sentiments have always pervaded regional planning and may be detected in, for example, the 1969 plan for the Mactaquac River Valley in New Brunswick.[4] This humanistic view, it must be noted, has not always been easy to reconcile with the rigidities of political boundaries, bureaucratic jurisdictions, and economic determinism. It is a major factor in the somewhat fitful history of regional planning in Canada.[5]

Characteristics of Regional Planning

In general, regional planning is rooted in the importance of using natural resources wisely. In Canada, this spawned three approaches to regional planning. One approach, as we have seen, is the **planning for watersheds** in the tradition of the TVA. Here the planning is for the control and use of water resources to prevent floods, to provide irrigation to agricultural lands, to generate electricity, to create recreational opportunities, or some combination of these. The conservation authorities that were established for a score of river basins in southern Ontario in the late 1940s epitomize this type of planning in Canada. Another approach is the **planning for rural land resources**, especially in the vicinity of large cities. Here the concern is to achieve a harmonious balance between urban and rural land needs. Two early examples were the Lower Mainland Regional Planning Board for the area around Vancouver and the regional planning commissions for the Calgary and Edmonton areas established about 1950.

Concerns over **economic development in resource regions** is a third approach to regional planning. This is a concern that has loomed large in many countries since the 1930s and is still prominent. Non-urban regions tend to depend heavily on the economic performance of their natural resource sectors. In many of these regions, the resources had become obsolete (as with coal) or depleted (as with minerals and timber), or the technology for exploiting them had become outdated (as with farming and fisheries). Many examples of this type of planning exist in Canada, from the Interlake Region of Manitoba to Cape Breton Island.

Even though the substantive concerns of each of these approaches of regional planning differ, certain common characteristics are evident. A prime characteristic is that regional planning deals with *large* areas— "supra-urban space," as John Friedmann has called it.[6] In other words, the scale of regional planning efforts encompasses areas larger than a single city, while that of city or community planning focuses attention on the space within the city. A second characteristic, closely associated with the first, is that regional planning is mostly concerned with the *location* of activities and resource development. This contrasts with the concern of city planning with the *allocation* of space among competing land uses.

Two other characteristics reveal social and political aspects of regional planning. On the one hand, regional planning is intimately tied up with social and economic questions, more so than is city planning. On the other hand, this concern involves regional planning in a special institutional setting. Quite commonly, regional planning is involved with more than one governmental jurisdiction, and very often with more than one governmental level. For example, water and other natural resource development is a provincial responsibility, while the necessary planning actions usually take place within municipal boundaries. Not infrequently, over the past few decades, the economic problems of many regions have become a national concern, thereby involving the federal government in planning for regional development, along with provincial and local governments.

Although regional planning is a public, governmental activity, it does not always take the form of direct government action. Many times, regional planning is only an *advisory* activity. This reflects the need to blend the governing powers of those public units that are involved with the planning needs of the region. Thus, regional planning in Canada has been undertaken under a variety of formats. There are those under which an agency has the authority both for planning and for carrying out plans, and those where the agency has only advisory powers on the implementation of plans. The former category includes the James Bay Development Corporation, which was established by the Province of Quebec to plan and develop the hydroelectric resources of an immense area in the northern part of the province. The latter category includes such regional planning commissions as those established in Alberta and New Brunswick, which have the authority to make plans for their regions but wield almost no powers of implementation. In between these forms fall a variety of other arrangements for regional planning: for example, corporations with limited powers, interdepartmental committees, and federal-provincial planning agreements. The second section of this chapter discusses examples of various regional planning efforts.

The Problem of Regional Boundaries

Often "regional planning" seems a nebulous term. This arises from the fact that what constitutes a region from one point of view may not constitute a region from another. Regional planning boundaries cannot be drawn with precision because of the variety of concerns involved. Even the boundaries of a watershed, which define the extent of water resources of a region, may not encompass the human interactions of commuting to work or the shipment of goods in and out of the same region. Moreover, since regional planning is a public effort to bring improvement to a region, that public effort will need to be expressed within the appropriate governmental jurisdictions: that is, regional planning boundaries must reflect the boundaries of the governments involved. This recognition often involves compromise between government units to determine an acceptable planning region. Moreover, governmental boundaries seldom follow the patterns of natural regions; when a river is used as a boundary between government units, the natural region is split.

The issue of regional boundaries for planning purposes can never be finally resolved. There may be a unique set of river basin regions, but human activities cannot be defined so neatly, and, significantly, their spatial configurations change over time. Political boundaries, meanwhile, tend to remain fixed over long periods of time. This ambiguity must be tolerated in regional planning. Rather than pursue the elusive ideal boundary for a planning region, it is more productive to plan explicitly for the boundary areas in conjunction with the adjacent region. It is wise to remember that wherever the region's boundaries are drawn there is another region on the other side.

CANADIAN EXPERIENCE IN REGIONAL PLANNING

Experience with regional planning in Canada can be dated, for the most part, from just after World War II. This experience shows regional planning to have taken four basic forms:[7]

1. Planning for regional resources development;
2. Planning for rural regions;
3. Planning regional economic development; and
4. Metropolitan-region planning.

Below we briefly describe examples of the first three of these basic forms. The aim is to show the kinds of problems regional planning tackles, the way in which planning efforts are organized, and the effects this may have on local community planning. The Canadian experience in metropolitan planning needs special consideration and this follows in a separate section.

Regional Resources Planning

Throughout the history of regional planning in Canada there have been many instances of concern over the quality and extent of natural resources development. It was one of the main stimuli for the creation of the federal Commission on Conservation in 1909 (see Chapter 4). Later, the unified planning of river basins approach, such as TVA, could be seen in this country.

Although there was nothing as grandiose as the TVA in Canada, its imprint can be seen in the establishment, also during the Depression, of both the Prairie Farm Rehabilitation Administration (PFRA) and the Maritime Marshland Rehabilitation Administration (MMRA). The PFRA sought to develop various measures for soil and water conservation in the then drought-stricken Prairie region, and MMRA's mandate was to reverse incipient salt-water intrusion into coastal agricultural lands in the Maritimes.

In 1946, something close to the "classic" form of river basin planning appeared in Canada. Ontario proclaimed a new Conservation Authorities Act. In it were provisions to establish regional conservation authorities to conduct multi-purpose planning for a dozen or more river basins in the province. The fruits of this planning are still enjoyed today in terms of flood-control measures, wetlands conservation, and water-based recreation, and future concerns are also being addressed.[8]

The doctrine of the connection between humankind and the territory it inhabits is also found to a greater or lesser degree in other regional planning efforts of the 1960s and 1970s. We see it clearly in the planning for the Mactaquac River Valley of New Brunswick,[9] in the planning for the impacts of the Diefenbaker Dam in Saskatchewan, in the plan for the Cumberland Sound region of the Northwest Territories, and in the Niagara Escarpment plan in Ontario.

These initiatives required planning boundaries that correspond to physiographic and social conditions, something not easy to reconcile with the rigidities of political boundaries and bureaucratic jurisdiction. Provincial and/or federal commitment to these "natural" boundaries was, therefore, of paramount importance to their being established and sustained. In each case, special agencies were created to carry out the regional planning (and often to construct facilities such as dams) and super imposed on existing local governments.[10] Contemporary efforts in the same vein can be seen in the federal-provincial-local-First Nations initiative to plan for the Fraser River Basin in British Columbia.

Rural Region Planning

One of the most successful and long-lived regional planning experiences in Canada is in physical planning for rural regions and small towns. Regional planning commissions in Alberta and New Brunswick, county planning in Nova Scotia and Ontario, and regional district planning in British Columbia are among the forms that provinces have devised to respond to the planning needs of low-density regions. Incidentally, these rural regions usually comprise about 90% of a province's territory.

The oldest of these agencies are the five non-metropolitan regional planning commissions in Alberta.[11] The reasons for their establishment in Alberta, and elsewhere later, are obscure, but it was probably a response to urban-type problems in rural areas, including overspill from growing towns and the consequences of subdivisions and ribbon development in the countryside. Curiously, they seem not to have been formed to deal with basic rural problems such as the lack of growth in towns and land use for rural production. Nevertheless, the planners recognized that their regions did not need conventional urban physical planning. Each town or township needed solutions to its specific problems such as the lack of basic utilities, disposing of trash, refurbishing Main Street, or reducing residential scatter (see Chapter 12). Several provinces also established agencies to provide planning services to small communities such as Prince Edward Island's Land Use Services Centre and Manitoba's and Newfoundland's field planning offices.

Worth special mention are the efforts of two provinces, British Columbia and Quebec, to conserve agricultural lands. In 1973, B.C. set up the Agricultural Land Commission which, in turn, established Agricultural Land Reserves (ALRs) to restrict urban development on areas with soil types that could support agricultural production (usually soil types 1, 2, and 3). The Land Commission continues to this day and has control over the subdivision of land in zones designated as an ALR inside and outside municipal boundaries. A similar step was taken in Quebec in 1978 with Bill 90, *An Act to Protect Agricultural Land,* that established a commission to protect agricultural land in "protected zones."[12] In both provinces there has been considerable success in preventing non-agricultural uses in protected areas.

Regional Economic Planning

Toward the end of the 1950s, Canada's economy entered a new spatial phase. Metropolitan regions were replacing rural resource regions in economic importance. And in the process, many of the country's agricultural, fishing, mining, and forestry regions exhibited signs of economic underdevelopment. Poverty, illiteracy, poor housing and infrastructure, inefficient technology, obsolete resources, and out-migration were in evidence. As these rural regions began to demand a share of the national prosperity, we entered a period of extensive regional planning, but of a different sort than those described above, that would last only into the early 1980s.

The awareness of unequal development between regions of the country captured the attention of people and politicians at both the provincial and federal levels. "Regional disparities" became a familiar phrase, and the concerns led to considerable amounts of mostly federal funds (some have estimated $15 billion) being devoted to mitigating regional economic differences. This, it should be noted, was not a new phenomenon in Canada as the Rowell-Sirois Royal Commission had pointed out in 1940 by saying that "income of the country is concentrated in a few specially favoured areas."[13] They were referring to the urban-industrial corridor from Windsor to Quebec City that Canadian geographer Maurice Yeates would later call "Main Street."[14]

The first major effort at countering regional disparities came in 1961, with the passage of the federal **Agricultural Rehabilitation and Development Act** (ARDA). Under ARDA, low-income agricultural regions were targeted for programs of farm enlargement, establishing community pastures, and improving farm market roads. Over the next few years, 40 regional planning efforts were undertaken. Three among them deserve mention to show both the scope and difficulties surrounding ARDA regional planning. One is the truly grass-roots redevelopment program in the Gaspé, the Bureau d'Amanagement de l'est du Québec (BAEQ), involving all sectors of the community in what nowadays would be called "self-management" of the region's future. A second is the "top-down" Newfoundland Outport Resettlement Program, which, while succeeding in relocating 300 outports (of the 600 that were targeted), caused numerous splits in families and communities still evident today. A third is the multifaceted Interlake Region program in Manitoba; it might be considered ARDA's success story.[15]

A host of other alphabetic agencies joined ARDA during the 1960s: ADA, the Area Development Agency; ADB, the Atlantic Development Board; and FRED, the Fund for Rural Economic Development. They were all gathered under the umbrella of DREE, the Department for Regional Economic Expansion in 1969.[16] DREE's approach was generally comprehensive in regard to a region's needs and included housing, municipal infrastructure, transportation, and education along with job creation. Throughout this period, the regional planning efforts involved both federal and provincial levels of government, for although the necessary funds were available at the federal level, the responsibility for regional resources lay with the provinces. This was, as Gertler notes, "a period of experimentation" in regional planning owing, as much as anything, to the need to evolve an approach to joint planning between two levels of government.[17]

Various planning paradigms were used by DREE and the agencies that succeeded it. At the beginning of the 1970s, 20 urban centres within problem regions were designated as regional **growth poles,** a concept popular at the time.[18] They became eligible to receive assistance to improve such services as roads, schools, transportation, water supply, and sewerage to enhance their capacity to attract industry, which would, in turn, spread benefits to the surrounding region. In 1974, General Development Agreements with each province replaced the previous highly centralized DREE approach and the provinces were encouraged to formulate plans for their designated regions. This approach remained in place until 1985 when the new federal government changed the emphasis to general economic growth rather than regional development.

This vigorous 25-year period in Canadian regional planning is hard to characterize. Some would ask: was it regional planning at all? There was seldom a permanent planning staff in a DREE-designated region. There were federal-provincial task forces, development corporations, and general funding agreements. But there was seldom a published regional plan. "Worst-first" concepts vied with growth poles in implementation. Not least, it was regional planning from *outside* the region. And this could sometimes be extremely upsetting to local councils and planners, as witness B.C. Hydro's plans to flood Arrow Lakes' communities[19] and the mega-industrial projects along the Canso Strait.[20] Only in a few regions was planning generated by local residents. In any case, the "experiment" Gertler spoke of is now far behind us and unlikely to rise again in an era when both bioregionalism and globalism vie for attention.

Other Forms: Past and Present

Brief mention needs to be made of a number of other forms of regional planning either for or affecting land use. One concerns the planning for regional transportation systems, especially expressway planning. While these are similar to the "functional" plans referred to in Chapter 6, they cover a much wider territory and involve many communities. Almost all the large metropolitan areas have had such plans prepared.

Less common is what might be called the regional policy plan such as that for the **Toronto-Centred Region** (TCR) prepared by a team of provincial planners for an area roughly within an 80 km arc around Toronto, or 22,270 km^2 overall. This plan from 1970 dealt with the location of future residential, commercial, and recreational areas and the basic transportation structure. The concept map of TCR is shown in Figure 11.3. The planners sought to align urban places in a linear fashion (see diagram "b" in Figure 11.4) in order, according to one planner, "to maximize the advantages of routing transportation and services along a line designed to serve several centres."[21] They sought to reduce the concentration of population and provide open space and recreational opportunities, along with making "careful use of resources."[22] Plans such as that for TCR represent a statement of provincial government policy, especially in regard to public expenditures for transportation and other costly regional utilities and open space. Such plans are also notable by their absence, and this frequently leaves municipalities wondering about provincial intentions.

Quebec took a major step in 1980 when its Regional and City Planning Act established a new regional planning framework.[23] It provided for the creation of 94 Regional County Municipalities (Municipalités regionales de comte, or MRC's), and one of their main tasks was to prepare a regional plan. The act defined very specifically the contents of such a plan. Briefly, the plan had to include proposals for land use, delimitation of areas to become urban, identification of environmentally sensitive, historical, and cultural areas, and the location of intermunicipal facilities and public utilities.[24] With this legislation, Quebec took the most comprehensive step in province-wide regional planning of any province because, significantly, it linked plan preparation to governmental powers of implementation.

More recently, **bioregional** approaches have begun to appear in Canadian regional planning. One of the first is found in the planning for the Kitimat-Stikine regional district in northwest British Columbia in the

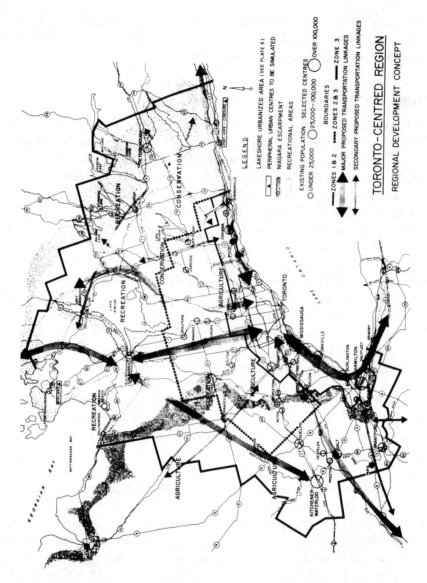

FIGURE 11.3   Plan for the Toronto-Centred Region, 1970
More than a metropolitan-area plan, this plan covered a region 80 km around Toronto, thereby recognizing the interactions and interdependencies that prevail in the region of a major metropolis—the urban field. This was a broad-brush strategic plan to signal the provincial government's intentions regarding urban development, transportation, agriculture, and open space. *Source:* Ontario, *Design for Development*, 1970.

late 1980s.[25] This and other initiatives draw upon the emerging field of bioregionalism, which is not a specific planning paradigm so much as an "action-oriented movement based on ecological principles."[26] It arises from a particular set of values regarding the quality of a region's living space. It is holistic in its outlook in that a bioregion is a system comprising three subsystems: a "biophysical" subsystem (i.e., the natural environment), an "inhabiting" subsystem (i.e., communities, agriculture, transportation), and a "network" subsystem (i.e., the economic and political systems).[27] Bioregionalism rejects existing political units in favour of "contiguous, mappable geographic regions" based on similarities of topography, plant and animal life, culture, and economy such as watersheds.[28] In many ways, this is a similar perspective to the "regionalism" of the 1930s alluded to earlier in this chapter.

What tends to be appearing in Canadian regional planning is not full-blown bioregionalism but rather the application of some of its principles. The Crombie Commission on the Toronto waterfront (which was referred to earlier) utilized the watershed bioregion notion as its organizing principle. The large municipality of Markham outside Toronto has conducted a comprehensive environmental planning study not only emphasizing environmental protection but also restoration of ecological diversity and integrating these with cultural patterns in the area.[29] A similar approach is taken in the recent plan of the greenbelt surrounding Ottawa, which propounds a "connected ecological system" and employs nodes, buffers, and links, as the bioregionalists call the landscape components.[30]

It appears certain that bioregional concepts and values will continue to influence both regional and local planning in the future. As that happens, there will be the need to re-examine some of the practices of conventional planning. For example, the bioregional approach links ecology and community and puts them at the centre of planning rather than, say, land use and economic development.[31] And not the least will be the need to negotiate new regional boundaries and implementation powers.

CANADIAN EXPERIENCE IN METROPOLITAN PLANNING

Canada is a leader in metropolitan planning in the Western Hemisphere. Almost all of the country's 25 metropolitan areas—the regions of our largest cities—have active planning agencies. This experience is now more than five decades old, having started with Winnipeg in 1943 and Toronto a few years later. In this section, we shall describe some of the highlights of Canadian metropolitan planning, with the aim of identifying the forms it has taken, the problems it has tackled, its accomplishments, and its relationship to local community planning. But before doing this, it will be helpful to examine the backdrop for metropolitan planning.

Nature and Origins

Metropolitan planning is a special form of regional planning. It not only deals with a large area, but it also deals explicitly with the growth and expansion of a major city on which the region is usually focused. Further, the planning normally is in an institutional setting involving several municipalities. Broadly speaking, metropolitan planning is concerned with the allocation of land uses and the location of major public works throughout the region of a metropolis. In this sense, it might be said that metropolitan planning is community planning "writ large."

Three factors must be remembered, however, about metropolitan planning. The first has to do with the scale of the area involved. Metropolitan planning areas are usually defined to encompass the potential spread of urban development, and this often means as much as 500 km^2. Moreover, the area will be developed at different densities and interspersed with agricultural areas and open spaces for recreation. The second factor also has to do with scale, but this time with the size of population. Planning for large aggregates of population requires a recognition of the increasing division of the metropolitan community into separate areas for work, residence, shopping, and leisure. Metropolitan planning must try to accommodate, as Hans Blumenfeld says, a number of "contradictory requirements," such as providing a "minimum need for commuting but maximum possibility for commuting."[32] The third factor is the intermunicipal setting for planning. Given the autonomy accorded local governments in Canada, the planning for several of them simultaneously must seek ways to blend competing aims for development in the interest of all the citizens of the metropolitan community. Achieving this planning blend requires special organizational arrangements, and these have taken a number of forms, as we shall see later.

The emergence of metropolitan planning in Canada coincides with the end of World War II, when cities all over the world began to have dramatic surges of population growth and commercial and manufacturing development. For example, in 1941 Canada had 15 metropolitan areas that comprised about 40% of the total population. By 1961, 5 more cities had been added to the metropolitan class, and metropolitan populations had become 51% of the total. Even more dramatic is the fact that in this 20-year period 5 million more people crowded into Canada's largest cities, more than doubling the population living there. Today, there are 25 metropolitan areas with nearly 17 million people, or 56% of the nation's total.

This vast growth created a host of problems for both the central city and the surrounding region in which the new suburbs were being built. In the central city, the problems were a combination of an aging physical environment and a lack of vacant land for new development. There was a deterioration of some older residential and industrial areas as populations and factories moved to the outskirts, thus leading to the need for rehabilitation and redevelopment. The new suburbs, at the same time, faced the problems associated with providing services, e.g., water, sewerage, garbage disposal, police and fire protection, roads, and schools. Their problems stemmed from the size of the new suburban growth and the meagre financial resources available to previously small municipalities. In addition, with the rapidly growing population and the vast areas being settled came the need for new facilities to serve the entire metropolitan area—among them hospitals, expressways, parks, airports, new sources for water supplies, and sewage treatment plants."[33]

Metropolitan planning originated in this complex, large-scale urban development. It grew out of the realization that no single municipality in a metropolitan area could deal with an array of problems as intertwined as these, with the need to balance growth and to provide metropolitan-wide facilities. For example, the location of a large subdivision or a shopping centre in one part of the area may generate the need for improved highway access, new schools, or new trunk sewers. While the new subdivision or the shopping centre may be a matter for local planning, it may also have repercussions at the metropolitan level. Conversely, local desires for development may depend upon the availability of metropolitan facilities and services. The latter are almost always very costly, especially for one community to provide, and it is important that they be properly located to serve the needs of all communities within the metropolitan area.

Achieving coordination in the land-use planning of diverse communities, thus, becomes a major aim of metropolitan planning. This was certainly the main stimulus prompting many provinces to establish, in the 1940s and 1950s, the means for metropolitan planning to occur in their burgeoning city regions. Manitoba, British Columbia, and Alberta were first, followed closely by Ontario. Their aim, it seems fair to say, was to rationalize the operation of various metropolitan functions (e.g., water supply and sewerage; public transportation and roads) in which the provinces were financial partners with the municipalities. Much effort has, therefore, centred on choosing the organizational approach to achieve effective metropolitan planning. We shall deal with this thrust first, but there is another to which we shall need to return. It concerns the physical form of the metropolitan community that is created out of these efforts, for Canadian metropolitan planners drew upon concepts developed abroad, and also contributed their own.

Organizational Approaches

The first formal metropolitan planning agency established in Canada (indeed in North America) was that created by the Manitoba government in 1943—the Metropolitan Planning Commission of Greater Winnipeg. The dozen or so municipalities that constituted the metropolitan area were members of the commission and contributed to its operation, as did the provincial government. It had a small and energetic staff, headed by Eric Thrift, that produced (by itself or with the help of consultants) an impressive series of reports on traffic, parking, the central business district, and parks. Although much was achieved through this intermunicipal effort, municipalities could choose whether to participate, and the plans that were made by the commission were not binding on any municipality. This same cooperative, advisory form of metropolitan planning was also adopted in Vancouver (1949), Edmonton (1950), and Calgary (1950).

It gradually became evident that metropolitan planning without a commensurate level of government authorized to implement planning policies could achieve only limited results. This was especially true in regard to decisions about the location and financing of facilities to serve the entire metropolitan area. It was also true for local land-use regulations and capital investments that could thwart the intent of the metropolitan plan. This division of authority among local units of government was, of course, the product of the primacy accorded municipalities by the provinces a half century or more earlier in handling their own affairs. The provinces, with the exception of Ontario, were slow to intervene in this tradition and form metropolitan governments.

Metropolitan Toronto

In 1953, the Ontario government established the Municipality of Metropolitan Toronto, the first metropolitan government in either Canada or the United States. It followed the form of a **federation** of the 13 local municipalities that made up the metropolitan area at the time. (The alternative form, an **amalgamation** of municipalities into a single unit for the entire metropolitan area, was debated and rejected.) Within the federation, each municipality retained responsibility for its own local planning and land-use regulation, and its own local public works. The metropolitan government ("Metro Toronto," as it has come to be called) assumed responsibility for major regional services and such facilities as public transportation, water supply, and expressways. Metro Toronto also had the power to raise its funds for capital works projects.

When it was established, the metropolitan municipality was provided with an Advisory Planning Board like those of other municipalities in the province. There was one major difference, however, because the Metro Toronto Planning Board had jurisdiction in planning over a surrounding area that was twice as large again as Metro. The planning area covered a total of 1,970 km^2, of which 620 km^2 comprised the 13 metropolitan municipalities, while the remaining area comprised 13 fringe-area local governments. The reason for establishing such jurisdiction was to give metropolitan planners some measure of control over the development occurring beyond their boundaries.

The Metropolitan Toronto Planning Board was charged with preparing an Official Plan, to which municipalities both inside and outside Metro were required to conform in their planning and public works projects. Within Metro the zoning of local municipalities had to conform to the Official Plan, and Metro had to approve local subdivision plans. It should be noted that the Official Plan of Metro is only advisory and cannot bind the local municipalities, but it has been a strong, persuasive force. An important reason for this, as Blumenfeld notes (he was Deputy Commissioner of Planning for Metro for many years), is that each municipality sent representatives to Metro Council where they had a voice in adopting the Official Plan.[34] As well, the debentures for public works of each municipality were underwritten by the metropolitan corporation. Further, from the metropolitan-area side, Metro had the power to fund and construct area-wide facilities and, thus, see its own plan become implemented.

There have been a series of changes to the metropolitan government of Toronto since its origin. The first was 15 years after its founding, when the continued pressure of the City of Toronto to consolidate all 13 municipalities into one single city resulted in a review of Metro's organization and functioning. The government structure was altered, the 13 local governments were reduced to 6, and a number of other refinements were made. In 1971, the province began instituting its program to establish regional governments, somewhat modelled on Metro, for all major urban areas in Ontario as well as for the urbanizing area surrounding Metro. The Regional Municipality of York was established to the north, Regional Peel was instituted on the west, and Regional Durham on the east. The significant change was the elimination of the fringe portion of Metro's planning area, thereby reducing it to the size of the metropolitan area.

The evolution of the structure of metropolitan government for the Toronto region continued again in 1997 with the amalgamation of the six constituent municipalities into one metropolitan unit. Twice before, in 1953 in the initial debates and again in 1968, amalgamation was debated and ruled out, but this time the province forced the issue. The debate was at times rancorous, often centring on the loss of democratic rights in the way the decision was made and the loss of presumably more responsive local government entities.[35] Curiously, the province's proposal barely touched on the impact of amalgamation on planning content or process.

A provincial task force in the previous year felt the need for an expanded view of metropolitan planning to what they called the Greater Toronto Area (GTA), a region only slightly smaller than the 22,000 km^2 Toronto-Centred Region set out in 1970.[36] The Toronto area, today, is unique among Canadian metropolitan areas because it comprises more than a single central city, its suburbs, and rural fringe. The GTA Task Force called it "a mixture of mature cities, growing suburbs, newer edge cities, and adjacent rural communities." Those planning its future form will probably need to look at newer models like the "dispersed metropolis."[37]

Metropolitan Winnipeg

Metropolitan planning in Winnipeg was given governmental backing in 1960 when the province created the Metropolitan Corporation of Greater Winnipeg, the second metropolitan government in Canada. The corporation was given responsibility for water supply, sewage disposal, transportation, and planning. Winnipeg chose a two-tier system of government, with the local municipalities remaining along with the new metropolitan corporation, yet it was not a federation as in Toronto. Metropolitan councillors were elected directly rather than drawn from local governments. This created a tension between the two levels of government. Further, the metropolitan corporation had no control over the capital spending of the local-level governments. These two conditions frequently resulted in a failure to implement metropolitan plans.[38] In 1971, Manitoba restructured the metropolitan government again, this time in the form of one single city, the City of Winnipeg, or Unicity as it is known. Now all levels of government and planning are integrated.

Other Metropolitan Areas

The approach of cooperative, advisory, intermunicipal planning remained in practice in the metropolitan areas of Vancouver and Victoria until 1966. Regional governments were formed and assumed the planning functions previously carried out by regional planning boards. Both the Capital Region District (Victoria) and the Greater Vancouver Regional District have prepared metropolitan-area plans. The Vancouver plan is based on the official plan prepared by the long-lived Lower Mainland Regional Planning Board to which we referred earlier. The metropolitan governmental set-up in Vancouver is a federation in the style of Toronto.

Two other early metropolitan planning efforts, in Edmonton and Calgary, did not evolve into metropolitan governments. In both cases, the regional planning commissions were continued but with increased powers. For example, not only are these commissions empowered to prepare a regional plan, but they are also the designated authority for approving subdivision plans for all parts of their respective metropolitan areas outside the central cities. As well, all cities in Alberta have planning authority over an additional 5 km zone outside their boundaries. Calgary is also a special case, as the city annexed large areas on its fringes in the 1960s to bring the potential urban area under a single jurisdiction.

In summary, while metropolitan planning in Canada differs from place to place in the details of its organization, a few common types may be discerned. One is the type that emerged earliest, the voluntary intermunicipal agency with advisory planning powers. This approach is still used in Halifax and Saint John. A variation on this approach is the metropolitan or regional planning agency with limited but substantial powers in land-use regulation, as in the case of Alberta cities. Another distinct type is where metropolitan planning is combined with a metropolitan unit of government. Besides Toronto, Winnipeg, Vancouver, and Victoria, this approach is used in Quebec's "urban communities" and in such regional municipalities in Ontario as Thunder Bay, Sudbury, Oshawa, and Hamilton.

Planning the Form of the Metropolis

The vast metropolitan growth of the 1950s and 1960s did not form compact cities as had been the case in the past. Rather, it dispersed new and old populations, businesses, and factories over large areas. Modern means of transportation—automobiles, trucks, and highways—and better communications systems came into their own in this period, enabling people and firms to seek an ever-widening array of locations. It seems that many people, wishing to live close to the countryside, sought the new suburbs, with country on one side and the city on the other. This creates a dilemma, as Blumenfeld notes, for "as more and more people move out into ever-widening rings of suburbs, they move farther and farther away from the city and country moves farther and farther away from them."[39]

This dilemma was evident to planners on both sides of the Atlantic. The planners recognized that the new forces of growth and expansion were creating new kinds of urban communities. To use an analogy, whereas urban development in earlier times resulted in large, compact cities like New York and Paris, it was now resulting in sprawling cities like Los Angeles. This perception led planners to propose new patterns of urban development that would be consonant with the new, large scale of cities, the need to blend the amenities of both city and country, and the necessity to provide a maximum of accessibility among all parts of the metropolitan area.

Planning Issue 11.1

A CASE OF DIVIDED JURISDICTION

The growth of Saskatoon after the war proceeded without threat to the riverbanks. However, in the 1960s and 1970s a number of proposed developments appeared to pose a threat to keeping the riverbanks in the newer areas in the public domain. As well, questions were raised about the ability of the river to sustain its many uses and to maintain its quality. The increased interest in the riverbank also raised concerns for the future of the heritage resources of the corridor.

These concerns were articulated in the 1974 Annual Report to Council by the city's Environmental Advisory Committee, which recommended that a riverbank study be undertaken and a comprehensive plan prepared for the river corridor. The city, the rural municipality, the province, and the largest landowner of the riverbank, the University of Saskatchewan (called the "participating parties") commissioned the recommended studies, and a visionary plan with a 100-year perspective was prepared by Raymond Moriyama and Associates of Toronto.

Planning for Conservation

The 100-year conceptual plan covered an 80 km stretch of the river corridor in the City of Saskatoon and the adjacent rural municipality of Corman Park. On the basis of an assessment of resources and needs in the corridor, it recommended a comprehensive strategy based upon a major restructuring of recreational use by relocating recreational activities from the environmentally fragile areas south of the city to the hardier glacial soils north of Saskatoon. It proposed a corridor plan characterized by linked nodes of development. The plan was based on the overall conservation concept of achieving "health" and "fit" through a balanced use of the resources. The report recommended that a special-purpose authority be established to oversee the conservation and development of the river corridor using the conceptual plan as a guide.

Central to the recommendation to create an authority was the recognition that, given the divided jurisdiction and the competing and often conflicting interests of developers, regulatory agencies and user groups, the implementation of the proposed 100-year conceptual plan would require the exercising of superior jurisdiction over land, water, and natural resources and the undertaking of developmental activities. Given the limitations of their respective mandates, it was not possible for the city or the province to accomplish this task.

Institutionalization and Implementation

On the basis of the recommendations of the report and the tasks inherent in the 100-year conceptual plan, the Province of Saskatchewan enacted legislation to establish the *MeewasinValley Authority* (MVA) in 1979, and gave to it jurisdiction over an 80 km stretch of the river and extensive adjacent lands. MVA was given wide-ranging powers to plan the river corridor, regulate land and water, acquire land (through purchase, expropriation and right of first refusal), and to develop, maintain, and police the area within its jurisdiction. The far-reaching powers given to it produced a backlash of opposition from the agricultural sector, property owners, the real-estate industry, and mortgage lending institutions. At its height, the opposition to the Authority was so great that there were serious doubts as to whether the newly created agency would survive. It received little support from City Council and most council members of the rural municipality were hostile and antagonistic.

There was, however, sustained support from the provincial government and from environment and heritage advocacy groups. MVA's powers became an issue at the provincial level of politics with the then official opposition aligned with its opponents. As a concession, the MVA Act was amended to remove private lands in the Rural Municipality of Corman Park from MVA's jurisdiction, the rural municipality withdrew as a participating party, and MVA's powers of expropriation (along with the right of first refusal on land) were repealed. A beleaguered agency, severely shaken by the beating it took, set out to improve its public image through benign projects. As it now stands, MVA is governed by a board of directors (hereinafter referred to as the Authority) consisting of representatives of three of its four original participating parties— the City of Saskatoon, the Government of Saskatchewan, and the University of Saskatchewan. Funds for operations are provided by the participating parties on the basis of a formula set out in the MVA Act.

MVA now has jurisdiction over the river channel in Saskatoon and Corman Park, publicly owned lands adjacent to the river in Corman Park and Saskatoon, and a small amount of private land in the city. For the present, at least, the bold restructuring of recreational activities to protect fragile areas seems to be impossible to implement, because MVA has no jurisdiction over most of the fragile areas and no means to acquire land for shifting recreational activities to the north of the city. It has also not had much success in convincing the rural municipality and other agencies to take action in this regard.

Source: Excerpted from Brijesh Mathur, "Conserving the Urban River Corridor: Experience from Saskatoon," *Plan Canada* 29, no. 5 (September 1989), 43–49.

In short, there was much seeking after urban forms that would give coherence and cohesion—a sense of community—to the "exploding" metropolis.

Four patterns gained prominence among planners: the "concentric" city, the "central city with satellites," the "star-shaped" or "finger plan" city, and the "linear" or "ribbon" city. These four patterns are illustrated in Figure 11.4. They are, of course, ideal types, and in practice they must be modified by the geography of the area and the past history of development. Nevertheless, each has had an influence in one or more metropolitan plans that have been drawn up in Canada in the past two decades.

The **concentric plan** is based mainly on sustaining the primary business centre by ordering new residential development and other activities at equal distance around the centre. The aim is to keep travel distances to the centre for work or business at a minimum for all sectors of the community. The main means for accomplishing this is by favouring transportation investments that concentrate travel movements in the centre, as with the subway investments in Toronto and Montreal and the light rapid transit (LRT) systems in Edmonton, Calgary, and Vancouver. In such large cities, the growth of suburbs gradually reaches limits where travel to the centre for all major activities becomes inefficient. At this stage, planners call for major subcentres of business, or "new towns in-town" as they are sometimes called. The 1976 plan for Metropolitan Toronto[40] follows this latter concept, with three new "town centres"—Scarborough, North York, and Etobicoke—each roughly 16 km from downtown Toronto.

The **central city with satellites** derives from Ebenezer Howard's idea of Garden Cities surrounding a major city, described earlier in this chapter (see Figure 11.1) and in Chapter 3. This metropolitan concept came to reality with Patrick Abercrombie's plan to guide the growth of London after World War II.[41] A greenbelt of parks, agriculture, and exurban development was established to limit the physical expansion of the central city about 16 km from the centre. Beyond the greenbelt, outwards about 30–40 km, a

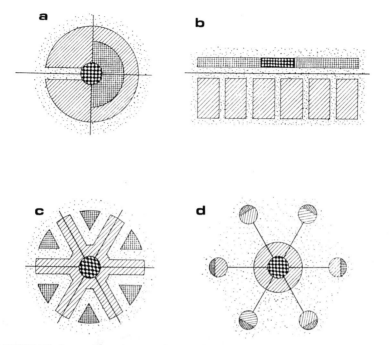

FIGURE 11.4   **Four Forms of Metropolitan Development**

Planners have evolved four patterns in coping with metropolitan expansion: (a) the *concentric city* (b) the *linear city,* (c) the *star-shaped city* or *finger plan,* and (d) the *city with satellites.* Each has been used as a model in planning for Canadian metropolises, suitably transformed to fit the prevailing topography. Each diagram is to the same scale, thus illustrating the amount of area consumed, the open space provided, and transport axes required.

Housing
Commerce
Industry
Open Space

dozen or more new satellite towns were planned to surround London and absorb its new growth, as well as decant some industrial development from the central city. The new towns were planned to connect with the centre by high-speed transportation, but were also expected to be relatively self-sufficient. The towns would not be large, ranging from 30,000 to 60,000 in population, and would afford residents quick access to the countryside.

The 1969 plan for the Vancouver metropolitan area proposed a satellite scheme with four "regional town centres" east and southeast of Vancouver, all connected to the central city by a rapid transit system. This plan was largely realized and the current Livable Region Strategic Plan, implemented in 1996, both expands and refines the concept. There are eight such centres in the new plan articulated by a more extensive transit system. Residential development will be focused on town centres with the aim of creating "complete communities" with a "better balance" in the availability

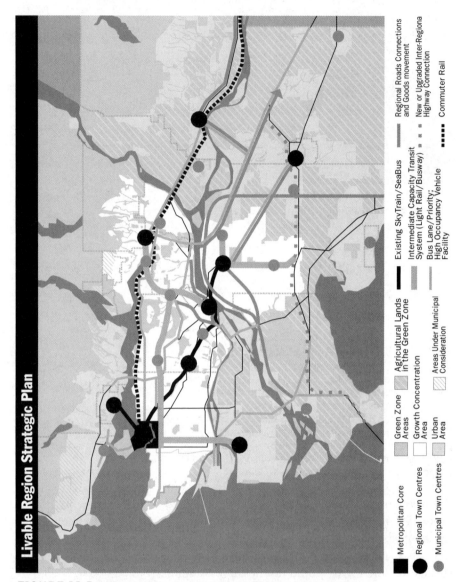

FIGURE 11.5   **Map of Vancouver's Livable Region Strategic Plan**
Source: Livable Region Strategic Plan (Vancouver: Greater Vancouver Regional District, 1996).

of jobs, housing, public services, and transportation.[42] There is no formal greenbelt in the Vancouver plan, although an extensive network of "green zones" (parks, wetlands, farming areas, and upland areas) are used to establish a "long-term boundary for urban growth" (see Figure 11.5).

The **star-shaped** or **finger plan** has as its best-known example the plan for Copenhagen of 1947. The essential feature of this concept is that development is confined to radial corridors emanating from the business centre, with green areas between each corridor. Major highway and rail transit routes serving the central city follow the corridors. This interpenetration of green space and urban development increases the distance to the city centre over that of the concentric plan, but also maximizes the access of city dwellers to the countryside. The 1974 plan for the National Capital Region of Ottawa-Hull employed the finger plan concept along with a greenbelt. The plan called for a continuous open space system with "the penetration of rural wedges" into the urban area.[43] A more detailed discussion of this region follows.

The **ribbon** or **linear city plan** proposes urban growth in modules along major transportation routes. A greenbelt would separate the major uses of industry, residences, and transport from one another in this concept. A variation on this type is used in one alternative plan considered for the Toronto metropolitan region in a major transportation planning report in 1967.[44] The concept was for a spine of transportation running east and west from the city along which would be arrayed, to the north and south of the spine, a series of communities separated from each other by greenbelts.

Ottawa and Its Greenbelt

Before leaving this section, we should note the special case of planning for the region of the nation's capital, Ottawa. The work of planning Ottawa goes back to 1899, with the establishment of the Ottawa Improvement Commission by the federal government. In 1915, a Federal Plan Commission prepared a plan for the city and its environs that proposed many of the projects that have since come to pass, for example, the relocation of railways out of the downtown area and the creation of the Gatineau Park greensward to the north. Following World War II, French planner Jacques Gréber was commissioned to prepare a plan that encompassed a region on both sides of the Ottawa River, including the City of Hull in Quebec. This plan, submitted in 1950, proved to be very influential in creating the present physical environment of the capital region. It proposed the development of a greenbelt around Ottawa, the expansion of Gatineau Park north of Hull, various urban parks and parkways, railway relocation, and the decentralization of federal government offices. The greenbelt covers about 20,000 hectares about 8 km from Parliament Hill and varies in width from 2 to 8 km.

In order to carry out the Gréber plan more effectively, in 1959 the federal government reorganized the capital region planning apparatus and created the present National Capital Commission (NCC). The planning area was extended to cover about 4,660 km^2 around both Ottawa and Hull. Winnipeg's metropolitan planner, Eric Thrift, was hired at this time to manage the NCC.

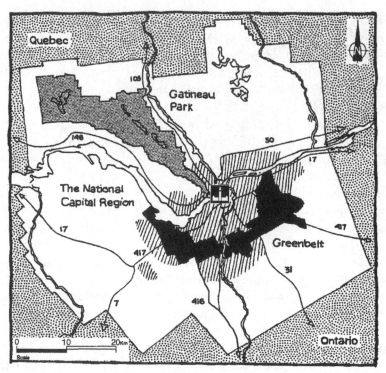

FIGURE 11.6   The Greenbelt in the National Capital Region
Source: Greenbelt Master Plan Summary (Ottawa: National Capital Commission, 1996), 7.

Unlike other metropolitan agencies, the NCC had special powers to purchase land for its projects in the name of the federal government and substantial funds provided by the latter for this purpose. As the NCC said in its 1974 plan for the region, "in implementing the Gréber plan ... the NCC used as its basic planning and development tool the ownership of land."[45]

The year 1996 saw the NCC adopt a brand new plan for the greenbelt, which one of the planners referred to as "reinventing" the Gréber plan.[46] The major need to do this was the rapid population growth not foreseen by the 1950 plan; already by 1970 the area's population had reached the level Gréber had predicted for the year 2000. Moreover, this greenbelt plan has some significant additions. It has become much more ecologically oriented. A primary component is its continuous natural environment which, in turn, is subdivided into several core natural areas (i.e., large sensitive natural environments), natural area buffers which surround the core areas, and natural area links for maintaining continuity of plant life and facilitating animal movement within and beyond the greenbelt.[47] This new orientation adds an important dimension to what was initially just a way of shaping urban form (see Figure 11.6).

Since 1970, the planning of the Ottawa-Hull metropolitan area has been facilitated by the inception of two regional municipal governments—the Regional Municipality of Ottawa-Carleton on the Ontario side and the Outouais Regional Community on the Quebec side. The latter agencies are responsible for the planning of all residential and commercial development and roads and parks, which are not part of the NCC system. In this endeavour, the regional governments share responsibility with the local municipalities. More will be said in the next section about the physical character of the metropolitan area that the NCC is hoping to create.

The metropolitan development of the 1950s and 1960s, which broke the bonds of familiar, compact city forms, was as new to Canada as elsewhere. It is to the credit of planners and government officials that they responded so well and so effectively. Plans have been prepared for all the metropolitan areas, and they are being implemented to a remarkably high degree. Probably the main reason for this has been the willingness of provincial governments to offer support either by granting regulatory powers to metropolitan planning agencies or by establishing full-fledged metropolitan governments. In North America, Canada has pioneered metropolitan government. In this, it indicates a willingness of Canadian communities to accept a high degree of societal intervention in their metropolitan development processes—certainly as compared with the U.S.—with the aim of creating a better environment for all citizens.

ENDNOTES

1. See Artur Glikson, *Regional Planning and Development* (Leiden: A.W. Sijthoff, 1955), 70–85, for an incisive description of Geddes' concepts.
2. Lewis Mumford, *The Culture of Cities* (New York: Harcourt, Brace, 1938).
3. For a Canadian statement see Doug Aberley, *Boundaries of Home: Mapping for Local Empowerment* (Gabriola Island, B.C.: New Society Publishers, 1993); the seminal work in bioregionalism is Kirkpatrick Sale, *Dwellers in the Land: The Bioregional Vision* (Philadelphia: New Society Publishers, 1985).
4. Cf. L.O. Gertler, *Regional Planning in Canada* (Montreal: Harvest House, 1972), 86–96.
5. Gerald Hodge, "Regional Planning: The Cinderella Discipline," *Plan Canada* 34, no. 4 (July 1994), 35–49.
6. John Friedmann, "Regional Planning as a Field of Study," *Journal of the American Institute of Planners* 29, no. 3 (August 1963), 168–178.
7. Hodge, "Regional Planning," provides the basis for this section.
8. Canada, Royal Commission on the Future of the Toronto Waterfront, *Watershed*, 2nd interim report (Ottawa Ministry of Supply and Services, 1990).

9. Gertler, *Regional Planning*.

10. Examples include the South Saskatchewan River Development Corporation and the James Bay Development Corporation (Quebec).

11. Alberta, Department of Municipal Affairs, *Planning in Alberta* (Edmonton, 1978), 77.

12. Evelyn Power Reid and Maurice Yeates, "Bill 90—An Act to Protect Agricultural Land: An Assessment of Its Success in Laprairie County, Quebec," *Urban Geography* 12, no. 4 (1991), 295–309.

13. Canada, Royal Commission on Dominion-Provincial Relations, *Recommendations*, Book II (Ottawa: King's Printer, 1940), 75.

14. Maurice Yeates, *Main Street: Windsor to Quebec City* (Toronto: Macmillan, 1975).

15. Helpful references for this period are T.N. Brewis, *Regional Economic Policies in Canada* (Toronto: Macmillan, 1969); Helen Buckley and Eva Tihanyi, *Canadian Policies for Rural Adjustment* (Saskatoon: Canadian Centre for Community Studies, 1966); and Economic Council of Canada, *The Challenge of Growth and Change*, 5th Annual Review (Ottawa: Queen's Printer, 1968).

16. Cf. John Perry, *Inventory of Regional Planning Administration in Canada* (Toronto: Intergovernmental Committee on Urban and Regional Research, 1974).

17. Gertler, *Regional Planning*.

18. For a full discussion of this concept, its roots and shortcomings, see John Friedmann and Clyde Weaver, *Territory and Function: The Evolution of Regional Planning* (Berkely, Calif.: University of California Press, 1980), especially 89–160.

19. James W. Wilson, *People in the Way* (Toronto: University of Toronto Press, 1973).

20. A. Paul Pross, *Planning and Development: A Case Study of Two Nova Scotia Communities* (Halifax: Dalhousie University Institute of Public Affairs, 1975).

21. G. Keith Bain, "The Toronto Centred Region: A Case Study in Regional Planning," *Nature, Science and Man*, n.d.

22. *Ibid.*

23. Gouvernement du Québec, *Guide explicatif de la loi sur l'amanagement et l'urbanisme* (Quebec: Ministère des Affaires municipales, 1980).

24. Jean Cermakian, "Geographic Research and the Regional Planning Process in Quebec: A New Challenge," *Proceedings of the New England St. Lawrence Valley Geographical Society*, 1984.

25. As described in Doug Aberley, "How to Map Your Bioregion: A Primer for Community Activists," in Aberley, *Boundaries of Home*, 71–129.

26. W. Donald McTaggart, "Bioregionalism and Regional Geography: Place, People, and Networks," *The Canadian Geographer* 37, no. 4 (1993), 307–319.

27. *Ibid.*

28. Stephen Frankel, "Old Theories in New Places? Environmental Determinism and Bioregionalism," *Professional Geographer* 46, no. 3 (1994), 289–295.

29. Ken Tamminga, "Restoring Biodiversity in the Urbanizing Region: Towards Pre-emptive Ecosystems Planning," *Plan Canada* 36, no. 4 (July 1996), 10–15.

30. Richard Scott, "Canada's Capital Greenbelt: Reinventing a 1950s Plan," *Plan Canada* 36, no. 5 (September 1996), 19–21.

31. Ian Wight, "Framing the Urbanism with a New Eco-regionalism," *Plan Canada* 36, no. 1 (January 1996), 21–23.

32. Hans Blumenfeld, "Metropolitan Area Planning," in Paul D. Spreiregen, ed., *The Modern Metropolis,* (Montreal: Harvest House, 1967), 79–83.

33. A good description of metropolitan conditions just after World War II is found in Albert Rose, *Problems of Canadian City Growth* (Ottawa: Community Planning Association of Canada, 1950).

34. Hans Blumenfeld, "Some Lessons for Regional Planning from the Experience ofthe Metropolitan Toronto Planning Board," in Spreiregen, *Modern Metropolis,* 88–92.

35. See, for example, John Sewell, "Thanks, Tories, for City Chaos," NOW, May 8–14, 1997; and Ken Greenberg, "Toward a Supercity That Works," *The Globe and Mail,* November 23, 1996, D3.

36. Greater Toronto Task Force (Ont.), *Greater Toronto* (Toronto: Publications Ontario, January 1996).

37. Cf. Peter Gordon and Harry W. Richardson, "Beyond Polycentricity: The Dispersed Metropolis, Los Angeles, 1970–1990," *Journal of the American Planning Association* 62, no. 3 (Summer 1996), 289–295.

38. George Nader, *The Cities of Canada,* Vol. 2 (Toronto: Macmillan, 1976), 293.

39. Blumenfeld, "Metropolitan Area Planning."

40. Municipality of Metropolitan Toronto, *Metroplan Concepts and Objectives* (Toronto, 1976), 2.

41. Patrick Abercrombie, *Greater London Plan 1944* (London: HMSO, 1945).

42. Greater Vancouver Regional District, *Livable Region Strategic Plan* (Vancouver, 1996), 2ff.

43. Canada, National Capital Commission, *Tomorrow's Capital* (Ottawa, 1974) 27ff.

44. Ontario, Department of Municipal Affairs, *Choices for a Growing Region,* a report of the Metropolitan Toronto and Region Transportation Study (Toronto, 1967).

45. Canada, National Capital Commission, *Tomorrow's Capital* (Ottawa, 1974), 8.

46. Scott, "Canada's Capital Greenbelt."

47. Ottawa, National Capital Commission, *Greenbelt Master Plan Summary* (Ottawa, 1996), 19.

Chapter 12 Planning for Canada's Small Towns

Planning becomes (n)either easier (n)or more difficult in the small community. ... Conditions are simply different and demand different approaches, not big-city hand-me-downs.

James Wilson, 1961

INTRODUCTION

There is a third type of Canadian community, actually the oldest type, which has its own special planning considerations—the small town. All of today's two dozen metropolises and 150 small and medium-size cities began as small towns. In addition, there are nearly 2,900 separate and distinct small towns in Canada with populations between 300 and 10,000. In these communities reside about four million people. Problems of land use, housing, traffic, public facilities, and population are there, too. But because of their small size, the planning problems of towns and villages manifest themselves in ways that are different from those of cities. The recognition of these differences in planning small communities concerns us in this chapter.

Planning Needs

The community-planning process we have discussed up to now would be initiated by a locally self-governed community, one with its own municipal council. But half the small towns in Canada (with populations over 300) have no self-governing structure. These approximately 1,500 small towns cannot, therefore, plan within the "umbrella" of the provincial planning act. The "parent" incorporated area—township, rural municipality, county, regional district, etc.—in which they are situated will normally be responsible for their planning.

Most planning practices have grown out of a concern about the problems that *cities* experience with rapid and large-scale growth. Although the planning problems of small towns fit the general categories of larger centres, they differ in scale, intensity, and pace of change. Thus, the typical land-use dynamics assumed by land-use control regulations found in most planning acts do not fit the mould of most small towns. There are, in addition, special planning problems that do not usually occur in cities, such as the provision of basic water and sewer services and the conservation of agricultural land.

Along with the above two factors that affect small town planning, there is the ever-present impact of senior government policies. In their pursuit of policies—for example, in transportation, energy, or agricultural support—the federal and provincial governments often overlook the effects on towns and villages. The small size and lack of resources of small communities put them in a dependent position relative to these senior levels, and affect their ability to plan for their own future.

Planning for small towns is assuming a new importance because, in the past 15–20 years, they have been growing. Although they are often pictured as "dying out," Canadian towns and villages, as a group, added more than one million additional inhabitants between 1961 and 1981.[1] Population growth is complemented by considerable expansion in the stock of new housing in small centres. While not all small towns are growing in size, more than half of them are, and almost all are adding new dwellings.

This buoyancy of towns and villages puts a new cast on their planning needs. The discussion in this chapter first addresses the nature of physical development in small towns, and then presents the planning and governing frameworks available to them. Lastly, we will review planning tools appropriate for small towns. This discussion is most relevant for the planning of towns above 300–400 population: at this level, a town begins to develop a distinctive street pattern and distribution of land uses, and planning approaches become pertinent.

Types of Towns

There are two broad types of small towns within the everyday experience of most Canadians: (1) those in rural regions and (2) those in the rural-urban fringe.[2] Probably the most widely perceived, and the most numerous, are towns that serve rural regions involved in agriculture (like Cabri in Saskatchewan and St. Mary's in Ontario). Of course, they have their counterparts in regions known for fishing (like Fogo Island in Newfoundland), forestry (like Hazelton in B.C.), and mining (like Fermont in Quebec), some of which have also pioneered new planning ideas (like Leaf Rapids in Manitoba).

The second kind of small town is situated within commuting distance of larger cities. These towns, in what has been called "the city's countryside,"[3] have often been transformed from their original rural functions under the influence of metropolitan growth. Many are former agricultural service centres that have become "dormitory" towns, among them Manotick, Ontario, and Cochrane, Alberta. Variants on this kind of small town are those located in high-amenity recreation areas near large cities, like many in the Laurentians, which have also found their growth patterns greatly changed.

We thus tend to know small towns by their economic function or regional location, and they differ substantially in these ways. However, in land-use patterns, in the process of their physical development, and in planning problems, most small towns are alike. Or, at least, they fit a similar set of dimensions. For example, a new resource town built all at once usually then settles into a long period of stability, just as do farm service centres and tourist towns. The approaches discussed below recognize the great diversity and individuality of small towns. What is propounded is a perspective through which planners can perceive the differences between planning for small towns and planning for large centres, and also recognize differences between small towns.

CHARACTERISTICS OF SMALL TOWN DEVELOPMENT
Land-Use Patterns

Small towns differ from one another, as any resident or observer can tell you. But in their physical development, there are a number of common characteristics that distinguish them from large communities and that also affect their planning. These relate to their size or area, density, and land-use patterns.

Size. It may seem self-evident to say that small towns occupy very little land area. It is, however, worth noting because this dimension is related to such issues as the provision of streets and public utilities, as well as to the accessibility of different land uses. Even the largest small towns, those 10,000 or so in population, occupy less than 5 km^2 of land. All the land uses would be within 1,300 m of the centre of the community. The typical small town of 500–1,000 population occupies less than 1.5 km^2 and has only 150–300 houses.

Density.   Despite their small size, small towns are usually not very compact. Development is spread out at gross densities of 2–5 dwellings per hectare. Only when the population of a small town approaches 5,000 is it likely to have a density near that found in city suburbs of 10–15 dwellings per hectare.

Vacant Land.   A factor that contributes noticeably to the low density is the large amount of vacant, undeveloped land found in most small towns. It is not uncommon to find as much as one-third of the land to be vacant, and not just on the fringes of the town. This is a reflection of the generally non-competitive land market. There is, indeed, plenty of land for all potential uses.

Commercial Development.   The land-use pattern characteristic of most small towns is one of residential areas concentrically arranged around a single commercial area. "Main Street" is both a retail and social focus for the town. The number of establishments is relatively small, and not infrequently, there are vacant buildings that attest to a slow-growing local market and the competition of urban shopping centres. There is, however, evidence of a stabilization, and even some growth, in the commercial base of many remote towns and villages.[4] And, of course, those within the orbit of a metropolis tend to show major expansion of shopping facilities.

Land-Use Diversity.   A mixture of diverse land uses characterizes all but the largest small towns. It is not uncommon to find on the principal commercial street stores, houses, service stations, churches, etc., juxtaposed. Even in residential areas, there is a diversity of uses. Yet these land-use patterns seem to function satisfactorily, suggesting that a high degree of tolerance is possible among land uses when the intensity of development is relatively low.

Physical Development Issues

To plan effectively for small towns one must recognize the issues that arise from their characteristics of small scale, small growth, and diverse land-use situations. These are not, it must be stressed, issues one normally addresses in city planning, which is more concerned with such matters as traffic congestion, rezoning for high-rise development, and the stability of residential areas. People in towns and villages tend to see their development in terms of a number of *specific problems* rather than broad issues.

The problems cited for the town of Clarenville in Newfoundland (population 2,800) indicate the types of small town planning issues that arise, especially in more remote rural regions:[5]

- The provision of an adequate water supply
- The provision of a sanitary sewer system
- Large areas of unsuitable building land
- The scattered nature of existing development
- The lack of industrial land
- Problems of the town centre
- Access from the Trans-Canada Highway
- Dangerous railway crossings
- Poor access to some existing houses
- Ugliness caused by lack of care, or indifference
- Garbage disposal.

The responses of town and village residents in Huron County, Ontario, in public planning meetings mirror the above list: "repair the sidewalks/provide more streetlights/get better recreation facilities/maintain the empty store buildings/fix the bridge."[6] City-oriented planners might tend to dismiss these issues as being trivial, and certainly, there is little place for them in conventional municipal plans. However, they are significant for small communities, and as the Newfoundland report notes, "If the day-to-day problems can be solved with the aid of a plan then ... the value of planning is established."[7]

One often finds, for example, that small town with 500 or fewer residents have no community-wide water supply system or sewage system. These services are usually provided by individual households and firms through wells and septic tanks. Even with the low-density development of most small towns, pollution problems may arise; thus, the common planning approach of increasing the density by in-filling on vacant lots either exacerbates these problems or necessitates costly utility systems. A related problem in providing basic water and sewer service is that dwellings are, very often, situated in areas of unsuitable building land (steep slopes, rocky, swampy). In addition, residences are often widely scattered, and this also contributes to the difficulty and cost of servicing them.

Small towns have their own forms of traffic and road problems. Within the community, both the unsuitable land and scattered residential development may lead to excessive and costly road building and maintenance. Traffic congestion may also occur in the business district because of the lack of adequate parking space. Inconvenient access for the community to a major highway nearby or the hazards of the highway running right through the community are two other burdens of small towns.

There are frequent complaints about the lack of care regarding the physical environment of a small town. The disposal of waste materials—

household garbage, worn-out vehicles, etc.—can pose a problem as to both the maintenance and the location of dumps. Unkempt cemeteries and playgrounds and derelict buildings are other common problems affecting the environment in a small community. That they often defy solution is due as much as anything to the community's meagre resources.

Social Development Issues

There are two demographic aspects of small towns that often have implications for planning their physical development. The first—the aging population—is more general and affects almost all small towns. The second concerns the social composition of towns in the rural-urban fringe. A brief description of these two situations will quickly reveal some of the land-use and development impacts associated with them.

First, **population aging**: whereas two decades ago people living in small towns often bemoaned the fact that they had little choice but to move to the city when they retired, today they are staying on and other elderly people from the city may be moving there, too. Smaller communities in all provinces, and in all locations except northern resource regions, tend to have considerably higher proportions of the elderly (those 65 and older) than do most cities.[8] Moreover, this tendency has been increasing such that many small centres have population concentrations of the elderly of 25% or more. Among British Columbia small towns, there have appeared two distinct types of retirement communities. One might be termed **indigenous** retirement towns where the retired population is primarily comprised of those who remain living in the community after retirement.[9] The other might be called **itinerant** retirement towns because most of the retirees have migrated there.

Regardless of the source of retirees, most small towns present some immediate problems in meeting the needs of older people. Whether it be health care, home support services, or transportation, there are usually few such services in rural areas and large distances to reach those that do exist.[10] Housing accommodation can also be problematic for the elderly living in small towns, mainly because of the lack of variety in housing types. Added to these, the local governments, as we have mentioned, have very limited resources to provide the services and facilities needed by their elderly.[11]

A second issue is the changing **social composition** of the population of towns in the rural-urban fringe and what it means for their physical development. The expansion of cities into the countryside often has the result of displacing the rural population that has lived there for, sometimes, generations.

Planning Issue 12.1

FARMERS SHAPE DEVELOPMENT TO MEET OWN NEEDS

TORONTO—David Bianchi talks knowledgeably about the intricacies of land development as he wheels his truck slowly along the laneways of the family farm, over the bed of the abandoned electric railway, through the irrigated apple orchards and the strawberry fields on the west bank of the Credit River.

Mr. Bianchi is the chairman of the largest corporate landowner on the northwest frontier of Greater Toronto. He is also a third-generation farmer.

The conversation and the truck both stop abruptly at the crest of a small hill, the windshield framing the view of a sparkling pond fringed by a mature maple bush and rolling pasture, a pair of turkey vultures casually circling above. Mr. Bianchi lets the view speak for itself.

"Does this look like it should be industrial land?" he asks. "You tell me."

It's not the kind of question normally posed in the development business on the fringes of Toronto, where "master planning" hammers raw land into the shape of 1,000-acre subdivisions with the precision of a stamping press,

and nature has made no views that can't be improved by the almighty bulldozer. But Mr. Bianchi and his group, the Huttonville Association for the Rights of Property Owners (HARPO), are changing all that.

Five years ago, they were just another bunch of farmers, caught in the usual squeeze play, facing a choice between going broke or selling out to the large corporate developers who were assembling land for the westward expansion of Brampton. Then a few of them had the radical idea of trying to shape the inevitable development to suit their own needs and vision.

"We've got all this natural beauty here and they were ignoring it," said Mary Lou Brown, a local bookkeeper and one of the group's founders. "We want to make sure it's not another standard subdivision."

That impression remains strong among some HARPO members, who nurse a lively resentment against a system that serves the needs of corporate developers so well but doesn't seem to have any regard for the local view.

"They don't see us as being a genuine case for development," complained Nigel Eves, Mr. Bianchi's neighbour. "Because we're not speculators, we're dismissed as rubes. But we don't think that way. We think we've got a better plan.

"We resent the notion that outside developers can establish the ground rules for the living conditions of a community that is over 200 years old."...

Together, HARPO's members own 1,000 acres in western Brampton, more than any of the speculators, and they have forced local politicians to listen. ...

... Council has already accepted most of the group's proposals, and in that it changed history. For the first time since master planning took hold in the Toronto area, local landowners have been able to play an important part.

Some of the landowners envisage a completely different type of place emerging on their holdings—not instantaneous, industrial-strength suburbia but a slowly developing, self-sufficient and beautiful new landscape. "What we're planning here is a different type of development than what the corporate developers are planning," Mr. Bianchi said. "It's a community development. We're part of the community. We live here." ...

"Who knows what kind of development is going on this property?" Mr. Bianchi said. "The whole thing is, we're doing it ourselves. A group of people who aren't developers. Just farmers and regular people."

Source: Excerpted from John Barber, "Farmers Shape Development to Meet Own Needs," *The Globe and Mail,* June 11, 1997, A2. Reprinted with permission from *The Globe and Mail.*

The pre-existing social networks of, say, farmers and traditional service people are changed by new arrivals (e.g., exurbanites, retirees, back-to-the-landers).[12] These newcomers, in turn, affect the political dynamics of the community and how it responds to development pressures and the need for additional services.[13] And even as newcomers become settled in, they are likely to be in the vanguard of resistance to further change. Therefore, one cannot overlook the social dimensions of what may seem to the outsider to be a relatively small change in the community environment.

Dimensions of the Development Process

Small towns are not just scaled-down versions of cities, and their development proceeds in distinctive ways. It is helpful, therefore, to have a perspective from which to assess their development. Four useful dimensions of physical development are:[14]

- *Scale* of development
- *Range* of types of development
- *Intensity* of development
- *Pace* of development.

And, especially for towns with adjacent farmlands, we need to add the dimension of *agricultural land* development. A brief elaboration of each will demonstrate the nature of the process of development in most small communities.

Scale. Smallness is an important dimension of several aspects of small town development. The level of density is low and the scale of population and of the built-up area is small in towns and villages. So, too, is the scale of change. The additions to a town's housing stock, for example, are likely to be relatively few in number, even though proportionately large for the community. A centre of 500 population experiencing a growth of 40% in dwelling units, as many did in the 1970s and 1980s, would have added only 50–60 new houses and required, say, 8 ha of land. This means, in general, that the scope of planning problems is usually small and their solutions should be appropriately scaled.

Range. Almost all small towns have only a small array of different activities and structures. From place to place, the range may vary according to the economic base of the community (a certain industry may predominate), the climate of the region, or the building materials available. There is seldom, however, a large variety in a town's residential, commercial, industrial, or public land-use areas. This is equally true when new development occurs: it will most likely bring the same kinds of activities and structures as have existed to that point. Thus, the planning implications of new development have ready precedents.

Intensity. Unlike the large-scale development of a city, a small town does not have either large areas covered with the same kind of development (such as residential suburbs) or highly concentrated activities (such as a cluster of apartment buildings). In most small centres, the development tends to be in discrete units in a more scattered fashion. Exceptions would be the mill, mine, cannery, transportation terminal, or other industrial enterprise in "single-industry" towns, the new shopping centre in a region-serving town, or the condo complex in a recreation town. The value of this dimension is in determining the effect that new physical development has on a community such as in the traffic generated, the utilities needed, and the schools and parks required.

Pace. There are two important facets of this dimension in regard to small towns. The first is that it is often misleading to view the pace of development in terms of percentage rates of growth. It is usually better with towns and villages to look at the actual amount of new development, or **absolute growth.** In the example used above of a town experiencing a 40% expansion in housing in a decade, not only was the number of houses built not very large (50–60), but also this was taking place over a 10-year span. The second facet is that seldom is this amount of change spread evenly over the 10 years. As we noted, with small town development occurring in discrete projects, all the houses quite likely were built in one or only a few years. Development activity is usually infrequent and irregular in commercial, industrial, and public building as well. Each project must, therefore, be planned on a more or less ad hoc basis because a continuous level of growth cannot be expected in small towns.

The process of development described within the four dimensions cited above pertains to most, but not all, small towns. There are some that are affected by rapid growth, a high demand for land, and major changes to their character. Resource towns like Fort MacMurray, Alberta, come readily to mind, as do towns on the outskirts of metropolitan centres, such as Markham, near Toronto. But this type of town and village development is an exception and probably affects no more than a few hundred of the 3,000 small centres referred to here.

Agricultural Land.   Although more of a contextual dimension than those above, the presence of agricultural land in its setting can be a significant factor in the physical development of a small town. In several provinces, notably Quebec and British Columbia, stringent limits are placed on the conversion of agricultural land to non-agricultural purposes, especially for residential development. In these two provinces, application must be made to a provincial commission for permission to further subdivide "protected agricultural areas," as they are called in Quebec, and "agricultural land reserves," as they are called in B.C.[15] Two major thrusts of this type of intervention are those aimed at (1) assuring current and future supplies of farm products and (2) preserving rural landscapes that symbolize rural ways of life.[16] Other measures to restrain town expansion onto farmland are generally weaker, such as the "urban containment boundaries" in Ontario.[17] Small towns in the rural-urban fringe are usually the ones most affected by such regulation because of the pressure on them for expansion.

PLANNING AND GOVERNING FRAMEWORKS

Community planning, regardless of the size of the community, is an integral part of the way a community governs itself and takes responsibility for its future. In the Canadian social and political milieu, local (municipal) government is the cornerstone for such community undertakings. All provinces have legislation that enables a municipality to make plans, regulate land uses, and make expenditures regarding future development. However, this provincial legislation is, by its very nature, meant to apply universally to all municipalities in the province, regardless of size, location, or resources.

Local Government Structures and Resources

Small towns exist within governmental milieux that put special constraints on their performance of the community-planning activity. Each province considers in its arrangements for rural settlements how small communities would obtain basic services (e.g., roads, public utilities, schools) and plan for future development. Essentially, the consideration is how to allocate resources and governmental authority in areas where people live in widely separated centres and in low-density settings in the countryside. The issues are those of determining at what population size a centre will be able to govern itself effectively and over what area governmental jurisdiction should prevail for countryside dwellers.

Rural Municipalities

There are distinctive arrangements from province to province, but certain common features also exist. Each province has provisions for according municipal status to towns and villages, usually based on population size. Thus, some small places may be **incorporated**, and others not. In Saskatchewan, the incidence of incorporation is very high among towns and villages, including small villages, whereas in New Brunswick and Nova Scotia, only the larger towns are incorporated. To provide government for dispersed rural populations, all provinces (except the Atlantic provinces) have **area municipalities,** known variously as townships, rural municipalities, and district municipalities, where settlement is widespread. These latter units often include smaller towns and villages that are not incorporated. As commonly found in Ontario, Quebec, and the Prairie provinces, they encompass about 260 km^2.

Both incorporated centres and area municipalities are local self-governing units with structures analogous to those of larger communities: that is, each would have its own council and constituent committees and boards, perhaps reduced in scale but with the same powers as city councils to raise taxes, to make expenditures, to pass land-use regulations, and to plan future development. The crucial difference is the much-reduced scale and quality of resources, both financial and human, that these small municipalities have available to them. Comprising, as they do, only a few hundred or a few thousand persons, their tax base is bound to be felt as small when monies are needed for new or renewed physical facilities. As well, they would have only a few technical and administrative persons on staff to carry out the regulative and planning tasks the community might wish. In the situation of the small town that is unincorporated, both the financial and staff resources are at the discretion of the council of the (also small) township or rural municipality.

It is only partly true, as it may be argued, that small towns and townships require much less in the way of resources and administrative structures because their needs are likely to be fewer. There often are fixed costs in providing such town facilities as a water or sewer system, streetlights, or sidewalks, and the modest local resources may not allow the community even to begin development of this kind. And, increasingly assigned to municipalities are such technical tasks as planning, or environmental protection, or energy conservation, which are administratively infeasible in small towns and townships. In these situations, either the task does not get done or the small community must rely on outside help from consultants, a regional government, the province, or all three. Rural local governments are thus often in a dependent position in regard to achieving their own goals for planning and development. Unincorporated small towns are always in this position in relation to their township or rural municipality.

Regional Government

Another structural form for providing governmental needs to rural regions is the **large area or regional government**. The county (in eastern Canada, except Newfoundland) and the regional district or county (in western Canada) are the various provincial counterparts. They may provide services and facilities—hospitals, parks, planning—directly to all communities because of the costs involved or the overriding regional need. They may, and often do, provide technical assistance to constituent communities; this is usually the case in planning. It should be noted that for most small communities the regional or county planning agency is not an alternative. The Alberta system gives the most coverage, with a set of regional planning commissions providing planning services to constituent communities across most of the province. The regional districts in B.C. provide nearly comparable coverage. But in provinces to the east, there is no consistent system of county or regional planning, and most small towns must rely on their own resources.

Planning Resources

It is assumed in all provincial planning acts that all (incorporated) communities are capable of establishing and maintaining a workable planning function. But, as we have indicated, the job of making community plans and land-use regulations and enforcing them in a small town falls to a small group of people. Typically, towns with populations below 2,000 people have fewer than five employees, and it is on them that the burden falls to make technical and administrative planning judgements. The key personnel on a small town staff are the town clerk, building inspector, and roads superintendent. Seldom does a town below 10,000 population have a municipal engineer much less its own professional staff planner.

To sum up, in the majority of small towns, resources are simply too meagre to permit a satisfactory planning process. Nevertheless, just as with large communities, both the plan-making and the plan-implementation phases must be undertaken. Some mechanisms exist to assist small communities to make plans and land-use regulations; these mechanisms include grants, which can be used to hire consultants, and technical assistance programs from provincial ministries and regional governments. But the job of plan implementation almost always falls to the community alone. This includes both the enforcement of land-use regulations and the programming of capital expenditures. Meanwhile, the intricacies of planning are increasing. Not only are provincial planning regulations and programs undergoing frequent change, but there are also new forms of legislation that impinge on such planning interests and resources as environmental assessment, farmland preservation, and coastal zone management. The small towns, which must exist within these dependent situations, must have mechanisms to complement their needs and compensate for their meagre resources. We shall now briefly explore several of the more significant supportive planning frameworks that have emerged for rural regions in Canada.

Planning Supports for Small Towns

There are two types of supportive frameworks that many small towns may call upon in their planning. Provincial ministries throughout Canada have increasingly, over the past decade or so, developed a variety of measures to assist small communities. In addition, many rural regions have formal frameworks for regional government or regional planning, as noted above. There is a great variety in these undertakings, but a brief sampling will indicate some of the sources of planning support to which small towns might turn.

Provincial Level
Ministries in all provinces have available technical assistance for planning in small towns and rural areas. These may take the form of providing

professional planning services directly to communities, financial assistance to obtain outside advisors, or technical assistance in the form of publications on relevant planning topics. The actual forms and the combinations available differ from province to province. For example, Manitoba operates community-planning field offices in several regional centres from which staff planners can assist small communities in preparing local planning instruments and acting as advocates at formal hearings. Land Use Service Centres fulfil much the same role for Prince Edward Island towns, while in New Brunswick planners are assigned from the ministry to assist designated rural areas and, sometimes, to become the resident staff in regional planning commissions.

Another form of planning assistance that many provinces provide to small communities is financial support to promote the preparation of general planning instruments and plans for specific kinds of projects. Ontario, for example, has a program of "community planning study grants," which are available only to its smaller municipalities (85% of Ontario's nearly 900 municipalities have fewer than 5,000 residents). This program allows them to obtain the services of consultants to conduct planning studies and to prepare community plans, zoning by-laws, etc. Aid is also available in most provinces for studies and plans for such specific kinds of projects as business-area revitalization, seasonal cottage areas, and housing needs statements. Saskatchewan's Main Street Development Program, which is designed specifically to assist small towns, is typical of these kinds of programs. Most planning assistance involving provincial grants is usually in the form of a shared-cost program in which the province contributes the major portion of the study and planning costs and the municipality the remainder. Provincial shares usually range from 50% to 80%.

Self-help planning manuals are available from provincial ministries to provide assistance in a wide range of planning needs. Many are designed specifically to help small communities or those that, according to a Newfoundland report, "may never become involved in a planning scheme larger than a subdivision."[18] The manuals show an encouraging tendency to avoid jargon and provide brief, coherent models for reports that are well within the capabilities of small towns and townships. Three other good examples are from Prince Edward Island, Saskatchewan, and Ontario.[19]

Technical assistance programs and services such as those described may play an invaluable role in planning small towns where resources are meagre. Their success, however, depends upon two factors. First, the provincial programs themselves must have continuity and also the capability of integrating the various elements of planning a community. This stems from the fact that the planning process for whatever size of community involves a long-term commitment on the part of the town: the adoption of a community plan, for example, is just the beginning of the next stage of implementing it. So it is important that provincial efforts do not diminish or languish; manuals should be kept up-to-date and, crucially, contact with professional planners should be facilitated because, as the community becomes more involved in its own planning, advice from and contact with planners become more necessary.

The second factor, and probably the most vital one in ensuring effective small town planning, is the capability of accessing provincial programs. A small town with few resources often lacks skilled personnel who can recognize the value of programs that are offered; it may lack funds even to participate in shared-cost programs, and its lack of municipal organization and other community institutions might make it incapable of sustained long-term planning. Well-intentioned programs tend to assume that all communities have similar needs and also capabilities. This can result in two problems: programs may not "fit" the character of communities needing assistance, and many communities may not seek solutions out of lack of awareness of how to adapt to the program.

Regional Level

Because of the great variety of small communities to be serviced, it is difficult for provincial programs of assistance to overcome problems of remoteness and lack of continuity. Planning support programs and services at the regional level can best provide assistance that is indigenous to the area of the small town. Regional planning commissions (Alberta), county planning departments (Ontario and Nova Scotia), and regional district planning departments (British Columbia)—the forms currently used in different parts of Canada—comprise all the communities in a defined area, often several hundred or even several thousand square kilometres in size. Such agencies can provide continuous planning staff support for individual communities, as well as for the interrelated services and facilities of the region. Importantly, this type of arrangement makes available to small towns their "own" staff planner, thus approximating the level of staff support needed to nurture a continuous community planning process.

Alberta's regional planning commissions are the oldest agencies of this sort, having been formed nearly five decades ago, and are probably the most successful at assisting small communities. The eight commissions each cover several thousand square kilometres and work as a loose coalition of municipalities. Professional planners assist communities in preparing their General Municipal Plans, ensuring that they meet the criteria of the Alberta Planning Act. They also act as facilitators in negotiations with such agencies as the provincial housing corporation and the highways department. Another function of the regional commissions is exemplified by the Oldman River Commission, near Lethbridge, which made plans for the provision to all communities of such services as libraries, ambulance, and garbage collection and disposal. The work of Alberta's commissions, as of regional-level agencies in other provinces, offers a supportive, participatory type of planning that most small towns cannot readily supply directly or obtain through outside consultants.

PLANNING TOOLS FOR SMALL TOWNS

The essential point to be made in planning for small towns is that planning approaches should be *small town* approaches. Most of our planning tools are more suitable for large communities than for small ones. Planners of small towns should consider whether the tools they propose to use are appropriate to the problems and capabilities of small communities. The planning situation usually features a distinctive set of easily identifiable problems that call for seemingly mundane solutions rather than an abstract arrangement of land uses. Moreover, plans and other planning instruments need to match the resources and the capabilities of a few hard-pressed and often untrained municipal officials.

In small towns, planning approaches can be simplified yet be appropriate to the situation; not infrequently, small town residents recognize this faster than city-trained planners who try to help them. There is, fortunately, growing experience in small town planning from which can be drawn examples of appropriate planning tools. Experience shows that the community-planning process is the same as for larger communities (as described in Chapter 7), but differs in the tools that are needed to make it effective. Thus, the community plan is a vital component, as are tools for analysis and implementation. The difference can perhaps be grasped as that between a large and a small wrench in a mechanic's toolbox; each is peculiarly suited to its task. The planner's toolbox in the small town setting need not contain as many or as wide a range of tools as for city planning situations. But given the uniqueness of each town and village, care must be taken in their application.

The Community Plan

The community plan for a small town deals with land uses, circulation, recreation facilities, and parks, just as a plan for a large city does, but it can be simpler and more direct both in content and style. Its objectives can address the problems residents would like to solve; it needs fewer analyses and fewer land-use categories; and it can be concise and brief. Experience in Newfoundland and Alberta demonstrates such principles of appropriateness.

In 1968, the Newfoundland government explored the special planning needs of small communities, using Clarenville (1981 pop. 2,800) for a prototype plan. The accompanying report advocated that such plans focus on a statement of community problems and possible solutions, noting that "if day-to-day problems can be solved with the aid of a plan then, even if they are of minor importance in themselves, the value of planning is established ... and there will also be an immediately beneficial effect on the physical environment."[20] The Clarenville plan begins with a listing of major problems that its citizens would like to solve: dangerous railway crossings, scattered housing, and unsightly areas and buildings. These are further described in photographs and located on a map. The land-use planning solutions suggested in the plan thereby have a clear connection with the felt needs of community members; they are not as abstract as the solutions in conventional municipal plans.

This concern over the style of presentation is not misplaced, for it is through its presentation that a plan achieves relevance for community members. A community plan is a way of demonstrating consensus, and a small town plan should heed this fact. Residents of small towns are usually intimately aware of land ownership patterns and the issues with which the town is concerned, and they will want to see these accurately portrayed. Moreover, there are likely to be few professional planning, administrative, and public media skills and resources available to interpret the plan if issues arise later. The danger in a poorly presented plan is that it may prove frustrating to officials and citizens; they may either ignore it or pay only lip service to it. A plan for High River, Alberta (population 4,800 at the time), is exemplary in its presentation style.[21] Vivid graphic techniques show new facilities, and the five major districts of the town have listed on the town map their main problems and proposed solutions.

Because planning practice in Canada is conducted within an elaborate statutory framework, as we have seen in previous chapters, this seems to have fostered the lengthy municipal plans one commonly finds. It is rarely apparent that these cumbersome, repetitive plans, so often given to legalistic language and jargon, are appropriate for any size of community, let alone small towns and rural municipalities. This conventional approach has produced a 50-page plan for a town of 400 people in New Brunswick and a 90-page plan for a community of 1,000 persons in Ontario, to cite just two examples. One has to wonder who, besides the planners, will read and use them.

The Alberta experience provides another positive example in the presentation of a small town plan. The staff of the Calgary Regional Planning Commission has developed a format wherein all the necessary parts of a plan, from objectives through forecasts, development policies, and the land-use design, are printed on one large, poster-size sheet. A portion of one of these poster plans—for the town of Crossfield (population 1,330 in 1983)—is reproduced in Figure 12.1. The plan adheres to the statutory provisions of the Alberta Planning Act and, at the same time, is presented simply and attractively; the design of each community's plan is distinctive. Such poster plans amount to the equivalent of only 16 pages. Another commendable plan of this type is one prepared for Terrace, B.C. (population about 12,000), which displays its land-use plan in a colourful aerial view of the town.

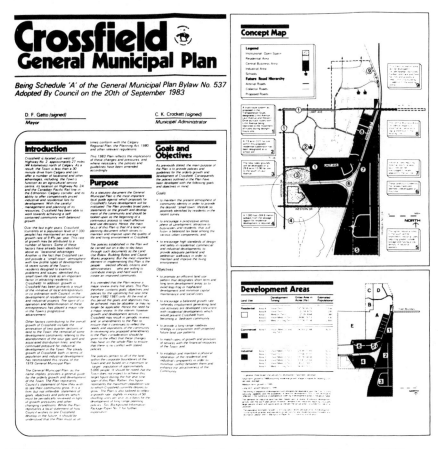

FIGURE 12.1   **Detail of a Poster Plan for Crossfield, Alberta (pop. 1,330).**
Source: Town of Crossfield, 1983.

Recent amendments to Saskatchewan's Planning and Development Act open up a new approach to small town plans. That province now acknowledges that not all municipalities may require a comprehensive municipal plan. Those communities that are very small or have a very low level of development activity may prepare a Basic Planning Statement. These are envisioned as short statements of municipal planning policy that would be sufficient to guide the local council in its (probably infrequent) deliberations over development proposals. The statements would play a role similar to that of a municipal plan in that they are a prerequisite to any intended zoning by-law.

The plans referred to above are for incorporated small towns; there still needs to be considered the planning situation of the 50% of small towns that are not municipalities. These towns would, at best, be included within the plans of rural municipalities, townships, or counties. The experience is that little consideration is given to preparing a special plan for them or giving them particular attention within the larger plan, despite the fact that they may be the most important centres in the locale. A way of rectifying this shortcoming is to prepare supplementary plans for unincorporated towns much as one makes special-area plans for downtown districts, historic neighbourhoods, and parks in large city plans. These are sometimes called "secondary plans," and they are used to good effect for planning small towns within the County Plan for Huron County in Ontario.[22] Planners of small towns are thus urged to find opportunities to make appropriate plans over and above the statutory requirements, where necessary.

Analytical Tools

With respect to the type of analytical tools that are required, the same general principles apply for small town planning as for community plans: that is, planners should strive for simple, direct methods of providing the base of knowledge needed for the plan's preparation. Many tools developed for city planning are simply not needed given the small size of towns and villages. For example, elaborate studies of land use and economic base will probably be irrelevant; similarly, statistical analyses involving correlations and sampling cannot provide reliable results because of the overall small size of the population. However, a concomitant of the small size that favours thorough understanding of the community is that the amount of data that is usually required can be readily obtained from field surveys and direct interviews. Information about housing, land use, jobs, age structure, and so forth will not be voluminous, and the direct contact can help elicit richer local information than is generally available to city planners. Moreover, the necessary studies may be conducted by community members, thus facilitating the task and engaging community interest in the plan-making process.

A **community profile** is a particularly appropriate approach to obtaining and presenting data for small town planning. This tool, as the name suggests, gathers together various data in a single document describing the community's present status, recent trends in population growth and structure, the environment, the local and regional economy, transportation, recreation, etc. Residents of small towns have a fairly unified view of their community; the profile makes use of this view, instead of fragmenting it with a series of separate studies. Furthermore, it promotes the holistic view that the community plan advocates.

The community profile lends itself as a community self-survey tool as well, especially in smaller towns. People of all ages, from schoolchildren to adults in service clubs, can participate in gathering the necessary data. It is helpful for the planner to incorporate issues into the profile that assist residents in identifying community problems and aspirations. Also worth incorporating is a historical overview of the community that provides both a sense of place and the factors that are important to the town's heritage. Historical photographs and maps may be used to advantage in conjunction with those of contemporary situations.

The planner also needs to make analyses and forecasts beyond those that citizens can help provide. The planner needs to know the size, composition, and trends in housing and population. These are probably the central kinds of knowledge a small town planner requires. An accurate survey of all households is the only sure way to acquire these data in a reliable form for analysis. The best analyses and forecasts use the simplest methods. It has been found that forecasts for small towns that use linear extrapolation—the projection of absolute increments in past change—are the most accurate. Because changes in population and housing can vary dramatically from year to year, projections based on percentage changes can be misleading.

Two kinds of economic analysis can prove useful in small town planning. One is a **locational analysis** of the residents' places of employment and shopping. People in small communities tend to interact over extensive areas, because they can seldom find a full range of employment and shopping opportunities right in their own communities. A knowledge of the extent to which residents commute to work in other places and shop in other centres will indicate the ways in which the town's economy is entwined with that of other communities. Such information could be helpful in forecasting the impact of changes occurring in the region of the town, for example, the opening or closing of a large plant or new shopping centre.

A method called **threshold analysis** is a second kind of economic analysis relevant to small communities and their business establishments.

Retail and other commercial firms are the economic backbone of most small towns because they provide goods and services and are major sources of employment. This tool calculates the amount of population required in the town and its trade area to support additional retail and service firms. It can be used to identify those types of firms that have good prospects and those for which the prospects are poor. If planning is conducted on a regional basis, threshold analysis can assist cooperative efforts to distribute firms equitably within reach of the residents of all small towns and the countryside.

Implementation Tools

As with other planning tools suitable for small town planning situations, one must consider the problems that implementation tools are intended to solve. The most familiar land-use regulatory tool—zoning—"grew up" in the city where there are large common-use districts and competition among land uses. How will zoning work in the small town context of low density and diverse land-use patterns? Given the small town's meagre resources for administering any kind of regulations, it may be important to avoid implementation tools that require continual and demanding administration. Then, too, the set of discrete problems to which most small communities give priority does not accord with a long-range capital investment program.

Making Zoning Appropriate

In the area of plan implementation, most of our tools have arisen in response to planning problems that are large in scale and tend to recur. The small town development perspective, as we have seen, is different. If one were to specify the needed characteristics of plan-implementation tools that would be most fitting for small towns, two of the most important would be flexibility and adaptability. It may be helpful to explore briefly the possibilities for achieving these qualities in such land-use regulation tools as zoning and subdivision control.

Zoning as commonly employed derives its usefulness from its ability to parallel the development patterns of cities, where land uses tend to sort themselves into districts of similar uses and types of structures. Only when population exceeds 2,500 does a small town's development pattern show evidence of homogeneous districts of different land uses. Even then, these districts are not large (perhaps less than 40–80 ha), and there are likely to be only a few of them (such as one each for the business area, the residential area, and the industrial area). Moreover, they will each probably accommodate a variety of uses. A general or comprehensive zoning by-law would be too cumbersome in this kind of situation. However, it may be pertinent to frame regulations for any special district where land development is more volatile and subject to conflicts with adjoining areas. There is often the need in small towns to control development along highways, watercourses, or in the business district.

The diverse and sporadic development process in small towns tends to accommodate problematic uses in close proximity, a practice about which city planners and city dwellers might be apprehensive. Conventional zoning tries to anticipate the activity effects of various classes of land uses, thereby predetermining allowable uses. In small towns, it is possible, and indeed commendable, to use a more flexible case-by-case approach that deals with the *effects,* or impact, of a proposed land use rather than with its *actual use.* For example, it is probably more important to know whether the proposed use will generate a lot of traffic, have abnormal hours of operation, create extensive noise or odours, or produce dangerous effluents, than to understand the use itself. A type of zoning originally used in industrial districts in cities, **performance zoning**, is being used in small towns in the United States to deal with the external effects of land uses.[23]

Rather than create districts, performance standards are specified to screen out uses whose effects may be offensive to surrounding properties. Criteria such as off-street parking requirements, external signs, hours of operation, noise levels, and size of structures may be established under performance zoning for the entire town or for specific districts. This kind of performance regulation of land uses is analogous to development control or site plan control used in Canadian cities. In the latter approaches, each proposal for a new or changed land use must receive permission to proceed. Performance zoning would simply require that specified criteria about external effects be met before a development permit is granted.

Land Subdivision

The subdivision of vacant land for new building lots and structures can pose special technical and resource questions for a small town. What may appear to be a boon in terms of new development and an expanded tax base may turn out to be a drain on financial resources and cause future problems for the community if not checked thoroughly at the start. All too often, the sites chosen for houses are on lands with poor buildability— steep slopes, floodplains, poor drainage, or subject to erosion. If the community is called upon later to provide adequate road access, public utilities, and proper drainage, the costs may be very high. Thus, subdivision proposals should be scrutinized for their relation to the development pattern envisioned in the community plan, for the provision of roads, parks, and utilities, and for the treatment of unique and hazardous topography.

Many technical and engineering questions arise in regard to subdivisions, and a small community may not have sufficient expertise on its own staff to deal with them. In many provinces, the final authority for approving subdivisions rests with the province or with the regional government, and advice will usually be available from these upper levels. However, it is still advisable for the town to be involved in reviewing such plans as thoroughly as possible. It may well be able to convene a review committee from among knowledgeable citizens. Such a group, or the council, could make good use of available provincial handbooks on the principles of good subdivision design when assessing proposals.

Cluster Zoning. A fairly recent planning tool for rural areas, especially in the rural-urban fringe, is one that blends both zoning regulation and subdivision control. Since expansion of many towns often means impinging on adjacent agricultural land, it is vital to try and reduce the impact that such expansion could bring through normal large-lot subdivision. The technique of cluster zoning, or open space zoning as it is sometimes called, groups the new development on a part of the property while the remainder is left for farming or other open use.[24] The "cluster" notion comes from the concept of having new development on several adjacent parcels be grouped together. This technique leaves larger blocks of open space, thereby maintaining a rural character to landscape and also making farms more viable.

The Role of Provincial Programs

Planning for the physical setting is only one of two important planning considerations in a small town. The other concerns provincial planning for transportation, economic development, and social services. Small communities are both more dependent upon such programs than cities and more apt to feel a strong impact from the program. Take, for example, major energy projects that aim to satisfy the needs of metropolitan and industrial areas in Canada (and sometimes abroad): hydroelectric dams, oil recovery projects, and coal mines. Construction workers throng to these areas, straining housing and social services. Permanent employees are usually fewer in number, yet their demands for permanent accommodation and services are different again. Further, the local community may be left with an aftermath of pollution problems. The discussion of impacts such as these is too extensive to pursue here, but just as we now perceive the need to ascertain the environmental effects of new programs and projects, so should we recognize the need to examine the impact of large projects on small communities.

There are two other facets of senior government programs of which small town planners should also be aware. The first is the large number of agencies that tend to be involved and that may simply overwhelm the administrative and technical resources normally found in small communities. The second is the problem of coordinating programs and activities of senior governments. All too common are duplication, interdepartmental conflict, and competition among programs and officials.[25] It is as if senior governments have extensive policy and program resources but a limited ability to deliver the programs effectively. There is considerable room for improving the coordination of senior government efforts so that they contribute positively to the development of towns and villages. Much small town planning may be rendered ineffective until this occurs.

ENDNOTES

The material in this chapter draws heavily upon Gerald Hodge and Mohammad Qadeer, *Towns and Villages in Canada* (Toronto: Butterworths, 1983), and on several other publications of the author.

1. Gerald Hodge, *The Elderly in Canada's Small Towns* (Vancouver: University of British Columbia Centre for Human Settlements, 1987), Occasional Paper 43, 5.
2. This follows the useful distinction made by Thomas L. Daniels and Mark B. Lapping, "The Two Rural Americas Need More, Not Less Planning," *Journal of the American Planning Association* 62, no. 3 (Summer 1996), 285–288.
3. Cf. C.R. Bryant, L.H. Russwurm, and A.G. McLellan, *The City's Countryside* (New York: Longmans, 1982).
4. *Ibid,* 12.
5. Newfoundland, Department of Municipal Affairs, *Planning for Smaller Towns* (St. John's: Project Planning Associates, 1968), 23.
6. County of Huron, *Howich Township Secondary Plan* (Goderich, Ont., 1976), 39–50.
7. Newfoundland, *Planning for Smaller Towns,* 7.
8. Hodge, *Elderly,* 14.
9. Gerald Hodge, *Seniors in Small Town British Columbia: Demographic Tendencies and Trends, 1961–1986* (Vancouver: Simon Fraser University Gerontology Research Centre and University of British Columbia Centre for Human Settlements, 1991), 10.
10. Ontario Advisory Council on Senior Citizens, *Towards an Understanding of the Rural Elderly* (Toronto, 1980).
11. Gerald Hodge, *Managing an Aging Population in Rural Canada: The Role and Response of Local Government* (Toronto: ICURR Press, 1993).

12. Gerald Walker, "Networks and Politics in the Fringe," in Michael Bunce and Michael Troughton, eds., *The Pressures of Change in Rural Canada,* Geographical Monograph No. 14 (Toronto: York University Department of Geography, 1984), 202–214.

13. Greg Halseth, "Community and Land-Use Planning Debate: An Example from Rural British Columbia," *Environment and Planning A* 28 (1996), 1279–1298.

14. Gerald Hodge, *Planning for Small Communities,* a report to the Ontario Planning Act Review Committee (Toronto, 1978), Background Paper No. 5.

15. Cf. Evelyne Power Reid and Maurice Yeates, "Bill 90—An Act to Protect Agricultural Land: An Assessment of Its Success in Laprairie County, Quebec," *Urban Geography* 12, no. 4 (1991), 295–309; and Christopher Bryant and Thomas Johnston, *Agriculture in the City's Countryside* (Toronto: University of Toronto Press, 1992), esp. 137–189.

16. Gerald Walker, *An Invaded Countryside: Structures of Life in the Toronto Fringe,* Geographical Monograph No. 17 (Toronto: York University Department of Geography, 1987).

17. Hugh J. Gayler, "Planning Reform in Ontario and Its Implications for Urban Containment and Agricultural Land Use," *Small Town* 26, no. 4 (January–February 1996), 4–13.

18. Newfoundland, Department of Municipal Affairs and Housing, *Residential Subdivision Design Criteria for Newfoundland* (St. John's, 1975).

19. Cf. Prince Edward Island, Department of Municipal Affairs, *Residential Subdivision Design Handbook* (Charlottetown, 1979); Saskatchewan, Department of Industry and Commerce and Municipal Affairs, *Guide to the Saskatchewan Main Street Development Program* (Regina, 1979); and Ontario, Ministry of Housing, *A Guide to Residential Planning and Design in Small Communities* (Toronto, 1980).

20. Newfoundland, *Planning for Smaller Towns,* 7.

21. Alberta, Task Force on Urbanization and the Future, *High River, Alberta* (Edmonton, 1973).

22. Cf. County of Huron, *Howich Township Secondary Plan.*

23. Cf. Judith Getzels and Charles Thurow, eds., *Rural and Small Town Planning* (Chicago: American Planning Association, 1979), 89–95.

24. Thomas L. Daniels, "Where Does Cluster Zoning Fit in Farmland Protection?" *Journal of the American Planning Association* 63, no. 1 (Winter 1997), 129–133.

25. A. Paul Pross, *Planning and Development: A Case Study of Two Nova Scotia Communities* (Halifax: Dalhousie University Institute of Public Affairs, 1975), 90.

PART 3

Participation and Decision Making in Community Planning

Source: Neil Lucente, *North Shore News*

INTRODUCTION

Planning for a community requires collective decision-making processes, usually within the framework of local government. There are a number of procedures, both formal and informal, often interwoven, that condition the processes of decision making. These involve a wide range of participants whose values, roles, and behaviour must be understood. Community planning does not operate independently from either the political arena or the economic marketplace. Reconciling these positions makes community planning a process in social cooperation.

Chapter 13 Deciding Upon the Community's Plan

Effective planning of human settlements ... will come to depend more on human relations in the process of arriving at decisions than it will on the planner's science and art of preparing plans.

Harry Lash, 1976

Community planning has been referred to as a social activity many times in the preceding chapters. It is the process of a community deciding upon its future environment. With this established, it is time to recognize the qualitative aspects of this process by which we may discern those individuals and groups who participate in plan-making. Community planning, after all, is concerned not just with planning *for* a community; it is equally concerned with planning *by* a community.

The planning process, as well as being a series of technical steps, is the process by which diverse people, firms, and institutions in a community make a decision. This diversity of participants is a primary characteristic of community planning. As compared to business planning or military planning, for example, there are many more participants with a variety of motives and goals involved in community planning. The various participants also have characteristic roles and enter into the process in different ways at different times.

The purpose of this chapter is to describe how the decisions are made in adopting a community plan. Against the series of technical and procedural steps, we shall array the principal participants and indicate the parts they play at different stages. Included here under the general rubric of plan-making are the complementary processes of amending the plan and implementing it. Both of the latter are considered part of the continuing process of a community that is planning its future. However, the set of participants and their actions are distinctive in each stage of the planning process.

THE DECISION SEQUENCE IN MUNICIPAL PLAN-MAKING

The Formal Steps

The community-planning process in Canada is highly formalized. The provincial planning acts prescribe for all communities a number of specific steps that must be taken, as well as the participants and their responsibilities at the various steps. The formal plan-making process does not contain all the steps that a community takes in preparing (or amending) its plan. Besides the steps legally required of the municipality, there are others of a technical, consultative, and deliberative nature that make up the planning process. The chart in Figure 13.1 contrasts the set of steps for municipal plan-making with those for the ideal community-planning process.

There are several general points of comparison between the two processes. First, the ideal planning process is a concept that does not specify participants, or specific decisions, or legal responsibilities. It is more like a reminder to a community of what to keep in mind when striving to prepare a plan. Second, the municipal plan-making process is concerned with defining the roles of public and private interests in the community in regard to the development of land. When the physical environment might be changed either by private initiative or by government action, many other interests are involved besides those who directly initiate change. There are the interests of other landowners and of the community as a whole. Thus, decisions must be specified so that all interests will be aware of their rights and responsibilities. Third, the formal process is concerned with establishing the balance between provincial and municipal authority in regard to private property rights. Since responsibility for these rights, when they are delegated to a municipality (as they are under the planning act), rests ultimately with the province, this shift in responsibility must be specified.

The municipal plan-making process shown in Figure 13.1 is a composite of steps found in various planning acts; actual steps may differ from province to province.[1] However, these slight differences only heighten the concern, to which we alluded above, over specifying steps and responsibilities. We may now describe briefly each of these steps in terms of the decisions that are made, the interests involved, and the planning objectives of the decision.

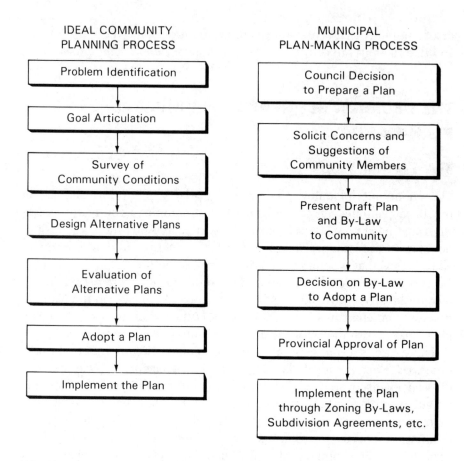

FIGURE 13.1 **Comparison between the Municipal Plan-Making Process and the Ideal Community-Planning Process**
The municipal process of plan-making explicitly takes into account the roles of public and private interests that participate in the development of the community's land base.

Decision to Prepare a Plan

Since a municipality's (or other local body's) plan becomes an official statement of policy, an explicit decision by the local council is required to initiate plan-making. Thereby all interests in the community, and those with an interest in the development of land in the community, are informed that the process is to begin. Such a decision to prepare a plan may arise from a sense in the community that development problems (or initiatives for major new projects) should be dealt with in a more comprehensive, logical framework.

Soliciting Concerns and Suggestions of the Community
Recognizing that there will be diverse opinions in the community concerning the future environment, most provinces require that these views be solicited. This input is usually obtained through one or a few public meetings held in the community. The objectives are democratic involvement of community members and the identification of goals for the environment. Professional planners or the local planning advisory committee usually conduct these meetings.

Presentation of Draft Plan
A proposed plan is submitted by the planners to the council or council committee along with a draft of the by-law that would officially sanction the plan. Public hearings are authorized to be held by the council or its committee. This provides a community evaluation of the plan proposals. Normally, only one plan alternative is presented.

Decision on Plan By-Law
The council's adoption of the community plan as a statement of policy about the physical environment is actually done through the formal process of voting on an implementing by-law. Thus, the plan becomes "official" and is legally binding on the council and all parties with interests in land development.

Provincial Approval of the Plan
Most provinces require that a community plan be submitted for review and approval to the provincial government department involved in planning matters. The plan is checked for the adequacy of its planning approach and its consistency with provincial government policies. The plan is usually not considered offcial, or the by-law in effect, until it has been approved and signed by the minister.

Implementation of the Plan through Various Instruments
The passage of a zoning by-law, the acceptance of a subdivision plan proposal, and, indeed, the amendment of the community plan tend to follow a set of steps similar to that for the original adoption of the plan. Each initiative of this sort is regarded as a supplementary process of plan-making in which the aims of the plan are reaffirmed, refined, and possibly revised. The initiative for many of the proposals in this phase of planning often originates with private land development interests.

It is this formal set of steps that gives structure to the planning process in a Canadian community. The formal steps act to ensure that the rights of property owners are properly considered and the democratic right of community members to participate is respected. They also prescribe the participants at each step and their responsibilities vis-à-vis the decision to be made. There are, basically, only three sets of participants at this formal stage: the members of the municipal council, the members of the general public, and provincial government officials. Of these three, the councillors and the provincial officials are charged with making binding decisions; although the citizenry participate, their role is only advisory. Another facet of these steps is that each consumes a relatively small amount of time in the total planning process. For example, there is the time taken by the council to debate the by-law that enacts the plan, the time for one or a few public meetings, and the time for provincial review of the plan. These formal steps are visible points of convergence of various technical and consultative planning efforts, at which decisions need to be taken. In the interstices of these formal steps, much planning occurs and many more participants are involved, as we shall now see.

The Informal Steps

While the formal steps tend to deal with *procedure,* with authority and responsibility of participation, there are other important steps that deal with the *substance* of the plan. These steps are concerned with the development of a community consensus about the need for a plan, the articulation of community goals based on community concerns, the survey of community conditions, and the design and evaluation of alternative plans. The latter steps consume the most time in the entire process, but are the least visible. However, the informal steps are crucial to the planning process, for through these steps the plan is actually formulated. Without the output from these steps, no formal decisions could be made. There are two main streams in this phase: (1) technical and (2) consultative or deliberative.

Technical Steps
A large part of the planning process, it will be remembered, is technical— for example, the studies and analyses that have to be done by the professional planners. Another large part is deliberative—for example, the discussions and consultations that need to occur among members and groups in the community. British planner Paul Cloke says that the steps that occur between the overt decision-making steps are often "obscure" to those outside the local government's planning apparatus.[2] Some steps may not be visible, such as those taken by the professional planners in their surveys and analyses, or they may not be clear as to purpose, such as when advice is being sought from local groups, developers, and other government agencies. In these phases, the professional planner and the politician are the

leading participants as they guide the plan-making process. There is no doubt that they are able to influence much of the approach and content of the plan. Where this happens unduly, it leads to a sceptical rejection of the objectivity and openness of the plan-making process and the charge that it is wholly "political." There is a challenge, therefore, to keep the plan-making process from becoming obscure in its informal phases; it is a challenge that falls on the planner and the politician alike. More will be said about this later in the chapter.

The planner may call upon the skills of a wide gamut of professionals, either employees of the municipality or consultants. This is the phase when analyses of economic and social factors must be done, and when the implications for public utilities, roads, and parks become evident, not to mention schools, libraries, and health facilities. As a result, individuals and groups outside the formal planning framework are drawn into the planning process. Except in the smallest municipalities, the planner will need to involve, at a minimum, the chief administrative officer, the public works director, and the director of parks and recreation. Some communities ensure this participation by forming a "technical planning committee," with the planner chairing it. It is important that the technical advice of specialists on city staff be available to the community, and also that there be a large measure of commitment to the emerging plan by those officials who will have a prominent role in implementing it.

In carrying out their role, planners frequently find themselves having to balance competing demands of other municipal departments, developers, politicians, and public advocacy groups. Sometimes, these demands are not readily reconcilable through technical or design analyses. Usually, this is because they are rooted in differences in basic attitudes and values. Dispute resolution methods are increasingly being used by planners to reach constructive solutions without going to costly litigation or to appeal tribunals.[3]

Two such methods being used are **negotiation** (where advocates for each side seek a mutual solution) and **mediation** (where a neutral third party assists each side in finding an acceptable solution). Planners trained in these methods find that they can help solve problems, enhance mutual understanding, and strengthen the planning process. Outside professionals may also be utilized by the planners to facilitate problem-solving between stakeholders.

Consultation Steps

This is also a phase for considerable consultation on community goals, needs, and development policies. Those consulted include the general public, public interest groups, community organizations, and other public agencies. There are usually several forms of consultation. For individuals and groups, there may be an organized public participation program conducted by the community's planners through public meetings, open houses, questionnaires, etc. Such public agencies as school boards, public utilities, and other levels of governments may be asked to react to planning proposals. Most communities establish a planning board or committee to channel the various reactions into the plan-making process. Such a committee is usually given a mandate by the municipal council to seek public reactions and to resolve these, along with the planner's advice, into a plan which then can be formally debated.

It will quickly be realized that this informal part of plan-making is a complex process of gathering information and giving advice. The information provided by individual specialists, agencies, and the public must be compounded until workable planning propositions are reached. This requires a high degree of social cooperation among the participants. Moreover, each participant brings to the consultations his or her own values, knowledge, motivations, and criteria for judgement. These perspectives may be personal, professional, or group views, or some combination of the three. Suffice to say at this point, the planner requires an acute awareness of the social relations inherent in the planning process, as well as a personal frame of reference regarding the social intervention inherent in plan-making.

Achieving consensus on planning proposals is a delicate task, but one that has become considerably more practicable and democratic in recent years.[4] The formal planning deliberations discussed above tend to start with planning solutions that are debated in some prescribed (i.e., parliamentary) procedure, whereas consensus techniques start with identifying options and criteria for choice and end with agreed-upon mutual solutions. These techniques are often invoked where there are multiple interests involved in reaching a planned solution to a problem. The siting of waste treatment facilities at a city-wide level or of group homes at a neighbourhood level are but two examples. The Islands Trust, which is a form of regional government for more than a dozen of B.C.'s Gulf Islands, uses this approach in developing community plans: a broad-based committee develops the planning options and criteria before they are submitted to the formal deliberative process.

Participants in consensual processes are usually referred to as **stakeholders**. In practice, this means individuals or groups "with something significant to gain or lose as a result of the deliberations."[5] Choosing stakeholders as participants is, in principle, a matter of being more *inclusive* with respect to different interests in the community—it involves including those often overlooked or inaudible in public debates, such as women and minorities.[6] It also means recognizing the value of a participant's practical experience and not just his or her formal knowledge.[7] Consensus building will be described more fully in the next chapter.

Making Supplementary Plans

Community planning does not stop with the formulation of the overall community plan. Once the latter step is completed there follows immediately a number of supplementary plans to bring the community plan to fruition. The most prominent is the zoning plan, which also addresses the entire area of the community. More specific plans that require decisions are the plans of subdivision for areas of undeveloped land and replotting schemes to consolidate and modernize scattered subdivision plans. Then there is the review and updating of the community plan itself. Most provinces require communities to review their overall plans on a regular basis, for example, every five years, as is the case in Ontario and B.C.

Each of these planning efforts supplements the community plan and refines its goals and policies. Supplementary plans are usually required by the provincial planning act to conform to the overall plan. Further, the decision-making sequence is formal and very similar to that for broad plan-making. Public meetings are held to solicit views about the draft plan; a planning advisory committee deliberates on the planning proposals, taking into account the views of the public, and makes a recommendation to the municipal council; the council debates the proposal in the form of an implementing by-law; and lastly, provincial approval is sought.

The array of participants is also much the same as in general plan-making, with the exception of a plan proposing a new subdivision or application for rezoning. In the latter cases, the plan is put forward by the individual or group wishing to modify the particular parcel. These proponents are commonly referred to as "developers," and in plans of subdivision and re-zoning they play a major role in propounding the merits of the plan in which they have an interest. All other supplementary plans derive from the community's planners, who assume the role of proponent.

RESPONDING TO DEVELOPMENT INITIATIVES

The community-planning process must be responsive to ongoing initiatives for urban development, as well as for the promotion of its own long-range goals. With regard to development on private land—the bulk of all community land—the initiatives that will result in new buildings or redeveloped older buildings come from a wide range of private sources. Implementation of much of the plan is thus effectively a function of decisions by diverse decision makers. And it is only in the course of these private decisions being taken that the vagaries of land development become apparent.

Three facets of land development affect the process of plan-making or, more specifically, call for modification of the plan's policies:

1. Inherent differences among pieces of property that could affect the type of development;
2. The ways different developers view the potential for land development on specific sites;
3. The ways other landowners or the public view development initiatives.

None of these potential situations can be ignored. To do so would be not only unrealistic but could also deny "natural justice" to participants. Formal planning frameworks thus provide the means by which these various differences can be reconciled.

Differences in Developability

Zoning by-laws treat each property within a zone as equally developable. Occasionally, one or a few properties may differ from their neighbours by topography, size, shape, and location, such that the norm of development of the zone cannot be met without causing their owners hardship. For such cases, provision is made to vary, or adjust, the zoning regulations on the basis of an appeal to a special committee established for this purpose. In some provinces, these committees are called a **Committee of Adjustment**, in others a **Zoning Appeal Board.** They are appointed by the municipal council.

The decision sequence and the set of participants in the process of applying for a variance from zoning regulations are distinctive. The process is initiated by a landowner through an application to the appeal committee. Other landowners in the same vicinity (usually within a 100 m radius) are advised that the application has been made, and that they may make submissions (pro and con) at a scheduled hearing before the committee. A hearing is held, and the committee can decide to allow or disallow the appeal. The committee's decision can usually be appealed to a provincial planning appeal body.

It will be noted that in the case of variances, neither the municipal council nor the advisory planning committee plays a specified role. The zoning appeal process is considered to be largely a judicial rather than a planning process. It is not unknown for decisions of appeal committees to have major planning consequences such that the municipal council may feel disposed to appeal the ruling of its committee. The most contentious appeals are for variances in the permitted land uses, which usually arise because a desired use is neither specifically allowed nor disallowed. A very common case is the request to carry on an occupation in one's home in a residential zone.

Differences in Developers' Perceptions

The land-use designations in a community plan and zoning by-law are the planners' *estimate* of the development potential of properties at particular locations. But not until a developer takes the initiative to build a new building or refurbish an old one on a site can the accuracy of that estimate be determined. Further, it is difficult to imagine all the uses that could be appropriate for a site, even within generally acceptable uses. For example, the properties adjoining an intersection may appear to be appropriate for retail commercial uses, such as a shopping plaza. The same properties may, however, appeal to a developer as a good location for a motel or an office building.

In the above case, all the possible uses are commercial. But take another example where the plan envisions, and the zoning allows, a site to be developed for residential use, and a developer comes forward with a proposal that a shopping centre be built there. In order to accommodate these sorts of possibilities, planning regulations provide for applications to amend the plan and/or the zoning by-law. The proponent of the project usually initiates this process and becomes a key participant throughout.

The examination of proposals to amend the plan and zoning by-law is analogous to their original formulation; that is, almost the identical formal decision-making process is invoked because it is felt that the plan or zoning by-law should represent a solid commitment by the community, and that it should not be modified without proper study and extensive deliberation. Thus, a proposal for development that would require amendments to existing planning policy receives technical scrutiny by the planning staff and other officials, a public hearing to receive citizen comments, debate by the municipal council, and final approval by the province.

In contrast to original plan-making, the process of amending a plan or by-law is usually initiated by someone external to the local government, such as the developer. The developer must make the case with various public bodies for changing the already agreed-upon planning policy. This, then, casts the staff planner in a different role, for, in such instances, he or she is required to appraise the merits of the proposed development and advise the municipal council on the desirability of modifying the plan or by-law. Here the planner is expected to act in the public interest and not on behalf of the developer or any other interests. Much has been written on the delicate balance of roles of various participants in these planning actions. There is probably no initiative in planning that can generate as much controversy as one to change existing planning policy.

Different Reactions to Development

An essential feature of community planning is the consideration given to how development on one site might affect surrounding properties, as well as the community as a whole (if the project is large). It is also in the nature of community planning that there is the right of appeal of planning decisions. This serves not only the democratic rights of citizens in the community but also the rights of natural justice of the property owners, who are directly affected because their property rights may be infringed upon by the decision.

It is something of a truism in planning that reactions to planning decisions become intense only when a proposal for development appears about to become an actual project. Thus, if we take the example in the preceding section, where a developer proposes a project that differs from what is allowed at a location under the plan and by-law, we have one of the classic situations where strong reaction emerges in the planning process. The reactions may, of course, be varied and may come from diverse and sometimes unexpected sources. But our planning statutes allow for these reactions to be channelled formally into the plan-making process.

There are three general mechanisms by which reactions to development proposals may be expressed. The first is through the public information meetings in which applications for rezoning and amendments to the community plan are deliberated. The second is through the filing of formal objections against the planning decision of the council with the provincial ministry or a provincial appeal board. The public meeting allows for a variety of reactions, pro and con, to be expressed about development proposals and the impending planning amendments. This forum mainly serves to allow the community's planners to assess the amount and type of reaction to a proposed project. Thereby they will be able to modify the formal planning policy and the by-law that the council will debate so that it better reflects the interests of affected property owners as well as the mood of the community. A third method is to use negotiating or mediating techniques for resolving such conflicts prior to formal appeals.[8]

The appeal process allows a formal objection to be filed against the decision of the municipal council. The objection must be heard in a judicial setting (unless the appeal board considers it trivial or simply dilatory). Those who would file an objection must be prepared to enter into the legalistic setting and, in some cases, to pay a fee to do so. Lawyers usually need to be retained, and this tends to limit appeals to those individuals, firms, or groups that can afford to appeal. There is generally provision for individual citizens or groups of citizens to be heard, but the format is so highly structured that unless their representations are well organized, they tend not to have much effect. Appeals are most often undertaken either by a developer whose proposal has been denied or by organized citizen groups objecting to a municipal planning decision. A common sort of appeal is that by a citizen group against a private development project or a project of a local or regional government, such as the location of an expressway, a waste disposal site, or an airport.

The amount and type of reaction that will emerge in response to a proposed development are not easily predicted. There are a variety of possible sources—adjacent property owners, competing property owners, citizen groups—but whether any or all of them will come forward with their concerns and objections, and with what degree of vociferousness, is unknown until the proposal is in the public arena. Also, the reactions may emerge from some individuals or groups at the public meeting stage and from others at the stage of an appeal.

WHO GETS INVOLVED

The field of participants in the various processes of plan-making in a community is, indeed, large. Potentially, every household may be involved, along with the local government, the provincial government, community planners and other professionals, business interests, land developers, and appeal bodies. This wide range of participants, so characteristic of modern democratic communities, contrasts with planning in cities of the past. The planning of these, described in the first few chapters of this book, was the responsibility of a few people—it is actually possible to identify who in those cities planned this or that element—and they usually had some official capacity. Not so today, for the planners now are more diverse than ever.

Let us try to define who the "planners" are nowadays. In large part, they may be inferred from the decision process itself, as described above. If we were to list the participants in order of their likelihood to become involved, it would look as follows:

- Politicians (members of the local council)
- Planning advisory board

- Professional planners
- The public
- Private developers
- Other professionals
- Extra-local agencies
- Appeal bodies.

This list indicates a hierarchy of participants, with those who are either responsible for or representative of community interests dominating community planning. But while this is true, one can easily imagine the great mixture of participants within the politicians, public, planners, and among the other participants. All come from different backgrounds and play different roles in the planning process. Thus, a simple listing conveys the complexity of community planning. Achieving a viable planning process in a community requires an appreciation of and an ability to work within such a complex of participants: who gets involved, and what is the quality of their involvement?

The Key Participants

We have seen that planning is not a monolithic process but rather a group of subprocesses, each concerned with different phases of the decision making. Each of these subprocesses has its own distinctive set of participants. Our listing of participants may be better appreciated within the context of the following three subprocesses, which reflect the basic decision sequences in community planning. The first set of participants would be concerned with plan-making, the second with plan implementation, and the third with plan clarification. Figure 13.2 shows the composition of participants in each set; the reader will note that they overlap to some degree with each other.

Participants in Plan-Making

As this is the pivotal phase of planning in a community, it is understandable that the key participants are community members and community advisors. Although in formal terms the local councillors initiate the making of an overall plan and the zoning by-law, the stimulus may arise from the public or from the planners employed by the community. Moreover, once the phase has begun, all three of the major participants become highly dependent on one another. Members of the business community or an environmental protection group may urge the making of a plan, but they will have to persuade the council. The planner, acting as advisor to the council, will need ideas and comments from the public in order to put forth politically

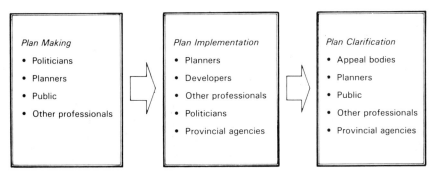

FIGURE 13.2   Key Participants in the Three Phases of Community Planning
Each of the three phases of community planning has its own distinctive set of participants, although some are involved in more than one phase. Within each phase, there is considerable interdependency among participants in their aims and decisions.

acceptable proposals. This very special relationship between politicians, planners, and the public is highlighted in the next chapter.

A few other points about the participants in this phase need to be made. First, the *politicians* on the council are representatives, as well as members, of the public. They are elected by their fellow citizens to represent the views of citizens in council deliberations. Second, the *public partici-pants* comprise many elements: individuals and organized groups within the community, as well as those representing their personal interests and those espousing community interests. All can claim, with some justification, to reflect the interests of the community. Reconciling these diverse and often conflicting views of the public is a major task of this phase. Indeed, *citizen participation* in plan-making has developed a special place in planning processes in Canada in the last two decades. The next chapter provides an in-depth look at citizen participation.

A third point is that, in the plan-making phase, *other officials of local government* are involved along with the politicians, planners, and the public. In roles such as city engineer, solicitor, parks director, traffic engineer, etc., they can affect the form and content of planning proposals, and also, as advisors to the council, they can influence the debate about the plan. Lastly, although the *planning advisory board* has not been mentioned explicitly, it should not be overlooked. It can be a major mediating factor both through its membership, which usually includes citizens, and through its review of planning proposals before they go to the council. Thus, planning advisory boards blend the elements important to community plan-making in their composition and their procedures. Where they are used, they can promote community cooperation.

Source: Hellman cartoon from *Built Environment* 22, no. 4 (1996), "Theory and Practice in Urban Design," reproduced by permission of Louis Hellman and Alexandrine Press.

Participants in Plan Implementation

With an overall plan and zoning by-law in place, the planning decisions in this phase have mostly to do with responding to development initiatives. These may come both from private land developers and from public agencies, including the local government itself. The community's staff planner or consultant is primarily responsible for determining whether these initiatives correspond to the intentions of the plan and by-law. If they do, the next steps tend to be routine, with various approvals for development being granted. In many communities, development proposals are subject to further scrutiny and approval, even though they conform generally with the plan and by-law. Plans showing the siting of new structures must be submitted to a site plan or development permit committee for approval of building location, traffic access, etc. The latter committee is usually composed of council members, and its approval, in the form of a site plan agreement or development permit, is usually submitted to the council for concurrence. Many other communities administer development proposals through special departments, sometimes called development departments, or through their building inspection departments.

When development initiatives do not conform with the community's planning policies and regulations, the developer has the option to petition council to amend the plan and by-law. In this instance, formal processes are set in motion and the planner becomes responsible for orchestrating the various steps until the proposed amendments can be put before the council. Studies are often undertaken to determine the impact of the development, and officials in city hall and in other public agencies are consulted. Hearings before the planning advisory committee may need to be arranged, and lastly, the amendments are sent to the council for decision. The developer appears at each formal hearing to advocate acceptance of the amendments. The planner also appears before council to give an opinion, which may be either pro or con, depending on whether he or she feels the proposal unduly compromises the plan. If the decision of the council is to accept the amendments, provincial officials are then given the opportunity to comment upon and accept them.

Participants in Plan Clarification

For a variety of reasons, the intent of planning policy in the plan and the provisions of the zoning by-law may need to be clarified. The simplest case is the exemption of a single property from some of the requirements of the zoning by-law—that is, the variance. The most complex are those where either a developer feels a project should be allowed within the plan and the council disagrees, or where the council has passed an amendment to the plan and by-law and members of the community disagree. The appeal processes provided for in planning legislation thus serve to clarify the current thinking with regard to planning in the community.

The appeal bodies are not only a focal point for participation in this phase, but also by their procedures they define the participants. For example, those that deal with variances tend to have participants who are closely associated with the property for which changes are requested, such as the property owner, owners of neighbouring properties, or other neighbourhood residents. However, appeals of council decisions involve a wider array of participants: the community's planner, other professionals appearing as expert witnesses (either for the community or for the appellant), and members of the public. In most instances, the decision on the appeal is reviewed by provincial officials, and sometimes even further appeal—to a court or provincial cabinet—is possible.

The Milieu of Roles

The quality of the involvement in the planning process is affected by the nature and extent of the participation of those involved. The *formal* agents (councillors, planning advisory board members, provincial officials) have defined places and functions in plan-making. Others act in an *individual* capacity (professional planners, other professionals, private developers, members of the public). And some act in *both* capacities, in particular the politicians and professional planners, especially when they are on the staff of the local government. This mixture of participants automatically means that the people involved will act from a variety of personal and professional backgrounds and have different perceptions of the aims of planning.

Those who participate in the various processes of planning do so much as actors play roles in the theatre or in a film. But planning processes are complex dramas, with each participant possibly playing several roles. Moreover, some of the roles are prescribed by the planning statute or

Planning Issue 13.1

COUNCIL BARS PUBLIC INVOLVEMENT

View Royal council excluded the public Tuesday from a special meeting on community plan proposals.

The reason, said Ald. David Burns, was that "if someone is self-serving in a letter, we should be able to bring that up, but it is not something that we should be airing publicly."

Five residents, who last week were accused of being "misinformed" about community plan proposals, were asked to leave Tuesday's meeting after council unanimously passed the motion to exclude the public.

"We're told we don't know what is going on—that we are misinformed—but when we come here to get informed we find ourselves turned out," commented View Royal Ratepayers Association president Barbara Munton outside the meeting.

Council has been struggling for several months to come up with a new community plan, and keeps postponing the date for the plan's adoption.

Two weeks ago council decided to delay presentation of a by-law for 60 days and to set June 26 as target date for its final adoption.

Meanwhile, March 27 and 31 and April 10 were set as dates for special planning sessions of council.

Representatives of the Advisory Planning Commission and the Parks and Recreation Commission were allowed to stay at Tuesday's planning session.

Burns said council would be considering letters from the public, and "there is a lot of stuff here I don't think the general public should have at this present time."

Source: "View Royal Bars Public from Planning Session," *Victoria Times-Colonist*, March 28, 1990.

regulation, while many are not. Each participant plays at least one formal and one informal role. The formal roles come from legal and institutional definitions of the participant, while informal roles arise from cultural norms of the situation, as well as from the personality and behaviour of the participant. For example, the local councillor's formal role is to debate and decide on the by-law that implements a plan, a role that no other participant shares. A citizen is ascribed a role at public meetings to comment about the plan. The local planner has a formal role, not by legal definition but by professional status, to advise the planning board and council on the technical matters pertaining to the plan.

Each of these participants also "acts out" informal roles. A municipal councillor may, for example, champion development interests in debates because the district he or she represents is populated by voters known to profess this orientation. The way in which the councillor plays out this role is further shaped by his or her own personality, which may range from that of an aggressive participant in council debates to that of a contemplative, behind-the-scenes participant. Beside these facets of a councillor's role playing, the person's actual behaviour comes into play: how he or she reacts to crises, to personal stress, to political changes, to pressure by interest groups, etc. In an analogous way, citizens and planners have their roles shaped by these informal factors. A citizen participant with professional qualifications as, say, a lawyer is likely to pursue things differently from a retired schoolteacher or blue-collar worker. If a planner is personally convinced of the need for citizen participation in planning, he or she will respond differently from one who sees the planner's role as strictly technical and neutral.

One final point needs to be made about differences in the involvement in planning from one community to another. These arise from the simple fact that the composition of persons and groups and the cultural norms of the community determine who becomes involved in plan-making in any of its phases. The presence or absence of persons with certain skills or of specific interest groups can affect the quality of involvement in community planning.

But more than this, each community will differ in its inclination to become involved in planning issues and in the intensity of that involvement. A community that prizes the operation of the economic marketplace and individual initiative to solve problems may not be willing to consider planning proposals that involve large public expenditures. Some communities may prize broad democratic principles favouring consultation of all sectors of the community, while others may operate mostly through a small, influential group of persons who make planning decisions. The particular configuration of interests and inclinations will affect both the behaviour of participants and the consequences of planning proposals. In short, though we may establish formal structures that afford opportunities for involvement—such as consultation, debate, deliberation, and appeal—in planning matters, we cannot know the nature and extent of that involvement until we know the particular community with which we are planning.

PLANNING AS SOCIAL COOPERATION

There is, perhaps, one overriding impression about community planning that is evident by now in our discussion: *there is no single decision-making entity in control of the process.* The local council may seem to have a central role in making planning decisions, but it depends upon advice from others and reactions from still others, and its decisions are often subject to appeal. The planner is involved in almost all phases of plan-making, but is not in a position to direct the process of carrying out the plan. One observer calls this diffuse undertaking of community planning a process in "social cooperation."[9]

Social cooperation is an apt term for this diffuse community activity, for community planning involves the processing of information, ideas, and reactions among a diverse group of participants who, it is likely, do not fully share each other's values about the development of the community. Furthermore, the decisions that must be made concern future physical patterns about which there will be considerable uncertainty. The choices in community planning are always based on incomplete information. This being the case, there must be a sharing of information among all participants at all levels. But more than this, there needs to be the opportunity to refine proposals and place new alternatives into the discussion. The open forms of decision making in community planning reflect this need for a large measure of feedback so that goals and courses of action may be re-examined and, where necessary, modified.

The ungainly process of deciding upon the community plan is the subject of much discussion. On the one hand are those who would streamline it and make it more efficient; they favour a corporate or management model of planning. On the other hand are those who wish to clarify and demystify the community-planning process; they see it not as a rational, objective process, but rather as one of political choice. Both these perspectives need to be examined in order to round out our discussion.

The Limits of the Corporate Planning Model

For many decades, going back to at least the 1920s, there has been considerable pressure to model community planning decision making after the process followed in private business firms. Early initiatives in this regard sought to "keep politics out of planning" and to "get on with making decisions." More recent initiatives, recognizing that community planning is, essentially, a process of political choice, seek rather to improve the information on which councillors base their choices and to organize the process of implementing decisions.

Much of this effort focuses on improving budgeting and financial planning. Various new approaches to budgeting that are being introduced into local government decision-making aim to improve the link between the service and programs being provided and the goals of the political decision makers. Performance budgeting (which looks at the output obtained by expenditures), program budgeting (which looks at the output of groupings of expenditures), and zero-base budgeting (which requires all operating units annually to justify expenditures against community goals) are all adding significantly to the effectiveness of local governments.[10] It is through the budget that actions of officials are controlled to achieve policy objectives.

The proponents of improving local government performance and planning advocate the use of corporate planning models. These latter models aim at a rational selection of effective means to obtain predetermined ends. At first glance, their paradigms seem to mirror the rational-comprehensive model of community planning. Plunkett and Betts, for example, propound a four-stage model: (1) *policy planning*, for the purpose of defining priorities and selecting objectives; (2) *action planning*, for the purpose of establishing program alternatives and budgets; (3) *operations*, which involves carrying out program activities; and (4) *feedback and review*, which involves assessing program impacts.[11] But these models start with the assumption that the ends (goals) are given and that the need is to activate an administrative structure to achieve these designated ends. They further assume that the tasks of the organization can be subdivided and delegated for their implementation.

A typical corporate planning model is that offered by Redman, illustrated in Figure 13.3.[12] It also is a four-stage model; it includes a feedback loop for plan modification and relates the tasks of the chief executive officer(s), the managers, and the department heads. This model puts into operation the sequence of decision making implied in the typical organization charts made for firms and governments: from chief executive to staff officers to line departments. It is a *hierarchical* model in which administrative responsibilities may be specified progressively from the highest to the lowest levels of the organization. It further assumes that problems or tasks may be handled simultaneously and independently from each other.[13]

Although the corporate planning model is suited to some facets of local government operations, there are several important ways in which it is not consonant with physical planning for a community. A rather obvious difference is in the time horizon of corporate planning, which is much shorter (i.e., 3–4 years) than that of most community-planning activities (i.e., 10–20 years). Further, there is the assumption in corporate planning that

Phase	Function	Responsibility	Time Horizon
1. Strategic planning	Establishes objectives, strategies, goals and policies to govern acquisitions, use and disposition of resources and *provides* resources to business units.	Executive management	Long term 4+ years
2. Management control	Establishes objectives and strategies relating to implementation of strategic plan and *allocates* resources.	Managers	Long and short term 1 month to 3 years
3. Operational control	Develops programs to *utilize* resources effectively and efficiently.	Department heads	Short term 1 month to 1 year
4. Plan modification	*Assesses* performance of resource use.	Executive management	Short term

FIGURE 13.3   Model of the Planning Process Used in Corporations
This model is essentially hierarchical and allows responsibilities for achieving objectives to be specified from the highest to the lowest levels of the organization. Such a division of labour does not usually exist within community planning. *Source:* Louis N. Redman, "The Planning Process," *Managerial Planning* 31, no. 6 (May/June 1983), 24–40.

the goals will be established by the top executive of the organization and that these will be agreeable to all other participants. Given the inherent democratic milieu of community planning, community goals are a product of extensive deliberation at all levels as well as subject to debate between levels. Another difference between the two is related to this: corporate planning assumes a hierarchy of responsibilities between participants, but such a division of labour does not exist within community planning.

And, lastly, the corporate model assumes that tasks can be divided in such a way as to allow participants to act independently. An essential feature of community planning is a concern that almost all initiatives of physical development will have an impact on other land uses and activities. Although it is tempting to want to adapt the efficient means of decision making in corporations to community planning, it is clear that the operation of the two spheres and their basic aims are fundamentally different.

Planning and Political Choices

Context: The Local Political Economy

One of the main reasons community planning decision making is not easily adaptable to corporate or other organizational planning models is its inherent involvement with *plural* political choices. Or, put another way, community planning is a mode of decision making peculiar to the needs of diverse interests to decide upon their community's future. There are, thus, a multiplicity of goals to be satisfied representing a plurality of interests. There is no viable hierarchical structure for channelling initiatives or commands. What regularity there is comes from the ever-present competition between economic and social interests.

Before the advent of community-planning institutions early in this century, decisions about the future development of a city or town had to be resolved by one of two mechanisms: either the **economic marketplace** or the **political arena**. These mechanisms still exist, of course, and play a prominent role, but are now joined by the approach of community planning. It will help in understanding the special character of decision making in community planning to look at these counterpart mechanisms and their relationship to planning. Figure 13.4 attempts to portray the situation.

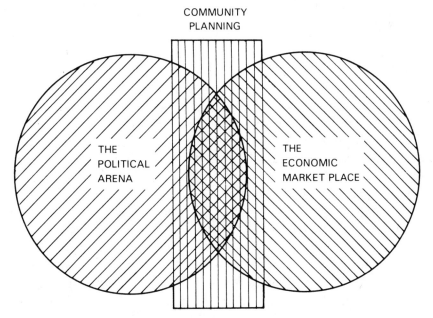

COMMUNITY
PLANNING

THE
POLITICAL
ARENA

THE
ECONOMIC
MARKET PLACE

FIGURE 13.4   **The Place of Planning in Community Decision Making**
Community planning plays a role in reconciling political and economic interests affecting the development of the physical environment in the interest of the community as a whole.

The physical development of a community results from choices made either by private landowners and project developers or by public agencies. The former build the homes, apartment buildings, shopping centres, and factories, while the latter build the roads, schools, parks, utility lines, and other public buildings. The decisions of private developers are largely motivated by economic considerations—how much will a home cost? how much profit can be realized by erecting an office building? Such decisions are articulated by mechanisms of the economic marketplace like the residential real estate market or the commercial and industrial land markets. The marketplace in our society is not controlled by any central mechanism, but is open for the participation of all who have the financial resources and the will to risk them. Decisions are made on the basis of resources that are bid for houses, properties, etc., and on the asking price for these. Transactions of this sort are made all the time in the typical Canadian community, the outcome of which determines much of the character of the physical environment—its appearance, location, and stability. The essence of the marketplace mechanism is the contention that the development of a community's land is most likely to occur, and in the best fashion, through the efforts of buyers and sellers who most fully appreciate their own interests—this is the so-called neoclassical model.

The political arena exists to make those decisions about the development of the community that affect the entire populace. On the one hand are those decisions about facilities and services whose provision is the responsibility of the community, such as the street system and the public utilities. On the other hand are those decisions about steps that are taken to protect the interests of all citizens, such as building and traffic regulations and waste disposal services. Provincial statutes provide local councils with the authority to raise money through various taxes to pay for facilities and to pass regulations in the general interest of the community. Further, the council's decisions frequently affect development in the private sector, such as decisions about the basic infrastructure and regulations that might constrain the quality of development.

It is important to note the inherent differences in the form and basis of decision making in the political arena and the marketplace. It might be said that both involve **voting.** In the council's milieu, the voting is done by a group of people who must publicly declare their position. Councillors are elected to represent the values and interests of the community, so that when they decide upon matters affecting physical development, their vote is expected to be for the general good. In the economic marketplace, the voting is done with money and the transactions are conducted in private, with only the interests of the participants at stake. In both arenas, the decisions are the same in that they tend to be concerned about short-term considerations: concluding a deal, passing the annual budget, establishing a regulation.

We call this milieu, using the older tradition of the social sciences, a **political economy.** The decisions of local councillors are seldom made without either explicit or implicit reference to economic consequences: what will be the impact on jobs with or without this new project? will we drive investors away if we don't approve this project? And, as has been seen at least in this century, those involved in developing land and trading real estate have taken an explicit interest in the workings of local government—running for council, getting appointed to planning boards, not to mention lobbying. Indeed, some politicians may have an inherent interest in furthering marketplace solutions to community development issues. Conversely, many councillors have been elected in recent years on "reform" platforms that espouse more social content in decisions, for example, housing programs for the poor and protection of the environment. The task of local government is to find the appropriate balance between the two realms, between the competing values of each. Community planning is the governmental activity that attempts this reconciliation. This intermediate position imparts special characteristics and tensions to the practice of planning as well as subjecting it to the vagaries of political power.

Planning, Politics, and Power

Community planning grew up and persists as a distinctive mode of decision making because neither of the two traditional modes deals effectively with all the concerns that arise when deciding upon the future environment. Developers usually have their eyes on short-term economic gains from a particular project. And politicians often have their eyes on an upcoming election. The approach of community planning is to employ a more pervasive rationality than either of the other two modes in those situations where future-oriented, community-wide interests are at stake.

Thus, community planning is an integral part of the political life and machinery of the municipality wherever it is in use. This means that the planners play a political role, an attribute that planners themselves have often had difficulty accepting. For many planners "politics has meant conflict," to quote Forester.[14] And, he continues, "conflict has meant irrationality ... [and] loss of control." It is virtually impossible for planners, or any others who become involved in planning decisions (e.g., citizens, business-persons), to shun the politics entwined in community planning. To quote Forester again:

We often have to interpret what a goal, policy, regulation of by-law means. Once we do that, knowing that multiple and conflicting interpretations are always possible (some favouring some people, others favouring others) we're right back to politics.

This is nowhere more evident, nowadays, than in environmental issues. Whether it concerns protecting trees in North Vancouver or storing PCBs in Baie Comeau, these issues are highly politicized. "No matter what position planners take in an argument concerning environmental policy," Friedmann suggests, "they are certain to antagonize important segments of the population."[15]

Both Forester and Friedmann conclude that planners must establish relationships with key participants in order to function effectively. This is due largely to the fact that working in a political milieu means coming to terms with power—the power of others as well as one's own power. Planners in Canada have little political power in the conventional sense (i.e., they are able only to give advice) and cannot control political outcomes. But planners are able to wield considerable influence on those who can (the politicians) and those who try to influence politicians (developers, citizens, business interests, etc.). Much more will be said about the role of planners and other participants in the next chapter.

Community planning seen this way does not operate independently of either economic or political outlooks and criteria, for planning does not entirely replace either of the modes and must draw upon them, thereby reducing the extent to which it can adhere to its own rational-comprehensive ideals. Those involved in community planning cannot help but bring their biases and interests into the process. Some would argue that since not all segments of the community are likely to be able to participate, planning outcomes tend to favour the interests of the more powerful over those of the weak and disadvantaged.[16] From this perspective, community planning is a political activity in all respects, because every planning alternative comes down on only one side of a development issue. Plans are, thus, not just neutral technical solutions. And when planners advocate a planning solution, they are in effect taking a stand that will affect different groups in different ways.

The potential for planning decisions to be discriminatory is very real. When a stable neighbourhood is divided by an urban expressway, or tenants with low incomes have their rooming houses demolished for high-rise apartments, or small businesses on downtown streets are forced to compete with modish underground shopping malls, it is clear that there are some who gain from a planning decision and some who lose. These sorts of situations create tensions in the planning process and affect the behaviour of participants. The long-standing utilitarian ethic of planners—to produce the greatest good for the greatest number—is often found wanting, since those who gain may be benefited differently from those who lose.

A graphic illustration of this kind of planner's dilemma is found in the situation that faced the Victoria Park neighbourhood on the southeast edge of downtown Calgary in 1992. The Calgary Stampede Board proposed an expansion of the Stampede Grounds over the entire 32 ha, 1,000-person older community that had undergone some gentrification. The main justification offered by the board was the need to sustain the economic contribution of the Stampede to the local economy, reputed to be about 20% of all tourist revenues.[17] The city's planners supported this plan and, further, argued that the community was marginal and did not deserve protection, even though their previous redevelopment plan had tried to do this. They chose to support the position the "developer" (albeit a public one) weighing the whole city's supposed economic gain against the needs of the citizens of Victoria Park, who would lose their homes and community.

The reconciliation of such positions in the realm of community planning is never easy. It is, however, to be hoped that planners recognize the moral side of issues in which they frequently find themselves working. At its best, community planning is a process in social cooperation and it will always be somewhat ungainly and time-consuming. Moreover, the search for a more effective process in social terms continues and one can expect modes of participation to be further adapted and present roles of planners and others to be further questioned.[18]

ENDNOTES

1. A useful review of the formal processes in use in each province is found in R. Audet and A. Lettenaff, *Land Planning Framework of Canada: An Overview,* Lands Directorate, Environment Canada (Ottawa, September 1983), Working Paper No. 28.
2. Paul J. Cloke, *An Introduction to Rural Settlement Planning* (London: Methuen, 1983), 3.
3. Richard B. McLagan, "Custom Negotiation and Mediation: Updating Our Planning Toolkit," *Plan Canada* 36, no. 4 (July 1996), 26–27.
4. Judith E. Innes, "Planning through Consensus Building," *Journal of the American Planning Association* 62, no. 4 (Autumn 1996), 460–472. See also Larry Susskind and Jeffery Cruikshank, *Breaking the Impasse: Consensus Approaches to Resolving Public Disputes* (New York: Basic Books, 1987).
5. Innes, "Planning through Consensus Building," 460–472.

6. Mary Gail Snyder, "Feminist Theory and Planning Theory," *Berkeley Planning Journal* 10 (1995), 91–106.

7. Penelope Gurstein, "Gender Sensitive Community Planning: A Case Study of the Planning Ourselves In Project," *Canadian Journal of Urban Research* 5, no. 2 (December 1996), 199–219.

8. McLagan, "Custom Negotiation."

9. Rolf-Richard Grauhan, "Notes on the Structure of Planning Administration," in Andreas Faludi, ed., *A Reader in Planning Theory* (Oxford: Pergamon Press, 1973), 297–316.

10. Cf. T.J. Plunkett and G.M. Betts, *The Management of Canadian Urban Government* (Kingston: Queen's University Institute of Local Government, 1978), 230–249; and C.R. Tindal and S.N. Tindal, *Local Government in Canada,* 2nd ed. (Toronto: McGraw-Hill Ryerson, 1984), 207–224.

11. Plunkett and Betts, *Management,* 247.

12. Louis N. Redman, "The Planning Process," *Managerial Planning* 31, no. 6 (May/June 1983), 24–40.

13. Grauhan, "Notes," 299.

14. John Forester, "Politics, Power, Ethics and Practice: Abiding Problems for the Future of Planning," *Plan Canada* 26, no. 9 (December 1986), 224–227.

15. John Friedmann, "Planning, Politics, and the Environment," *Journal of the American Planning Association,* 59, no. 3 (Summer 1989), 334–338.

16. Among many writers recently concerned with this issue is Matthew Kiernan, "Ideology and the Precarious Future of the Canadian Planning Profession," *Plan Canada* 22, no. 1 (March 1982), 14–24; and T.I. Gunton, "The Role of the Professional Planner," *Canadian Public Administration* 27, no. 3 (Fall 1984), 399–417.

17. Barton Reid, "The Death of Victoria Park Neighbourhood, the State of Urban Reform and the Battle of Mythologies in Calgary," *City Magazine* 13, no. 1 (Winter 1991/92), 36–42.

18. Beth Moore Milroy, "Some Thoughts about Difference and Pluralism," *Planning Theory* 7–8 (1992), 33–38.

Chapter 14　The Texture of Participation in Community Planning

Challenging public decisions could be viewed as a form of Kafkaesque base-ball. Citizen groups are always the visiting team in their own home town.
Linda Christianson-Ruffman, 1977

In the end, the effectiveness of planning in a community is more a function of the participation in the decisions about plans and regulations than of any other factors. Planning acts may prescribe a planning process, but it is people who make it a reality. A well-designed plan and a thoughtfully drafted zoning by-law must be approved and applied by members and officials of the community. And, as we have seen, the texture of participation in planning is coarse-grained. It arises out of a network of relationships among participants that can be only partially specified in advance. Ultimately, it depends upon the expertise, values, and personal characteristics of the individual participants and how they choose to play the roles assigned to them in the planning process.

Within this variegated texture of decision making for community planning there are several key participants whose behaviour is crucial to an effective planning process. Politicians, professional planners, the public, and developers compose this group. We may learn a great deal more about participation in planning, its characteristics, complexity, and vagaries, by examining these participants singly and together. This chapter provides perspectives, first, on the relationships between politicians, planners, and the public; second, on the unique role of professional planners; third, on the special place of developers; and fourth, on the need and prospects for citizen participation.

LINKING THE PUBLIC, POLITICIANS, AND PLANNERS

In this process of social cooperation called community planning, participants become linked together as they seek the common goal of an improved community. The key interrelationship is between the members of the community, the members of the local governing body, and the professional planners. The effectiveness with which this triad—public, politician, and planner—can work together will largely determine the success of the planning process in a community. Their situation is not unlike that of the distinctive Russian sleigh (*troika*). It is pulled by three horses whose energies must be balanced to achieve both forward motion and the desired direction of the sleigh. So, too, the citizenry and the municipal planners and councillors are dependent upon one another in the process to attain a plan that embodies an acceptable direction for the future of the community.

The concept and style of how to achieve a harmonious and productive blend of all participants has undergone some change in recent decades. Prior to 1960, community planning was a relatively sedate activity. Politicians received and accepted the "expert" advice of the planners; the public seemed willing to let their elected representatives judge the appropriateness of planning proposals. However, the disruptions to neighbourhoods caused by the planning responses to urban growth and deterioration—especially large redevelopment and expressway projects—changed the way in which these relationships worked. Citizens confronted politicians over proposed projects, rezonings, etc., and more workable solutions were sought from the planners by the politicians. But three decades later, in the 1990s, many of these kinds of confrontations continue. In only a few cities have the major impediments to effective citizen participation been removed, as witness the stories of meagre participation measures in recent plan-making in Winnipeg and Montreal.[1]

Two lessons for planning emerge from this experience. The first is that community planning is a *political* activity that makes choices among values and affects different segments of the community in different ways. Thus, people, groups, firms, etc., demand a voice in the decision making consistent with the venerable democratic aspirations of community planning. The second is that participation in planning decisions is not just a one-way process of communication. There needs to be a *dialogue* among all three interests. These lessons have been learned only grudgingly in some communities, especially by planners and politicians. Where they have been absorbed, the planning process features a high degree of interaction between the public, the politician, and the planner—a "six-sided triangle"

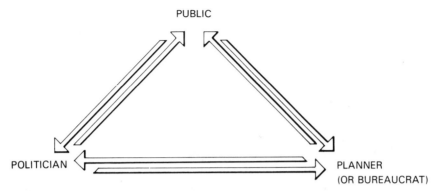

FIGURE 14.1   The Six-Sided Triangle of Planning Participation
The effectiveness of the community-planning process is largely determined by the degree to which this triad—public, politician, and planner—can work together. It may be called a process of social cooperation. *Source:* Adapted from Harry Lash, *Planning in a Human Way* (Ottawa: Ministry of Urban Affairs, Cat. No. SU32-3/1976–9). Adapted with the permission of the Minister of Public Works and Government Services 1997.

of communication, as Harry Lash has called it.[2] Figure 14.1 depicts the six important links of communication in community planning; every interest must have the potential of dialogue with each of the other two. Anything less and the effectiveness of the planning process is diminished.

But achieving a good working relationship among all three sets of participants is not a simple matter. Personal and professional expectations, mutual trust, and communications skills and preferences are at the heart of making the six-sided triangle work effectively. Planners must consider whether their role is to be that of a neutral technical advisor to the politician or that of an advocate of particular positions held within the community. Politicians must consider how and whether to invite citizens into the decision-making process, to share some of their power. Citizens must consider how to work in a constructive way with planners and politicians who make a place for them in the planning process. These are some of the threads in the fabric of this important part of the planning process. A brief examination of a few of the interrelationships between these constituencies will help fill out the pattern.

Politicians and Planners

The relationship between the politician and the professional planner is complex and, in some ways, paradoxical. It has several aspects, one of which is that of employer (politician) and employee (planner), because the planner is either on the staff hired directly by the local governing body or is hired as a consultant to the council. Another aspect is that of expert (planner) and client (politician), because the planner comes to the situation with certain socially sanctioned skills from his or her education and professional experience. In the planning process, they are each dependent upon the other, for both seek the similar end of coordinating diverse interests in the community and achieving a good quality of environment generally. Yet in this relationship tensions exist, and politicians and planners can find themselves in conflict over who should give leadership in plan-making.

The job of the politician is not well understood. Nominally, elected officials are there to represent the interests of the people in the community. But those interests are diverse and often compete with one another. Thus, the job of "representing" becomes one of reconciling and integrating the many competing demands that citizens, groups, firms, and other officials place on the local councillor. This role of the politician has been called that of "broker-mediator."[3] The politician also has to provide leadership as to the direction in which the community's development should be going, so that the competing private interests are merged into a general, community-wide interest.

The politician's job of providing leadership and resolving conflicts has some incompatible aspects. If there is conflict around an issue—for example, the closing of a neighbourhood school—the politician must try to hear as many of the competing views as possible and not make up her or his mind too early. This uncommitted stance may be scorned as failing to show leadership. But when the politician decides on a possible solution to an issue he or she may then be rebuked for being biased toward one interest. As Lash says, "On any given issue in the community, he/she cannot *lead* unless he/she is *committed* to a solution, but if there is serious conflict around an issue, he/she cannot *resolve* it if he/she is *committed*."[4]

The interests that the politician tries to bring together generally fall into two sets. One set comprises the views held by members of the community. The other comprises the advice given by the community's planners and other technical advisors. In reconciling the diverse interests in the community, the politician is very dependent upon the local staff. The issues often require an almost immediate appreciation of technical matters. It is the duty of the planner to present all the options to the politician. But, with the recommendation of one course of action, the planner then becomes a competitor for the politician's attention. This situation raises at least two ethical dilemmas for the planner regarding the option he or she advocates in the political debate. On the one hand, if the planner's position seems to support that of the politician, then citizens may lose confidence in his or her impartiality. And, on the other hand, too vociferous support for citizen positions on an issue may be seen by the politician to be at issue with those of the planner's "employer." And for the politician, it leaves the difficult task of bringing together the judgement of the "expert" and the "will of the people." At some point in the process, the relationship between the politician and the planner may shift from employer-employee to client-expert. The ease with which this shift of roles occurs depends a great deal upon the planner's concept of leadership in community planning. The planner's essential contribution to the planning process is to be able to prepare a plan for a physical development situation that integrates a multitude of public and private interests and concerns. Through training and experience the planner is in a position of "intellectual leadership" in plan-making.[5] But this training seldom equips the planner for political leadership.

Conflict can arise between the planner and the politician if the planner thinks herself or himself best fit to serve the community needs and assumes a measure of political leadership. This potential conflict is, of course, associated with the relationship that each has with the other set of participants—the public. In playing out their respective roles, the politician and the planner have both an obligation and a need to involve the public, in order that both can say they hold planning positions reflecting the community at large. The competition for the public's attention simply indicates the high degree of interdependence of the three sets of participants in the community-planning process. It can also be seen that there are few formal specifications for making these relationships work. Hence, our stress in the preceding chapter on the need for **social cooperation.**

Including the Public

There was a long democratic tradition of the community making plans for its own future through its locally elected councillors. There was likewise a tradition of public participation, where public-spirited citizens and groups advocated the need for a community plan. However, neither of these traditions provided for the direct participation of the public in actually making a plan. (The citizen participation movement will be put in perspective in the next section.) When the public is included in the making of decisions about the plan for the future community environment (as is the expectation nowadays), the relationships among all three sets of participants are affected. Both the politician and the planner must redefine their roles. With citizen involvement, the politician may no longer assume that he or she provides the best reflection of the views of the public in the planning process; the planner may no longer assume that he or she serves the public by serving only the politician.

Involving citizens in plan-making constitutes a sharing of power over the content and implementation of the plan and over the process of getting to the plan. In recent years, formal avenues of communication between the public and local government officials have been established such as public meetings and hearings. These permit the citizen to be heard, but not necessarily in a comprehensive or continuing way. Effective and full participation involves more than such one-way flows of information and also implies some citizen influence on subsequent developments in the plan.

As a result of past practices in citizen involvement, there is often the apprehension among citizens that they will be used for the politicians' own ends if they participate. As for planners, citizens often feel "talked down to," or ignored, or hampered in obtaining information. Many may feel they are not listened to at all, as numerous feminist critics have pointed out with respect to the participation of women and persons from marginal groups in planning processes.[6] (A later section discusses this more fully.) These tensions are an inevitable part of any political process where those with power are being asked to share it. Further, the planning process does not assign power to citizens, only the right to be consulted. Even though provision may be made for including citizens in plan-making decisions, the final responsibility rests with the politicians and planners to see that effective participation occurs.

Despite the conflicts and difficulties, the relationships between citizens, politicians, and planners are essential to the planning process. The reasons are quite simple. The citizens are a primary source of information about the problems that are being experienced by the community, about the impacts of proposed solutions, and about the values and aspirations of community members. The politicians and planners, on the other hand, know the resources that are available to solve problems, the limits of knowledge about project impacts, and the institutional and procedural avenues that must be observed.

The politician is the key actor in determining the form participation will take and whether it will be positive, for it is the politician's ultimate decision-making prerogative, with regard to issues and options, that would be opened up to scrutiny. The politician must come to believe that public participation will enhance his or her ability to resolve conflict and provide leadership, in other words, to know the community better. When the public is included, there are sometimes risks for the planners: "expert" opinions may have to be justified to "non-expert" citizens, uncertainties may have to be acknowledged, and information may have to be shared. In short, another party is brought into the decision making, and this always complicates the resolution of issues. As the six-sided triangle in Figure 14.1 shows,

"We want real community participation in this decision. Plan A is too expensive. Plan C is inefficient. Now, which plan do you prefer?"

there are *three times* as many interactions to consider if citizens participate than if the planner and politician are the only participants.

The triangle of public-politician-planner can lead, as does any three-sided relationship, to unequal coalitions and resulting stress. If the politicians come to rely more on the citizens' views than on those of the planner, the latter may feel that his or her technical competence is being devalued. Politicians may come to distrust their staff planners, fearing that they will cater to citizen groups espousing different political ideas. Citizens, for their part, often learn that they cannot expect their recommendations always to be accepted by politicians and planners. Indeed, each of the participants has much to learn, not only about the others, but also about the planning process and its possible outcomes when seen through others' eyes.

Thus, to social cooperation must be added **social learning** as another important characteristic of community planning.

ROLES OF THE PLANNER

In many ways, the community-planning process centres upon the professional planner. Although not necessarily the one to initiate the process, the planner soon becomes responsible for sustaining it, for shaping it so that plans, policies, and programs emerge to guide future physical development. It can be said that it is in the planner's own interest to carry out the task. Nevertheless, it is a demanding task, involving interaction with all the other participants in the planning process. The planner, it must not be forgotten, plays a multifaceted role in a political milieu.

Four basic roles, as originally identified by Daland and Parker, constitute the scope of the planner's task: (1) the planner as leader (or representative) of the planning agency, (2) the planner as representative of the planning profession, (3) the planner as political innovator, and (4) the planner as citizen educator.[7] Each of these roles may be played differently, depending upon the individual planner's personal disposition. Different communities may call for the emphasis to be placed on one role rather than another, and in some cases other participants might substitute for the planner. Also, the emphasis has changed, and continues to change, as planning theory and ideology evolves. Gunton has identified eight variations of planners' roles, for example.[8] However, this four-role model is helpful, as variable as the circumstances may be, in examining the range of relationships that the planner maintains with others in the planning process.

As **planning-agency leader**, the planner must be concerned with the organizational base from which he or she operates. This involves not only the staffing and morale of the agency but also its status and relationships with community groups, governmental organizations, and developers. The planning agency must be accepted as an essential part of the governmental machinery if the goals of planning are to be achieved. Thus, the planner must develop the confidence of elected and appointed officials and the public about the necessity of planning. The stance of the planner in regard to private developers must also be measured here. This means developing relationships of trust, cooperation, and encouragement with each of these groups. It means being able to obtain a budget for the planning agency that is adequate and, just as important, to cultivate channels of communication for obtaining information for planning and directing attention to planning problems.[9]

The effectiveness of the planner, whether as director or staff member, is closely linked with the credibility of the planning agency. The maintenance or improvement of the credibility is, in turn, affected by the conduct of the planner in the course of carrying out each planning task. The social and political relations of the planning agency itself, by which it is either welcomed or excluded in promoting planning solutions with developers, other agencies, or the public, must be perceived by the planner as a routine part of the task. Allies as well as enemies, cooperators as well as antagonists, must be located. Planners thus need skills that go beyond the technical knowledge of planning. They need to be able to work with others and develop trust and support for the agency and its views. This is especially cogent for planning professionals whose agency's development proposals will not be carried out by them but by others (e.g., engineers, lawyers, architects).

Not to be overlooked in this particular role is the bureaucratic milieu in which the staff planner works. Municipalities and other forms of government that employ planners have hierarchical structures which assure that major decisions are taken by elected officials and tactical decisions within the agency are taken by department heads. As Filion notes, this hierarchical form of decision making "slows the planning process and reduces planners' capacity to make commitments."[10] Another Canadian observer points out that "senior managers and department directors usually have far more experience in government than the politicians and considerable skill in exercising control outside the purview of the elected officials."[11] So, being a "leader" for some significant reform may be a challenge for the planner.

As **technical advisor**, the planner brings to the community-planning job the values and standards of the planning profession. By virtue of education and training, she or he learns how to approach planning situations, each of which is unique in some respect. It is the planner's knowledge of theory and practice that helps to bridge the gap between current planning needs and circumstances and the longer-run need of preparing viable plans. The community looks to the planner to provide these skills and experience to organize the particular planning task. In doing so, the planner employs approaches that are consistent with the outlook and practice of the planning profession. In an important way, a planner is a representative of professional mores and doctrine as well as a member of the community's technical staff.

It will be recalled that planning practice involves both technical and social organizing skills. On the one hand, the planner uses accepted technical skills in research and design. On the other hand, the planner must also organize the process that will be followed, including who will participate, when, and to what extent. In the latter case, the planner generally will invoke the professionally accepted values of governmental responsibility, democratic planning, public participation, etc. These values also change. Thus, planners tend nowadays to advocate widespread public participation on the principle that this will make planning more effective. This may draw objections from politicians who wish a narrower context for planning decisions. It is a delicate, if not impossible, task for the planner to balance the value of being a neutral technical advisor and the social values of the profession. Thus, planners often refine this role according to the theoretical or ideological view they espouse. Gunton, recognizing this tendency, has identified such roles as "social reformer," "advocate," "referee," and "social learner."[12]

A dominant view of the planning profession is that the planner's primary obligation is to serve the public interest.[13] This is related to the notion that community members share certain underlying personal and group interests with regard to the subjects that planning deals with as well as the way it deals with them. For example, it may be argued that it is in the interests of all the community to acquire parkland today to ensure that it is available for future generations and, similarly, that means of public participation are in everyone's interests to ensure that issues are properly aired. The planner adopts this stance in order to fulfil the mandate of serving all the community and not only the interests of one group. But it is not an easy stance to defend because it depends upon deciding *who defines the public interest.* Quite simply, there is no ready mechanism for doing this. Politicians will argue that voters have sanctioned their views; citizen groups will argue that their grass-roots views truly reflect the public interest; and planners may argue that their comprehensive view of the community provides the basis for such a definition. Clearly, there is ample room for conflict among participants in whichever definition the planner adopts. Probably most important in this tenuous situation is that the planner does not argue for his or her own purposes, but for openness in hearing all interests and facing all issues.[14]

As a **political innovator**, the planner pursues the acceptance of planning ideas and proposals by those persons in the community with the influence and authority to act on them. All planning activity involves changes in the community, either in the short or long run, and requires approval by the governing body. Even where the changes are slight, there will be some political pressure to resist or delay the change. Affected landowners may protest; politicians may be reluctant to commit capital expenditures; other department heads may have competing proposals. Getting planning proposals accepted often means changing the political climate in the community toward new ideas. The planner, therefore, is frequently called upon to promote proposals in such a way as to bring about political innovation.

In general, in every community there is a reasonably well-defined group whose support is crucial to those political innovations that would interest the planner. They are sometimes referred to as the "influentials," and may comprise elected politicians and appointed officials, as well as others outside the local government whose views are often sought. In some situations, the influence of such special groups as chambers of commerce, environmental organizations, property owners, and tenant associations may also have to be taken into account in order to gain acceptance of planning proposals. The planner will usually try to identify all actors with a specific interest in a proposal and predict their reaction to it. Then the planner will have to consider the steps to take that will improve the chances that the plan or other proposals will be accepted. These may include the timing of proposals, the structure of participation, the use of outside advisors, the establishment of elite advisory committees, selected pre-release consultations, and even overt political pressure. This role implies the possible need of the planner to adapt to political realities. There are limits to this adaptation, however, as modifications to plans may begin to conflict with the planner's professional standards or the integrity of the planning agency start to be threatened.

As **citizen educator**, the planner seeks to affect the basic attitudes and values of the community at large regarding the benefits and consequences of planning. The planner is obliged to do this given his or her commitment to the broader public interest. The extent to which it is undertaken will depend upon the degree of tolerance for new ideas in the community. Communities vary in this regard depending upon their previous experience with planning and development, their cultural milieu, and their perception of resources that might be needed. The planner needs to be aware of the factors affecting attitudes toward planning and also of the avenues available to enlarge the area of tolerance in the particular community.

Specific techniques include publications about planning, dissemination of information through the media, personal contacts by the planning staff, speeches, public meetings, neighbourhood drop-in centres, and provision of planning services and information to citizen groups. Some planners have become quite inventive in seeking widespread participation. Vancouver's planners, when preparing CityPlan in the mid-1990s, the new overall plan for the city, created the opportunity for small groups of people to discuss planning issues. Each group, called a CityCircle, was supplied information kits and a facilitator and the language of the community was used when requested.[15] Over 200 such groups formed; they made submissions that were put into an "Ideas Book," which was then used in a city-wide Ideas Fair. It is estimated that 20,000 citizens (out of 400,000) took part in this process. Calgary followed a similar process in its GoPlan transportation planning.[16]

The citizen-educator role is an extension of the planner's professional ethos in democratic planning. But it may also be related to the need for political innovation so that community influentials will feel more prone or able to accept planning proposals. In a community without previous experience with planning, a public education program may be essential at the outset along with efforts to build confidence in the new planning agency. Indeed, all four roles tend to be played concurrently, with the emphasis shifting as the planning needs change.

The four roles we have been describing provide only the broad institutional parameters of the planner's participation in the planning process. Within this institutional context, there are a number of specific roles that a planner might play. In a planning agency requiring several planners, some will function as plan-makers and others as researchers, regulators, or managers. The scope of their contacts with other participants outside the planning agency will differ, and so too their possible perception of the outcome of the process. Some will come in contact more with the public, with developers, with elected officials, or with other agencies. Increasingly in recent years, it has been noted that planners practise in relation to a variety of special interest groups, settings, and regulatory systems, and may be seen as technical staff, evaluators, and advocates.[17]

In turn, each planner brings to the particular role individual differences in outlook that affect the way in which the role is actually played. Research into planning practice indicates that the individual planner tends to fashion his or her own concept of how the role should be played.[18] Planners thus "frame their role" according to personal views of the problem at hand and to preferred courses of action in solving problems, especially in conjunction with others. Planning practice is still evolving, both in relation to changes in the role that planning plays in our society and in relation to planners' own understanding of planning processes.

ASPECTS OF DEVELOPER PARTICIPATION

A very large part of community planning is involved with anticipating and responding to the initiatives of persons and firms outside the institutional milieu whom we may call **developers.** This is a generic term referring to those individuals and groups who make the decisions to convert raw land to urban use and/or to convert an already existing use to a different use (sometimes called redevelopment). The developer's role, broadly, is to satisfy the demand for new space for such establishments as homes, factories, stores, offices, schools, etc. This is a key role in the overall process of cre-

Steps Taken by Developer	Participants				
	(a) Active	**(b)** Passive	**(c)** Consultants	**(d)** Intermediaries	**(e)** Regulators
1. Land acquisition	–land owner(s) –land developer	–lenders	–appraisers –lawyers	–realtors –lawyers –assembly agents	
2. Site preparation	–land developer	–land owner(s) –lenders	–planners –engineers –architects –lawyers		–planning board –council –ministry –appeal body
3. Project production	–builder	–land developer –mortgage lender	–architects	–mortgage brokers	–building inspectors
4. Project marketing	–builder –consumer	–mortgage lender	–lawyers	–realtors –lawyers	

FIGURE 14.2   **Participants in the Development of an Urban Project**
Many different individuals, groups, and professions participate in bringing a project to fruition, and their roles differ according to the stage of development: (a) *active* participants have a financial interest in the land and are directly involved in improving its value; (b) *passive* participants also have a financial interest in the land and/or improvements, but are not actively involved in the development; (c) *consultants* are called in by active participants to advise on technical and legal aspects; (d) *intermediaries* act as a liaison between active and passive participants; (e) *regulators* represent the public's interests, and their approval is required for the project to go ahead. *Source:* Simon B. Chamberlain, *Aspects of Developer Behaviour in the Land Development Process* (Toronto: University of Toronto Centre for Urban and Community Studies, 1972), Research Paper No. 56.

ating the future physical environment. Thus, community planning and **community building,** the activity of the developer, are closely entwined.

The developer is the central actor in the process by which a piece of land is turned into buildings and other usable spaces. It is a complex process that usually involves a number of persons and firms—land assemblers, builders, site planners, mortgage lenders, and realtors among them. However, it is the developer (an individual or a firm) who makes the decisions about whether a project will go ahead and when. The process of development occurs in a series of four discernible stages, each of which comprises its own set of participants (Figure 14.2): (1) land acquisition, (2) site preparation, (3) project production, and (4) project marketing.[19]

Planning Issue 14.1

PLANNING OR BLACKMAIL?

In the City of Toronto, a group known as Downtown Action agreed to withdraw an appeal respecting an approval of a 68-storey $400,000,000 development known as Scotia Plaza, if the developer, Campeau Corporation, paid $2,000,000 to the Cooperative Housing Federation of Toronto for building low-income housing. There was no authority in legislation for demanding the payment of the money. Prior to its approval of the same development, the City of Toronto secured an agreement from Campeau to build a day-care centre in the Scotia Plaza. There is no provision in the Ontario Planning Act for the imposition of such a condition upon the approval of a development. Have we reached the situation where planning has become blackmail? The payment of the money and the building of the day-care centre were both for the same purpose—to secure a speedy approval of the project. Are we in a situation where developers have to buy planning permission? Should developments not be accepted or rejected on their merits, and not upon the extra legislative concessions forced out of a developer?

These questions raise fundamental issues regarding rule of law values, fairness, and equity in planning. One goal of the legal system is to insure those persons subject to legal rules—be they zoning by-laws, tax legislation, or contract law—have an opportunity to know what the rules are and to have the rules apply uniformly. If this happens, then individuals will not be granted favours or have inordinate burdens placed upon them. This value is clearly at the basis of zoning. Zones are supposed to be set out in advance. Regulations are to apply uniformly to all property owners in a zone, and development occurs not because of blackmail or favouritism but because of the uniform application of zoning laws. The imposition of requirements on a case-by-case or negotiated basis for the payment of money or the construction of non-authorized facilities runs sharply against this value.

However, it is also clear that negotiations dealing with developments on a case-by-case basis are an important part of planning today. All provinces have subdivision control procedures that allow the imposition of conditions, which may vary from subdivision to subdivision. Indeed, the Ontario Municipal Board, in reviewing the imposition of lot levies pursuant to subdivision approval, has stated that levies must be reasonably related to development. This is an attempt to individualize the levies and not have a levy of uniform application.

Yet there are some serious concerns about the Toronto situation in particular and the imposition of conditions generally. Firstly, it is important that where publicly elected bodies such as municipal councils are exercising authority, they do so within the legislative power given. They should not consciously attempt to exceed their powers and impose conditions not authorized by legislation. If no authority is granted to impose levies, for example, they should not be imposed. If day-care centres cannot be required under the law, they should not be required.

Secondly, because a system of discretionary control is open to abuse, the imposition of conditions should only be done in accordance with the provisions of an official or municipal plan, and as much information as possible should be made public before and after a deal is made.

In conclusion, negotiations, the imposition of conditions, and the treating of different developers and developments differently is not in itself wrong. These powers are important aspects of discretionary planning control, although they do not reflect rule of law values. There is great benefit from the $2,000,000 payment and the day-care centre extracted from Campeau. It is important, however, that these controls, since they are open to abuse, are exercised within the scope and purpose of planning legislation and adopted plans and in an open and accountable manner.

Source: Excerpted from Stanley Makuch, "Planning or Blackmail?" *Plan Canada* 25, no. 1 (March 1985), 8–9.

The stage at which a developer usually becomes involved in the planning process is **site preparation**. When it has been decided to proceed with a project, the next steps will require some physical and legal changes to the parcel of land. Physically, the site may require existing buildings to be demolished, excavations, and provision of roads, sewers, and water supply. Legal changes may be needed in the form of official approvals for subdivision, zoning, and building construction. Most of these physical and legal changes are under the control of public bodies. Municipalities may exer-

cise various kinds of development control as well as require financial contracts to provide basic utilities.

Each application for approval by the developer involves personal interaction with public officials, especially planners. What ensues is a complex
negotiation-bargaining situation. The developer seeks approvals that
will keep the project plans intact. The municipality seeks, where necessary,
to modify any aspects of a project that will require undue expenditures of
public funds or infringe on public rights of access. The planners may also
try to persuade the developer to include more amenities in the project for
the occupants and the public, such as more open space. In large cities and
in large projects in particular, the bargaining between developers and planners has become very complex, with various trade-offs being made.[20]

Planners may offer bonuses, such as additional height on office building
projects, in return for the provision of a public plaza; or land may be given
by the developer in return for closing a public right-of-way; or a heritage
building may be retained in return for other concessions. Even citizen
groups may become involved in such bargaining, as when a large office project in Toronto was stalled in order to obtain money from the developer for
low-income housing[21](see Planning Issue 14.1).

The often intense negotiations between developers and planners in the
site preparation stage indicate the strong mutuality of the two participants.
One observer has termed it a "symbiotic interrelationship" in which the following occurs:[22]

1. Planners prepare plans basically intended to modify, but heavily influenced by and building on, what developers already do; and
2. Developers make their development decisions based on their interactions with planners and their knowledge of what planners will accept.

In situations involving the development of raw land, most of the bargaining will be done by the developer and the planner, along with other
municipal officials, and be "obscure" to both politicians and the public.[23]
In redevelopment situations, where the local populace has a strong interest in maintaining the status quo, a good deal of the bargaining may be subject to public scrutiny and public input as well.[24]

INVOLVING THE COMMUNITY IN PLANNING

Some Precedents

The participation of citizens in community planning, which today is common in Canada (although to varying degrees), has taken several different

forms over the history of modern planning. In the first decade of this century, the impetus for planning often arose from such community groups as boards of trade and arts organizations. Influenced by City Beautiful concepts and impressed by the progressive image of planning, these elite groups hired planners to prepare a plan that could be presented to the community to persuade it to launch its own planning activities. Thomas Adams, while with the Commission of Conservation in the century's second decade, actively promoted the formation of "civic beautification committees" that might lend support for planning in their municipality. In the 1920s, using the provisions of new planning acts, many municipalities established town-planning commissions to prepare master plans and zoning by-laws. The appointed members of these commissions were usually selected from the real estate and construction industries or other lines of commerce. (See chapters 3 and 4.)

Immediately after World War II, with the financial support of the Central Mortgage and Housing Corporation, a nation-wide citizens' planning organization was established. The **Community Planning Association of Canada** (CPAC) functioned to promote the advantages of planning for Canadian cities and towns with citizens, local and non-local government, and the business community. It published a national magazine, organized national planning conferences as well as regional ones, and lobbied all three levels of government about good and bad planning practices. CPAC was organized with a national office and staff, provincial divisions, and local chapters. Membership was open to everyone and comprised citizens, planning professionals, municipal councillors, planning board members, and representatives of business and industry.

In the 30 years of the group's existence, CPAC was influential in many ways in creating a favourable climate for community planning in Canada. It promoted changes in federal legislation, advocated the introduction of planning education programs, led efforts to establish local planning departments, and lobbied for metropolitan government, to list a few of its accomplishments. No little credit is due to the CPAC volunteers who dedicated much time and effort to making people and governments more accepting of community planning throughout Canada. CPAC was an appropriate vehicle for its time, when awareness about planning was needed and elementary structures had to be established.

It is something of a paradox that the success of CPAC in promoting planning contributed to the decline of the organization. CPAC advocated planning when little or none was being done, in the 1940s and early 1950s. By the late 1960s, when planning was quite pervasive, proposals by planners began to be questioned, often vociferously, by citizens. CPAC was at a disadvantage in the emerging era of "citizen activism," "participatory democracy," and "advocacy planning." In part, this was due to its role as handmaiden to the planning establishment. It was also due to CPAC's organization, which favoured provincial and national levels rather than local involvement. The new citizen participants offered instead a critique of community-planning concepts and practice, and they often started with a very local perspective.

Although community planning developed with strong democratic principles, its early years did not feature a high degree of citizen involvement. The traditions it followed were those of *representative* local government, using advisory groups where elected and appointed officials felt the need of their support. It was more planning *for* people than *with* them or, as it was once referred to, "participation by invitation." To be fair, the same tendencies pervaded almost all government activities at the time.

Pervasive Participation

For a variety of reasons, there was dissatisfaction over the outcome of much planning in the 1945–1965 period. In coping with vast urban growth, the planning solutions were often large scale and disruptive: expressways sliced through residential and park areas; old neighbourhoods were levelled for new office and apartment complexes or public housing projects; new shopping centres either displaced old commercial areas or dispersed the new populations, or both. Moreover, the solution to one planning problem not infrequently created other problems for which "more of the same" seemed to many citizens to be the planners' prescription. And, in the wake, public transit was usually ignored if not dismantled, farmland was forced out of production if not built over, and air and water environments deteriorated.

Incongruous though it may seem, the advent of widespread public participation was not a movement against planning. Successful planning efforts were visible, and the benefits of planning public expenditures and private development amply demonstrated. The concern was mostly over the conduct of planning—that it was too limited in the alternatives it considered and that it left out of the decision-making process those most likely to be affected. The call for public participation was, in effect, a demand to share in the decisions over planning goals, policies, and programs. Planning decisions were seen not only as important in themselves, but also as crucial to the multitude of regulatory and administrative decisions needed to implement a plan.

Throughout Canada, planning proposals became issues for public debate. Beginning in the larger cities, projects for new expressways, residential redevelopment, high-rise offices, civic centres, and airport extensions were criticized by citizen groups. Some protests were protracted and rancorous. Many of the disputes became nationally known and celebrated in books.[25] Their names were synonymous with the victory or defeat of planning ideas, depending upon which side one was on in the strenuous political debate that surrounded them: for example, the battles over the Spadina Expressway and Trefann Court urban renewal in Toronto, over the redevelopment of such neighbourhoods as Quinpool Road in Halifax, Lower Town in Ottawa, and Sunnyside in Calgary, over Pacific Centre in Vancouver and Concordia Village in Montreal, to cite some of the well-known ones. Smaller cities had their instances of confrontations over development proposals and rural areas, too, as environmental concerns became more prominent.

As citizen participation became more pervasive, it stimulated a number of significant changes in the conduct of community planning. Some were formal, such as new provisions that were written into provincial planning acts to ensure avenues for public comment and consultation. Many municipalities instituted new channels of communication with citizen groups and, in general, made their planning processes more open with public meetings, newsletters, etc. Citizens learned how to organize themselves to work within the various political and legal arenas of planning, as well as to draw attention to their views outside institutional venues. Not a few ran for municipal council and were elected. Professional planners mounted public participation programs to tap more effectively citizen views and to involve citizens in planning decisions. In other words, the traditional participants— the politicians, the planners, and other bureaucrats—began to shift their positions in order to accommodate citizens at the plan-making table.

Degrees of Participation

The successes of citizen participation have not always been easily won, and there is still less than unanimous support for the practice. While participation of community members in their government is applauded in principle, it is not always so in actuality. The reason for the restrained acceptance is that public participation amounts to citizens being able to share the power over planning decisions. It means that citizens can join politicians, planners, and other bureaucrats in determining how goals and policies are set regarding the future of the community. Of course, those mandated to make such decisions may find this a difficult situation, especially given that the citizens, in the end, have no legal or ethical responsibility for the outcome.

Citizen participation is not a unitary concept: that is, power may be shared with citizens in different degrees. It may vary according to the needs of the decision situation and the disposition of those in control of making decisions. In its most modest form, citizens are informed of planning proposals and asked to respond. More power is shared when, for example, citizen advisory committees are employed in the planning process; still greater power is shared when citizens are delegated to make plans. Again, legal and practical considerations may limit the sharing of planning power, but participation may also be deliberately constrained by those holding power so that it becomes nothing more than an empty ritual.

The different degrees of citizen participation are readily discerned in a "ladder of citizen participation," a still-valid concept propounded by Arnstein almost three decades ago.[26] There are eight rungs on the ladder, each corresponding to the degree to which citizens could share power in government decision making (Figure 14.3). This broad typology has been widely used in other areas besides planning in which citizen involvement has become an issue, for example, health care, education, and the environment.

The two bottom rungs describe levels of "non-participation," or ways of avoiding sharing any planning power:

1. **Manipulation** may be practised when participation is organized to "educate" and persuade citizens to already decided-upon plans and programs in order to gain support for them. Citizen committees with no mandate, even to give advice, may be simply "public relations" vehicles for plans and planners.

2. **Therapy** refers to the practice of engaging citizens in diversionary activities that will "cure" them of their concerns over basic flaws and injustices. This rung is seldom encountered in community planning in full-blown form, but there may be gradations of it in "workshops" provided for citizen members of planning boards.

3. **Informing** is the first level at which the planning process is opened up to citizens. Information is supplied to them on the nature of the planning task, its schedule, and the role of citizens. At its best, responses of citizens will be sought and facilitated. At its worst, this stage will feature only one-way means of communication, such as the use of printed or news media formats, combined with legalistic and technical jargon.

4. **Consultation** occurs when there are explicit means used to obtain the views of citizens, such as through attitude surveys and public meetings. However, while at this level citizens are given the opportunity to be heard, they are not assured of being adequately understood. The design of questionnaires and their interpretation may require some forms of feedback and additional dialogue with citizens, for example.

5. **Placation** refers to forms of participation where citizens are heard but may not be heeded. A notable effort at this level of participation was

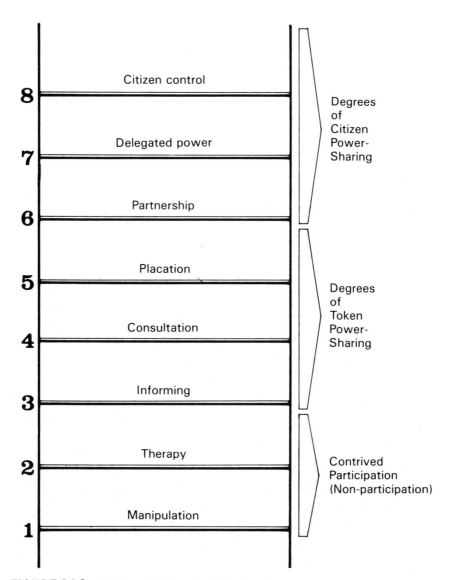

FIGURE 14.3   **Ladder of Citizen Participation**
Citizen participation involves the sharing of power over planning decisions with members of the community. This may vary according to the needs of the decision situation and the disposition of those in control of planning decisions to share their power. *Source:* Adapted from Sherry R. Arnstein, "A Ladder of Citizen Participation," *Journal of the American Institute of Planners* 35 (July 1969), 216–224. Adapted by permission of the Journal.

the system of nine citizen policy committees used to advise the governing board of the Greater Vancouver Regional District in the preparation of its 1970s metropolitan planning policies. Committees were provided with technical assistance by staff planners; however, the politicians only "received" their reports and did not debate them, thereby relegating the citizens to a token advisory role.[27]

6. **Partnership** involves an agreement to share responsibilities for planning through joint policy boards or committees. Often used to resolve impasses, such mechanisms allow citizens to influence the outcome of the plan by their votes (on preliminary if not final versions). The City of Toronto successfully used working committees a number of times in the 1970s in contentious planning situations. All neighbourhood interests were invited to sit on a committee, with area aldermen and planning staff, to formulate an acceptable plan that could be presented to the city council.

7. **Delegated power** gives citizens dominant decision-making responsibility over a plan or program, usually from the outset. The traditional planning board or commission, with a majority of appointed citizen members and legislative authority to prepare the community plan, is an ideal example of this level of participation. More recently, many communities with urban renewal grants under the federal Neighbourhood Improvement Program established committees dominated by residents of the designated area to recommend program expenditures.

8. **Citizen control** is a level at which citizens govern a program or project in all its policy and managerial aspects. Although this is not likely in regard to preparing a community-wide plan, instances of citizen control are found in cooperative and other citizen non-profit housing developments throughout the country. Community groups that obtain grants from senior governments for recreation facilities also operate at this level, as did for example a group in Kingston, Ontario, that designed and constructed a public waterfront walkway.

Using Public Input

There is little question that community planning will continue to draw citizens to participate in it. If they are not accorded a viable role, they may unceremoniously insist on it. People nowadays are reluctant to give up full control over their environment. Nevertheless, how to include citizens effectively is yet another question. It is a process that involves a good deal of mutual trust and confidence among all participants, characteristics that cannot be legislated or easily institutionalized.

Given the inherent value of including citizens, participants from the political and professional realms will, therefore, need to cope with a number of aspects that can never be fully resolved. One that frequently surfaces is the **representativeness** of those citizens who participate. Experience shows that they are bound to be small in number and proportion of the population. But counting heads will not ascertain whether they are an isolated activist faction or a good cross-section of the public. Regardless of whom or how many they represent, those who do get involved bring the views of truly interested citizens, and these are valid in and of themselves. The issue of representativeness is possibly more crucial when it comes to selecting a few citizens to sit on committees. For those making the appointments, there will be questions of the completeness of the representation; for those appointed, there is the matter of to whom they are accountable.

The issue of **accountability** pervades the practice of citizen participation, because citizens cannot be held legislatively or professionally responsible for their decisions. This should not, however, be used to restrict public participation, since final authority in municipal matters always rests with the elected council. It may simply require a limitation to participation no higher than the partnership level. On the part of citizen participants, they will want to be assured that any limits placed on their role are not just a form of co-optation, where their involvement mainly serves the purpose of making the decision process appear broad-based. And, it must be noted, citizens have a duty to act responsibly when they become involved. There are many incidents of neighbourhood "protectionism," sometimes referred to as NIMBY-ism ("not-in-my-back-yard"), that seem ill-informed. This facet of participation is discussed more fully in the next chapter.

Not only may public participation not occur in the scope and form hoped for; it may not happen at all. Participation is a voluntary act; it can be promoted but not guaranteed. Given their experience, the poor and cultural or ethnic minorities may feel powerless to influence decisions. Middle-class citizens may choose not to participate out of cynicism or apathy. Deliberate efforts to promote participation have had only limited success, especially where the plans are for the distant future. People respond much more readily to changes in their immediate environment than to large, remote projects or abstract plans. Moreover, organized groups of citizens are known to avoid devoting much time to pre-planning exercises, preferring to save their resources for more immediate decision-making stages.

WOMEN AND COMMUNITY PLANNING

Public participation in the planning process has, until recently, not distinguished the nature of the participants except by their place of residence.

While attention came to be paid to neighbourhood differences, differences between "neighbours" were not usually considered. Neither gender nor other human characteristics such as age, economic status, literacy, and cultural background were taken into account by officials when framing provincial procedures for participation or by most local planners when conducting participatory processes in their communities. There was just the *public* being involved, an undifferentiated human category. Yet the public is a very diverse collectivity.

Many women, for example, are excluded from public participation processes, as feminist critics freqently note.[28] This exclusion can come from two sides. It may happen because the process is not made physically accessible to women (the time of day of meetings, the need for child care, the availability of transportation, etc.). The planning process may also fail to take into account women's knowledge of the city, their experience from their daily lives.[29] Planners have tended to rely on expert, technical data about land use that can result in so-called objective, rational, universal knowledge. Thus, the knowledge that comes from the personal experience of women —such as safety on the streets, difficulties with mass transit, or scarcity of affordable housing for a single-parent family—has had little or no place in the planning process. In the eyes of some observers, the knowledge planners do use, therefore, has a male/professional bias.[30]

There are a number of cogent issues regarding community planning that arise from this critique. Perhaps the primary one is the need to shift the perspective on the substance of planning from mainly land use and spatial relations to include social and personal relations: that is, to consider relations that come out a perspective of "home" and its role in people's lives rather than the physical attribute of "housing"; relations that come out of a "community" perspective rather than just a physical "neighbourhood" perspective. Such perspectives call for dealing with **aspatial** concerns, things that one can't always put on a typical planning map. A Vancouver project that involved women in the planning of their own neighbourhood alerted planners about the need for things like crosswalks, street lighting, community meeting spaces, "latch key" programs, recycling, and a crisis centre.[31]

This relates to another major issue about how to obtain such "data" through public participation processes that may be either physically or intellectually inaccessible. This applies often to women, as we noted, whose knowledge from personal experience is undervalued. It argues for citizen participation in planning to be able to acknowledge "alternative images" of the community, to become more interactive and collaborative.[32] Both these issues presage a more general issue of accommodating a broader, less

Planning Issue 14.2

SAFE CITY IDEA SPREADS—WINNIPEG WORKSHOP
The Urban Safety Project

On April 25th, 1991 at a midday forum and an evening workshop on the theme "A Safer City for Women," a group of about seventy persons, mainly women, were informed about the Urban Safety Project that has been underway in Winnipeg during the winter of 1990–91. ...

The plenary and group discussions covered a multitude of issues and possible improvements for a safer city. As a way of representing the discussion I have created the following interview with a woman "participant."

Interviewer: Is Winnipeg a safe city?
Woman: Winnipeg is still considered to be a fairly safe city but when you consider the rising crime statistics against women and children it is hard to ignore the fact that there is good reason to be concerned about violence both in the public streets and in the privacy of people's homes.

Interviewer: Is sexual assault the most serious crime against women?
Woman: Statistically sexual assault and rape are rising and there is a greater number of cases of women being beaten and murdered. The target is women, young and old alike. Sadly too many women are dying after violent attacks from partners and men they have trusted. But in my opinion, as terrible as the truth about violence is, I think the worst crime against women is the fact that we have not been listened to and not been taken seriously when we have been telling our women's experiences and justifiable fears of living in urban areas that are not suited to our needs as single women, mothers and older women. We haven't been able to tell our whole story or to relate our true fear.

Interviewer: Why is this important?
Woman: The issues of violence against women and children whether it is sexual assault, family violence, economic assault, or social degradation, are just the outward signs that women do not have a safe place in society as equal and full human beings. Women do not have the economic and social status that men enjoy and as a result continue in a cycle of poverty and victimization. Our

needs have been made invisible. Even the women who have 'made it' are part of the statistics—violence knows no class or racial boundary. The target is women.

Interviewer: You had a chance to hear the speakers at the midday panel and in the evening, what impressed you the most?

Woman: I have always been comfortable living and working in the downtown area of the city. The core area was the neighbourhood where I was raised and where I chose to return to raise my children. We like to walk, bike ride and be part of the hubbub, using some common sense and a belief that we had a right to move freely. ... A work sheet we were asked to fill out asked "What are 5 things that I do on a regular basis to ensure my safety?" I was amazed to discover how many things easily came to mind. Over the years I had developed so many safety strategies that really limited my freedom and enjoyment of life in the city, day or night. It reminded me that women start to learn fear early and need to protect themselves for the rest of their or their children's lives. ...

Interviewer: What are the areas of concern?

Woman: Public transportation and access to help, prevention programs and street-proofing for children, design problems, police responsiveness, issues of family violence and not being listened to. Of major concern in Winnipeg was violence against native women.

Interviewer: What is going to happen to the report of the Winnipeg Fact Finding Group on Urban Safety for Women and Children?

Woman: ... The Winnipeg group will make its own recommendations for planning policies and implementing municipal strategies for preventing public violence and making our neighbourhoods safer. Finally they will be listening to women—*for a change!*

Angela Mulgrew is a community consultant in Winnipeg and a Masters student in City Planning at the University of Manitoba.

Source: Excerpted from Angela Mulgrew, "Safe City Idea Spreads—Winnipeg Workshop," *City Magazine* 12, no. 3 (Summer 1991), 6–7. Published with permission of *New City Magazine* (formerly *City Magazine*).

routine, more subjective approach in planning practice. The ideals of social justice, equity and democracy are not foreign to planners, but they are often not manifested in actual practice. If they can be realized, then, not only women but other marginalized citizens (e.g., the elderly, youth, ethnic minorities, the disabled) will also benefit.

PLANNING AND CONSENSUS BUILDING

In the end, a community plan's success will be determined by the extent to which individuals and groups in the community agree with it, especially when it comes time to implement it. Many a plan remains on the shelf because key interests did not have a direct role in framing it and will not support it. Much has been written in the planning literature about how to achieve agreement,[33] or about whether it is even possible to do so.[34] The issue that has arisen more and more in the past two decades is how can the overall community plan achieve support from individuals and groups that make up the community? And this support, or agreement, is vital if the plan is to come to fruition through community discussion and actions.

In many fields besides community planning (e.g., health care, the environment, the economy), the promise of order and certainty have been competing with stagnation and conflict and pressures to re-examine fundamentals, as the past two decades have unfolded. The need to confront these unsettling conditions, fortuitously, has spawned a variety of ways to address complex and controversial public issues that involve multiple interests. Methods of negotiation and mediation referred to in earlier chapters grew out of the need to resolve disputes that occurred during implementation of a plan or other public policy.[35]

Refinements to these methods have led to broader, more democratic approaches that can be used at the beginning of the planning process and and that have the result of achieving agreement and support among the various interests about implementation. In general, these **consensual approaches,** as we call them, aim to reach mutually beneficial agreements about planning issues.[36]

Most of these methods have two essential features. The first concerns process: rather than the formal, vertical approach where, typically, "solutions" (i.e., motions) are debated using parliamentary procedures, consensus building tends to work horizontally, with discussion, not votes, on principles and criteria that would provide a framework for reaching agreement on solutions to issues. The former generates and heightens differences among participants and does not ensure that all viewpoints will be expressed and explored. The latter, consensus building, provides for knowledge, experience, ideas, and concerns to be shared among equal participants and accumulated as part of the solution. A consensus is thus achieved in which all participants have been partners and share a concern over the solution, say, the community plan, and its future disposition.

The second major feature of the consensus-building approach is the extensive array of participants who are involved, who tend to be referred to as **stakeholders**. Indeed, consensual approaches are assumed to work best when the discourse is broad and not limited by professional rank or social or electoral status. So, if all groups or individuals "with something significant to gain or lose by the deliberation" are included as stakeholders, the process has the highest chance of success.[37] Agreement is facilitated and implementation more assured because participants are, essentially, the authors of the planning decision.[38]

This approach to participation is increasingly being used in community planning in Canada and elsewhere. A compelling example is given in the description of the "community strategic planning" process in Port Colborne, Ontario (population about 18,000), in the early 1990s.[39] The process they set up ensured that anyone who was interested could become "a fully-participating member of the planning process." Further, the planning exercise was not the product of one single body in the community but rather evolved from a partnership of groups. The result, in their words, was that such a process "enhances communications and mutual awareness among its stakeholders." Another outcome was that this consensual process permitted both difficult issues (like the allocation of scarce resources) and a wider range of issues to be addressed than in a typical physical plan for a community. For example, the Port Colborne plan comprises themes like economic development, physical infrastructure, social development, and commercial revitalization.

Unquestionably, the consensus-building mode enhances the role of citizens in community planning. But it also raises concerns about the role of planners. Some wonder whether they are losing their leadership role and "becoming mired in the citizen participation quagmire" and just "brokering among fragmented short-term points of view."[40] Another observer, citing the integral nature of conflict among planning goals—environmental protection vs. economic efficiency vs. social justice—suggests that planners can decide either to remain outside the conflict as mediators or to be inside promoting their own visions.[41] (More will be said about the future role of planners in the concluding chapter.) There can be little doubt as we approach the millennium that the texture of participation in community planning is changing.

The vagaries of citizen participation simply reflect the complexity of the actual choices to be made in planning for the future physical environment

of a community. Irksome though it may sometimes be to other participants, the advent of direct involvement of citizens has revealed the paucity
of the notion of one correct plan and the suppression of relevant value
positions often associated with it. At the same time, it helps reveal the
wider range of possibilities for action that exist in reality. The substantive
side of planning is thereby enriched. Probably most important, many community members are involved in decisions about their environment.
Notably, this includes women, who provide much of the initiative and leadership in citizen participation efforts. Through citizen participation, the
planning for our cities and towns becomes much more a process in community planning.

ENDNOTES

1. Kent Gerecke, "Plan Winnipeg—Towards 2010," *City Magazine* 13, no. 3–4 (Summer–Fall 1992), 21–24; and Joshua Wolfe, "Montreal's Master Plan: Long on Text, Short on Results," *City Magazine* 14, no. 2 (Spring 1993), 23–25.
2. Harry Lash, *Planning in a Human Way* (Ottawa: Ministry of State for Urban Affairs and Macmillan Canada, 1976), [Cat. No. SU32-3], 9–13. The following paragraphs in this section draw heavily upon Lash's monograph, especially Chapters 3 and 5.
3. Norman Beckman, "The Planner as Bureaucrat," *Journal of the American Institute of Planners* 30, no. 4 (November 1964), 323–327.
4. Lash, *Planning in a Human Way*, 75.
5. Melvin M. Webber, "Comprehensive Planning and Social Responsibility," *Journal of the American Institute of Planners* 29 (November 1963), 267–273.
6. Cf. Susan Fainstein, "Planning in a Different Voice," *Planning Theory* 7–8 (1992), 27–31; and Penelope Gurstein, "Gender Sensitive Community Planning: A Case Study of the Planning Ourselves In Project," *Canadian Journal of Urban Research* 5, no. 2 (December 1996), 199–219.
7. These categories derive from Robert T. Daland and John A. Parker, "Roles of the Planner in Urban Development," in F. Stuart Chapin, Jr., and Shirley Weiss, eds., *Urban Growth Dynamics* (New York: Krieger Publishing, 1962), esp. 190–196.
8. Thomas Gunton, "The Role of the Professional Planner," *Canadian Public Administration* 27, no. 3 (Fall 1984), 399–417.
9. John Forester, "Know Your Organizations: Planning and the Reproduction of Social and Political Relations," *Plan Canada* 22, no. 1 (March 1982), 3–13.

10. Pierre Filion, "The Weight of the System," *Plan Canada* 37, no. 1 (January 1997), 11–18.

11. Torvald Viland, "The Bureaucratic Barrier," *City Magazine* 12, no. 4 (Fall 1991), 30.

12. Gunton, "The Role."

13. The extent to which this value pervades the Canadian planning profession may be seen in the survey results of John Page and Reg Lang, *Canadian Planners in Profile* (Toronto: York University Faculty of Environmental Studies, 1977), a report to the Canadian Institute of Planners.

14. The debate over the public interest criterion is far from resolved; witness a recent view that society is fundamentally conflictive rather than consensual: Matthew Kiernan, "Ideology and the Precarious Future of the Canadian Planning Profession," *Plan Canada* 22, no. 1 (March 1982), 14–24.

15. Barton Reid, "Looking into the Future: Vancouver's City Plan Attempts Innovation," *City Magazine* 14, no. 2 (Spring 1993), 11–12.

16. Calgary, City Planning Department, *Public Participation in the Planning Process* (Calgary, 1993).

17. Donald A. Schon, "Some of What a Planner Knows," *Journal of the American Planning Association* 48 (Summer 1982), 351–364.

18. *Ibid.*

19. This classification is derived from two sources: Simon B. Chamberlain, *Aspects of Developer Behaviour in the Land Development Process* (Toronto: University of Toronto Centre for Urban and Community Studies, 1972), Research Paper No. 56; and Urban Land Institute, *Residential Development Handbook* (Washington, 1978).

20. A penetrating review of such negotiations and their consequences for city development in Canada is found in James Lorimer, *The Developers* (Toronto: James Lorimer, 1978).

21. Stanley Makuch, "Planning or Blackmail?" *Plan Canada* 25, no. 1 (March 1985), 8–9.

22. Chamberlain, *Aspects of Developer Behaviour,* 45.

23. Paul J. Cloke, *Introduction to Rural Settlement Planning* (London: Methuen, 1983), 3.

24. An excellent description of bargaining between developers and municipal planners in Scarborough, Ontario, is given in Hok Lin Leung, "Mutual Learning in Developmental Control," *Plan Canada* 27, no. 2 (April 1987), 44–55.

25. Illustrative of this Canadian "participation literature" are the following: Graham Fraser, *Fighting Back: Urban Renewal in Trefann Court* (Toronto: Hakkert, 1972); Jack Granatstein, *Marlborough Marathon* (Toronto: James, Lewis and Samuel, 1971); Donald Gutstein, *Vancouver Ltd.* (Toronto: James

Lorimer, 1972); Donald Keating, *The Power to Make It Happen* (Toronto: Green Tree Publishing, 1975); John Sewell, *Up Against City Hall* (Toronto: James, Lewis and Samuel, 1972); and, not least, *City Magazine*.

26. Sherry R. Arnstein, "A Ladder of Citizen Participation," *Journal of the American Institute of Planners* 35 (July 1969), 216–224.

27. Lash, *Planning in a Human Way, 35.*

28. One of the earliest critiques is J. Leavitt, "Feminist Advocacy Planning in the 1980s," in Barry Checkoway ed., *Strategic Perspective in Planning Practice* (Lexington, MA: Lexington Books, 1986); two later valuable sources are, Leonie Sandercock and Ann Forsyth, "Gender: A New Agenda for Planning Theory," *Journal of the American Planning Association* 58, no. 1 (1992), 49–59; and Clara Greed, *Women and Planning: Creating Gendered Realities* (London: Routledge, 1994).

29. Fainstein, "Planning", and Mary Gail Snyder, "Feminist Theory and Planning Theory," *Berkeley Planning Journal* 10 (1995), 91–106.

30. Suzanne Mackenzie, "Building Women, Building Cities: Toward Gender Sensitive Theory in Environmental Disciplines," in Carolyn Andrew and Beth Moore Milroy, eds., *Life Spaces: Gender, Household, and Employment* (Vancouver: University of British Columbia Press, 1988), 13–30.

31. Karen Hemmingson and Leslie Kemp, "Planning Ourselves In: Exploring Women's Involvement in the Community Planning Process," *City Magazine* 14, no. 4/15, no. 1 (Fall/Winter 1993), 14–17.

32. Beth Moore Milroy, "Some Thoughts about Difference and Pluralism," *Planning Theory* 7–8 (1992), 33–38.

33. Among the best and most hopeful is John Friedmann, *Planning in the Public Domain: From Knowledge to Action* (Princeton, NJ: Princeton University Press, 1987).

34. Among the most withering critiques is that of Alan Alschuler, *The City Planning Process: A Political Analysis* (Ithaca NY: Cornell University Press, 1965).

35. Cf. William H. Taylor, "Planners as Negotiators: Practice and Preparation," *Plan Canada* 32, no. 2 (March 1992), 6–11.

36. An excellent overview is provided in Judith Innes, "Planning through Consensus Building: A New View of the Comprehensive Planning Ideal," *Journal of the American Planning Association* 62, no. 4 (Autumn 1996), 460–472.

37. *Ibid.,* note 5.

38. Larry Sherman and John Livey, "The Positive Power of Conflict," *Plan Canada* 32, no. 2 (March 1992), 12–16.

39. Manfred Fast, "Communities Can Make It Happen: Forging the Port Colborne Ontario Strategic Plan," *Small Town* 26, no. 1 (July–August 1995), 10–15.

40. Michael and Julie Seelig, "Can Planners be Leaders?" *Plan Canada* 36, no. 5 (September 1996), 3–4; and Alan Artibise, "Challenging the Profession's Values," *PIBC News* (June 1995), 10-13.

41. Scott Campbell, "Green Cities, Growing Cities, Just Cities?: Urban Planning and the Contradictions of Sustainable Development," *Journal of the American Planning Association* 62, no. 3 (Summer 1996), 296–312.

Chapter 15

Canadian Community Planning at the Millennium

... in the large-scale task of putting cities together in which we all live and work, we have not yet stretched our abilities.

Humphrey Carver, 1955

APPRAISING THE PROGRESS

The advent of a new millennium marks also the beginning of the second century of public planning for communities in Canada. Two such momentous transitions are ample stimulus to appraise the progress of community planning in Canada. Starting with Humphrey Carver's challenge above, of more than four decades ago, it seems we must still let it stand as we move into this new era. We have accomplished much of what he saw the need for then, but not all, and new tasks have emerged that will confront us in the decades to come. Cities and towns continue to develop, informed by both their past and their future, regardless of millennial expectations.

So our progress in community planning is not a simple one to render, not just a matter of toting up the successes and the failures. There have been many achievements in Canadian planning in the 40 or so years since Carver issued his challenge (and, indeed, over the past century). In terms of physical products of community planning we can see such achievements as Market Square in Saint John, High River Alberta's downtown, and the False Creek development in Vancouver. In these and dozens of other cases, planners, politicians, and citizens have taken important initiatives toward putting cities together. And other communities, like Montreal, Sudbury, and White Rock, have demonstrated vital innovations in their planning processes to their own and others' benefit.

And there have been shortfalls such as the continuing problems of providing affordable housing, dealing with "gridlock," (the name of today's traffic congestion), and disposing of human and industrial wastes. The promises of planning's advocates to deal with such basic problems, as long as a century ago, still need to be fulfilled. But no small part of the difficulty is due to the changing nature of these problems. Housing for the homeless has been added in the last two decades, gridlock is found in the suburbs as well as downtown, and consumer and industrial products are more toxic today than ever. Not only is community planning a "large-scale task," as Carver noted, it is also a task that evolves as society evolves. New problems arise along with new versions of old problems. Thus, old objectives, principles, and processes may not suit new conditions. The true progress of community planning would seem to be as much a measure of how well it anticipates future conditions as how it deals with existing ones.

This final chapter will discuss a number of salient issues that will challenge the content and style of Canadian community planning as it moves into its second century and a new millennium. We shall need to look back at issues that have not yet been resolved: citizen participation (especially as seen in NIMBY and LULU) and environmental protection. And we shall consider issues that will become more insistent in the years ahead, such as the aging of the population, the expanding multicultural population, and the future of the suburbs. The chapter concludes with reflections on the adequacy of planning practice to provide guidance in the coming decades.

CONTINUING DILEMMAS

NIMBY and LULU

A not untypical public meeting in Vancouver in the early 1990s heard objections from residents of the city's East End to city council's plans to locate a plant for recovering recyclable materials from city garbage *in their neighbourhood.* Sceptics at city hall, and in other neighbourhoods too, probably classed this as just another case of NIMBY (not-in-my-back-yard).

Community objections to planning decisions that are perceived as damaging neighbourhood quality (through noise, traffic congestion, decreased property values, etc.) are frequently heard today. However, NIMBY is not new. It was documented in the early 1950s by Meyerson and Banfield in their pioneering study of planning for public housing in Chicago.[1] They found that Chicagoans, in general, favoured the establishment of housing projects for low-income people. But the Housing Authority was rebuffed by many neighbourhoods in its search for sites, a reaction that recalls, in many ways, demands by affluent property owners, decades earlier, for protective zoning regulations.

Regardless of its history, NIMBY is becoming more frequent and more frustrating to planners, politicians, and developers. Together with its sister-reaction LULU (locally unacceptable land use), NIMBY is blamed for costly delays in formulating plans and by-laws and for holding up construction projects. While this is undoubtedly true, from the neighbourhood perspective it is the *residents* who have to live with the outcome of the decision. Projects visualized in plans become actual buildings, traffic, and so forth in someone's neighbourhood. The need for a project (e.g., recycling) may be accepted by the whole Vancouver community as meeting its value for a better environment. While the affected neighbourhood may share this value, it may also have values that are unique to it. NIMBY is, thus, a new name for one of the basic tensions in the planning process (see Chapter 7) between neighbourhood and city values.

NIMBY and the Planning Process

NIMBY is more prominent today because the planning process has become more open. This raises the question, should citizen participation be constrained? On a basic level, the public participates because it satisfies one of planning's primary values—**democratic participation** (see Chapter 4). Before the late 1960s, it is useful to recall, public participation was extremely limited in planning matters. That neighbourhood groups have taken to it with such alacrity and become so adept at it suggests three things:

1. Citizens strongly desire to be *partners* in making planning decisions affecting their "turf";
2. The planning process in its present form invites stalemate; and
3. The process does not enable neighbourhood/city value conflicts to be resolved.

In order to be full partners in the process, citizens would have to share in planning power. As the situation now stands, citizens usually are allowed no higher than the middle rung of Arnstein's "ladder of participation"; that is, they are only *consulted* (see Chapter 14). Provincial legislation specifies consultation through public meetings, but it does not require municipalities to take the advice generated from such meetings. Since the public meeting is usually the only formal means citizens have to share in planning decisions, citizens often choose to exercise their democratic right to speak up strongly and loudly (and sometimes interminably). They are aware that politicians, for obvious reasons, are disinclined to prevent them from doing so.

The result of many NIMBY protests is an aborted planning process. Politicians may make hasty decisions (for or against the neighbourhood) or none at all. Or they may plan a new round of meetings, which further protracts the process; this is one of the most common outcomes of a planning process that still only accords citizens a token role.

Why NIMBY?

At its simplest, NIMBY is the desire to alert planners and politicians to local concerns, and to bring local knowledge, which is often invaluable, into the process. On other occasions, NIMBY is the reaction of a neighbourhood or a community to not having been informed, or only at the last minute, about a planning decision affecting it. Yet another NIMBY message urges politicians to stick to the official community plan and not to revise it in light of each new development proposal. To long-time civic activist Jim Green, "NIMBYism arises from a perceived feeling of powerlessness. It is often the result of the failure of those in power to allow a democratic planning process."[2] Accordingly, the more the local planning process allows access to decision making, the more the NIMBY factor will be reduced.

More problematic are the messages of "slow growth," "no more development," and so forth. Planner Peter Hall suggests that these are deep-seated reactions of people in all walks of life to endless growth and the spread of development.[3] This form of NIMBY challenges planners and politicians to answer a fundamental question: why is more growth needed? The motivations are diverse, sometimes altruistic (e.g., about the environment) and sometimes selfish (e.g., about lifestyle), but seeking motivations is only a distraction from this basic question, one which communities have a right to expect planners, politicians, and developers to debate.

The fact remains, however, that NIMBY reactions are not always informed or generous. Citizens have become adept at using the planners' lexicon, especially about density and traffic congestion, but the results are often facile and misleading. Housing projects for senior citizens have frequently been opposed on the grounds of increased density and traffic in the neighbourhood. Yet it takes little research to show that, although such projects represent a higher density of dwelling units than usual for, say, a single-family dwelling area, the number of residents per unit is usually half (or less) that of the surrounding area. Further, the percentage of automobile ownership among seniors would be considerably less than half that of the neighbours. A more benign land use seems scarcely imaginable, on top of which it seems a cruel hoax to deny our less affluent elders decent shelter.

No less distressing are the tribulations of a Winnipeg clergyman who tried for four years to find a site for a seminary to train native people. Urban and rural municipality alike refused the necessary land-use permission, citing increased traffic and lowered property values.[4] This story is shared by many who have sought to establish group homes in Canadian communities even though the effect on neighbouring land values has been shown to be almost non-existent.[5] Paradoxically, the opposite situation can occur as it has in an old downtown neighbourhood in Toronto that is the location of several drop-in agencies for many of the city's destitute. The downtown location and solid old housing have attracted middle-class residents who are starting to gentrify the area, resulting in a schism between the agencies and their clients and the new residents (see Exhibit 15.1).

There is no technical rationale for resolving such conflicts. The issues are moral ones as much as anything, and planners have no mandate when it comes to individual and public morals. However, planners do have a heritage of social justice in their professional ethos and the kind of NIMBY situations portrayed here demand it be considered. Both the Winnipeg and Toronto cases illustrate a fundamental tension that one planner calls "the property conflict."[6] Each case concerns a situation of competing claims on neighbourhood land from contrasting value positions: our capitalist, democratic society sees land as a *private* commodity, while our social welfare system sanctions *public* intervention on behalf of the needy. Planners will increasingly find that they will face such dilemmas in the future.

To sum up, NIMBY contains three major challenges for Canadian planners:

- to establish and maintain consistent and consensual public participation processes;
- to provide intellectual clarity in the debate about the need for growth, as well as viable alternatives for community development; and not least
- to join the moral debates that frequently arise in cases of NIMBY.

The Environment and Sustainability

Over the course the first century of Canadian planning, a number of issues have been transformed and become more complex, but none more so than environmental protection. The long-standing planning traditions of conservation, park planning, and open space preservation began to give way, about two decades ago, to concerns over ecosystems and biodiversity. The planners' response to ecological concerns in many ways has been commendable.[7] Among them are the District of North Vancouver's Alpine Area

Planning Issue 15.1

TORONTO'S DESTITUTE WEAR OUT WELCOME

BY MARGARET PHILP
Social Policy Reporter
Toronto

Some drop-in programs serving homeless people in downtown Toronto are in jeopardy because residents weary of so many dishevelled and drug-addicted people wandering their neighbourhoods have mounted a determined campaign to shut them down.

A fierce battle is raging between residents and social agencies in an east-end neighbourhood near Parliament and Dundas Streets, where an enclave of stately three-storey Victorian houses abuts a skid row of gritty rooming houses and drop-in centres for the city's most destitute.

It is a touchy problem that has pit middle-class residents fed up with people urinating on their lawns against overworked social agencies swamped by an increasing homeless population relying on their drop-in services.

"This has been a gigantic struggle, I'll tell you," said Ruth Mott, executive director of Central Neighbourhood House, an east-end social agency whose drop-in for homeless men is under threat. "Never have I put in so much time and felt like I've come out with so little."

The building that houses the agency's weekend drop-in is slated for demolition next week,

---

Downtown middle-class residents fed up with people urinating on their lawns want to evict drop-in social agencies from their neighbourhoods.

---

and residents associations, which have the ear of city politicians, are flatly opposing a possible move back to the agency's main building on a nearby residential street where more genteel services such as child care and Meals on Wheels are run.

With nowhere else to go, the drop-in has secured permission to operate temporarily in downtown St. Michael's Hospital until October.

After that, doubt surrounds the future of the program. Its director has tendered her resignation as of October in protest. Although Central Neighbourhood House's board of directors has vowed to keep the drop-in alive, it is looking for space strictly on commercial streets—a concession to its powerful neighbours—when it can scarcely afford the rent.

"This has given me nightmares like nothing I've ever worked on," Ms. Mott said.

"The number of people on the street is greater than we've ever seen it. We're watching people physically and emotionally deteriorate, and our ability to meet their needs is really marginal. I've always been able to find a way to hustle up money and resources when I had to. But that's not the barrier here. For the first time, the barrier is finding a place to be able to do it."

For the residents, the problem boils down to the massive concentration of social agencies serving homeless people in their neighbourhood. With drop-ins and hostels on almost every corner, they argue that it is no wonder the streets are crowded with homeless people, drug dealers, pimps and prostitutes.

Peter Stranks, head of the social-services committee of the Seaton-Ontario-Berkeley Residents Association (the name derives from the three main residential streets in the neighbourhood), said not a day passes when he isn't chasing a crack-cocaine addict from his property.

He describes a litany of daily grievances: needles and used condoms tossed onto the street, garbage heaved onto front yards and prostitutes plying their trade on the sidewalk at night.

Mr. Stranks, a professional photographer, knew the neighbourhood was tough when he got a bargain on the purchase of his house. Still, he wants to raise a family in that house, he said, and no one should have to endure the level of depravity that slaps him in the face every day.

"I have a four-day-old daughter," he said. "That's why I've been fighting so hard.

"Just because I choose to live downtown, why should it be acceptable to have prostitutes and drug dealers run my life? If you live here, you have to accept illegal activities going on. I don't know anywhere else in Canada like that. No child should have to be raised in an environment like that."

But workers at some of the social agencies under fire insist that their dispute with the residents reflects a classic case of not-in-my-back-yard attitudes on the part of people fussing more about their property values than the social upheaval around them.

Since a number of the neighbourhood agencies first hung out their shingle, they say, the nearby streets have become gentrified as former rooming houses were converted into fashionable single-family homes.

"People have moved into this part of town and they want the garbage out," said Joy Reid, founder and executive director of 416 Drop-In Centre, an agency that provides meals, clothing, health care and a place to sleep during the day for homeless

---

"They feel I'm responsible for all the drugs and hooking in town. No, I can't solve the problem. I have to work with the problem."

---

women, usually prostitutes and bag ladies. Some men are also allowed.

"They feel I'm responsible for all the drugs and hooking in town," she said. "No, I can't solve the problem. I have to work with the problem." ...

More than the others, it is Ms. Reid's drop-in centre that has incurred the neighbours' wrath. In the opinion of residents and city politicians, the agency enforces no ground rules to control its clients' antisocial behaviour, in utter disregard for the neighbours.

"In the middle of a row of Victorian houses, you have a property that's been turned into a social agency that looks like a flop house," Toronto Councillor Kyle Rae said.

"They consider themselves to be indispensable. But I wonder, is the 416, in the middle of a residential row, is that a great place for a drop-in? Maybe the answer is no." ...

Source: Excerpted from *The Globe and Mail*, July 18, 1997, A6. Reprinted with permission from *The Globe and Mail*.

Official Community Plan in 1989,[8] the Markham (Ontario) Plan for the Environment in 1995,[9] and the 1996 Greenbelt Master Plan for Ottawa.[10] Each of them addressed the need to maintain or restore biodiversity.

Nevertheless, environmental planning is still probably the "weak link" in land-use planning.[11] Traditionally, land-use planning is about improving the physical environment, but this has mostly been limited to the built environment and the defence of nature has been secondary. An inherent difficulty in planning for the two environments—natural and built—is that it raises an underlying conflict of "protecting the natural environment vs. land development," as the North Vancouver planners realized.[12] Acting within basic precepts and existing mandates, local planners can apply sound environmental criteria and principles to many of their normal tasks. But the underlying tension will still be there to address and be resolved.

Planners will need to decide about joining, if not initiating, the debate, a debate that will become larger as we confront questions of sustainability.

The Dilemmas of Sustainability

The environmental side of community planning has shifted once again from environmental and ecological maintenance to the broad concerns encompassed by the concept of **sustainable development,** now so widely used. As the implications of the work of the United Nations' World Commission on Environment and Development (the Brundtland Commission) are more fully absorbed, it is becoming clear that they reach beyond simple questions of ecosystems protection and resource conservation.[13] Sustainability is turning out to be a much more complex issue whose debate is far from concluded. Canadian planner Nigel Richardson observes that it involves three major facets—economic growth, social development, and environmental protection—whose "precise linkages and interrelations" are still to be defined.[14]

A quick glance at these facets of sustainability indicates that even though each of them is integral to the planning of cities, towns, and regions, there is rarely mention of such entities. Is there such a thing as a "sustainable city"? Richardson and others wonder. Or is there just sustainable development within which community planning and development is one part? The sustainable development concept has caught the attention of the whole world because of the holistic vision it projects of economics, the environment, intergenerational equity, and social development.

The Brundtland Commission defined sustainable development as "development that meets the needs of the present without compromising the ability of future generations to meet their own needs."[15] The building (and planning) of a community constitutes "development," so how can it be sustainable? And what are the implications of such a goal on planning practice?

The over-arching nature of sustainable development has the effect of presenting the planner with the three broad goals of community planning that are its integral parts, even if not always made explicit, namely:

1. Economic growth and efficiency;
2. Environmental protection (natural and built); and
3. Social justice and equity.

American planner Scott Campbell suggests that one imagine these as three points of a triangle in which each point, or goal, is linked to the other two.[16] In this form, one can quickly grasp the conflicts inherent in attaining each planning goal, much less all three. Campbell identifies them as:

1. The **property conflict** between economic growth and social justice;
2. The **development conflict** between environmental protection and social justice; and
3. The **resource conflict** between economic growth and environmental protection.

The ideal position for the planner, the sustainability position, is at the centre of the triangle balancing off each of the goals. At least two of these dilemmas have been evident to planners for some time. One is the "property conflict, which goes back to the earliest days of zoning and other public land-use regulation as well as the social intervention in established neighbourhoods mentioned above. And John Friedmann, in 1989, addressed the "the resource conflict,"[17] the relationship between economic growth and environmental quality. As he pointed out, with economic growth comes **capital accumulation** and the use of resources in the natural environment to attain capital assets. Commonly this is presented to planners in the addition of new houses, commercial buildings, roads, schools, etc., to a city or town (i.e., capital accumulation). To add to the physical environment of cities and towns, thus, requires the supply of resources from the natural environment. Timber, mineral aggregates, petroleum products—not to mention water, air, and energy—are needed for the production of lumber, wall board, plastics, and so forth. A plan that promotes an increase in a community's density or otherwise expands its physical environment forecasts the need for natural resources to achieve economic development.

Political and Moral Issues

It is evident that community planning functions at a strategic point in the economic development process as well as in the process of environmental conservation and protection and of attaining social equity. Community planners—whether they are on staff, acting as consultants, or serving on an advisory planning board or as members of a municipal council—are in a position to make significant decisions about each of these. Take, for example, the modish style of very large houses ("big houses" or "monster homes"), which are beginning to replace much more modest 1950s dwellings in many communities (see Figure 9.4 and Exhibit 6.1), and which require two to three times the materials of the homes they are replacing while performing the same residential function and often housing fewer people. Clearly, there is a market for such housing, but is that sufficient reason to permit such a grandiose use of resources? Ordinary zoning can control for the bulk of buildings and thus affect the amount of resources consumed (or destroyed) to meet the functional needs of the community.

Up to now, environmental protection has not entered into the concern over the new large houses, except for preserving views. There are, of course, analogous issues associated with other kinds of new construction, like contemporary "big box" retail outlets.

Planning issues are inherently political. As Friedmann points out, they involve "questions not only of the physical environment but also of investment and production, quality of life, and the distribution of costs and benefits among different sectors of the population."[18] Planners are likely to "antagonize important segments of the population" whichever position they take on environmental issues. Not infrequently, it is lower-income segments that must bear the burden of reducing capital accumulation or effecting conservation measures. They lose the jobs that would have come from new construction—and thus the opportunity to upgrade their quality of life—or are cut back in order to reduce the harvesting of natural resources. On the other side, investors and developers may also lose in these situations. These conflicts are breeding new alliances between workers and corporations against conservation and environmental protection measures.

The fundamental question in all planning endeavours—*who benefits and who pays?*—is even more complex when it comes to sustainable development. However, planners cannot long avoid these questions and their related political and moral aspects. Matters of power and equity are involved in framing environmental policies and in the location and nature of their outcomes. It all comes down to how we live with one another and with our local environment and, ultimately, with that of our globe. Distressingly, this message is not much different than the apprehensions voiced by those at Canada's Commission on Conservation 90 years ago! (See Chapter 4.)

Affordable Housing

The problem of providing affordable housing for people of lesser means plagues planners and city councils today as it has periodically through the past century. Slums, and what to do about them, comprised one of the prime planning issues of the turn of the century and of the post-World War II period (see Chapter 4). Besides the persistence of this problem in inner-city areas, one now finds versions of it in the suburbs and even in older affluent neighbourhoods.

Why is this problem so resistant to solution? Ensuring the availability of affordable housing is a complex problem. It is what some call a "wicked problem" because dealing with one aspect can unleash a host of other problems, often of a fundamental nature, that we are neither equipped nor prepared to tackle. Even in its earliest versions, the issue of making afford-able housing available went beyond the physical problem of constructing dwellings to encompass both social and economic components, involving as it did the economically and socially vulnerable—the poor, recent immi-grants, the elderly, the disabled. Attempts to ameliorate the housing needs of these groups rapidly expose poverty, discrimination, and an unrespon-sive economic marketplace.

The affordable housing problem is not easily resolved given the nature of city and town development in our society. Urban economic growth and development, which we prize so highly, aims to replace, expand, and change physical environments. Those without the economic wherewithal to participate in the bidding in the marketplace, owners and tenants alike, are destined either to live under miserable circumstances or to be dis-placed from their homes (and businesses). The problem presents itself in many different ways in the course of urban development, as examples from Toronto and Vancouver demonstrate. (Although the following portraits are not new, they are still a reflection of current realities.)

Don Vale, a neighbourhood close to downtown Toronto, had been for sev-eral generations prior to 1970 a haven for low- and moderate-income renters. Its location close to the burgeoning core area and its stock of ample Victorian houses drew new owners and speculative renovators desir-ing to restore the dwellings. In just 10 years, its population shrank by 36%, it lost one-third of its rental units, and rents on remaining units doubled and, in some cases, tripled. The process is called **gentrification;** its result in Don Vale was as devastating to tenants as if the area had been cleared for high-rises (a fate the area barely escaped in the mid-1960s).[19]

Kerrisdale, a well-to-do residential area about four miles from downtown Vancouver, was built up mostly in the 1920s and 1930s. Later, some 3–4-storey apartment buildings were added, which attracted older people from the neighbourhood who were no longer able or willing to care for their single-family houses. In 1988, owners of the buildings began to apply for demolition permits that would allow them to raze the apartment build-ings and take advantage of the demand for upscale condominiums. The zoning allowed this change, since a condominium building is still for multi-family use. The dilemma was greatest for older tenants, as there were fewer apartment rental units in the area to choose among (to stay meant buying an expensive unit) and no new rental accommodation being built nearby.

As most city newspapers show, these are not isolated cases but rather one of the inevitable consequences of urban growth and change. The economic marketplace is indifferent to these consequences, and the political arena, while it is obliged to listen, is not required to act to redistribute the costs of displacement. Moreover, the social and human consequences are often not evident until the new development thrust is a *fait accompli,* by which time the constituency of the displaced must overcome the community's heady expectations of increased profits from economic development and an increased tax base.

Although many of the consequences of city change cannot be anticipated, planners can predict with little difficulty the kinds of displacement discussed above. The crucial question with regard to maintaining and even increasing the supply of affordable housing is: *where does the planner stand on the issue?* Will he or she help enact land-use regulations to mitigate the social consequences of proposals that affect affordable housing? The problem, one can predict with certainty, will reappear in the future.

The mundane planning issue of maintaining a supply of good-quality affordable housing is, in a paradoxical way, the factor that helps bring to fruition the grandiose schemes of downtown development for the creation of a great city. It permits underclass as well as overclass to participate in the benefits of growth and development. The success of affordable housing ultimately comes down to the vision of the community planner and his or her ability to transmit that vision to others effectively.

IMPENDING CHALLENGES

Community planning in Canada must continue to evolve as it contends with old and new issues alike. The new issues, which arise from changes in society as a whole—**contextual changes**—hinge on such factors as the rapidly aging population and its increasingly multicultural texture. Communities usually have no control over such trends but must respond to them as they occur. Other new issues for community planning arise from societal predispositions to change—**consensual change.** Thus, communities or regions may agree that living environments would benefit from the preservation of heritage buildings or from planning designed to provide greater personal safety.

The makeup of the future planning agenda for specific communities will differ depending upon which changes occur and how the community decides to respond to them. Although it is not possible to predict all of the changes that will occur, three seem destined to demand responses from community planners in most cities and towns: (1) the increasing numbers of elderly, (2) the increasing multicultural diversity of the population, and

(3) the future of post-war suburbs. Each poses special challenges for community planning. And though other, now latent, challenges will undoubtedly arise, these will suffice to show the ways in which community planning can be affected. Each, it should be noted, challenge planners to consider the nature of the community they are helping to build. It is an opportunity for planners to tackle the "unfinished task of community planning" that Kent Gerecke, rightly, admonished them for abandoning.[20]

The Seniors' Surge

The rapid increase in the number of elderly people in cities and towns is well known to most Canadians. However, this trend and its implications have received little attention in the planning literature despite the fact that those 65 and older are the fastest-growing age group in our society.[21] In 1996, there were just over 3.5 million persons 65 and older in Canada. This represents a growth in numbers of the elderly of almost 30 percent from a decade earlier. And, as substantial as the seniors' surge has been in the past, it will be even greater in the future. When the baby boom generation reaches senior citizen status in 2011, the numbers of elderly will grow even more spectacularly.[22]

But numbers alone are not what make the surge in seniors' population relevant for planners. Just like the booming population of children three and four decades ago, elderly people have special needs regarding city and town environments. Studies have shown for some time that the three major needs of the elderly that impinge on the domain of the planner are housing, transportation, and community support services.[23]

Regarding housing, seniors require a variety of options that take into account changing circumstances of physical ability, household composition, and income. Seniors need to be able to continue to make choices about their residence—*to remain independent as long as possible*.[24] Collective transportation is also an essential element in the seniors' environment where one-quarter or more are unlikely to have the ability or desire to drive.[25] Community support facilities constitute a high priority for seniors' well-being and independence. These facilities should be broad in range (including, for example, seniors' centres, adult day-cares, and medical clinics). As well, shopping, banking, and dining facilities should be easily accessible by foot and transit.[26]

The need for planners to take into consideration the rapidly aging population has particular urgency for certain communities. Winnipeg and Vancouver metropolitan areas already have concentrations of those 65+ that are nearly one-fifth higher than the Canadian average. Among medium-size cities, Kingston and Victoria have an even higher concentration of the elderly. For nearly 3,000 towns and villages, especially in Saskatchewan and Manitoba, proportions of seniors already exceed that projected for the nation 20 years from now. [27] And the seniors' surge has already hit the suburbs in most Canadian metropolitan areas. In 1991, for the first time, the number of seniors living in metropolitan suburbs exceeded that living in central cities.[28] This change, it should be noted, has come about not through migration of the elderly to the suburbs as much as through simple "aging-in-place" of young adults who moved to the suburbs when they were being built 35 or more years ago.

The main challenge for community planners is to design (or, more likely, redesign) communities that accommodate the needs of seniors. Forty years ago, the demographic imperative was families with children. The components involved in meeting the needs of seniors are much the same—housing, public transportation, walking environments, and community facilities—although, of course, the configuration is different. Planners must reconsider the meaning of community for older people, as a prescient Ontario report noted over a decade ago.[29] Land-use regulations must be re-examined. A planning report for the Vancouver area observes, for example, that zoning has not responded to needed innovations in seniors' housing densities, parking, and on-site services.[30] Next to health care professionals, planners probably have the greatest influence over the ability of seniors to maintain their independence.

Multicultural Diversity

Hardly a community in Canada is not seeing its cultural identity being reshaped by new immigrants to this country. This is also a phenomenon that communities have faced more than once in the past. The difference this time is the scale and the diversity of immigrants, not to mention their diffusion throughout the country. More and more of Canada's immigrants are from Third World countries, and more and more of them do not feel bound to settle where they land, whether in Toronto, Vancouver, or Montreal.

This raises new challenges for planners to broaden their social perceptions and the perceptions of those whom they are advising. The issues that emerge with expanding cultural diversity cover the spectrum from housing and transportation to employment and community services. A sensitive review of the topic by a Toronto planner notes, for example: "A parking problem can become a race relations problem if the opponents on the issue are members of different racial groups and mediation has been mishandled."[31] In other words, the content of the planning agenda is much the same as for other members of the community. What differs is the need for planners to be able to cross cultural boundaries in seeking to understand ethnic community concerns, as well as expectations of the planning process. The new awareness of the planner will not be sufficient if it does not recognize the *diversity* among cultural groups. The needs of one ethnic community will likely be significantly different from those of others. Incomes may differ, as may language, family composition, class divisions, housing customs, and mobility. Even the concept of "neighbourhood" may have different spatial dimensions and land-use composition from one ethnic community to another.

The fact that planners can't do this alone provides an opportunity to broaden planning processes, as well as planners' cultural sensitivity. Information can be translated into the language of the neighbourhood, as is already done in several cities. But translation will undoubtedly raise questions of interpretation of planning concepts and procedures that will help the planner better understand his or her tools and position. Planning staffs should be augmented to include people who understand ethnic community concerns. And the mode of public consultation may have to be adapted to the means of communication with which the community is most able to articulate its aspirations. Planners have had to devise various modes of obtaining public input over the years (public meetings, open houses, storefronts)—the challenge is to continue to innovate in the style of planning. There are relevant lessons in the feminist critique of how planners "listen" to the experience of people to which we referred in Chapter 14.[32]

Retrofitting the Suburbs

The growth of cities after World War II was unprecedented, not just in numbers of people and houses but also in the spatial dimensions of urban community life. Traditional urban nodes were surrounded by ever-expanding rings of suburbs. This dramatic change is often viewed in a pessimistic light with the new suburbs being stereotyped as undifferentiated streetscapes that are inconvenient and energy inefficient and that promote social anomie and gender discrimination.[33] Regardless of this conventional picture, most people who live there tend to like it, as both early and more recent studies show.[34]

Why this difference in viewpoint about the suburbs? Largely it is because those who lament the passing of the traditional single-centre community fail to appreciate the major transition that was going on in the structure of urban communities. Essentially, people made conscious choices to move into the new communities that were being formed. Shopping and work opportunities also began to appear in the suburbs, as did various social institutions like hospitals, colleges, and recreation and sports facilities. As suburbs matured, this meant that almost all major land uses could be found there and, thus, residents could, and do, conduct most of their daily lives within these "urban realms" or "urban communes."[35]

Nevertheless, a vast amount of housing in suburban areas is already 40–50 years old and much is considered obsolete. Today's housing markets demand both larger detached houses and smaller attached dwellings and apartments, thereby presenting planners with new dilemmas.[36] Many such neighbourhoods are being redeveloped to accommodate higher densities at the same time as residents ask for maintenance of low densities. As Skaburskis and Geros note about suburban Burnaby, B.C.: "The objectives of the city's planners and of its established suburban residents are at odds."[37] We have here yet another instance of planning conflict that will require resolution in the future both in social terms and in terms of new physical designs.

Responding to Change

Although a community plan is a forecast for the future shape and functioning of a city or town, the future is never fully known. Even the challenges we have noted will impinge in different ways in different communities. Other challenges may appear on the scene rather abruptly, as the energy crisis did in the early 1980s and fiscal restraint in the 1990s, and add new elements to the picture. What impact will free trade with the U.S. have on resource communities? How will the reduction of Via Rail service affect small towns? What about the consequences of Indian land claims on various regions? Yet other alterations in plans may be necessary as a result of changes in local preferences, pollution controls, densities, or safety standards.

In short, some changes can be anticipated, but not their final effect, while others cannot be anticipated in either timing or effect. Moreover, there are outcomes from plans that may be both unintended and unanticipated. These conundrums are illustrated in the following classic planning diagram (Figure 15.1):

	ANTICIPATED	UNANTICIPATED
INTENDED	1	3
UNINTENDED	2	4

FIGURE 15.1 **The Consequences of Planning Action**

It is not always possible for the planner to function in the mode of Box 1, but it is important to try and avoid Box 4. To do this requires a strategy for confronting change. The guidelines might proceed as follows:

1. Expect that some change will occur in the planning period.
2. Be aware of broad societal tendencies as they emerge, and estimate their possible impacts on the community.
3. Be aware of changes in local preferences about the quality of the environment.
4. Develop mechanisms for the regular review of plans that involve the entire community in the process.

Planners have long perceived that planning problems follow a cyclical pattern: problems emerge, pressures grow to have them solved, solutions are formulated, policies and programs are adopted, and/or the problems wane. American planner Bernard Frieden suggests that planners (and politicians) tend to respond at the height of housing crises, when shortages and inflated prices are already set in place.[38] With knowledge of the cyclical nature of housing demand, Frieden argues, planners should better anticipate housing problems and plan for them in the "troughs" of the cycle, especially in regard to low-income housing. Canadian planners, Tom Gunton concludes, often do not get involved in a planning problem until the need for planning has begun to recede.[39] He urges planners to "begin their analysis as soon as the problem emerges instead of waiting for a formal request from politicians." In this way, their planning capability is strongest when the need for planning is strongest.

THE SUFFICIENCY OF PRACTICE

The topics in the foregoing section raise a basic question: *is planning practice sufficient to meet the kinds of challenges that have been posed?* Community planning has established itself as part of the social and political fabric in most parts of this country. Although most planners would demur, they are a part of institutional structures and thereby enjoy the power that accompanies official status. Still, planning will need to adapt itself further if it is to respond effectively to the issues of its second century and the new millennium. This high degree of institutionalization means that any changes to planning practice will have to be *adaptations* of structures and styles that currently exist. It is important, therefore, to understand the underlying dimensions of planning practice in Canada and those aspects that need to be changed. This is the final task of this chapter.

The Roots of Practice[40]

Community planning, like most Canadian institutions, derives in considerable measure from both British and American influences.[41] It is a unique amalgam adapted to Canadian cultural and constitutional circumstances; Canada has adopted, for example, zoning, the important handmaiden of planning in the U.S., but at the same time it employs development control, a British tool. However, one must go beyond the tools to determine the essential elements of Canadian practice.

Henry Thoreau, on a visit to Canada 100 years ago, observed an element vital to the development of Canadian planning practice: "in Canada you are reminded of the government every day. It parades itself before you. It is not content to be the servant, but will be the master."[42]

Thoreau sensed a quality of Canada that is pervasive, that informs the life and times of the country. Perhaps instead of referring to this as a "government" orientation it could be more aptly called a "corporate" orientation to Canadian institutions, for, historically, it has been the fur-trading companies, churches, railroads, and mining and forestry companies that have, as much as government, established the modes of development. Municipalities, too, at their outset were corporations rather than governments.[43] This corporate orientation did not so much affect the content of Canadian planning solutions—the problems of cities, after all, were much the same as elsewhere—as affect the style of practice and the decision-making environment.

Planning practice and institutions in Canada took different routes to solving planning problems than those followed in the United States and Britain. For example, in Canada, for constitutional reasons there is not an integral partnership role for the federal government in planning urban development. The provinces avidly protect their rights with regard to land, thus limiting the federal government to providing funding and/or advice. It is somewhat paradoxical that the strong parliamentary power of the federal government cannot be translated into a strong planning presence, as the role of Canada Mortgage and Housing Corporation exemplifies.

The provincial governments are the fulcrum of planning practice in Canada. This is demonstrated by the amount of effort eight of the provinces put into revising their planning acts in the 1970s and into building extensive planning staffs. Further, the provinces establish the ground rules for local planning and end up becoming, in many respects, the ultimate "clients" of local planners. Local planners, in turn, ply a process that is not essentially a public process. The development permit system (adopted from Britain) that is used so widely in Canadian planning can be characterized as a system of "contracts" between developers and the municipal corporation. They are formulated by officials and their bases are legal, not planning, institutions. Public scrutiny and debate are highly constrained at this stage of the planning process. A concomitant effect of this discretionary system is that the Canadian planner spends considerable time at the "operating" end of the planning process rather than in goal-setting, plan-making, and learning or expressing public views in other ways.

One cannot help but be struck by Canadian planning's pervasive bureaucratic orientation and by its much greater acceptance of government involvement.[44] Concern among Canadian professionals over the plan-vs.-process debate has been minimal, which has not been the case among U.S. practitioners. The emphasis has been on accomplishment, not theory. Practice has meant planners finding technical and administrative solutions to urban problems. In short, one should be aware that this is a major part of the context from which Canadian planners will confront the challenges the new millennium will pose.

Whither Planners and Planning?

The various challenges posed in this chapter make demands on both the *substance* and *style* of planning practice. The issues, which range across housing, the environment, the elderly, and multiculturalism, involve not only the planning process but moral questions as well. There is today far greater community consciousness about both the potential for planning and its limits. This consciousness has given rise to concerns about the livability of communities and, more specifically, about economic opportunities and social equity, as well as congestion and amenity. These two tendencies argue for a planning process that is more fine-grained—one that, on the one hand, means more participants actively involved in planning solutions and, on the other hand, means planners working more and more with custom-made plans for particular neighbourhoods, locales, and projects.

Leaders or Followers?
Even this minimum agenda will require transformations in planners' styles and planning-agency relations. It will, increasingly, demand that planners acknowledge that planning and politics are linked. More importantly, it will demand that planners know how to make their efforts politically effective, which includes encouraging citizen empowerment. Given the bureaucratic orientation planners have adopted, can such changes be attained? Can (and will) planners share power with other participants? Not easily, if some recent reactions of planners are indicative. Many planners are frustrated by

ungainly citizen participation processes and see themselves as becoming subordinated to the lay public,[45] while others urge planners to renew their "leadership and visionary skills and lead from in front."[46] Planners may not, however, have the luxury of entertaining the issue of leadership in an increasingly complex world that demands a greater variety of expertise and a broader range of involvement. The most effective future role for planners may be in assembling and facilitating the range of interests in working toward agreement on planning issues.[47]

Short Term vs. Long Term?

Nor is this the extent of the challenges planners will face. A dilemma for many planners is how to achieve more timely and more certain implementation of plans and policies. From within the profession, there are calls to abandon long-term comprehensive planning in favour of a "short-term problem-oriented" stance.[48] It would probably be relatively easy for Canadian planners, with their bureaucratic leanings, to shift to such a perspective. While this may result in more rapid implementation of policies, it could lead to a less open planning process at a time when public sentiment is for more, not less, citizen participation. An approach such as strategic planning, which deliberately links a plan and the means for its implementation, might offer a way out of the dilemma, providing, of course, it allows adequate time for participation.

If planners gravitate toward short-term planning, long-term planning will be weakened. The major conceptual argument against long-term planning has been its inability to take into account unanticipated changes within its time frame, for example, the failure of projects to materialize, the emergence of new opportunities, and even disasters. However, the solution is not to substitute short-term planning (where vagaries also occur) but to institute *contingency* planning. To this one might add regular plan reviews, which planners in many communities today seem to do grudgingly, if at all. The weakening of planners' concerns for the long-term future also means, as Harvey Perloff notes, a lessening of planners' "capacity to deal with it."[49] If not the planners, who will deal with this important dimension? Who will supply the images of the future?

How We Know What We Know

Regardless of the level at which they practise, planners must work to improve their means of analysis, of relating means to ends. The dearth of case studies in the planning literature means that there is no easy way for planners to know what works. In the training of planners, insufficient attention is paid to developing skills in critical appraisal of data and research findings. This, in turn, leads to highly variable planning research. One necessary step is to illuminate the presuppositions that guide much practice. (A few of these are examined in Exhibit 15.2.) Further, even though planners pioneered rigorous methods of evaluation, little use is made of them by practitioners—we just don't test practice.

A FUTURE OF CHALLENGES

As we head into the 21st century, there can be little doubt that communities and planners will be confronting very different conditions than were encountered even just three decades ago.

We have come to see many issues in their true complexity and have identified more clearly the competing choices, as is the case with the meta-problem of *sustainability*. The active discourse about *gender issues* serves to alert us that other groups and interests need to be included in planning theory and process. And while the planning process in most communities tends to involve more people, it usually is still at the middle-rung—consultation—of Arnstein's ladder of participation, and hence there is the consequent, and often valid, complaint that the process is not much more than "public nattering."[50] Add to these the globalization of the economy and fiscal constraints and there is no doubt that planners face a future of challenges.

Canadian planners have reflected on many of these challenges and a sampling of their thoughts may help illuminate the role of planners in the path ahead in community planning. The quotations are taken from a special issue of *Plan Canada* that celebrated the 75th anniversary of the founding the Canadian Institute of Planners.[51]

> **Jill Grant:** Planners have a role to play in helping people to understand the implications of the choices they make today for achieving their aspirations for tomorrow.

> **Jeff Fielding and Gerry Couture:** Our role is to open up public debate on opportunities for change that will result in real improvement.

> **David Witty:** What all this suggests is the need to develop a better understanding of the organizational milieu that encompasses planning practice and an awareness of the emerging politics of power and conflict that drive the agendas of community evolution.

> **Hok Lin Leung:** Planners should not have extravagant expectations, but be ready to take small steps and win small battles. In the end, how a city looks and functions should really be the choice of its citizens. But choice depends on the availability of options.

Planning Issue 15.2

EVERY PLANNER KNOWS ...*

Every field of activity is based on *presuppositions*. It is important in reading this book, or any other planning document, to know the presuppositions of planners, to insist that they be articulated. Some of the presuppositions listed below may challenge accepted propositions. The aim is to improve the basis on which we do community planning.

1. To Make a Plan Is to Advocate a Position

A plan constitutes a combination of all the elements of land use in a workable relationship. If it is workable, it is defensible. It constitutes one position regarding how the urban pattern could work. Alternative plans constitute other preferred combinations. One should also ask: can a planner truly recommend more than one plan?

2. Planners Cannot Keep All Their Options Open

In the face of the uncertainties that abound in planning it is tempting not to make a plan for the future. Some would contend that this allows them to deal with new events and conditions when they arise. This approach means, of course, that at least one major option—making a firm commitment to attain desired future conditions—has been foreclosed.

3. One Rezoning Does Not Lead to Wholesale Rezoning

By convention, rezoning is considered for one project at a time through variances or the recognition of changed conditions affecting viability of a project. That it will be seen by other landowners in the same zone as a precedent depends upon their individual aims and available resources. In any case, a precedent only exists if the zoning authority wishes to treat the particular situation that way. If a plethora of other rezoning applications arise, the zoning regulations probably should be changed for all landowners.

4. Zoning is Necessary, but Not Sufficient for Development

Grandiose development schemes and a sense of urgency usually accompany (re)zoning applications. All too often, no construction follows a successful application. Since zoning confers development value on a property, this usually results in large potential profits being made merely by getting zoning approval. That is as much the aim as actually building something, at this stage of the process.

5. Public Approval Processes Do Not Slow Down Development

Government regulations regarding subdivisions and zoning are an easy target for those desiring to expand development. However, studies have failed to confirm that such regulations have been the culprit, to any appreciable degree, in reducing the pace of development. The development process involves many actors, besides planners, who have the ability to slow a process, not least those providing financial backing.

6. A Shortage of Subdivided Land Does Not Cause the Price of Housing to Rise

The cost of housing is a function of location, cost of commuting, amenities, types of housing, and consumer preferences exercised in many geographic and social submarkets that have few substitutes. It is essentially behavioural. Subdivided land is a physical entity that will create yet another

submarket, on the periphery, if it gets built upon. Subdivided land is to housing costs what a sperm bank is to the birth rate. They are different logical types, as Bateson would say.

7. The Home-to-Work Journey Seldom Exceeds 40 Minutes

For over a century, through changes in city size and modes of transportation, the vast majority of commuters have chosen not to travel more than 40 minutes to or from work. This self-imposed limit is achieved through personal adaptations to the urban environment such as changing residences and/or jobs, modifying working hours, and finding new routes and modes.

8. Things Have to Get Better before They Get Worse

Hans Blumenfeld many years ago observed that traffic congestion in cities seldom improved for very long by adding more capacity. Cities are self-adjusting systems of land use and those seeking access to it thereby generate a certain level of congestion. It won't worsen unless steps are taken to reduce it by adding more lanes to the freeway or improving public transit that make the land use more accessible and more in demand.

9. Rapid Transit Stations Do Not Cause High Density Nodes

Rapid transit stations are located at accessible junctions to serve existing activity centres and/or link with surface transportation. These are usually traditional nodes that have reached a level of development commensurate with their locale. All a rapid transit line does is bring people to the junction more efficiently so that they may be dispersed more efficiently by bus or car to surrounding areas. Dreams of high-rise development around stations are just that. The political will has to be there, the zoning has to be in place, and the developers have to see the potential. Consider the surroundings of so many stations that never see much change at all.

10. Canadian Cities Will Never Have the Densities of New York and Paris

Toronto, Montreal, and Vancouver are not simply at a lesser "stage of development" than New York or Paris, such that they will eventually have the latters' densities of people and buildings. Population densities of cities and their Floor Space Indexes are a product of the local, perhaps even national, cultural milieu. They reflect cultural norms on residential development and building bulk. In effect, city growth and density do not have a linear relationship over the long run.

*A variation on Lord Macaulay's favourite phrase—"Every schoolboy knows who imprisoned Montezuma." Adapted from Gregory Bateson, *Mind and Nature* (New York: Dutton, 1979).

John Dakin: Planners will have to get into such matters in depth and prepare concrete offerings particularly about how our urban regions can be planned to meet the new conditions.

John Sewell: The best we can do is get all the different interests together around the table and see what can be agreed upon.

Lastly, if planners are to respond to these challenges, they will need to become more self-conscious of their practice and develop a firmer philosophical foundation for it. Planning practice, following John Friedmann's paradigm, comprises *technical, moral,* and *utopian* dimensions.[52] All of these dimensions—not least the moral dimension—must be part of the planner's response. If planners are prepared to address the moral issues, they will also see the necessity of re-establishing an ideology, or philosophy, to inform practice. Utilitarianism no longer seems sufficient for this purpose as it did 100 years ago. The notion of community has long been used to characterize planning for Canadian cities and towns, but it seems to have little currency in today's practice.[53] Perhaps the solution lies in redeeming and regenerating *community* planning.

ENDNOTES

1. Martin Meyerson and Edward C. Banfield, *Politics, Planning and the Public Interest* (Glencoe, IL: The Free Press, 1955).
2. Jim Green, "Regional Government, Revolution and Nimbyism," *City Magazine* 13, no. 2 (Spring 1992), 29.
3. Peter Hall, "The Turbulent Eighth Decade: Challenges to American City Planning," *Journal of the American Planning Association* 55 (Summer 1989), 275–282.
4. "Native Seminary Meets Only Rejection," *The Globe and Mail*, Toronto, January 1990.
5. Tom Goodale and Sherry Wickware, "Group Homes and Property Values in Residential Areas," *Plan Canada* 19, no. 2 (June 1979), 154–163.
6. Scott Campbell, "Green Cities, Growing Cities, Just Cities?: Urban Planning and the Contradictions of Sustainable Development," *Journal of the American Planning Association* 62, no. 3 (Summer 1996), 296–312.
7. Cf. Marie Lessard, ed., special issue of *Plan Canada* devoted to conservation: 29, no. 5 (September 1989).
8. Desmond Smith, "Local Area Conservation," *Plan Canada* 29, no. 5 (September 1989), 39–42.
9. Ken Tamminga, "Restoring Biodiversity in the Urbanizing Region: Toward Pre-emptive Ecosystems Planning," *Plan Canada* 36, no. 4 (July 1996), 10–15.
10. Richard Scott, "Canada's Capital Greenbelt: Reinventing a 1950s Plan," *Plan Canada* 36, no. 5 (September 1996), 19–21.
11. Michael D. Jennings, "The Weak Link in Land Use Planning," *Journal of the American Planning Association* 55, no. 3 (Summer 1989), 206–208.
12. Smith, "Local Area Conservation."
13. World Commission on Environment and Development, *Our Common Ground* (Oxford and New York: Oxford University Press, 1987).
14. Nigel H. Richardson, "What Is a Sustainable City?" *Plan Canada* 36, no. 5 (September 1996), 34–38.
15. World Commission, *Our Common Ground*, 8.

16. Campbell, "Green Cities."

17. John Friedmann, "Planning, Politics and the Environment," *Journal of the American Planning Association* 55, no. 3 (Summer 1989), 334–338.

18. *Ibid.*

19. The plight of Don Vale and other Toronto neighbourhoods is described in Leigh Howell, "The Affordable Housing Crisis in Toronto," *City Magazine* 9, no. 1 (Winter 1986), 25–29.

20. Kent Gerecke, "Resurrection of Community," *City Magazine* 10, no. 2 (Fall 1988), 33–35

21. Gerald Hodge, "The Seniors' Surge: Why Planners Should Care," *Plan Canada* 30, no. 4 (July 1990), 5–12.

22. Leroy Stone and Susan Fletcher, *The Seniors' Boom* (Ottawa: Ministry of Supply and Services, 1986), Cat. No. 89–815.

23. Maurice Yeates, "The Future Urban Requirements of Canada's Elderly," *Plan Canada* 18, no. 2 (June 1978), 88–104; and reiterated in Larry Orr, "An Aging Society: A Municipal Social Planning Perspective," *Plan Canada* 30, no. 4 (July 1990), 42–45.

24. One Voice, The Canadian Seniors Network, *Habitat: A National Seniors Housing Consultation* (Ottawa, 1989).

25. For a suburban area study of this, see Gerald Hodge and Stephen Milstein, *Serving Seniors Better,* a report to Peace Arch District Hospital (Vancouver: Simon Fraser University Gerontology Research Centre, 1989).

26. James Wilson, "Assessing the Walking Environment of the Elderly," *Plan Canada* 21, no. 4 (1982), 117–121.

27. Gerald Hodge, *The Elderly in Canada's Small Towns* (Vancouver: University of British Columbia Centre for Human Settlements, 1987), Occasional Paper No. 43, 20.

28. Gerald Hodge, *The Greying of Canadian Suburbs: Patterns, Pace and Prospects* (Ottawa: CMHC, 1996), 5.

29. Ontario, Ministry of Municipal Affairs, *Towards Community Planning for an Aging Society* (Toronto, 1983).

30. Michael Geller and Associates et al., *Development Control for Seniors Housing,* a report to the Greater Vancouver Regional District, November 1989.

31. Mohammed A. Qadeer, "Pluralistic Planning for Multicultural Cities: The Canadian Practice," *Journal of the American Planning Association* 63, no. 4 (Autumn 1997), 481–494.

32. Cf. Susan Fainstein, "Planning in a Different Voice," *Planning Theory* 7–8 (1992), 27–31.

33. One recent sample of the lament about suburbs is found in John Sewell, *The Shape of the City: Toronto Struggles with Modern Planning* (Toronto: University of Toronto Press, 1993).

34. Marion Clawson, *Suburban Land Conversion in the United States: An Economic and Governmental Process* (Baltimore: Johns Hopkins University Press, 1971); and Andrejs Skaburskis and Dean Geros, "The Changing Suburb: Burnaby BC Revisited," *Plan Canada* 37, no. 2 (March 1997), 37–45.

35. James E. Vance, Jr., *The Continuing City: Urban Morphology in Western Civilization* (Baltimore: Johns Hopkins University Press, 1990), esp. 503–505; and John Friedmann, "Urban Communes, Self-Management and the Reconstruction of the Local State," *Journal of Planning Education and Research* 2, no. 1 (Summer 1982), 37–53.

36. Michael Mortensen, "Retrofitting Suburbs: Windows of Opportunity," PIBC *News* (December 1996), 13–14.

37. Skaburskis and Geros, "The Changing Suburb."

38. Bernard Frieden et al., *The Nation's Housing, 1975–1985* (Cambridge, MA.: MIT Press, 1977).

39. Tom Gunton, "A Theory of the Planning Cycle," *Plan Canada* 25, no. 2 (June 1983), 40–44.

40. This section is adapted from Gerald Hodge, "The Roots of Canadian Planning," *Journal of the American Planning Association* 51 (Winter 1985), 8–22.

41. Although there were extensive French influences in developing settlements in Canada, Anglo-American tendencies have dominated planning institutions and practice.

42. Henry D. Thoreau, *A Yankee in Canada* (New York: Haskell House, 1892).

43. Harold Kaplan, *Reform, Planning, and City Politics* (Toronto: University of Toronto Press, 1982).

44. The same conclusion is reached in Michael Goldberg and John Mercer, *The Myth of the North American City: Continentalism Challenged* (Vancouver: University of British Columbia Press, 1986), 129ff.

45. Alan Artibise, "Challenging the Profession's Values," PIBC *News* (June 1995), 10–13.

46. Michael and Julie Seelig, "Can Planners Be Leaders?" *Plan Canada* 36, no. 5 (September 1996), 3–4.

47. John Sewell, "Slip-Sliding into the Future: Issues and Problems Facing the Profession," *Plan Canada* special edition (July 1994), 144–147.

48. Gunton, "A Theory."

49. Harvey S. Perloff, *Planning the Post-Industrial City* (Washington: American Planning Association, 1980), 87.

50. John Dakin, "Heading for New Minds?" *Plan Canada,* special edition (July 1994), 93–98.

51. *Plan Canada,* special edition (July 1994). Individual quotes are found on the following pages: Jill Grant, "Visions of the Future," 93–98; Jeff Fielding and

Gerry Couture, "Reflections on the Profession," 148–152; David Witty, "Taking the Pulse of Canadian Planners: A Snapshot of the Profession," 153–159; Hok Lin Leung, "Planners and City Future," 113–115; John Dakin, "Heading for New Mind?" 93–98; and John Sewell, " Slip-Sliding into Future Issues and Problems Facing the Profession," 144–147.

52. John Friedmann, "Planning in the Public Domain: Discourse and Praxis," *Journal of Planning Education and Research* 8, no. 2 (Winter 1988), 128–130.

53. This worthy theme is found in Gerecke, "Resurrection of Community"; Harold Chorney, *City of Dreams* (Toronto: Nelson Canada, 1990); and Scott Peck, *Different Drum* (New York: Simon and Schuster, 1988).

APPENDIX A: A NOTE ON "COMMUNITY" PLANNING

The term "community planning," used throughout this book, deserves some explanation. Although one does not encounter the term very often nowadays, it is peculiarly Canadian and especially appropriate to describe the activity of planning living environments in our variously sized settlements. "Community planning" entered the Canadian lexicon not long after World War II, when the Community Planning Association of Canada (CPAC) was formed. In the United States, the comparable term is "city planning"; it has been in use since shortly after 1900. The British have used the term "town planning" since the late 19th century. In the academic world in Canada and the United States, "urban planning" has been the accepted term since 1960.

There is no record available to explain why the Community Planning Association chose "community planning" for use in Canada; the term "town planning" was in widespread use from the turn of the century. Provinces had their town-planning acts, cities their town-planning commissions, and the professional planners had their town-planning institute. The first significant use of the term "community planning" appeared in a report to the Canadian government by a committee giving advice on the problems the country would face when World War II ended. The 1944 Advisory Committee on Reconstruction report *Housing and Community Planning*[1]—which came to be known as the "Curtis Report" after its principal author, Professor C.H. Curtis of Queen's University—argued that town planning had two distinct but complementary meanings. Town planning, they felt, should encompass not only the "rational physical organization" of a city but also the concept of "better community living."[2] Perhaps this was the stimulus to adopt the term "community planning" when the CPAC met two years later, for many of the members of the Curtis committee were founding members of Canada's first (and only) nation-wide citizen organization in planning.

It is worth noting that, prior to World War I, Thomas Adams urged Canadians to use the term "town planning" in preference to the American term "city planning."[3] He contended that the American term gave too much emphasis to the physical side of city-building and did not seem to acknowledge the human side of city life. He felt that the British term "town planning" was more encompassing of the social, physical, and environmental qualities of human settlements. His preference is understandable, as he had begun his career in planning with the founders of the English Garden City movement, who advocated building new communities that integrated human and physical factors. This latter dichotomy has for a considerable time been a source of debate among the professional planners and others involved in planning for our communities. The physical factors are the facets of a community that can be planned, regulated, and shaped most easily, so the practice of community planning quite naturally gravitates in this direction. Every so often, planners are accused of emphasizing physical factors at the expense of human factors in their planning solutions. While the emphasis ebbs and flows between the human and the physical factors, our planning efforts seldom comprise only one. Thus, community planning has merit in that it brings the human or community aspects clearly into the picture.

"Community planning" seems to be the most salutary term to use for two other reasons. First, in the Canadian setting, a town is usually seen as a small-size settlement and a city, by contrast, a large one. However, Canadian settlements of all sizes are involved in planning, as are many rural areas that are not clusters of populations. But all may rightfully be called communities. Second, "community planning" conveys the idea that modern planning is an activity by the community involving all who live in it. Both city planning and town planning suggest a technical activity dominated by professional planners. Humphrey Carver, one of the founders of the CPAC, says that one of the main aims in establishing the association was to create "a framework of discussion in which laymen, professionals, and politicians could meet on equal terms to talk about their aspirations for Canadian cities."[4] The polite phrase "a framework for discussion" evolved into the more vigorous one of "citizen participation" as a way to describe the involvement of more than just planners and politicians in planning activity. Even though the involvement of community members is not uniformly practised, the question is not whether it should happen, but how and when. "Community" planning thereby signifies the importance of the aspiration that the community should be doing the community planning.

ENDNOTES

1. Canada, Advisory Committee on Reconstruction, *Housing and Community Planning*, vol. 4 (Ottawa: King's Printer, March 1944), report of the Subcommittee.
2. *Ibid.*, 178.
3. Thomas Adams, "What Town Planning Really Means," *The Canadian Municipal Journal* 10 (July 1914).
4. Humphrey Carver, *Compassionate Landscape* (Toronto: University of Toronto Press, 1975), 90.

APPENDIX B: HIGHLIGHTS OF CANADIAN COMMUNITY PLANNING

Historically, the achievements in Canadian community planning fall into four distinct periods of development. There was, first, a *formative period* in which the perceived problems of cities were allied with planning solutions, and institutional arrangements began to be put in place to facilitate community planning. This period began in the final decade or two of the 19th century and lasted until 1930 in Canada. A second, the *transitional period*, spanning the years 1930 to 1955, saw steps to build an infrastructure for community planning at the national, provincial, and local levels. The period from 1955 to 1985, the *modern period*, was an era of putting planning ideas into practice on a widespread basis, a period of experimentation and innovation, of trial and error, and notably of the acceptance of the approach of community planning. There are indications that community planning has, since the mid-1980s, moved into a new period that could be called the *post-modern period*. Many planning initiatives in this period are moving beyond previously single-problem formats and linking factors in broader-based approaches, as with healthy communities and bioregionalism.

The evolution of community planning in Canada may be seen in the sets of important events constituting each of the four periods shown in the following chronology.

The Formative Period, 1890–1930

1896   Herbert Ames' study of Montreal slums.
1904   City Beautiful plan for Prince Rupert, British Columbia.
1906   Toronto Civic Guild of Art prepares City Beautiful plan for city.
1908   Garden Suburb plans prepared for Shaughnessy Heights in Vancouver, Mount Royal in Calgary, etc.
1909   Commission of Conservation formed by the federal government.
1911   City Planning Commissions established in Winnipeg and Calgary.
1912   New Brunswick passes first provincial planning act.
1913   Alberta's Town Planning Act allows municipalities to acquire 5% of subdivisions for parks.
1914   Thomas Adams appointed Town Planning Advisor to Commission of Conservation.
1914   Sixth National City Planning Conference held in Toronto.

1914   *Conservation of Life* begins publication for seven years (Thomas Adams, ed.).

1915   Local planning boards required in Nova Scotia.

1915   Plan prepared for National Capital area of Ottawa and Hull.

1917   Thomas Adams submits plan for rebuilding the Richmond District in Halifax devastated by a wartime explosion.

1917   Garden City plan prepared by Thomas Adams for new resource town (Temiskaming, Quebec).

1919   Town Planning Institute of Canada founded with 117 members; publishes its own journal.

1921   Commission of Conservation disbanded.

1923   First zoning by-law adopted for Kitchener and Waterloo; drafted by Thomas Adams and Horace Seymour.

1929   Provincial Planning Office established in Alberta; Horace Seymour first director.

The Transitional Period, 1930–1955

1935   Prairie Farm Rehabilitation Administration established.

1935   Housing Centre formed at University of Toronto by Humphrey Carver and Harry Cassidy.

1938   National Housing Act passed.

1939   National Housing Conference held in Toronto.

1943   Metropolitan Planning Commission for Greater Winnipeg formed; Eric Thrift, director.

1944   Report on the Advisory Committee on Reconstruction (the "Curtis Committee").

1945   Central (now Canada) Mortgage and Housing Corporation established.

1946   Founding of Community Planning Association of Canada; publishes *Community Planning Review* for 25 years.

1946   Ontario Planning and Development Act passed.

1948   Regent Park North slum clearance project built in Toronto.

1949   Lower Mainland Regional Planning Board formed; James Wilson, director.

1951   Plan for Kitimat, B.C., by Clarence Stein, using the neighbourhood principle.

1951   University of Manitoba establishes first graduate program in planning education.

1953   Metropolitan government instituted for the Toronto area and given wide planning powers; Murray Jones, director.

The Modern Period, 1955–1985

1955   Macklin Hancock's plan for Don Mills "New Town" is implemented.

1959   National Capital Commission founded to implement Gréber plan and acquire the Greenbelt.

1961   Resources for Tomorrow Conference held in Montreal.

1961   Agricultural Rehabilitation and Development Act passed.

1964   National Housing Act, 1964, enunciates new housing and urban renewal policies.

1964   Establishment of le Bureau d'aménagement de l'est du Québec for regional planning in the Gaspé.

1966   Trefann Court urban renewal citizen protest begins in Toronto.

1967   Mactaquac Regional Development Plan unveiled in New Brunswick by Leonard Gertler's team.

1970   Ontario government presents plan for 14,250 km^2, Toronto-Centred Region.

1971   Spadina Expressway (Toronto) ordered stopped.

1972   Federal government organizes Ministry of State for Urban Affairs, based on recommendations by Prof. Lithwick in his report, *Urban Problems and Prospects.*

1973   B.C. Agricultural Land Commission instituted.

1974   Niagara Escarpment (Ont.) Plan initiated.

1975   Greater Vancouver Regional District unveils "Proposals for a Livable Region."

1976   United Nations' Habitat Conference held in Vancouver.

1978   Quebec moves to protect agricultural land with its Loi sur le protection du territoire agricole.

1978   In Toronto, plans for Harbourfront and new inner-city housing in the St. Lawrence precinct.

1978   In Vancouver, False Creek redevelopment, including Granville Island's unique industrial-commercial-artistic mix.

1979   Meewasin Valley Authority established to plan and develop 80 km of riverbank in the Saskatoon area.

1980   Revitalization plan begun for Market Square in Saint John.

1981   The Core Area Initiative to redevelop downtown Winnipeg agreed to by three levels of government.

1982   Light Rapid Transit systems built in Edmonton and Calgary.

The Post-Modern Period, 1985 to the Present

1985   Canadian Institute of Planners Conference, "Sustainable Community—The New Frontier," Sudbury.

1987   Introduction of the City of Sudbury Strategic/Corporate Plan, encompassing physical, economic, human, and organizational development.

1988   Hans Blumenfeld dies in Toronto at age 96.

1988   Healthy communities initiative launched by Canadian Institute of Planners.

1990   Waterfront planning for the Toronto region by the Crombie Commission recommends a bioregional perspective.

1992   Montreal's first complete city plan is adopted.

1993   Highly participative planning process in the preparation of Vancouver's CityPlan and Calgary's GoPlan.

1993   Regional planning commissions are disbanded in Alberta.

1994   75th anniversary of the founding of the Canadian Institute of Planners.

1996   New Greenbelt Plan for Ottawa embraces ecosystems approach.

1996   City of Toronto modifies zoning regulations in two "reinvestment areas" to promote diversity and adaptation of uses.

1997   Municipal governments within Metropolitan Toronto amalgamated.

INDEX

Page references in italics indicate an illustration or a diagram.